D1475920

THE POLITICAL ECONOMY OF TURKEY

The Political Economy of Turkey

Debt, Adjustment and Sustainability

TOSUN ARICANLI
Assistant Professor of Economics

and

DANI RODRIK
Assistant Professor of Public Policy
both at John F. Kennedy School of Government
Harvard University

Theodore Lownik Library
Illinois Benedictine College
Lisle, IL 60532

St. Martin's Press   New York

338.9561
P 769

Tosun Arıcanlı and Dani Rodrik 1990

All rights reserved. For information, write:
Scholarly and Reference Division,
St. Martin's Press, Inc., 175 Fifth Avenue,
New York, N.Y. 10010

First published in the United States of America in 1990

Printed in Hong Kong

ISBN 0–312–03596–9

Library of Congress Cataloging-in-Publication Data
The Political Economy of Turkey: debt, adjustment and sustainability
[edited by] Tosun Arıcanlı and Dani Rodrik.
    p.   cm.
ISBN 0–312–03596–9
    1. Turkey—Economic policy.   2. Debts, External—Turkey.
    I. Arıcanlı, Ali Tosun, 1947–.   II. Rodrik, Dani.
HC482.P68   1990
338.9561—dc20   89–34980
                                                        CIP

Contents

Contents

List of Figures

List of Tables

Acknowledgements

Most of the chapters included in this volume were originally presented at a conference at Harvard University on 'The Political Economy of Turkey in 1980s: Changing Strategies and Prospects for the Next Decade' held on 22–23 April 1988. Without the financial and moral support that we received from the University community this conference could not have been organized. We would like to thank Roy P. Mottahedeh and William Graham of the Center for Middle Eastern Studies, David S. Landes of the Department of Economics and the History Workshop, Richard J. Zeckhauser of the John F. Kennedy School of Government, the Japanese Corporate Associates Program, and Andrew W. Mellon Awards of the Faculty of Arts and Sciences for their interest and support.

While their names do not appear in the volume, the discussants at the conference provided vital input to the preparation of the final version of the papers. We thank them all: Ataman Aksoy, Henri Barkey, Cihan Bilginsoy, Susan M. Collins and Tevfik F. Nas.

We are grateful to the organizational assistance provided by Colleen Mac Donald and Cisley Malmi. Last but certainly not least we should mention the meticulous work of Jane Trahan who undertook the arduous task of preparing the manuscript for publication. Without her unyielding effort and good cheer the volume could not have been put together.

Tosun Arıcanlı
Dani Rodrik

Notes on Contributors

Yılmaz Akyüz   UNCTAD, Geneva
Ritu Anand   The World Bank
Tosun Arıcanlı   Department of Economics, Harvard
                                University
İzak Atiyas   The World Bank
Tercan Baysan   The World Bank
Charles Blitzer   The World Bank (on leave from Center
                                for Energy Policy Research, MIT)
Korkut Boratav   Turkish Social Science Association,
                                Ankara
Merih Celâsun   Department of Economics, Middle East
                                Technical University, Ankara
Ajay Chhibber   The World Bank
Patrick Conway   Department of Economics, The University
                                of North Carolina at Chapel Hill
Emine Kıray   Department of Economics, Wellesley
                                College
Dani Rodrik   John F. Kennedy School of Government,
                                Harvard University
Fikret Şenses   Department of Economics, Middle East
                                Technical University, Ankara
Lance Taylor   Department of Economics, MIT
Sweder van Wijnbergen   The World Bank

Introduction and Overview

Tosun Arıcanlı and Dani Rodrik

As these words were being written (in October 1988) the Turkish economy stood at a crossroads. A model of stabilization and adjustment for long, Turkey had been perceived as one of the few examples of a successful transition from inward- to outward-oriented policies during the turbulent economic conditions of the 1980s. But the strains accumulated in this transition were now becoming all too evident. The opening-up of the political system following the military rule of the early 1980s had led to a series of hotly contested elections, exerting growing pressure on fiscal balances. As the public-sector deficit had started to get out of control, so had the inflation rate, reaching all the way to its levels in the pre-adjustment period. The trend deterioration in real wages had accentuated political conflict and led to demands for compensatory policies. Added to the growing burden of external debt service, these developments now. raised serious doubts as to the sustainability of the strategy.

The alternatives appear to be clear. In the favorable scenario, a combination of budgetary conservatism, continued export boom, and some debt relief (presumably under a different name) would enable Turkey to grow steadily at 5–6 per cent per annum, ultimately reversing the steady increase in principal debt ratios. On the other hand, growing doubts about Turkey's creditworthiness could put a quick end to the present level of inflows ($3–4 billion annually from private sources), precipitating a payments crisis and some forced reversal in current policies. It is hard to know which scenario is more likely at present. Much depends on imponderables, such as bandwagon expectations in world capital markets and developments in domestic politics.

The implications of the outcome extend far beyond Turkey. By virtue of having gone through her debt crisis relatively early (in 1978–80, as opposed to after 1982) and having achieved respectable growth rates by the mid-1980s, Turkey remains the major example of a country which has managed (so far) to recover from a debt crisis. This relative success has been linked to the outward-oriented policies put in place since 1980: flexible exchange rates, export subsidies and liberalization. The uncertainty regarding Turkey's fate can lead to legitimate doubts as to whether such policies are either necessary or sufficient to grow out of a debt crisis. If Turkey fails, much of current orthodoxy regarding adjustment via liberalization will be regarded as having failed as well.

Taken together, the papers collected in this volume — most of which

1

were initially presented at a conference at Harvard on 22–23 April 1988 — present a comprehensive evaluation of Turkey's recent experience and her prospects in the near future. The papers demonstrate both the extensiveness of the transformation having taken place, and the seriousness of the internal conflicts generated by such comprehensive reforms. With practically no exception, the authors raise doubts as to the sustainability of the current set of policies. The key issues are the budget, private investment, and, of course, domestic politics.

Tercan Baysan and Charles Blitzer outline the basic approach taken in the post-1980 reforms, focusing on exchange-rate policy, import liberalization and export promotion. Their chapter highlights the policies of steady (almost) real depreciation, explicit export subsidization, and gradual import liberalization. As explanations of the export boom they point to exchange-rate policy and the fall in marginal costs faced by Turkish firms in the early 1980s as a result of the prohibition on layoffs, which transformed labor into a fixed factor. Noting that there has already been some backsliding in the trade regime, Baysan and Blitzer raise a critical question: will the government be able to pursue its objective of a neutral trade regime in an environment still characterized by macro instability (high inflation, low levels of private investment, and a large debt burden), and if so how? An increase in private investment in manufacturing, necessary for sustained export performance, will require reducing the uncertainty regarding future trade policies, an uncertainty which is fostered by the frequent changes recently in commercial policies.

The chapter by Merih Celâsun focuses on the fiscal dimension of the post-1980 performance. As his discussion makes clear, after eight years of adjustment, a concerted fiscal retrenchment still remains imperative. Such a retrenchment will prove difficult to implement without aggravating socio-political conflict. Celâsun finds that public-sector revenue mobilization has been achieved in large part thanks to increases in public-enterprise (SEE) prices, rather than via productivity improvements. He draws attention to the role of extra budgetary funds (EBFs) as instruments of unencumbered spending. Major areas of concern are distributional effects and the need to transform the recovery into self-sustaining growth.

The chapter by Fikret Şenses documents and evaluates the phenomenal rise in Turkish exports from $2.3 billion in 1979 to $10.2 billion in 1987. This performance was the consequence primarily of the rise in *manufactured* exports, which accounts for four-fifths of the increase. Textiles, clothing, and iron and steel constitute around two-thirds of total manufactured exports. Şenses finds a sharp distinction between exports to EEC, which consist primarily of labor-intensive goods not requiring a high level of skills, and exports to the Middle East, which consist of more capital-intensive categories with higher skill content. These Middle Eastern markets have therefore played an important role as a vent-for-surplus of the import-substituting industries erected under the previous policy regime. Like other authors, Şenses stresses the importance of increasing private investment in exportables, and suggests that direct investment incentives may be needed.

The determinants of private investment behavior are the subject of the chapter by Patrick Conway. In what is perhaps the most in-depth analysis of Turkish private investment to date, Conway finds that private investment has been discouraged by real currency depreciations, high inflation and high nominal interest rates. It is not entirely clear why real depreciations hurt manufacturing investment, but it is possible that the operative channel is through the prices of imported machinery. The negative effect of inflation is also surprising at first sight, but the increased relative-price variability (and hence uncertainty) fostered by inflation may be the reason for it. The spurt in private investment since 1985 has been disappointingly limited to the housing sector. Conway points out that concern with private investment is a new feature of economic policy, as it is *public* investment which has played the leading role so far. He concludes that '[p]resent Turkish economic policy has not yet provided investors with a stable and profitable environment. The evidence suggests that the important components to such an environment will be greater stability and lower absolute levels of inflation and nominal interest rates and a slower rate of exchange rate depreciation'.

Yılmaz Akyüz documents and evaluates the bewildering array of experiments in financial liberalization undertaken since July 1980. These reforms have affected the banking sector, capital markets and external financial transactions. Akyüz finds a large substitution in private portfolios from narrow money to interest-bearing time deposits and foreign exchange deposits. Disappointingly, private bond and equity issues have not partaken in the growth of financial assets. Quite contrary to the McKinnon-Shaw presumption that financial deepening would go hand in hand with increased long-term finance of private investment, Akyüz discovers that the effect has rather increased short-term indebtedness of the private sector. He also calls attention to the distributional effects of interest rate increases: by redistributing income from high savers (corporations, government) to low savers (rentiers), interest-rate liberalization may have actually reduced the savings rate. Akyüz then provides suggestive evidence of the low propensity to save in the household sector: it appears that households are running down their real wealth by consuming the inflation component of nominal interest payments. This redistributive aspect provides a plausible channel through which positive real interest rates may be conducive to lower rather than higher savings. Akyüz's verdict on financial deepening is that it has led to: erosion of small savings and greater concentration of wealth, drastically increased short-term indebtedness of corporate and public sectors, and no tangible improvement in savings rate. The Turkish experience here demonstrates the inherently destabilizing nature of financial deregulation and capital-account liberalization when the economy is still gripped by inflation, fiscal crisis, and continuous real depreciations.

İzak Atiyas focuses more narrowly on the sources of the 1982 financial crash. By analyzing a panel data set of firms, he shows that firms received a double shock: one to interest rates and another to sales. Hence the financial distress. This double squeeze has been revisited in 1988, by virtue of an orthodox monetary shock designed to ease pressure against the lira. What was perhaps unexpected was the response of commercial banks to the difficulties of their clients. Instead of letting firms go bankrupt, banks continued to refinance non-performing loans. This required fierce competition for deposits, which in turn raised interest rates further. Atiyas highlights a dilemma that financial liberalization has forced policy-makers to confront ever since 1980, that of advocating free interest rate determination on the one hand, and promoting collusion and 'responsible' behavior among banks on the other. He also draws attention to the weakness of the regulatory framework to deal with the financial instability created by de-facto deposit insurance.

Ritu Anand, Ajay Chhibber, and Sweder van Wijnbergen focus in their chapter on two crucial questions: first, how did Turkey, unlike so many other countries, manage to grow at respectable rates in the 1980s?; second, can she sustain her growth rate into the future? With respect to the first question, the authors point to the generous capital inflows, the shift in composition of public expenditures towards investment, and the interest-rate policy which prevented private savings from falling. Using an econometric framework, they are able to quantify the linkages among fiscal policy, investment and growth. With respect to the second question, the authors calculate that if Turkey can grow at a rate of 6 per cent she can run current account deficits of up to 2.5 per cent of GNP without deteriorating a simple creditworthiness indicator, the debt-resource ratio. They suggest that this is attainable provided there is a reduction in fiscal deficits of a few percentage points, which by reducing real interest rates would boost private investment sufficiently to offset the impact on growth of reduced public investment. The caveats are that the real exchange rate is assumed to stay constant, foreign finance is presumed readily available, and the fiscal cuts are supposed to be heavily biased against current expenditures. Provided the requisite fiscal retrenchment is undertaken, the authors are moderately optimistic about the prospects for sustaining growth.

The chapter by Dani Rodrik addresses some policy dilemmas created by the use of exchange-rate and interest-rate policy when the fiscal situation is still unstable. He argues that export performance on its own is insufficient to sustain external debt service; the export effort has to be complemented by a comparable fiscal effort. The problem is that some policies currently in use have contradictory effects on these two targets. Real exchange-rate depreciations tend to hurt the fiscal effort by eroding the real revenue base of the government. So do high interest rates, as they add to the cost of servicing the internal debt. This paper complements the contributions of Akyüz and Atiyas by questioning the wisdom of having undertaken financial liberalization prior to fiscal consolidation.

The chapter by Korkut Boratav is devoted to the distributional implications of the post-1980 policy reforms. Boratav's main argument is that 'changing and redefining the policy parameters regulating and shaping income distribution against labor in general was a major goal of the structural adjustment program of the 1980s'. He documents the regression in real wages since the late 1970s, and links this to the 'reactionary/ authoritarian' ideology of the official circles, as exemplified by the severe restrictions imposed on union activities in the early 1980s and the curtailment of the scope of collective bargaining in the 1982 Constitution. Boratav indicates that the substantial reduction in real wages that has already taken place now makes employers willing to consider indexation-type mechanisms which would freeze such losses. Complementing Akyüz's analysis, he finds that the benefits of wage regression have been captured mostly by rentiers through higher interest income. With respect to agriculture, there is also a sizable deterioration in the terms of trade with industry, comparable in magnitude to that experienced by Turkish farmers during the great depression of the 1930s. Despite the great increase in marketed output, Boratav finds that the purchasing power of the countryside has fallen during the 1980s. Disconcertingly for the outward-oriented strategy, part of the problem has been that the benefits of higher lira prices at the border do not appear to have been passed on to the farmers.

Tosun Arıcanlı traces the effect of exogenous variables on the Turkish debt crisis and the adjustment process. An outcome of the first oil price shock was the austerity program in Europe that put an end to Turkish labor migration. Domestic political pressures during mid-1970s led to an economic policy that attempted to accomodate the resulting rise in unemployment rate. He argues that in this period adverse conditions in international politics closed alternatives for Turkey in seeking financial relief through official sources. To the extent that entry into the crisis coincided with exogenous factors with negative effects, the period of adjustment corresponds to a period of turmoil in the Middle East, such as the Iranian revolution and the war between Iran and Iraq, which helped enhance Turkey's position in the Middle East. Huge capital inflows that Turkey received during this period — with a positive net resource transfer until 1983 — is explained by these factors. Arıcanlı evaluates the recent past as a period of lessening conflict in the region and therefore promising lesser windfalls for Turkey in the future. More than ever, future capital infusion will depend on economic performance which does not look promising on the basis of recent records of domestic investment and public sector deficits.

Emine Kıray provides a historical perspective on Turkey's experience with foreign debt and conditionality. Her focus is on the stabilization program recommended by a British mission in 1860, following Turkey's very first debt crisis. Despite the 120 years that have intervened, Kıray finds a remarkable degree of similarity with present-day IMF-World Bank programs. The British mission identified fiscal deficits as the root cause of the problem, and recommended real depreciation, deregulation and liberalization. Disconcertingly, the economic outcomes were similar as well: private investment did not recover, and the debt burden grew further (eventually taking the Ottoman Empire to the default of 1875).

Lance Taylor closes the volume by synthesizing some of the major conclusions of the preceding chapters, and by placing the Turkish experience in comparative perspective. He stresses that Turkish policy has been only partly orthodox in its design and implementation. This stance, in turn, has been made possible by the fact that Turkish policy-makers have been on a 'long leash' from the IMF and the World Bank. Now that the cheap money is gone and Turkey is, in the words of Taylor, borrowing from Mastercard and Visa, there is the possibility of a vicious circle if private investment in exportables does not pick up. Depressed investment may choke off exports while fragile fiscal balances prevent the government from attempting to crowd in additional private investment. Taylor warns that as the policy dilemmas mount, the government may be forced increasingly towards the extremes of austerity and further liberalization, neither of which will make the problems go away.

What do we learn from the Turkish case? First, the importance of having access to substantial inflows in the early stages of adjustment cannot be underestimated, as this allows a spurt in output by increasing foreign exchange availability. Second, export promotion very early on can also help growth, even if it is accomplished through rather unorthodox means such as subsidies. Third, financial liberalization tends to have destabilizing consequences if implemented in an environment where fiscal stability is tenuous. Fourth, the relative-price changes needed to validate the adjustment process can have vast redistributive implications which may well render the reforms unsustainable. Fifth, the ability to control and stabilize the public-sector deficit is the *sine qua non* of successful adjustment. Sixth, trade and price reform is not sufficient to get the desired private investment response if such reform comes at the cost of high levels of uncertainty and continuous policy tinkering.

As these papers demonstrate, the final verdict on the Turkish experience of the 1980s is yet to come. Yet it should not be forgotten that Turkey did manage to recover in the early 1980s in a difficult world environment, in which a generalized world debt crisis and macroeconomic imbalances in the industrial countries had rendered an outward-looking strategy particularly risky. That she succeeded where so many others have failed is telling on its own. And whatever outcome ultimately awaits the Turkish economy, it is unlikely that there will be a complete reversal from the present strategy: a flexible (nominal) exchange rate has proved too useful a tool to abandon entirely; the almost total neglect of exports in the 1960s and 1970s is unlikely to recur; and for good or ill, some of the financial liberalization will no doubt survive.

If the Turkish experiment does not eventually succeed, we should also not be too hasty in blaming government policies for the failure. As the papers collected in this volume demonstrate, the debt overhang and the associated reticence on the part of creditors to increase exposure impose extremely tight constraints on what can be achieved. As more countries are discovering, it may well be that, even with the best of policies, there is no conceivable 'life after debt' without some large-scale debt relief provided by creditors.

1 Turkey's Trade Liberalization in the 1980s and Prospects for its Sustainability

Tercan Baysan and Charles Blitzer[1]

I INTRODUCTION

Turkey entered the 1980s facing dire economic circumstances. Inflation was accelerating, unemployment was rising, shortages were common, and labor unrest had reached crisis proportions. Even worse, political violence was rampant and spreading throughout Turkey. Leading up to this had been six years of external shocks, macroeconomic mismanagement, and severe political/social instability.

Despite unfavorable external circumstances, in part due to higher world oil prices, successive coalition governments attempted to maintain or even accelerate aggregate economic growth. Inflationary policies, foreign borrowing, and postponement of structural adjustments were used to sustain this effort. Economic policy-making was often inconsistent, unstable and irrational. As a result, economic performance — as measured by the trade deficit, debt, inflation, unemployment and real economic growth — rapidly deteriorated after 1976, culminating in a foreign debt crisis in 1979.[2]

As the growth process became unsustainable and the debt problems worsened, various *ad hoc* adjustments were tried. These included maxi-devaluations in 1978 and 1979, additional measures to restrict imports, and half-hearted austerity programs undertaken in conjunction with two separate stand-by arrangements with the IMF (April 1978 and July 1979). In a period of serious political instability and violence, these proved ineffective in reversing the balance-of-payments and other macroeconomic problems. This necessitated long and detailed negotiations with Turkey's official and private creditors for rescheduling debt servicing, and with her NATO allies for large amounts of increased financial aid.

In the face of these problems, the need to undertake *immediate* and *substantial* reforms in economic management became crucial. Turkey's creditors were insisting on steps to reduce the trade deficit and to improve efficiency in resource use. Perhaps more importantly, the Government, too, became convinced that fundamental changes were required. Beginning in January 1980, a series of economic policy changes were introduced to achieve a turnaround in Turkey's economic performance. These included strong macroeconomic stabilization measures, as well as more fundamental reforms aimed at liberalization and improving the efficiency of the economic system.

While the reforms were comprehensive, this paper focuses primarily on those aspects of Turkey's post-1980 economic policy having to do with foreign trade, export promotion and liberalization of imports. In Section II, these aspects of the January 1980 decisions and the post-1980 measures are reviewed and assessed in terms of their relative importance, timing and sequencing. The impact of trade policy reform on Turkey's economic performance in the 1980s, with particular emphasis on the role of export performance, is assessed in Section III. Various explanations for the strong export performance after 1980 are reviewed in Section IV. Finally, in Section V we discuss some implications of the current macroeconomic situation for the sustainability of trade policy reform and liberalization.[3]

II ECONOMIC POLICY REFORMS SINCE 1980

In January 1980 the Government announced a major stabilization and economic liberalization program. The short-term objectives of the January 1980 decisions were to reduce the rate of inflation, improve the balance-of-payments situation through rapid export-growth and, thereby, re-establish Turkey's international creditworthiness. What differentiates the 1980s from earlier adjustment periods is that Turkey for the first time embarked on a set of policies aimed at a permanent transformation of the economy and the nature of government-economic relations. Since 1980 the explicit long-term objectives have been to adopt a more market-directed system of resource allocation in general, and an outward-oriented trade strategy based on comparative advantage. Trade strategy has shifted from indiscriminate import substitution to export-oriented development.

When the stabilization-cum-liberalization program was launched in 1980 with the initial set of policy measures, no specific plans, timetables, or sequential order of long-run change were announced. It is unlikely that such a detailed timing/sequencing plan was ever formulated. Nonetheless, subsequent actions revealed the basic elements of a reasonably coherent plan, incorporating an impressively comprehensive set of policy measures. The specific policy objectives included: (i) the adoption of a realistic and flexible exchange rate policy; (ii) more effective export promotion measures to encourage rapid export-growth; (iii) gradual import liberalization, including the dismantling of quantitative restrictions and the rationalization of the tariff structure; (iv) improved external debt management and information systems; (v) tight monetary controls and discipline to restrain domestic absorption and reduce the rate of the inflation; (vi) deregulation of interest rates to encourage private savings; (vii) rationaliz- ation of the public investment program; (viii) a greater role for the private sector by encouraging privatization and limiting the range of sectors dominated by public enterprises; (ix) reform of the State Economic Enter- prises (SEEs) to reduce their burden on the budget and improve their efficiency; and (x) steps to improve institutional efficiency in key sectors.

In this section, we concentrate on the first three of these objectives because they are directly related to foreign trade. Associated policy reforms are only briefly reviewed since they are discussed extensively in other chapters in this volume.

Exchange Rate Policy

The January 1980 reforms immediately devalued Turkey's exchange rate by 48.6 per cent. This was followed by seven other devaluations in 1980, with an average rate for the year of TL 76 per dollar. The nominal devaluation was 144 per cent for 1980, giving rise to a 30 per cent real devaluation, with inflation running at more than 100 per cent that year. Average real exchange rates from 1979 to 1987 are summarized in Table 1.1.

After May 1981, the exchange rate was adjusted daily and, since then, the underlying policy followed in nominal devaluations has been the gradual depreciation of the real exchange rate. From May 1981 to May 1987, the average annual rate depreciation rate was 4.2 per cent. Nonethe- less, there have been short periods during which the steady real de- preciation pattern was broken. These have been caused by optimistic inflation 'targets' and concern about the feedback between the exchange rate and inflation rate. For example, from November 1981 until April 1982, the real exchange rate appreciated 17 per cent, and between February 1984 and February 1985 real appreciation was 13 per cent. Nevertheless, the overall trends shows that the policy of real exchange rate depreciation generally has been adhered to in the 1980s.

Adoption of an actively managed, flexible exchange rate system was one of the most significant positive steps undertaken in the early 1980s, and it has remained a central instrument in the trade liberalization program. Real depreciation of Turkish lira has contributed to strong export growth in recent years, and it has also played an important role in restraining growth of *ex ante* import demand.

However, the policy of real depreciation increasingly is in conflict with aggregate demand and debt management objectives. Briefly, these con- flicts arise through the following linkages. First, real depreciation leads to capital losses by increasing the real burden (in terms of domestic goods) of external debt. This acts to increase the government's budgetary deficit, and

TABLE 1.1   *Real Exchange Rate*, 1979–87 (monthly index and Annual Averages) December 1982 = 100*

	1979	1980	1981	1982	1983	1984	1985	1986	1987
Jan.	150.4	139.6	111.9	110.1	107.8	93.8	101.0	95.0	82.3
Feb.	153.4	101.9	109.5	110.1	107.9	92.0	103.7	94.7	82.4
Mar.	163.4	111.1	106.4	113.0	107.8	92.2	103.7	88.9	83.3
Apr.	171.5	107.6	105.8	113.4	105.1	95.7	100.8	86.7	83.1
May	177.3	107.6	106.2	111.6	104.7	97.6	98.5	86.8	82.8
Jun.	151.4	102.8	106.9	108.4	103.9	99.1	94.8	86.5	
Jul.	140.8	101.6	104.2	106.9	102.3	96.5	93.2	86.7	
Aug.	146.7	100.6	101.7	105.4	100.6	97.6	93.2	85.2	
Sep.	148.9	104.7	101.9	105.5	98.8	98.2	93.8	85.0	
Oct.	155.7	110.3	98.9	105.3	98.7	98.5	95.3	86.0	
Nov.	158.5	110.1	96.7	103.7	99.5	100.3	95.6	83.2	
Dec.	164.2	111.4	101.9	100.0	99.2	99.3	94.0	82.3	
Annual average RER	156.9	109.1	104.3	107.8	103.0	96.7	97.3	87.2	
Memo item: Nominal exchange rate (TL/$) period average	31.1	76.0	111.2	162.6	225.5	366.7	522.0	674.5	789.6 (Apr.)

* Derived by adjusting the nominal exchange rate for the inflation differential between Turkey and six countries (USA, UK, France, Germany, Switzerland and Italy). Decrease indicates real depreciation. Trade weights are averages for 1983–5).
SOURCE   World Bank Estimates.

adversely affects international creditworthiness, unless offset by improved export performance.[4]

Second, once a policy of real exchange rate depreciation is maintained for some time, economic units start anticipating future real depreciation. If the financial system is relatively free, such that interest arbitrage activity in financial assets denominated in foreign and local currencies is possible, then domestic real interest rates will remain above the world rates, with the differential determined by expected real depreciation and a risk premium, which itself may rise with the debt-to-output ratio. This interest arbitrage condition suggests that domestic real interest rates may have to be raised further if capital inflows are stimulated by making domestic-currency-denominated financial assets more attractive. Higher real interest rates, in turn, may retard structural adjustment in the real sector by slowing down investment in export industries.

Export-Promotion Policies

Rapid export growth has been one of the principal objectives of the economic reform program. The Government's emphasis on this objective was indeed crucial. Export growth was essential to improve the balance of payments situation, to gain international creditworthiness, to compensate for the depressed domestic demand caused by the austerity program, and thereby, to secure the survivability of the entire economic reform program.

A variety of incentives have been used to promote manufactured exports. These have included tax rebates, credit subsidies, and foreign exchange allocations that allow for the duty-free import of intermediates and raw materials. The value of these direct subsidies has averaged about 20 per cent of value of manufactured exports (Table 1.2), although they have varied considerably across different commodity categories.

Tax rebates on exports grew rapidly in the early 1980s, both in absolute terms and as a share of total exports. Manufactured commodities receiving rebates were grouped into 10 lists, where the rebate rates varied from up to 20 per cent.[5] The (weighted) average tax rebate rose from 9 per cent in 1980 to 23 per cent in 1983. The total coverage of the rebate system (measured by the share of manufactured exports eligible for rebates) rose from about 61 to 87 per cent in this period. As shown in Table 1.2, the (weighted) average subsidy component of the tax rebates went from 3.6 per cent of the fob value of manufactured exports to 11.5 per cent. This was due to increases in the rates themselves, their coverage and shifting composition of exports.[6]

The value of export credit lies in the interest rate subsidy. The differential between the rates charged on general short-term credit on export credits was over 30 per cent in 1981 and 18 per cent by the end of 1983. This decrease, due to reductions in the general rate and increases in the export rate, reflected the Government's desire to reduce interest rate differentials across the board as a policy for improving aggregate efficiency.

As shown in Table 1.2, the relative importance of export credits has declined since 1981 in comparison with the tax rebates or foreign exchange allocation and duty-free imports. The foreign exchange allocation is intended to meet import needs of exporters. Under this scheme, exporters receive the right to import raw materials and intermediate inputs duty free, up to the amount of allocated foreign exchange. The maximum amount of foreign exchange allocation was 60 per cent of the pledged export value until the end of 1983. This was reduced to 40 per cent in December 1983. The subsidy element of this export incentive resulted from any remaining foreign exchange premium and access to duty-free imports.

In late 1983, the Government announced its intention to stimulate exports less through direct export subsidies and more through active

TABLE 1.2 *Export Incentives, 1980–86: Weighted Average Subsidy Rates on Manufactured Exports (Per cent)*

	1980	1981	1982	1983	1984	1985	1986
*Elements of Subsidy**							
Export tax rebates	0.64	3.60	10.07	11.50	11.07	9.70	7.55
Preferential export credits	15.93	12.56	7.23	6.47	1.07	0	–
Foreign exchange allocation and duty-free imports	5.48	4.49	4.21	5.47	2.98	4.90	6.22
RUSF cash grants[†] (Uniform, flat rate)	–	–	–	–	–	4.00	2.18
Total subsidy*	22.05	20.65	21.51	23.44	15.12	18.60	15.95

* Subsidy rates are weighted averages, and weights are the export shares of manufactured goods in total manufactured exports.
† RUSF: Resource Utilization and Support Fund.
SOURCES Branko Milanovic, *Export Incentives and Turkish Manufactured Exports, 1980–1984*, (1986) World Bank Staff Working Paper, no. 768, World Bank reports: *Turkey: The 1986 Import and Export Regimes: Developments and Policy Recommendations* (September 1986), and *Trade Policy in Turkey in 1986 and 1987: An Evaluation* (March 1987) (mimeo).

exchange rate policy and import liberalization. This policy shift was intended to serve the long-term objective of creating a more neutral trade regime, as well as holding down government expenditures. The Government intends to reduce or eventually eliminate these subsidies.

Although no changes were made in the structure of the system, the rebate rates were uniformly lowered 20 per cent in April 1984, and an additional 25 per cent in September. In 1985, export tax rebates on 35 commodities were eliminated and those of textile exports were lowered. In July 1986 the rates were lowered to 55 per cent of their 1983 levels, and textiles were removed from the list of eligible products. The number of export tax rebate lists were reduced from 10 to 5, and the range of the tax rebate rates was lowered to a maximum of 8 per cent from 14 per cent at the beginning of 1987.

However, as shown in Table 1.2, the subsidy element in the export tax rebates has fallen less than proportionately. This is due to shifts in manufactured exports toward higher rebate categories, and the introduction of VAT rebates in 1985. Although the Government had announced its intention of removing export tax rebates by the end of 1989, reaching this target may not be feasible given the experience of rather poor export performance in 1986.

As for export credits, their costs were raised and maturities shortened four times in 1984. Also, steps were taken to reduce red tape. In January 1985, the Central Bank abolished the preferential export credit facility.[7] Thus, the subsidy element of export credits fell to 1 per cent in 1984 and to zero in 1985. But in November 1986, in a policy reversal, the Government reintroduced the export credit scheme, with the interest rate set at 38 per cent as opposed to normal short-term credit rates of 54–65 per cent.

Additionally, in 1985 the Government introduced a 4 per cent across-the-board cash premium to exporters. This new export incentive, financed from the Resource Utilization and Support Fund (RUSF), was intended as a compensation for reduced tax rebate rates and removal of export credits. The latter were reduced to 2 per cent in March 1986 and the scheme was abolished in November that year.

As a result of these changes in the export incentive schemes, the overall export subsidy rate, after reaching a high level of 23.4 per cent in 1983 fell to 15.2 per cent in 1984, rose to 18.6 per cent in 1985, and then fell again to 16 per cent in 1986.

A new system of cash incentives was introduced in January 1987. This is a selective system of export subsidies, covering 110 commodity categories. The rates of payments are specific and, in principle, determined on the basis of comparison of domestic costs and international prices. This new scheme is financed from the Support and Price Stabilization (SPSF). Data on its implementation are not yet available.

Import Liberalization

Policy reform was more gradual for imports, although the Government never hid its long-term objective of liberalization in general, and elimination of the QR system in particular.[8] Perhaps the main reasons for the slow pace in the case of imports were the worry that rapid import liberalization would contribute to the balance of payments problems and also exacerbate unemployment.[9]

The most important changes in the import regime between 1980 and 1983 were: (i) the reduction of the stamp duty from 25 to 1 per cent in January 1980;[10] (ii) gradual shifting of goods from the more restrictive Liberalized List II to Liberalized List I (see Table 1.3); (iii) reduction of pre-deposit (guarantee deposit) rates; (iv) simplification of import procedures; and (v) the abolishment of the explicit import quota list, which accounted for 13 per cent of the programmed imports in 1980.

However, significant import liberalization measures were delayed until the end of 1983. With the announcement of the 1984 Import Program, the Government introduced dramatic policy changes, the most significant being reform of the remaining elements of the QR system. Previously, commodities not explicitly included on the Quota or Liberalized Lists could not be imported. This system was replaced with a negative list system that included three different lists. The first list, the Prohibited List, included some 219 explicitly banned commodities, initially including mainly consumer goods. The second list, the Approval List (or, as alternatively

TABLE 1.3 Turkey's Import Regime in the 1980s: Liberalization of the QR System

Import Lists and Quantitative Restrictions (In terms of numbers of commodity categories)	1979	1980	1981	1982	1983	1984	1985	1986	1987
A. Under the 'Positive List' System (until the end of 1983):									
Liberalized List I	[Approx. 1600]	653	942	956	956				
Liberalized List II		958	835	821	821				
Quota List	345	312	–	–	–				
'Fund' List (introduced with the 1982 Import Program)		–	–	23	28				
B. Under the 'Negative List' System (from Jan. 1984 onwards):									
Prior Approval List* (share in 1984/85 imports)						369 (28%)	523 (25%)	290 (NA)	111 (18.6%)
'Fund' List (share in 1985 imports)						77	152	347 (28%)	572 (30%)
Prohibited List†						219	– May 1985	–	–

* Somewhat misleadingly, this list is sometimes referred to as the *License List*. Actually all imports require an import license, but in the case of Approval List items issue of a license requires obtaining a permit ('approval') from the Undersecretariat of Treasury and Foreign Trade.

† For all practical purposes, the Banned List was abolished in May 1985, as only three items were kept on the list: weapons, ammunitions and narcotics.

SOURCES *Official Gazette*, issues: no. 16880, Jan. 25 1980; no. 17208, Jan. 2 1981; no. 17565, Jan. 5 1982; no. 17919, Jan. 5 1983; no. 18266, Dec. 29 1983; and World Bank reports: *Turkey: The 1986 Import and Export Regimes* (September 1986) (mimeo); and *Trade Policy in Turkey in 1986 and 1987: An Evaluation* (March 1987) (mimeo).

referred to, the License List), requires prior approval for the issuance of import licenses. This list included 369 items initially, which accounted for about 28 per cent of 1984 imports. The third list, the Fund List, was introduced in 1983 to cover mainly luxury goods, which could be freely imported after the payment of a special levy. In contrast with the previous system, the new system allowed all other goods to be freely imported. In addition, the licensing procedures themselves were further eased.

The new system liberalized about 60 per cent of 1983 imports. Table 1.4 shows the sectoral composition and percentage of liberalized goods. Almost all consumer goods were liberalized, although this accounted for only about 5 per cent of total imports in 1983. Intermediate goods were liberalized far more than capital goods. In total, liberalized goods accounted for 43 per cent of 1984 imports.

Concurrently, significant changes in the tariff structure were made, which reduced tariffs for the majority of imports to about 20 per cent. While the announcement of the new set of lists drew stronger criticism from affected sectors than the announcement of the tariff reductions, the latter probably was more significant in reducing protection levels. As such, it should have been interpreted as strong evidence of the new Government's determination to move forward with import liberalization.

Table 1.5 summarizes the sectoral pattern of those goods whose tariffs were changed. Customs duty rates and production tax rates were reduced simultaneously for 331 commodity categories, mostly at the 6-digit level of disaggregation. Reductions ranged between 5 and 100 percentage points. The production tax rate alone was lowered for another 56 commodity categories. At the same time, customs duty rates were raised on 52 commodity categories, mostly consumer durables. On average, nominal protection increased for domestically-produced goods, due to the new levies imposed on consumer goods and tariff increases for consumer durables. Tariffs decreased for other categories, most sharply for intermediate goods, by 16 per cent on average for the affected items. The overall reduction in the statutory tariff system was 3.3 per cent.

Some of the Government's strategy was revealed in how these changes were made. In an obvious attempt to cushion the impact of liberalization, there appeared to be an inverse correlation between which sectors were hit hardest by the loss of licensing/ban protection and which had tariffs reduced. For instance, consumer imports were almost completely liberalized, but their level of tariff protection was increased. The reverse occurred for capital goods, where tariffs were reduced to a greater degree, but most capital goods remained on one or another list. Only intermediates seem to have faced lowered protection on both counts.

This is consistent with the Government's announced intention of continuing with an escalating protection system, with the lowest levels of protection provided for raw materials and intermediate goods.

18

TABLE 1.4 *1984 Changes in Protection**

	Elimination of QRs	Estimated Overall Tariff Change	Estimated Change in Nominal Protection
Agricultural products	69.3%	7.4%	Uncertain
Live animals, plants	2.6%	1.1%	Increase
Fruits and vegetables	93.3%	31.9%	Probable increase
Meat products	100.0%	0.8%	Decrease
Sugar, confectionary	100.0%	9.9%	Uncertain
Beverages and tobacco	14.2%	86.7%	Increase
Textiles and clothing	95.8%	2.8%	Uncertain
Textiles	98.0%	3.2%	Uncertain
Clothing	0.6%	-3.6%	Decrease
Total Consumer Goods	93.6%	4.5%	Uncertain
Metal ores	87.1%	0.0%	Decrease
Chemicals	81.8%	-3.8%	Decrease
Rubber and plastic	27.4%	0.9%	Decrease

Leather and furs	100.0%	4.9%	Uncertain
Wood and paper	78.5%	-18.9%	Decrease
Glass and ceramics	19.6%	-2.6%	Decrease
Iron and steel	0.1%	3.2%	Decrease
Non-ferrous metals	-2.2%	-27.4%	Decrease
Total Intermediate Goods	69.2%	-4.4%	Decrease
Metal products	6.5%	-2.7%	Decrease
Non-electrical machinery	11.9%	-0.1%	Decrease
Electrical machinery	60.2%	-14.9%	Decrease
Transportation equipment	14.3%	3.8%	Probable increase
Measuring equipment	45.8%	-10.3%	Decrease
Electronic equipment	100.0%	20.5%	Increase
Total Capital Goods	23.5%	-2.1%	Decrease
Grand Total	60.1%	-3.3%	Decrease

* The first column is the percentage of imports (in value terms) in each category that had Quota Restrictions removed in 1984. The second column is the nominal tariff reduction times the share of those categories' imports which had tariffs reduced. The third column combines these two measures. If QRs and tariffs declined, then so did protection. Other cases may be ambiguous.
SOURCE World Bank, *Turkey: Trade Policy Issues in the Structural Adjustment Process* (1984) (mimeo).

20

TABLE 1.5 *Changes in Nominal Tariff Protection, (1983–84)**

	(1) Average tariff Prior to Dec. 1983	(2) Average tariff After Jan. 1984	(2)−(1)
Agricultural products	11.1%	20.0%	8.9%
Live animals, plants	1.0%	71.6%	70.6%
Fruits and vegetables	20.6%	93.0%	72.4%
Meat products	3.9%	4.7%	0.8%
Sugar, confectionary	70.8%	80.9%	10.1%
Beverages and tobacco	128.9%	296.6%	167.7%
Textiles and clothing	26.1%	33.3%	7.2%
Textiles	24.9%	32.8%	7.9%
Clothing	67.6%	52.7%	−14.9%
Total Consumer Goods	18.0%	26.2%	8.2%
Metal ores	8.1%	2.7%	−5.4%
Chemicals	47.0%	22.5%	−24.5%
Rubber and plastic	43.8%	48.1%	4.3%

Leather and furs	4.0%	9.9%	5.9%
Wood and paper	42.0%	18.0%	-24.0%
Glass and ceramics	68.0%	2.1%	-65.9%
Iron and steel	19.7%	9.3%	-10.4%
Non-ferrous metals	41.4%	9.4%	-32.0%
Total Intermediate Goods	40.8%	18.6%	-22.2%
Metal products	31.3%	21.2%	-10.1%
Non-electrical machinery	40.3%	36.7%	-3.6%
Electrical machinery	44.5%	21.8%	-22.7%
Transportation equipment	42.6%	69.7%	27.1%
Measuring equipment	38.7%	9.9%	-28.8%
Electronic equipment	72.8%	94.9%	22.1%
Total Capital Goods	44.0%	32.0%	-12.0%
Grand Total	38.8%	22.3%	-16.5%

* The values are average weighted tariff protection for those items whose protection was affected by the changes.
SOURCE World Bank, *Turkey: Trade Policy Issues in the Structural Adjustment Process* (1984) (mimeo).

Since then, reductions in the QR system and rationalization of statutory tariffs have continued.[11] In May 1985, the Prohibited List was, for all practical purposes, abolished since only three items remained on the list — weapons, ammunition and narcotics. The number of items on the Prior Approval (License) List increased to 523 in 1985 from 369 in 1984. This was partly due to the transfer of previously banned goods into this list, and partly due to the increase in the number of tariff lines from 5000 to 8000 in January 1985, which led to the splitting of some categories into two or more categories. The size of the Approval List was reduced to 290 items in 1986 and to 111 in 1987.

Tariff rates were revised again in 1985 and 1986. Tariff categories affected by the 1985 changes accounted for 20 per cent of the imports in that year, without much change in the overall (weighted) average tariff rate, which remained at about 11 per cent. The 1986 tariff revisions were more comprehensive, affecting 1095 commodity categories which accounted for about 48 per cent of 1985 imports. As a result of these changes, the weighted average tariff for the affected items was reduced from 13.4 per cent to 11.5 per cent in 1986, and the overall (weighted) average tariff fell from 11 to 10 per cent.

These changes maintained tariff escalation, with the highest rates on capital goods (20.8 per cent), lower on non-durable consumer goods (8.2 per cent), and the lowest on intermediate goods (7 per cent). The escalation is further reinforced by the special levies mentioned earlier, increasing effective protection rates for the final products.

More recently, there have been some developments which have raised uncertainties about the future course of the import regime. First, the number of items subject to the special levy (Fund List) increased from 77 in 1984 to 152 in 1985, 347 in 1986, and to 572 in 1987. They now account for about 30 per cent of imports. Moreover, the levy rates have been changed frequently, with their overall tariff equivalent rising from 2 per cent in 1984 to 2.4 per cent in 1985, and to 5.2 per cent in 1986.

The Fund List was set up initially for the purpose of taxing luxury imports heavily and channeling the resources so collected to the newly established Mass Housing Fund. It would also serve as a vehicle for stabilizing domestic prices of certain agricultural commodities, which are susceptible to wide price fluctuations. However, as the recent developments show, the Fund List is being used as a back door method of providing greater price protection to an increasing number of domestically-produced manufactured goods. Frequent changes in the levy rates, and their rising trend, tend to indicate that the Government perhaps is giving in to demands for higher protection. This is supported by the evidence that the overall tariff plus levy rates have been rising, from about 12.8 per cent in 1984 to 13.4 per cent in 1985, and to 15.2 per cent in 1986.

A second set of policy reversals in the import regime concerns other import taxes and deposit requirements. Ostensibly, these have been raised in response to the worsening trade balance. The stamp duty was raised from 1 per cent to 4 per cent in 1985, and to 6 per cent in December 1986. The two per cent import surcharge, whose revenues are transferred to the Support and Price Stabilization Fund, was raised to 4 per cent in 1987. Also, import guarantee deposit rates, after being reduced to 3 per cent in 1985, were raised to 9 per cent in July 1986, and then reduced to 7 per cent in October 1986. In February 1988, this rate was raised to 15 per cent and was then reduced to 7 per cent in May.[12]

III TRADE AND BALANCE OF PAYMENTS PERFORMANCE IN THE 1980S

In the 1980s, trade and macroeconomic policy changes, debt relief and new foreign lending, and external developments have all affected economic performance in Turkey. Therefore, an exact attribution analysis for assessing the impact of each policy change is difficult, if not impossible. Nonetheless one can speculate on the general direction of some of the crucial interactions and linkages. In this section, we review export performance, changes in imports, and the balance of payments.[13]

Exports

Export performance since 1979 is summarized in Table 1.6. The dollar value of exports grew very rapidly, at an annual average rate of 25.4 per cent in 1980–85, before falling by 8 per cent in 1986 due to a sharp fall in exports to Iran and Iraq associated with the depressed oil prices. Over the same period, volume growth averaged 30 per cent.[14] The commodity composition of exports has shown a dramatic change, as manufactured exports grew even faster, 44 per cent annually during 1980–85, raising their share in total exports steadily from 36 per cent in 1980 to above 70 per cent by the mid-1980s. As a share of total manufacturing output, exports went from 8.5 to 15.8 per cent in 1980–83. This performance is frequently cited in illustrating the success of the 1980 reforms, a topic which is discussed at greater length in the next section.

Exports of textiles, leather goods, chemicals, iron and steel products, non-ferrous metals, machinery, electrical goods, and transportation equipment grew faster than the average of total exports. Textiles have remained as the most important export category, with their share rising from 15 per cent in 1980 to 25 per cent in 1986, while the iron and steel industry has emerged as the second most important export industry. Export-to-production ratios increased in all manufacturing sectors, most rapidly in the basic heavy industries. During this period the economy-wide export ratio almost tripled rising from 7 per cent of GNP in 1980 to over 20 per cent by mid 1980s.

The country pattern of export sales also changed very rapidly (Table 1.6). Although exports to all regions grew substantially, trade with other countries in the region exploded. Exports to Middle Eastern Countries jumped from $400 million (17 per cent of the total) in 1979 to $3.2 billion (41 per cent of the total) in 1985, before falling to $2.3 billion (31 per cent of the total) in 1986. Iran and Iraq have emerged as one of Turkey's major export markets; the share of exports to these countries rose from about 6 per cent in 1979 to 26 per cent in 1985, then fell to 15 per cent in 1986 as a result of the fall in oil prices.

Imports

Over the 1980–85 period, merchandise imports (in current US dollar terms) grew at an average rate of 16 per cent per year, then fell by 5 per cent in 1986 when the cost of oil imports declined by more than $1.5 billion (Table 1.7). The bulk of the growth in imports was concentrated in the first two years, immediately after the foreign debt crisis, and 1984. Real imports in 1980 and 1981 grew more slowly than dollar costs, and afterwards faster, reflecting the reduction in global inflation and world oil prices.

Many factors affected aggregate imports in this period. These included debt relief, new foreign lending, rapid export growth, and relaxation of import restrictions which interacted to allow import growth, while devaluations, and the austerity program of earlier years acted to reduce the *ex ante* import demand. Fluctuations in oil prices have also been an important factor. In any case, despite slower aggregate import growth in this period than in the second half of the 1970s, it was sufficient to support increased capacity utilization in the economy. The import-to-GNP ratio rose from 15 per cent in 1980 to 21 per cent in 1986. The composition of imports underwent some modest changes (Table 1.7). Since 1984, when the import liberalization began, imports of consumer goods have grown extremely rapidly, although from a small base.

Balance of Payments and Foreign Debt

Table 1.8 summarizes the movements in the balance of payments and external debt since 1980. As a result of rapid export growth, the trade deficit declined from $4.6 billion in 1980 to the $3 billion range in more recent years, whereas the current account deficit fell to below $1.5 billion range from $3.4 billion in 1980, thanks to sizeable remittances.

Workers' remittances, however, have fallen after reaching a level of $2.5 billion in 1981. This is partly explained by the fact that a portion of remittances are placed in the attractive foreign exchange deposit accounts and the Central Bank's Dresdner accounts, therefore appearing as capital account inflows. The other reason for falling remittances is the falling stock of Turkish workers in Western Europe. Finally, it is highly likely that significant amounts of remittances have been diverted to the black market away from official channels.

The non-interest current account was in deficit in 1980 and 1981, following the debt crisis of 1979. It showed a surplus in 1982, and also in 1984–86. However, growing interest payments on increasing stock of external debt led to a persistent deficits in the overall current account, although as a ratio of GNP, it fell from 5 per cent in 1980 to 2.6 per cent in 1986 (Table 1.8).

Between 1980 and 1983, outstanding foreign debt increased from $16.3 billion to $18.2 billion, while the debt-to-GNP ratio rose from 28 per cent to 35.6 per cent (Table 1.8). However, rapid export growth led to a sharp reduction in the debt-to-exports ratio. It is the latter improvements that have allowed Turkey to increase net foreign borrowing sharply since 1984 from both multilateral and bilateral sources as well as from private sources. External debt has increased by 79 per cent since 1984, reaching $32.5 billion during 1986. The share of short-term debt went from 13 per cent to 21 per cent between 1983 and 1986.[15] By the end of 1986, the debt-to-GNP ratio reached 42 per cent, the debt-to-export ratio reached 261 per cent, and the debt-service ratio reached 37 per cent.[16]

IV ANALYSIS OF EXPORT PERFORMANCE

The most frequently cited positive result of the liberalization program is Turkey's spectacular export performance, particularly the growth of manufactured exports. In this section we examine various supply-side and demand-side explanations for this rapid growth.

The period of export growth, beginning in 1980, coincided with substantial real depreciation and expanded export subsidies, implying a clear statistical correlation between improved incentives for exporters and export growth. But correlation is not proof of causality and other supply and demand factors undoubtedly were very important as well.

In particular, depressed domestic demand and excess capacity have also been crucial supply-side factors. It is important to recognize that the growth in manufactured exports did not stem from the establishment of new export industries, but from existing capacity in industries that before had been producing mostly for the domestic market (that is, industries which had originally been established for import substitution). The period after 1980 was one of macroeconomic stabilization, characterized by austerity policies that depressed domestic incomes and demand. In this

TABLE 1.6 Export Performance, 1979–86

Export Performance	1979	1980	1981	1982	1983	1984	1985	1986	1980–85
Merchandise Exports (fob)	2 261	2 910	4 703	5 890	5 905	7 389	8 255	7 583	
Growth Rate:									*(percentage change from previous year)*
Total Exports:									
Value		28.7	61.6	25.2	0.3	25.1	11.7	–8.1	25.4
Price					–12.5	1.2	1.5	–9.0	
Volume					14.6	23.6	10.1	+1.0	30.3
Industrial exports:									
Value		33.4	118.6	49.7	6.7	40.6	16.2	–11.2	44.2
Commodity Composition									*(percentage shares in total)*
Agriculture and livestock	59.4	57.4	47.2	37.3	32.8	24.5	21.6	25.3	
Mining and quarry products	5.9	6.6	4.1	3.1	3.3	3.4	3.1	3.3	
Industrial products	34.7	36.0	48.7	59.7	63.9	72.1	75.3	71.4	

Exports by Destination

(In millions of US dollars; percentage shares in parenthesis)

	1979	1980	1981	1982	1983	1984	1985	1986
OECD:	1 446	1 680	2 264	2 556	2 760	3 740	4 106	4 292
	(64.0)	(57.7)	(48.1)	(44.5)	(48.2)	(52.0)	(51.6)	(57.6)
EEC	1 132	1 300	1 564	1 802	2 066	2 781	3 204	3 263
	(50.0)	(44.7)	(33.3)	(31.4)	(36.1)	(39.0)	(40.3)	(43.8)
Eastern Europe	333	516	353	333	265	286	336	311
	(14.7)	(17.7)	(7.5)	(5.8)	(4.3)	(4.0)	(4.2)	(4.2)
Middle East countries	382	625	1 894	2 544	2 442	2 826	3 247	2 306
	(16.9)	(21.5)	(40.3)	(44.3)	(42.6)	(39.6)	(40.8)	(30.9)
of which: Iran and Iraq	125	220	793	1 402	1 407	1 685	2 040	1 112
	(5.5)	(7.5)	(16.9)	(24.4)	(24.6)	(23.6)	(25.7)	(15.0)
Other countries	99	90	193	314	281	285	271	548
	(4.4)	(3.1)	(4.1)	(5.5)	(4.9)	(4.0)	(3.4)	(7.4)
Memo item								
Exports of G & NFS/GNP (%)	7.2	10.9	14.5	15.7	19.5	20.7	18.0	

SOURCES State Institute of Statistics, *Statistical Yearbook of Turkey*, (various issues); World Bank, *Turkey Annual Data Tables*; World Bank, *Turkey: External Debt, Fiscal Policy and Sustainable Growth*, (Feb. 1988) (mimeo).

28

TABLE 1.7 *Imports, 1979–86*

Imports	1980	1981	1982	1983	1984	1985	1986
			(in millions of current US dollars)				
Merchandise Imports (fob)	7 513	8 567	8 518	8 895	10 331	11 230	10 664
			(percentage change from previous year)				
Growth Rates:							
Total Imports:							
Value	56.0	14.0	−0.6	4.4	16.1	8.7	−5.0
Price	24.0	−3.0	0	−6.9	−2.1	0.3	−9.5
Volume				12.2	18.6	8.4	4.8
Oil Imports:							
Value	192.9	10.3	8.3	−8.1	−8.7	−1.1	−43.2
Volume	61.4	−4.9	21.8	−2.0	23.7	2.3	9.4
			(percentage shares in total)				
Commodity Composition	*1980*	*1981*	*1982*	*1983*	*1984*	*1985*	*1986*
Agriculture and livestock	0.6	2.1	2.0	1.5	3.4	3.3	4.1

	1980	1981	1982	1983	1984	1985	1986
Mining and quarry products	39.1	38.7	42.3	37.3	33.9	32.0	19.3
of which: Fuels	(37.3)	(36.2)	(39.9)	(35.1)	(32.8)	(30.7)	(17.8)
Industrial products	60.2	59.2	55.7	61.2	62.2	64.7	76.6
Imports by Origin:			*(percentage shares in total)*				
OECD:	45.3	47.9	50.1	48.5	51.7	56.1	65.8
EEC	(29.8)	(29.5)	(29.0)	(30.1)	(30.8)	(34.3)	(41.1)
Eastern Europe	10.5	9.5	4.8	8.7	8.8	5.8	7.9
Middle East countries	40.5	38.5	41.6	37.3	32.7	30.0	17.1
of which: Iran and Iraq	(25.7)	(23.3)	(24.5)	(23.5)	(23.2)	(21.1)	(8.9)
Other countries	3.7	4.1	3.4	5.4	6.8	8.2	9.3
Memo item							
Exports of G & NFS/GNP (%)	15.0	16.5	17.9	19.6	23.1	23.5	20.7

SOURCES State Institute of Statistics, *Statistical Yearbook of Turkey*, (various issues); World Bank, Turkey Annual Data Tables; World Bank, *Turkey: External Debt, Fiscal Policy and Sustainable Growth*, (Feb. 1988) (mimeo).

TABLE 1.8 Balance of Payments and External Debt Burden Indicators, 1980–86 (in millions of US dollars and percentages)

	1980	1981	1982	1983	1984	1985	1986
Balance of Payments							
				(in millions of US dollars)			
Merchandise Trade Balance	−4 603	−3 864	−2 628	−2 990	−2 942	−2 975	−3 081
Interest payments	−1 138	−1 443	−1 565	−1 511	−1 586	−1 753	−2 134
Workers' remittances	2 071	2 490	2 140	1 513	1 807	1 714	1 634
Current account balance	−3 408	−1 919	−935	−1 898	−1 407	−1 013	−1 528
Memo items:							
Current account balance/GNP (%)	−5.0	−2.8	−1.6	−3.6	−2.8	−1.9	−2.6
Non-interest current account							
Balance/GNP (%)	−3.9	−0.8	+1.2	−0.4	+0.4	+1.4	+1.0
Overall External Debt							
				in billions of US dollars			
Debt outstanding and disbursed (DOD)	16.3	16.9	17.6	18.2	20.8	25.5	32.5
Medium- and long-term	13.8	14.7	15.9	16.0	17.6	20.8	25.6
Short-term	2.5	2.2	1.8	2.3	3.2	4.8	6.9
Debt Ratios (%)				(in percent)			
Debt/GNP	28.0	28.6	32.8	35.6	41.5	47.9	55.9
Debt/export*	284.1	198.3	175.0	192.9	180.5	194.5	260.5
Total debt service/exports*	30.6	NA	28.5	30.3	26.1	33.4	37.2

* Exports include goods, factor and non-factor services plus workers' remittances.
SOURCES SIS, *Statistical Yearbook of Turkey*, (various issues); World Bank, Turkey Annual Data Tables; World Bank, *Turkey: External Debt, Fiscal Policy and Sustainable Growth* (Feb. 1988) (mimeo).

environment, exports provided an alternative to falling domestic demand. Diversion of production into exports may have been necessary for many firms to avoid bankruptcy or Government bailout.

In the short run, with capacity fixed and weak domestic demand, a sufficient condition for the profitability of exporting is that marginal export revenue (foreign exchange price times the effective exchange rate or EER) exceeds marginal costs. Although devaluations raised the costs of many intermediates, marginal costs that Turkish firms actually faced declined in late 1980, as a result of prohibition on layoffs which, in effect, made labor costs fixed, leaving only intermediate inputs and their costs truly marginal. Moreover, with excess capacity in almost all sectors, it is likely that marginal costs were quite flat and not rising significantly with export quantities.

In a period in which export supply functions were practically flat and shifting to the right because of weakening domestic demand, improved EERs provided the needed extra push on the supply side. At the same time, EERs above the level corresponding to the upward turning point of marginal costs (where unused capacity starts disappearing) would, in the short run, be expected to generate little additional supply response but would improve financial profits for the exporters, strengthening firms' balance sheets.

On the demand side, since Turkey's share of world exports in all exported manufacturing commodities is small, in general the effects of devaluation do not change the foreign exchange price of her exports. At the same time, it has certainly been the case that Turkey has faced stiff price competition, especially in the European textile markets, from Asian exporting countries. For these commodities, increases in real EERs would be expected to lead to some demand responses. Indeed, some regression results reported by Anand, Chhibber and van Wijnbergen (this volume) show that price competition in the major OECD markets with the other exporting countries has been important for Turkish exports.

Several other demand-side factors also are relevant. Perhaps most importantly, the Government was very actively involved in this period in arranging bilateral trade deals, especially in development of regional markets. For political and economic reasons Turkey's oil suppliers (Iran, Iraq, Libya and Saudi Arabia) became more willing to enter into what in effect were barter deals, in which crude oil would be exchanged for Turkish agricultural and manufactured goods.

Although export growth to the OECD countries has averaged almost 20 per cent annually since 1980, it is likely that exports could have grown even more rapidly if the macroeconomic situation (especially in Europe) had been more favorable.[17] Slow growth in aggregate demand for imports by these countries meant that, for several important Turkish exports, quantitative restrictions were often binding and increasing slowly, implying that the demand curves were kinked at the level of the QRs. For newer, or non-traditional, export commodities the short run demand functions may also be kinked, but the rate of outward shift would depend more on marketing and reputation building for quality and reliability.

Several statistical tests were attempted to measure a quantitative relationship between manufactured export performance and price incentives. One question was whether those sectors in which exports grew relatively rapidly since 1980 were also those sectors that received the most favorable treatment in terms of subsidy rates. Another important question was whether additional real devaluation after 1980 contributed to the aggregate or sectoral export performance.

Using cross-section, time-series data on sectoral exports, total subsidy rates, and real exchange rates for the period 1980–84, it was not possible to establish any statistically significant relationships among these variables.[18] Variations in EERs do not seem to explain the sharp differences among sectors in export growth performance.[19] These negative results provide weak support for the hypotheses that, in general, more uniform and somewhat lower export subsidies (or real EERs) would have been sufficient supply-side incentive for the export growth in the first half of the 1980s.

V   SUSTAINABILITY OF TRADE LIBERALIZATION

While the Government has generally maintained the process of export promotion and import liberalization, the recent policy reversals referred to in Section II raise questions about the Government's commitment to establishing a neutral trade regime. The key question is if, and how, the Government will attempt to deal with current macroeconomic problems — high inflation, low private investment in manufacturing industries, high unemployment, and a forthcoming debt-servicing bubble — without major policy reversals on the trade side. The interaction of these issues is briefly discussed here.

Rapid increases in the public sector's borrowing requirement in recent years have become a serious source of instability in the economy, fuelling inflationary expectations, pressuring the balance of payments and, with continued depreciation of the real exchange rate, keeping real interest rates high, thus leading to a crowding out of private sector investment.[20] A combination of revenue raising and expenditure cutting (perhaps a slow-down in infrastructure investments) effort is urgently needed. Trade liberalization may be directly threatened by the imposition of distortionary and protectionist import levies imposed for revenue raising.

It is equally clear that the Government has to take significant corrective measures to address the rapidly deteriorating foreign debt situation. While the option of rescheduling appears sensible, it may not be considered by the Government because of possible adverse implications for Turkey's international credit standing. The danger again is that *ad hoc* restrictions on imports will be used as a political expediency.

Thus, the immediate concern regarding import liberalization is the Government's readiness to use various import surcharges to redress its growing budget deficit problem, to raise funds for rapidly proliferating extra-budgetary accounts, and to restrict imports for balance-of-payments purposes. Such measures have been used more than once in recent years, as was described in Section II. The apparent arbitrariness of these changes also seems to point to increased rent-seeking behavior in the current import regime.

Maintaining strong export performance is crucial, not only for servicing the foreign debt, and thus protecting Turkey's credit standing, but also for the sustainability of the on-going import liberalization process. To achieve sustained export growth, continuing real depreciation may not be sufficient. Creation of new productive capacity in export industries will also be necessary. There is also inconsistency between the declared aim of a neutral trade regime and the policy of maintaining an escalating tariff structure.

While direct export incentives may result in short run efficiency gains in the utilization of existing capacity, long run export performance will depend on permanent changes in resource allocation, new capacity creation, product diversification and differentiation, information gathering, marketing, quality control and so forth. Turkey has only recently started learning the art of exporting as a business and so far there has been little in the way of new capacity creation. To stimulate the required private investment in manufacturing it will be necessary to bring down real interest rates and reduce the great uncertainty about future trade policy. This uncertainty has been fostered by frequent changes recently in export and import policies and tax/subsidy rates.

Finally, there is ample evidence from the trade liberalization experience of other countries that sound macroeconomic management is the key for avoiding policy reversals. Failure to contain the growth of domestic absorption when import liberalization is underway has often resulted in trade liberalization being blamed for macroeconomic difficulties. Therefore, improving macroeconomic management is a priority task for the Government of Turkey, not only to redress domestic macroeconomic imbalances but also to save trade liberalization from falling victim to macroeconomic mismanagement.

NOTES

1. The views expressed here are those of the authors and should not be attributed to the World Bank and its affiliated organizations or MIT.
2. The strategy followed in foreign borrowing is perhaps the best indicator of how badly the economy was managed. Successive governments assumed enormous risk by promoting short-term borrowing with the Central Bank assuming the full exchange risk. Celâsun and Rodrik (forthcoming) present an excellent analysis of the destabilizing effects of the borrowing strategy in the 1975–7 period.
3. This paper draws on our recent monograph *The Timing and Sequencing of Trade Liberalization Policies: The Case of Turkey*. That research was undertaken as part of a 19 country study of the timing and sequencing of trade policy liberalization episodes which was sponsored by the World Bank.
4. This points to potential conflict between the policy of boosting export competitiveness through exchange rate depreciation and attempts to reduce fiscal deficits.
5. Further details on the timing and magnitude of changes in export incentives during the 1980s are presented in: Baysan and Blitzer (forthcoming), Milanovic (1986), Şenses (1984), World Bank (1986, 1987).
6. The subsidy component of these depends on the average rebate rate, the proportion of eligible exports, and the indirect taxes actually paid during the production of exported goods. Note that in January 1985, a value-added tax (VAT) replaced all the indirect domestic taxes. Rebate of VAT on exports since the beginning of 1985 has made export tax rebates a direct subsidy by almost the full amount, since exporters have had access to duty-free imports of their inputs.
7. Commercial banks continued extending export credits at interest rates 4–5 percentage points below their non-preferential rates, with the understanding that exporters would sell their foreign exchange receipts to them.
8. The import regime is administered through annual import programs, which, through 1983, contained three lists under a 'positive' import list system. Liberalized List I contained the most freely importable goods, for which licenses were issued automatically. Liberalized List II was a restricted list, where obtaining an import license required prior approval. The third was the Quota List, which had dollar value limits for specified commodities, and predetermined shares allocated to industrialists and commercial importers.
9. See Baysan and Blitzer (forthcoming) for a detailed discussion of this issue.
10. In addition to customs duties, other levies on imports include: (i) a stamp duty (levied on the c.i.f. value of imports across-the-board); (ii) Municipal Tax (15 per cent of the applicable customs duty); (iii) a wharf duty (5 per cent of the sum of c.i.f. value plus customs duty plus municpality tax plus customs clearance expenses); and, until 1985, (iv) a production tax, ranging from 10 to 75 per cent (on the sum of c.i.f. value plus customs duty plus municipality tax plus clearing expenses plus wharf duty). Production taxes were also levied on domestically produced substitutes. In 1985, a VAT replaced all the domestic indirect taxes, including the production tax.
11. Starting in 1984, administrative procedures were centralized in the Treasury and Foreign Trade Undersecretariat, permitting more flexible and efficient running of the system.
12. Import guarantee deposits are kept with the Central Bank until imports are cleared, and they do not carry any interest. Occasionally, deposit rates are

raised not only to curtail *ex ante* demand for imports but also to reduce money supply.

13. Other aspects of economic performance since 1980 are reviewed elsewhere in this volume. Further details regarding trade and external performance can be found in Baysan and Blitzer (forthcoming).

14. There is some evidence that at least part of the export growth was actually due to inflated figures attributable to 'fictitious' exports and over-invoicing. Such abuse of the system was encouraged by export subsidies large enough to permit arbitrage on either black markets or in Europe where TL traded at a discount. It is estimated that during 1981–85, the average extent of over-invoiced/ fictitious exports to OECD was 12.6 per cent. On this subject, see Celâsun and Rodrik (forthcoming) and Milanovic (1986).

15. Over 90 per cent of the external debt is publicly owed or guaranteed.

16. These ratios understate the burden since they exclude short-run debt servicing. For further details, see Rodrik (this volume).

17. Regression results obtained by Anand, Chhibber and van Wijnbergen (this volume) indicate that income elasticity of import demand of the major OECD countries for Turkey's exports exceeded unity for the sample period 1968–84.

18. We used two estimation methods in our World Bank study of trade liberalization in Turkey. In one, Spearman rank correlation coefficients were calculated based on the rankings of the manufacturing sectors according to their export growth rates and their real EERs. In the other, ordinary least squares regression equations were estimated with the sectoral export levels, export growth rates, and export shares as dependent variables and with subsidy rates, real exchange rates and real EERs as independent variables. In both cases, we used yearly data for 1979–84.

19. Regression results obtained by Celâsun and Rodrik (forthcoming) also show that the exchange rate policy has played 'a comparatively small role' in affecting Turkey's export volume.

20. For a discussion of recent trends in private investment, see Conway (this volume).

REFERENCES

Baysan, T. and C. Blitzer (forthcoming) *The Timing and Sequencing of Trade Liberalization Policies: The Case of Turkey*, a World Bank research study.

Celâsun, M. (1986) 'Income Distribution and Domestic Terms of Trade in Turkey, 1978–83', *METU Studies in Development* 13, pp. 193–216.

Celâsun, M. and D. Rodrik (forthcoming) *Debt, Adjustment, and Growth: Turkey*.

Erdilek, A. (1986) 'Turkey's New Open-Door Policy of Direct Foreign Investment: A Critical Analysis of Problems and Prospects', *METU Studies in Development* 13, pp. 171–91.

Milanovic, B. (1986) *Export Incentives and Turkish Manufactured Exports, 1980–1984*, (Washington DC: World Bank) World Bank Staff Working Paper no. 768.

Şenses, F. (1984) 'An Assessment of Turkey's Liberalization Attempts since 1980 against the Background of her Stabilization Program', *METU Studies in Development* 10, pp. 271–321.

World Bank (1984) *Turkey: Trade Policy Issues in the Structural Adjustment Process* (Washington DC).

World Bank (1986) *Turkey: The 1986 Import and Export Regimes: Developments and Policy Recommendations* (Washington DC).

World Bank (1987) *Trade Policy in Turkey in 1986 and 1987: An Evaluation* (Washington DC).

World Bank (1987) *Fiscal Policy and Tax Reform in Turkey* (Washington DC).

World Bank (1988) *Turkey: External Debt, Fiscal Policy and Sustainable Growth* (Washington DC).

2 Fiscal Aspects of Adjustment in the 1980s

Merih Celâsun[1]

I INTRODUCTION

In the post-1973 era, Turkey faced her debt crisis before the second oil shock of 1979, and launched an outward-oriented and market-based program in 1980. Against the background of the rapidly worsening economic situation in 1978–9, the post-1980 adjustment effort produced credible results in a number of important directions. After a brief interval of output contraction in 1980, the program proved to be effective in relieving commodity shortages and hoarding, inducing an export-led recovery, and restoring creditworthiness just as other heavily indebted LDCs were entering into deepest crises in their recent history.

Ex-post assessments of her macroeconomic performance indicate that Turkey's post-1980 policy experiment benefited in a substantial way from sizable debt relief and new lending provided by the bilateral creditors (mainly OECD countries) and multilateral institutions (IMF and World Bank). During the difficult stage of 1980–3, the cumulative financial transfer (net foreign borrowing less interest payments) was nearly a positive $3 billion.

With the termination of debt relief in 1984, Turkey's debt-servicing burden sharply increased, and net financial transfer turned nearly negative in 1984–7. Nonetheless, Turkey's external debt stock increased in US dollars to about 38 billion in 1987 from 18 billion in 1983, largely reflecting the appreciation of the major European currencies against the US dollar after 1985.

At the end of 1987, the available indicators of Turkey's overall adjustment point out two major areas of concern for the policy-makers. First, there seems to be an emerging socio-political consensus that the distributional aspects of the adjustment program require a more sensitive policy treatment in the future, which is likely to restrict the scope for measures resulting in the further erosion of real incomes of unprotected groups in the society (mainly urban labor and agricultural producers). Second, the economic recovery and adjustment process needs to be transformed into a sustainable growth process to meet the pressing employment requirements of Turkey's rapidly expanding labor force.

A sustainable growth pattern with a strong export-orientation is also

37

essential for the servicing of external debt, which increased to about 58 per cent of GNP in 1987 from 36 per cent in 1983. Since the bulk of Turkey's external debt stock is held by the public sector (and Central Bank), the medium-term growth process needs to be strongly coupled with more efficient resource mobilization methods in the public sector, which takes the brunt of adjustment for debt repayments.

Under the economic conditions prevailing in 1987, establishment of a solid basis for sustainable growth faces, however, a number of interrelated constraints in the domestic economy. These constraints pertain mainly to firstly, persistently large fiscal deficits, which are increasingly financed by high-yield government securities, and secondly, excessively high interest rates, which threaten stability in the financial system, and inhibit new private investment in export-oriented activities, such as manufacturing, which relied on improved rates of capacity utilization in the 1980–87 period.

Besides reflecting the impact of bond financing of fiscal deficits, high interest rates are also affected by exchange rate depreciation as arbitrage equilibrium conditions appear to hold under currency substitution and financial openness.[2] While serving as the key mechanism to enhance international competitiveness, exchange rate depreciations generate yet another side effect by increasing the domestic currency value of external debt burden, which in turn leads to the widening of fiscal deficits.

These policy conflicts produce pressures on the prices, and weaken the foundations of macroeconomic stability, which is a precondition of sustainable outward-oriented growth in the late 1980s and early 1990s. Furthermore, the remaining imperfections in product and financial markets engender additional difficulties in inflation reduction, which has been an unsatisfactory component of macroeconomic performance in the mid-1980s. In such a policy setting, a more concerted effort for fiscal retrenchment appears to be a cornerstone of new policy initiatives required to restore macroeconomic stability in Turkey.

Against the backdrop of these policy concerns obtaining toward the end of 1987, the present paper aims to provide an interpretive review of the Turkish fiscal adjustment in the post-1980 period. Within the framework of national accounts, the paper focuses on the size, structure and macro-economy linkages of the Turkish public finance, and thus eschews disaggregated description of its particular components.[3]

From the methodological standpoint, fiscal adjustment may be analyzed on the basis of either flow-based or stock-based measures, which have varying limitations as well as advantages. The stock-based measures would allow a sharper focus on the structure of deficit financing, and its decomposition into real and nominal parts.[4] In turn, flow-based measures provide a more extensive base to interpret the nature of movements in public sector incomes and expenditures. Since a key objective of the present paper is to bring out and highlight the shifts in the size and patterns of public revenue, expenditure and savings, flow-based fiscal data are assembled to serve as a factual basis for our assessments.

The remainder of the paper is organized around six additional sections. Section II reviews the broad nature of background factors, overall adjustment and fiscal strategy in the 1980s. Section III examines public sector aggregates in relation to macroeconomic adjustment, deficit financing, and domestic credit patterns. Section IV analyzes the changes observed in the composition of public revenue, savings and investment. Section V draws attention to policy conflicts produced by revenue-raising processes in state economic enterprises (SEEs) and extra-budgetary funds (EBF). Following the evaluation of indicators of public debt in Section VI, concluding remarks together with a brief discussion of fiscal prospects are presented in Section VII.

II OVERALL ADJUSTMENT AND FISCAL POLICY: AN OVERVIEW

Background

In the aftermath of the 1970 devaluation, the Turkish economy experienced an unexpectedly large improvement in its external position in a favorable world economic environment. The reserve accumulation was impressive in 1972–73. Turkey's initial policy response to the external shocks of the mid-1970s was one of deferred internal adjustment, reserve decumulation and additional external financing to sustain a rapid inward-oriented growth until the emergence of a debt crisis in mid-1977. Why did the Turkish economic growth come to a grinding halt so early in the post-1973 era?

Two sets of key factors may be identified to explain Turkey's early debt crisis in the 1970s. The first set relates to the largely unnoticed build-up of price and incentive distortions in 1973–77, which caused not only a stagnation in exports, but also a rapid rise in the intensity of imported inputs in current production. The rising import dependence resulted in a negative import-substitution as a source of growth at the aggregate level. Against the backdrop of sharply deteriorating export performance, and reduced flexibility in the import-dependent productive structure, Turkey's short-term capability in debt-servicing was gravely impaired.

The second and more crucial set of explanatory factors for the early crisis pertain to the sudden ending of foreign lending in 1977, which had its major source in an ill-structured borrowing policy. In the context of overvalued currency, anticipated devaluation and stagnating exports, Turkey's debt management relied strongly on exchange rate guaranteed short-term debt instruments, which quickly destabilized macroeconomic balances through an uncurbed over-borrowing by the private sector.[5] With the sudden loss of creditors' confidence in Turkey's ability to service its debt, all bank lines were abruptly terminated in mid-1977.

The elasticity of substitution between domestic output and imported goods proved to be too low in coping with foreign exchange shortages from mid-1977 onwards. The suddenly reduced foreign lending, and subsequent import compression in 1978–79 caused large dislocations in domestic production.

The 1978–79 episode was successful in negotiating a massive restructuring of Turkey's external debt, but failed in three respects. First, it could not produce a coherent policy package for adjustment. Second, it could not adequately curb nominal expenditures and monetary expansion. Third, it could not secure sufficient new lending from abroad. A heavy reliance on import compression via rationing produced output contraction and high inflation.

Overall Adjustment in the 1980s

As described in detail elsewhere, Turkey introduced a comprehensive set of policy measures in early 1980.[6] These measures were consolidated and extended in successive stages in 1980–5. The contents and modalities of the policy measures were substantially shaped by the conditionalities of a three-year IMF stand-by arrangement and five World Bank structural adjustment loans.

Viewed as a whole, the new policies aimed at two broad objectives: stabilization combined with export-led recovery; and liberalization of the Turkish economy. The process of liberalization featured the following sequence: (i) deregulation of industrial product prices; (ii) considerable decontrol of the financial markets through an interest rate reform; (iii) trade liberalization in stages; and (iv) partial decontrol of the capital account of the balance of payments.

The initial conditions required large price corrections to reduce SEE deficits, promote exports and stimulate financial savings. After a steep initial devaluation and switch to positive real interest rates for time deposits, flexible exchange rate and industrial price policies were adopted. In a lurching general equilibrium framework, these price policy adjustments were validated by real wage cuts and reduced terms of trade for agriculture, which were engendered through a semi-formal incomes policy under the transitional military government from September 1980 to November 1983.[7]

Somewhat in contradistinction to the policy guidelines of the multilateral agencies, the Turkish policy-makers showed a growth-bias in two areas. First, by shifting the burden of fiscal correction to cuts in SEE deficits and current outlays, the real growth of public investment was maintained in 1980–81 to offset the contractionary output effects of falling private investment. Second, import liberalization was gradual in 1980–83 to avoid output losses and/or further decline in real wages. The anti-export trade-regime bias implied by the remaining non-tariff barriers during 1980–3 was substantially reduced by large export incentives. Thus, an early resumption of export-led growth was helpful in restoring policy credibility at home and external creditworthiness abroad.

Turkey's GNP growth averaged around 5.7 per cent in 1981–87. In current prices, the ratio of merchandise exports to GNP increased from 5 per cent in 1980 to more than 15 per cent in 1985. From the viewpoint of price-level stabilization, Turkey's recent adjustment experience contains, however, some disappointing characteristics. The inflation rates hovered around 30–40 per cent in 1985–86, reaching nearly 50 per cent in 1987. Large fiscal deficits, exchange rate adjustments, and non-competitive pricing in industrial and financial markets appear to be the major underlying factors for persistent inflationary pressures.[8]

Overall Fiscal Policy

From 1973 to 1977, public spending was accelerated, and widening deficits were financed by domestic credit expansion. Under reserve decumulation and heavy short-term borrowing, which caused a decline in net foreign assets of the Central Bank, credit expansion to the public sector was largely sterilized, producing only a moderate monetary expansion and inflation.

In turn, with the reduced foreign borrowing in 1978–9, deficit financing through Central Bank credits could no longer be sterilized, leading to an unprecedented rise in money supply and domestic inflation. The reduction of public sector deficits and creation of more sustainable fiscal conditions became therefore a key concern of the post-1980 adjustment effort.

In the 1980s, the fiscal policy as a whole evolved in response to (i) stabilization, output recovery and liberalization objectives of the overall adjustment program, and (ii) policy-makers' desire to remove structural weaknesses in Turkey's public finance system.

In the early 1980s, to accommodate a restrictive monetary stance and reduce deficits, the fiscal strategy relied on resource mobilization through SEE price hikes, real wage cuts, and expenditure restraint on public consumption to provide room for public investment expansion. In response to overall policy emphasis on export promotion and financial liberalization, fiscal burdens and incentives were modified in appropriate directions. In the post-1983 period, bond financing of deficits became a complementary tool of fiscal policy.

For the removal of deeper structural weaknesses in Turkey's public finances, policy initiatives strived to achieve acceptable results in the following areas: (i) reforming of the tax system; (ii) systemic improvement of the SEEs; (iii) rationalization of public investment; and (iv) fiscal decentralization away from the central government in favor of a greater fiscal autonomy for the local authorities. After 1983, ostensibly to increase fiscal and allocational flexibility, the Özal administration expanded the scale and number of extra-budgetary funds, which quickly became a significant segment of public sector resource management. The structural change in public finance is discussed further in Sections IV and V.

In terms of generating new employment, the public sector has played a restrained role in the post-1980 period. In the mid-1980s, the shares of public services and SEEs in non-agricultural employment (totaling about 6.5 million workers) were nonetheless sizable, about 20 and 11.5 per cent, respectively. While maintaining the level of employment, the public sector resorted to real wage cuts to reduce the share of wage bill in its total spending. In the absence of an effective labor union activity, real wage flexibility was also observed in the private sector as an adjustment mechanism to accommodate high interest rates and exchange rate depreciations in the economy. Consequently, the share of formal wage income in GDP declined from 33 per cent in 1979 to about 18 per cent in 1985–86 (See Özmucur, 1987).

After this brief outline of initial conditions, overall adjustment and fiscal policy, we now turn to the review of various sets of fiscal data processed for the 1980–87 period.

III MACROECONOMY AND PUBLIC SECTOR

In Turkey's recent macroeconomic history, the public sector as a whole has played a significant role in domestic investment effort. The traditionally activist role of the government in investment may be explained partly by the huge infrastructure requirements of Turkey's semi-developed economy, and partly by policy concern to offset the low investment propensity of the private sector. The policy commitment to rapid industrialization was also an underlying factor for the rise in public investment in the 1970s. While its composition was restructured toward non-industrial sectors, public investment nevertheless served, in addition to exports, as a demand-side source of growth in the post-1980 period.

In the Turkish macroeconomic setting, the traditional emphasis on public investment exacerbates the difficulties that surround the matching of internal and external adjustments in the economy. The socio-political constraints on raising public revenues and moderating current expenditures often result in large public sector savings gaps, which absorb private-savings surpluses as well as external savings. Prior to 1983, the resource transfers from the private to public sector were effected mainly through new money creation by the Central Bank, which intensified inflationary pressures. After 1983, the bulk of such resource transfers takes place through the channels of bond financing at high interest rates as noted previously in the introduction to this paper.

Public Sector and Internal Adjustment

Table 2.1 presents data on the public and private sector components of savings, investment and real expenditure growth in the Turkish economy from 1976 to 1987. These data show that the share of total investment in GNP dropped from 25 per cent in 1976–7 to 18.4 per cent in 1978–79, and then recovered to 20.7 per cent in 1980–85. The rapidly falling share of private investment in GNP contributed to proportional downfall in total investment, which was prevented from a further decline by public investment activity in the post-1980 period.

The sectoral savings balances shown in Table 2.1 indicate that the counterpart of reduction in foreign savings (that is, current account deficits) was the contraction of public savings gaps. This was achieved not by reducing public investment expenditure, but through raising the share of public savings in GNP. The nature of this adjustment may be clarified by the analysis of fiscal aggregates assembled in Table 2.2.

Table 2.2 data point to an increase in aggregate public revenue (as per cent of GNP) from 1981 onwards. This was, however, offset by the rapid rise in current transfers (to private sector and abroad) to produce a fairly constant share of public disposable income in GNP, as measured in current prices, especially after it reached its peak in 1981–82. In turn, the share of public consumption in public disposable income was reduced to give scope for the expansion of public savings.

The characteristics of the adjustment process become magnified when the relevant aggregates are measured as percentages of GNP in constant 1983 prices, which reflect the effects of post-1980 relative price changes. Panel B data in Table 2.1 bring out the large real volumes of current deficit reductions from 1976–77 onwards. During 1978–79, current deficit was sharply reduced through import compression. From 1980 on, current deficit was lowered by export expansion, which enabled a rise in real imports to relieve imported-input constraint on domestic production. In constant price terms, the improvement in public savings gaps comes out more sharply in the post-1980 period.

Memo items in Table 2.2 measure (as per cent of GNP) public disposable income and its constituent parts in constant 1983 prices. These figures point to a significant real income shift toward the public sector in 1980–81. Symmetrically, private disposable income declined in relation to GNP in

TABLE 2.1 *Macroeconomic Balances and Public Sector, 1976–87*

	1976–7 Average	1978–9 Average	1980	1981	1982	1983	1984	1985	1986	1987‡
A. % GNP, Current Prices										
Investment	24.9	18.4	21.4	21.5	20.3	20.6	19.6	20.5	24.1	25.0
Private	12.5	8.9	9.9	8.3	8.3	9.1	9.6	9.5	11.0	11.5
Public	12.4	9.5	11.5	13.2	12.0	11.5	10.0	11.0	13.6	13.5
Domestic savings	19.1	16.0	15.9	18.0	18.1	16.5	16.8	18.6	22.0	23.5
Private	11.9	12.0	10.6	9.4	9.2	9.2	9.2	9.4	11.7	16.0
Public	7.2	4.0	5.3	8.6	8.9	7.3	7.6	9.2	10.3	7.5
Foreign savings*	5.8	2.4	5.5	3.5	2.2	4.1	2.8	1.9	2.6	1.5
Sectoral savings − investment balances										
Private	−0.6	3.1	0.7	1.1	0.9	0.1	−0.4	−0.1	0.7	4.5
Public	−5.2	−5.5	−6.2	−4.6	−3.1	−4.2	−2.4	−1.8	−3.3	−6.0
Total (= − foreign savings)	−5.8	−2.4	−5.5	−3.5	−2.2	−4.1	−2.8	−1.9	−2.6	−1.5

B. *% GNP, Constant 1983 Prices*

Sectoral savings – investment balances

Private	-9.1	-1.1	-0.4	0.4	0.4	0.1	1.0	0.8	1.6	1.1
Public	-10.7	-7.7	-7.2	-5.3	-3.5	-4.2	-3.9	-2.7	-3.5	-4.7
Total (= – foreign savings)	-19.8	-8.8	-7.6	-4.9	-3.1	-4.1	-2.9	-1.9	-1.9	-3.6

C. *Growth of Real Expenditures (% per year)*[†]

Private	8.2	-3.5	-6.3	-0.3	4.3	4.7	5.9	4.0	8.4	8.2
Public	11.4	-0.5	2.0	5.2	2.1	1.5	2.3	8.9	9.0	0.2
Total	8.9	-2.9	-4.7	0.8	3.8	4.0	5.2	5.0	8.6	6.3

Memo item (% growth per year)

Real GNP	5.9	1.2	-1.1	4.1	4.6	3.2	5.9	5.1	7.8	6.8

* Current account deficit (after debt relief). The 1984–7 figures follow the revised presentation of the Central Bank for the balance of payments.

† Domestic final expenditure excluding inventory changes.

‡ Provisional estimates.

SOURCES Celâsun and Rodrik (forthcoming, Table 5.5); SPO (1988) for 1986–7 data.

TABLE 2.2 *Fiscal Aggregates, 1978–87*

	1978–9 Average	1980	1981	1982	1983	1984	1985	1986	1987*
Public Sector (% GNP, current prices)									
1. Revenue[†]	20.3	19.8	22.2	22.9	22.4	21.8	23.8	28.7	28.0
2. Current transfers[‡]	2.9	2.3	2.9	3.2	5.0	5.2	6.1	9.3	11.0
3. Disposable income (=1–2)	17.4	17.5	19.3	19.7	17.4	16.6	17.7	19.4	16.9
Consumption	13.4	12.2	10.7	10.8	10.1	9.0	8.5	9.1	9.4
Savings	4.0	5.3	8.6	8.9	7.3	7.6	9.2	10.3	7.5
4. Final expenditure[§] (consumption+investment)	22.9	23.7	23.9	22.7	21.6	19.0	19.5	22.7	22.9
5. Total expenditure (=2+4)	25.8	26.0	26.8	26.0	26.6	24.2	25.6	32.0	34.0
6. Savings-investment balance (=3–4)	−5.5	−6.2	−4.6	−3.1	−4.2	−2.4	−1.8	−3.3	−6.0
Memo items									
Wealth tax (% GNP)	0.2	0.1	0.1	0.1	0.1	0.2	0.2	0.4	0.4
Public disposable income (% GNP, 1983 prices)	12.4	15.5	18.6	18.8	17.4	16.2	17.4	17.9	15.4
of which									
Consumption	9.8	10.9	10.5	10.2	10.1	9.8	9.6	10.0	10.0
Savings	2.6	4.6	8.1	8.6	7.3	6.4	7.8	7.9	5.4

* Provisional estimates.
[†] Includes factor income from property and net surplus of social security institutions; excludes wealth tax and capital flows.
[‡] Includes subsidies and interest payments; excludes capital transfers.
[§] Excludes capital transfers and debt (principal) repayment.
SOURCES   SPO (1985 and 1988); Central Bank (1987); Celâsun and Rodrik (forthcoming, Table 8.1).

real terms, leading to reduction in private expenditures in 1980–81 to provide room for export expansion promoted by exchange rate depreciation and other supportive measures.

The constant price data also suggest that the absolute level of public consumption did not decline in real terms, while its nominal share in GNP was lowered from 13.4 per cent in 1978–79 to 8.5 per cent in 1985. This was engineered mainly through real cuts (about 48 per cent from 1978 to 1983) in government employee salaries, which make up a large portion of public consumption expenditure.[9] The latter development has caused a general worsening in the quality of government services, particularly in the education and health sectors. The nominal shares of public expenditures on education and health in GNP came down from 3.3 and 1.1 per cent in 1980 to 2.4 and 0.6 per cent in 1985, respectively (see OECD, 1987, p. 54).

A further point of interest attaches to the nature of internal adjustment in the post-1983 period under the Özal administration. After showing a drop in 1984, the public revenue/GNP ratio (in current prices) increased from 21.8 per cent in 1984 to about 28 per cent in 1986–87. Besides the continued reliance on SEE price hikes, the boosted public revenue performance benefited from the introduction of value added tax system in 1985, and extended operation of extra-budgetary funds in 1985–87.

The rising public revenue in 1985–87 could not however be translated into public disposable income, because of surging interest payments, which are included in the category of current transfer expenditures. The accelerated public investment and increased availability of non-oil imports (made possible by the fall in world oil prices) induced a rapid expansion of private savings and investment in 1986, which saw a domestic demand led growth of GNP around 7.8 per cent.

Fiscal Deficits

Following Celâsun and Rodrik (forthcoming), Table 2.3 presents two variant sets of estimates for fiscal deficits, that is, overall public sector borrowing requirements (PSBR) as per cent of GNP in current prices. PSBR(A) estimates are arrived at by adjusting public savings gaps for three factors: (i) non-debt capital transfers (involving grants, sale of property and so forth); (ii) valuation differences for the end-year SEE inventories; and (iii) changes in the arrears of the central government budget. PSBR(B) figures are consolidated cash deficits of the central government and non-financial SEEs, excluding cash balances of other public sector agencies.

As shown by data in Table 2.3, fiscal retrenchment was quite sizable in 1981–3 compared to a huge PSBR in 1980. This is also reflected in inflation reduction in this sub-period. The year 1984 saw a rise in fiscal deficit and intensified pressures on prices, the major source of which was the large

TABLE 2.3 *Public Sector Borrowing Requirement (PSBR), 1980–87*

	1980	1981	1982	1983	1984	1985	1986	1987*
PSBR Estimates				*(% of GNP)*				
1. *Variant A*								
PSBR(A)	9.9	3.7	5.0	5.3	7.9	4.9	6.0	8.2
Financing (net):								
External borrowing	3.2	2.5	1.0	1.4	2.7	0.5	2.8	4.1
Domestic borrowing								
(Treasury)	1.1	1.4	1.5	0.9	2.3	2.7	2.9	2.9
Budget, long-term	0.2	0.8	0.6	1.8	0.7	1.9	1.2	1.4
Budget, short-term	0.9	0.6	0.8	–0.9	1.6	0.9	1.7	1.5
Central Bank	3.5	2.0	0.3	0.6	0.7	1.3	0.7	1.0
Other	2.2	–2.2	2.2	2.3	2.1	0.4	–0.4	0.2
2. *Variant B*								
Cash deficit								
a. Central government								
budget	5.0	1.3	2.1	2.1	5.2	2.8	4.1	3.9
b. SEEs[†]	6.6	4.7	3.9	2.9	2.8	2.8	3.7	4.7
c. Total (=a+b) = PSBR(B)	11.6	6.0	6.0	5.0	8.0	5.6	7.8	8.6
Memo items								
Interest rate on government								
bonds (%)					45	59	56	50	52
Increase in WPI (%)	107	37	25	31	52	40	27	46

* Provisional estimates.
† Cash deficit of non-financial SEEs after budgetary and extra-budgetary transfers and before arrears and State Investment Bank Credits.
SOURCES Celâsun and Rodrik (forthcoming, Table 8.3); SPO (1988) for 1986–7 data.

drop in the central government budget revenue. Fiscal retrenchment was quite encouraging in 1985, but available estimates point to a rapid widening of PSBR in 1986–87, which saw a relatively lax fiscal stance due to two successive elections held in these years.

The changes in the financing pattern of PSBR, as shown in Table 2.3, point to the decline in the share of Central Bank financing, and the rise in the corresponding share of domestic borrowing at high rates of interest as explored further in Section VI. The prospects for deficit reduction are briefly discussed in the final section of the paper.

Impact of Fiscal Adjustment on Domestic Credits

Fiscal adjustment affects macroeconomic performance also through its impact on money and credit markets. A reduced reliance on Central Bank financing strengthens the basis for a restrictive monetary stance to control inflation. Changes in the mix of bank lending influence credit availability

TABLE 2.4   *Money, Domestic Credit and Public Sector**

	1979	1980	1981	1982	1983	1984	1985	1986
A. *Income Velocity*								
GNP/Monetary base	6.8	9.3	8.0	7.4	7.3	6.7	6.4	7.4
GNP/M1	5.0	6.3	6.7	6.5	5.9	8.1	8.6	7.8
GNP/M2	4.2	5.0	4.0	3.4	3.5	3.5	3.4	3.4
GNP/Domestic credit	2.8	3.3	3.2	3.3	3.3	4.3	3.9	3.2
B. *Domestic Credits* (%)[†]	100	100	100	100	100	100	100	100
by : Deposit money banks	56	59	64	66	70	72	77	78
Investment banks	17	13	12	13	13	11	8	10
Central Bank	27	28	24	21	17	17	15	12
to : Public sector	50	48	40	37	32	28	29	28
Treasury	13	14	13	12	10	12	11	11
Public enterprises	37	34	27	25	22	16	18	17
Private sector	50	52	60	63	68	72	71	72
Memo item								
Real interest rate (%)[‡] (1-year deposits)	−31	−38	0	8	5	4	8	16

* Figures are rounded to the nearest unit.
† Net of Central Bank advances to the banks.
‡ Annual averages of highest quarterly net returns deflated by the wholesale price index.
SOURCES   Central Bank of Turkey; OECD (1986).

for production and trade expansion. An increased dependence on bond financing affects interest rates, which exert a pervasive impact on the financial and real spheres of the economy.

Table 2.4 shows selected indicators of money and credit over the 1979–86 period. As these indicators bring out, monetary contraction and squeeze on the banking system were highly severe in 1980, the first year of the adjustment program.

With the deregulation of bank deposit rates, real balances for broad money increased at a much faster pace than real money base, contributing to a larger availability of domestic credit for the private sector. The reduced access of public enterprises (including agricultural support agencies) to Central Bank was also instrumental in increasing the share of private sector in total domestic credits from 50 per cent in 1979 to about 70 per cent in 1983–84.[10]

While the post-1980 fiscal adjustment and interest rate reform contributed to the avoidance of a relatively larger credit squeeze on the private sector, the lending rates for non-preferential credits soared to about 25–30 per cent in real terms, leading to a rise in the share of non-performing loans in the banking system. The refinancing of interest payments placed a large claim on the nominal expansion of private sector credits, and widened the illiquidity problems of the private corporate sector. In such an environment, the unregulated activities of the brokerage firms produced a financial crisis in mid-1982.[11] After 1983, non-preferential lending rates continued to remain sticky at inordinately high levels, producing a highly vulnerable banking system in the late 1980s.

IV STRUCTURAL CHANGE IN PUBLIC-SECTOR RESOURCE MOBILIZATION

Composition of Public Revenue

As the fiscal data presented in Section III indicate, the public revenue/GNP ratio mildly improved from 20 per cent in 1979–80 to 22.5 per cent in 1981–83. After featuring a fall in 1984, this ratio increased rapidly to 28 per cent in 1986–87. Panel A in Table 2.5 gives the breakdown of public revenue by its major categories for selected bench-mark years during 1979–87. Among the public revenue categories, factor income from property corresponds basically to the consolidated (after tax) profits and depreciation allowances of the SEEs, including the net surplus of social security institutions.

Panel A data in Table 2.5 bring out the significant compositional change in public revenue mobilization, which strongly relied on factor income generation by the SEEs. The tax reform initiative did not produce the expected rise in the tax burden of the country. OECD (1987, p. 58) provides the following estimates for tax elasticities with respect to GNP:[12]

	Total	Total Direct Taxes	Personal Income Tax	Indirect Tax
1978–9	0.95	1.11	1.83	0.79
1980	0.85	0.99	0.99	0.65
1981	1.22	1.29	0.95	1.07
1982	0.84	0.74	0.61	1.02
1983	0.89	0.61	0.61	1.35
1984	0.52	0.43	0.87	0.64
1985	1.37	0.71	0.47	2.20

After producing a temporary tax buoyancy in 1981, the tax reform process centered in 1982–84 mainly on the removal of bracket creep (fiscal drag) in personal income taxation, and provision of tax relief to export activities, financial intermediation and financial earnings. The tax relief accorded to private firms in payments difficulties was also substantial. After the introduction of the value-added tax system in 1985, the tax effort began to recover. The stepped-up levy collection by the extra-budgetary

TABLE 2.5 *Structural Change in Public Revenue, Savings and Investment,*
1979–87

	1979	1982	1985	1986	1987*
A. *Public Revenue (%)*					
1. Taxes					
a. Direct taxes	56.6	46.3	25.7	26.4	27.7
b. Indirect taxes	43.7	32.2	38.1	37.5	42.2
Subtotal	100.3	78.5	63.8	63.9	69.9
2. Non-tax budget revenue	3.5	7.1	9.2	13.4	8.4
3. Factor income from property[†]	−3.8	14.4	27.0	22.7	21.7
4. Total	100.0	100.0	100.0	100.0	100.0
B. *Public Savings*					
1. Central government budget	107.4	68.7	16.1	9.7	9.6
2. Local government	−8.1	6.2	14.2	18.1	29.5
3. State economic enterprises (non-financial)	−24.7	13.9	49.6	32.1	32.5
4. State economic enterprises (financial)	19.6	9.2	1.2	1.2	1.8
5. Revolving fund agencies	5.7	2.1	6.8	3.8	3.9
6. Extrabudgetary funds	–	–	12.2	35.0	22.7
7. Total	100.0	100.0	100.0	100.0	100.0
C. *Public Investment*					
1. Central government budget	33.6	39.3	32.3	30.3	31.0
2. Local government	3.8	4.7	9.6	14.3	18.5
3. State economic enterprises (non-financial)	60.0	54.1	50.8	45.8	41.6
4. State economic enterprises (financial)	0.2	0.3	0.4	0.3	0.4
5. Revolving fund agencies	2.4	1.6	1.4	1.8	2.2
6. Extrabudgetary funds	–	–	5.5	7.5	6.3
7. Total	100.0	100.0	100.0	100.0	100.0

* Provisional estimates.
† Including net surplus of social security institutions.
SOURCES Celâsun and Rodrik (forthcoming, Tables 8.2 and 8.6) for 1979–85;
SPO (1988) for 1986–7 data.

funds also contributed to the expansion of indirect tax revenue in 1985–87.

Adjustment in tax schedules proved to be effective in reducing bracket creep in personal income taxation, particularly in wage earners' tax liabilities. The share of wage earners in personal income tax revenue came down to about 46 per cent in 1985–6 from nearly 70 per cent in 1979–80. This shift should not be interpreted, however, as an indicator of enhanced equity in the tax system. As pointed out at the end of Section II, the share of formal wages in GDP declined to 18 per cent in 1985–86 from 33 per cent in 1979. Recalling also the regressive features of indirect taxes and SEE price hikes, it may be inferred that a partial removal of bracket creep did not achieve an overall tax equity in the country. A more effective taxation of non-wage income remains a challenging task for future tax policy initiatives.

Structural Shifts in Public Savings and Investment

Changes in the composition of public revenue and its collection patterns gave rise to important shifts in the intra-sectoral structure of public savings and investment as shown in Panels B and C of Table 2.5.[13] With the increasing shares of SEEs, local government and extra-budgetary funds in revenue raising, the relative contribution of the central government budget to savings generation rapidly declined, especially during 1986–87.

Within the framework of its overall political program, the Özal administration attached importance to the removal of deficiencies in urban infrastructure systems. Local administrations (in particular big city municipalities) were given an extended autonomy in tax collection, borrowing and expenditure decisions.

The proliferation of extra-budgetary funds (EBFs) under the Özal administration reflects basically the policy-makers' preference for administratively unconstrained and politically popular spending on special purpose programs. Among the newly established funds, the particularly significant ones are the Mass Housing Fund (for residential construction), the Public Participation Fund (for public infrastructure investment), the Resource Utilization Support Fund (for investment and export incentives), the Mutual Assistance and Support Fund (for income transfers to the poor), the Petroleum Consumption Fund (for municipal and highway investments) and the Defense Industry Support Fund.

Changes in the intra-sectoral pattern of resource management were accompanied by shifts in the allocation of public investment among major activity sectors. The following data show the lowered priority of manufacturing and agricultural sectors in public investment:

| | Public Investment (%) | |
	1980	1985
Agriculture	7.1	6.6
Manufacturing	28.8	12.0
Energy and mining	32.1	32.5
Transport and communications	18.1	29.8
Other services	13.9	19.1
Total	100.0	100.0

SOURCE   State Planning Organization.

V   REVENUE-RAISING IN THE SEES AND EBFS: CONFLICTS IN ADJUSTMENT POLICY

SEEs

The review of compositional change in public revenue and savings in Section IV points to the prominent role of SEE factor income mobilization in Turkey's post-1980 internal adjustment process. In this context, a question may be raised as regards the relative contributions of output change, productivity improvement, price hikes and wage cuts as sources of financial improvement in the SEEs.

Lacking an adequate data base for a proper decomposition analysis of overall SEE performance, Table 2.6 presents selected aggregate indicators for non-financial SEEs. These data indicate that the SEE sales revenue showed about 96 per cent cumulative rise in real terms in 1980–82, while the SEE real wages dropped more than 30 per cent in this sub-period. The growth of labor productivity averaged around one per cent per year in 1981–83. The real value-added data suggest that sales revenue increases originated mainly from price hikes rather than output changes.

The implication of price hikes serving as the main source of SEE sales revenue expansion is that demand functions for most SEE products were largely inelastic in the medium-run. Thus, the emphasis on SEE price hikes accentuated imperfections in product markets. The private industrial and trading firms followed suit by continuing with their mark-up pricing, which weakened the effectiveness of anti-inflationary demand management policies (see TÜSİAD, 1986).

The data on the new wholesale price index (WPI) of the State Institute of Statistics, which do not cover the pre-1981 years, shed some light on the relatively more rapid cumulative rise in the prices of public sector goods in the post-1981 era, following the huge inflationary impulse of initial SEE price hikes in 1980. The relevant data are summarized as follows (TÜSİAD, 1986, p. 28):

	1981	*1985*
General WPI	100	357
Private sector goods	100	350
Public sector goods	100	372
of which: electricity	100	666

Since the bulk of SEE products serve as intermediate inputs in industrial production, their price adjustments closely affect the sources of price changes in private firms. TÜSİAD (1986, p. 26) provides the following decomposition of the sources of price level change in the private manufacturing industry:

	Per cent Contribution to Price Rise, 1980–84
Labor cost	10.7
Profits and indirect taxes	21.3
Intermediate inputs	68.0
of which: Agricultural inputs	11.6
Industrial inputs	31.3
Services inputs	15.5
Imported inputs	9.6

TABLE 2.6   *Selected SEE Prices and Indicators*

| | Percent Annual Increase | | | | |
	1979	1980	1981	1982	1983
A. *SEE Items*					
Electricity	38	153	49	61	10
Lignite	72	131	101	18	40
Fertilizer(TSP)	0	824	52	10	0
Cement	62	177	39	30	27
Sugar	62	171	82	12	19
Diesel Fuel	72	225	64	32	28
Paper	21	231	39	40	14
Pig iron	89	121	46	66	21
B. *Non-financial SEE*					
Sales revenue*	69	163	53	51	35
Value added (real)			−4.4	3.5	5.7
Employment	2.4	0.0	−4.6	1.3	4.7
Per worker value added (real)			0.2	2.2	1.0
Real wage index	−12.0	−19.5	−2.7	−7.7	−7.1
Memo items					
Wholesale price index[†]	64	107	37	25	31
GDP(real)	−0.6	−1.0	4.7	4.3	4.1

* Excluding budget transfers that cover duty losses.
[†] Treasury price index.
SOURCES   SPO (1985); High Control Board (1987).

As the preceding decomposition shows, upward adjustment of industrial input prices, influenced largely by the SEE revenue-raising policies, account for about 31 per cent of the cumulative rise in the gross output price of private manufacturing from 1980 to 1984. In this context, it is evident that wage repression sharply reduced the relative contribution of nominal wage adjustments to upward shifts in the price level.

The reform legislation for the SEEs came rather late in 1983–84.[14] The new legislation delineated the particular SEEs which would function on the basis of market criteria. Privatization studies for the SEEs were initiated in

TABLE 2.7   *EBF Levies and Import Protection, 1985**

Sector	Import Duties	Nominal Protection Rates Imported Duties plus EBF levies
Agriculture	0.22	0.25
Industry	0.25	0.30
Mining	0.16	0.18
Manufacturing	0.29	0.36
Consumer goods	0.51	0.58
Intermediate goods	0.25	0.30
Capital goods	0.31	0.39

* EBF denotes the Extra-Budgetary Funds.
SOURCE   Turhan (1986).

1985–86. The Özal administration proclaimed its intention to proceed in stages in privatizing SEEs, starting with the sale of financially most attractive units.

EBFs

The revenue-raising schemes of extra-budgetary funds (EBFs) have also caused conflicts in the adjustment policy process. Besides the issue of revenue sharing certificates of public utilities and enterprises, foreign borrowing, and interest income on their financial assets, the EBFs strongly rely as sources of revenue on earmarked levies on foreign trade, bank credits and other transactions.

As shown in Table 2.7, the EBF levies on imports have been quite substantial. They increased the nominal protection on manufactured products from 29 per cent to 36 per cent in 1985, producing conflicts with trade-liberalizing steps taken at the end of 1983. The increased protection on domestically produced goods broaden the scope for non-competitive pricing in product markets. Moreover, the arbitrary and opaque way in which fund levies are administered generates additional channels of rent-seeking activity in the economy.

VI PUBLIC DEBT

The major indicators of public debt are summarized in Table 2.8 for the 1981–87 period. In this table, public external debt (A.1) excludes debt stock held by the Central Bank. Since the valuation changes for a portion of external debt held by the Central Bank (such as rescheduled convertible TL deposits) become a Treasury liability in monetary accounts, they are

TABLE 2.8   *Indicators of Public Debt, 1981–87*

	1981	1982	1983	1984	1985	1986	1987*
A. *Public Debt Stock*							
1. Public external debt[†]							
a. billion $	10.3	11.6	11.6	13.0	14.9	18.1	22.2
b. trillion TL	1.1	1.9	2.6	4.7	7.7	12.1	18.4
2. *Public domestic debt*							
(trillion TL)							
a. Consolidated debt[‡]	0.5	0.7	1.7	2.5	3.9	7.1	7.3
b. Non-consolidated debt	0.5	0.7	0.8	1.0	1.8	2.8	5.0
Subtotal	1.0	1.4	2.5	3.5	5.7	9.9	12.3
3. *Total public debt (=1b+2c)*							
a. trillion TL	2.1	3.3	5.1	8.2	13.4	22.0	30.7
b. % GNP	32.0	37.7	44.4	44.8	48.5	56.2	55.1
c. % public revenue	144.1	164.6	198.2	205.5	203.8	195.8	196.8
B. *Debt Service in*							
***Central Government Budget (% GNP)*[§]**							
1. External debt service	0.9	1.5	2.4	2.7	3.1	3.7	3.4
2. Domestic debt service	0.9	0.8	0.7	0.9	1.2	3.0	4.3
3. Total debt service	1.8	2.3	3.1	3.6	4.3	6.7	7.7
Memo items (% GNP)							
Central Government Budget							
Revenue	20.3	19.6	20.0	15.5	16.1	17.2	18.2
Non-interest expenditure	21.9	21.5	21.0	18.6	16.9	17.4	18.5
Interest payments (total)	1.0	1.1	1.6	2.0	2.1	3.4	4.1
Budget balance	−2.7	−2.0	−2.6	−5.1	−2.9	−3.6	−4.4

* Provisional estimates.
[†] Excluding external debt held by the Central Bank.
[‡] The bulk of consolidated debt covers devaluation-induced valuation changes in external debt held by the Central Bank.
[§] Including principal and interest payments.
SOURCES   Celâsun and Rodrik (forthcoming, Table 8.4) for 1981–5 debt stock data; SPO (1988) for budget figures in 1986–7; Central Bank (1987) for other data.

included, however, in domestic consolidated debt. The aggregate figures show that Turkey's public debt increased from 32 per cent of GNP in 1981 to about 55 per cent in 1987.[15]

With the termination of OECD debt relief in 1984, Turkey began to face a hump in external debt service in 1985–87, which may persist several more years in the absence of a rescheduling exercise. Besides creating the need to generate trade-surpluses in the balance of payments, a heavy load of external debt service gives rise to additional resource requirements in the public sector. Exchange rate depreciations (undertaken for trade improvement) increase the domestic currency value of external debt burden.[16]

Within the Turkish public sector, the central government budget carries the major burden of servicing external debt. As pointed out in the discussion of fiscal deficits in Section III, an increasing recourse to bond financing of deficits at high interest rates since 1983 adds to the government's debt servicing problem. The ratio of total debt service to revenue in the central government budget increased to nearly 40 per cent in 1986 from about 15 per cent in 1981–83.

Besides limiting the scope for government spending on essential services such as education and health, the debt overhang increases potential fiscal instability, because of a large reliance on high-cost domestic borrowing. The predominance of public sector in the issue of securities crowds out suitable domestic financing for export-oriented investors who lack a sufficient capability for self-financing.

VII RECAPITULATION AND PROSPECTS

After outlining Turkey's economic policy concerns obtaining toward the end of 1987, this paper has discussed background factors and fiscal aspects of the post-1980 adjustment process. The review of macroeconomy and fiscal policy linkages has brought out the critical role played by public-sector savings generation in promoting an internal adjustment pattern that matched export-oriented external adjustment. The evaluation of compositional changes in public revenue and savings has suggested that a prolonged reliance on SEE price hikes for resource mobilization produced conflicts with price-stabilization objectives of the adjustment program.

Turkey's post-1980 fiscal policy experience indicates that the reduction of tax evasion and broadening of the tax base are lengthy processes, which are prone to disruptions by supply-side concerns. The introduction of the value-added tax system in 1985 was the most notable achievement in the tax reform process. A more adequate taxation of non-wage income remains a central task for future fiscal policy initiatives.

With the termination of external debt relief in 1984, government's debt burden soared in 1985–87. The task of external adjustment was eased in 1986 by the drop in world oil prices. Because of an inadequate fiscal retrenchment, an opportunity was missed in 1986 to achieve a sizable inflation reduction under falling import prices. In 1987, the fiscal policy stance was relaxed further with an eye for political advantage in November 1987 parliamentary elections.

The preliminary estimate for PSBR(A), that is, the wider concept of the overall public sector deficit, is around 8.2 per cent of GNP in 1987. Measured before the budget arrears, the size of the 1987 deficit reaches nearly 9 per cent of GNP. The observed macroeconomic data for the 1980–87 period broadly suggest that fiscal deficits need to be reduced to about 5 per cent of GNP for the inflation target of 30–35 per cent per year.

The Government's 1988 Annual Program calls for a reduction in fiscal deficit to 6 per cent of GNP in 1988 in combination with the 5 per cent growth rate and 50 per cent inflation rate targets. In terms of percentage points of GNP, the Program projects 2.2 per cent rise in public disposable income, and 0.7 per cent cut in public investment, with no change in the proportion of public consumption. Because of the rising share of current transfers (including interest payments) in GNP, the required increase in the ratio of public revenue to GNP is estimated as 3.5 per cent. The major sources of additional revenue mobilization are specified as indirect taxes, fund levies and state enterprise factor incomes.

Although the 1988 Program attempts to come to grips with the deficit-reduction problem, the projected revenue-raising measures portend policy conflicts in the stabilization, liberalization and distributional processes. An increased direct tax burden on non-wage income is eschewed on political grounds. For a more effective drive to reduce deficits and inflation rates, the policy-makers may eventually be forced to resort to larger expenditure cuts, and a more consolidated use of EBF resources in the overall budgetary process. In the medium-term, the deficit-reducing measures will definitely lead to intensified socio-political tensions in the country.

NOTES

1. The work reported here is partially based on a joint research project with Dani Rodrik in the context of the NBER project on Developing Country Debt. Research support by Tevfik Yaprak and helpful suggestions by Dani Rodrik are gratefully acknowledged.
2. For the review of data on interest rate, exchange rate and inflation, see Chapter 4.8 in Celâsun and Rodrik (forthcoming).
3. The present paper draws heavily on Chapter 8 in Celâsun and Rodrik (forthcoming). For disaggregated data on government revenues, expenditures and SEE accounts, see the public finance reviews included in OECD (1984 and 1987).
4. In their analysis of fiscal deficits, Anand, Chhibber and van Wijnbergen (this volume) adopt stock-based measures.
5. For an analytical modeling of exchange rate guaranteed borrowing by Dani Rodrik, see Chapter 2 in Celâsun and Rodrik (forthcoming).
6. For detailed accounts of post-1980 policies, with varying points of emphasis, see Şenses (1983), Öniş (1986), Kopits (1986), Wolff (1987), Celâsun and Rodrik (forthcoming) and Baysan and Blitzer (this volume).
7. See Kopits (1986) for a discussion of wage settlement arrangements and agricultural support policies in 1980–85; Celâsun (1986) provides a general equilibrium analysis of the Turkish economy from 1978 to 1983.
8. See Fry (1986) and TÜSİAD (1986) for analyses of Turkish inflation.
9. See Celâsun (1986) for labor market and wage data.
10. If bonds, bills and other forms of advances are added to credits, banks' total advances to the public sector increased more rapidly, however, than advances to the private sector during 1984–86, as pointed out by Akyüz (this volume).

11. See Atiyas (this volume) for an analysis of private sector's response to financial deregulation in the early 1980s.
12. For a detailed classification of tax revenues, see OECD (1984 and 1987).
13. From 1984 on, social security institutions, which were previously included in financial SEEs, became revolving fund agencies.
14. See Karataş (1986) for a detailed review of SEE reform efforts.
15. End-year external debt stock has been valued (for item A.1.b) at the annual average exchange rates.
16. See Rodrik (this volume) for a wider discussion of the net budgetary impact of exchange rate depreciation.

REFERENCES

Celâsun, M. (1986) 'A General Equilibrium Model of the Turkish Economy, SIMLOG 1', *METU Studies in Development* 13 (1, 2) pp. 29–94.
Celâsun, M. and D. Rodrik (forthcoming) *Debt, Adjustment and Growth: Turkey*.
Central Bank of Turkey (1987) *Annual Report* (Ankara).
Fry, M. (1986) 'Turkey's Great Inflation', *METU Studies in Development* 13 (1, 2) pp. 95–116.
High Control Board (1987) *General Report on State Economic Enterprises, 1986* (Ankara: Prime Ministry) in Turkish.
Karataş, C. (1986) 'Public Economic Enterprises in Turkey: Reform Proposals, Pricing and Investment Policies', *METU Studies in Development* 13 (1, 2) pp. 135–69.
Kopits, G. (1986) 'Structural Reform and Economic Stabilization: A Case Study of Turkey', (Washington DC: International Monetary Fund Institute) paper presented at a seminar on the Role of the Fund in the International Monetary System.
OECD (1984, 1986, 1987) *OECD Economic Surveys: Turkey* (Paris: Organization for Economic Co-operation and Development).
Öniş, Z. (1986) 'Stabilization and Growth in a Semi-Industrial Economy: An Evaluation of the Turkish Experiment, 1977–1984', *METU Studies in Development* 13 (1, 2) pp. 7–28.
Özmucur, S. (1987) *Milli Gelirin Üç Aylık Dönemler İtibariyle Tahmini, Dolarla İfadesi ve Gelir Yolu ile Hesaplanması* (Quarterly National Income Estimates, in US Dollars and by Income Types) (Istanbul: Istanbul Ticaret Odası Yayınları).
Şenses, F. (1983) 'An Assessment of Turkey's Liberalization Attempts since 1980 against the Background of her Stabilization Program', *METU Studies in Development* 10 (3) pp. 271–321.
SPO (1985) *V. Beş Yıllık Plan Destek Çalışmaları: I* (Fifth Five Year Plan Supplementary Studies: I) (Ankara: State Planning Organization).
SPO (1988) *1988 Annual Program* (Ankara: State Planning Organization) in Turkish.
Turhan, A. (1986) 'İthalatta Sektörel Vergi Tahsilat Oranları, Ağırlıklı Vergi Oranları ile Koruma Oranları' (Sectoral Tax Collection Ratios, Weighted Tax Ratios and Protection Ratios on Imports), *Planlama Dergisi*, no. 20 (Ankara: SPO).
TÜSİAD (1986) Inflation in Turkey, Report T 186, 7, 90 (Istanbul: Turkish Industrialists' and Businessmen's Association) in Turkish.
Wolff, P. (1987) *Stabilization Policy and Structural Adjustment in Turkey, 1980–85* (Berlin: German Development Institute).

3 An Assessment of the Pattern of Turkish Manufactured Export Growth in the 1980s and its Prospects

Fikret Şenses

I INTRODUCTION

Turkey's trade and industrialization policies until 1980 were characterized by strong inward-orientation. All indices of trade orientation put her well behind cross-country norms with exports in 1979 constituting only 3.2 per cent of GNP. Although a wide range of export promotion policies were in operation since 1963, the trade regime remained heavily biased against exports. Consequently, exports were dependent on a handful of traditional commodities like cotton, tobacco, hazelnuts, dried figs and raisins while manufactured exports constituted only 27.4 per cent of the total as late as 1979.

A major objective of the Stabilization Program introduced in early 1980 in response to domestic financial instability and a full scale external payments crisis was to generate a policy shift towards export orientation. Apart from short-term components like domestic demand restraint, the Program included medium and long-term components such as the provision of extensive tax and credit incentives to exporters, real effective depreciation of the exchange rate through daily adjustments after 1981, substantial steps taken towards import liberalization especially after December 1983, and strong encouragement of direct foreign investment.[1] Incentives provided by these policies contributed to a spectacular increase in exports unparalleled by any other country in the protectionist and largely stagnant international environment of the 1980s,[2] especially during the first half of the decade. Exports registered nearly a five-fold increase in only eight years rising from $2.3 billion in 1979 to $10.2 billion in 1987, accounting in 1985 for 14.9 per cent of GNP. This not only surpassed Turkey's previous record by a substantial margin but was also well above the rate of growth of world trade and exports by the newly-industrializing countries. The main engine of this growth was the upsurge in manufactured exports which was accompanied by a strong diversification in markets towards neighboring Middle Eastern countries.

The significance for our purposes of this rapid growth of exports, which witnessed the rapid transformation of economic policies from arch-type inward-orientation to 'moderate outward orientation', is manifold with strong implications also for the future. First, export growth along with inflows from international organizations like the IMF, World Bank and the OECD, played a crucial role in facilitating imports of key raw materials and intermediate goods, the shortage of which had brought production to a virtual standstill. Still on the balance of payments front, rapid export growth was largely responsible for the smooth repayment of external debt, the steady fall in the debt/export and debt-service/export ratios in the critical period until 1984, and the improvement in external credit-worthiness, facilitating a steady inflow of resources from private as well as official sources. Second, exports have been a major factor behind rapid economic growth, partly compensating for shortfalls in other major components of aggregate demand like government expenditure and investment. Finally, and most importantly, sustaining export growth over a period of more than eight years has gone a long way in removing the export pessimism of the pre-1980 period and led to the emergence of a new group of entrepreneurs with a strong international outlook. An important element in this new understanding was the active role played by the government in developing new trade channels through bilateral agreements and trade missions.

As for the future, export growth is likely to remain the single most important factor in the sustainability of Turkey's liberalization attempts and indeed the whole Stabilization Program still in force, especially in view of the growing external indebtedness with a term structure shifting towards short-term debt.[3] Similarly, export growth at such a rapid pace would have implications for employment and requires detailed study of the factor intensity of exports to different destinations.

Previous studies of Turkey's manufactured export growth were largely confined to identifying the main factors responsible at the global level.[4] My earlier work on the subject was directed at assessing the nature and main characteristics of this growth at a lower level of aggregation using mainly 1984 data (see Şenses, 1989). In this paper, updating my earlier work, I shall aim to reinterpret this phenomenon in light of more recent data, carry out a disaggregated analysis of factor intensity of manufactured exports, and explore further the extent to which exports to different destinations incorporate differences in factor content. A related objective is to evaluate the prospects for manufactured export growth and assess the likelihood for its sustainability in the future.

Manufactured exports are defined to include Standard International Trade Classification (SITC) groups 5 to 8 less SITC 68. Three-digit SITC data for 1985–87 obtained from the data tapes of the Under-Secretariat of Treasury and Foreign Trade and the State Institute of Statistics will be used to supplement our earlier findings based on United Nations Commodity Trade Statistics. More recent data covering the first half of 1988 will be employed to capture the current trends in tackling the sustainability issue. The so-called fictitious exports representing the abuse of the export incentives system are left outside the scope of the paper as the extent of this phenomenon (let alone its sectoral and commodity composition) is not known.[5] The analysis of the direction of manufactured exports will be based on two major groups of countries, the Middle East and the European Economic Community which together represented 75.3 per cent of total manufactured exports in 1987. The first of these groups, apart from its importance in recent growth, comprises countries with close cultural ties with Turkey and a similar stage of development. The second group, on the other hand, represents Turkey's traditional export markets which may gain further prominence in future depending on the outcome of her application in April 1987 for full membership.

The plan of the paper is as follows. In Section II, I shall examine the structure, pattern and direction of manufactured exports and their factor content. In Section III, I shall give a brief account of the main factors responsible for the upsurge in manufactured exports and the emerging pattern. Finally, in Section IV, I shall assess the likelihood for the sustainability of export growth in the future and present my main conclusions.

II   THE STRUCTURE AND PATTERN OF MANUFACTURED EXPORT GROWTH

Extent and Main Features

The data on manufactured exports by major category (corresponding to one-digit SITC categories) for the 1963–87 period are presented in Table 3.1. As it is clear from the Table, there has been a long-term tendency for steady export growth with a corresponding rise in the share of manufactured exports in the total; a tendency strongly reinforced in the post-1980 period. The sharp rise in total exports during 1980–87 was accompanied by an increase in the share of manufactured exports from 26.9 per cent to a massive 66 per cent. One can therefore argue that the export boom of the 1980s was, by and large, due to an upsurge in manufactured exports which represented 81.6 per cent of the total absolute increase during the same period. Although there was rapid growth in all major categories, manufactured exports remained heavily concentrated on basic and miscellaneous manufactures which together accounted in 1987 for 73.8 per cent of the total. Further disaggregation of these broad categories, on the other hand,

TABLE 3.1 *Manufactured Exports,* * 1963–87 (million dollars)*

	1963	1969	1973	1979	1980	1981	1982	1983	1984	1985	1986	1987
Chemicals	2.1	8.9	14.0	23.7	76.5	99.6	161.7	151.1	199.6	298.5	409.9	675.0
Basic manufactures†	3.7	20.6	141.0	446.0	474.3	1 051.0	1 533.9	1 514.6	1 910.6	2 520.8	2 106.4	2 553.3
Machinery and transport equipment	–	0.9	8.9	43.6	83.5	208.6	301.4	263.7	353.1	644.9	414.6	1 085.5
Miscellaneous manufactures	0.4	2.5	57.6	107.1	147.8	388.6	477.4	713.7	1 385.6	1 387.4	1 399.9	2 411.1
Total manufactured exports (1)	6.2	32.9	221.5	620.4	782.0	1 747.7	2 474.4	2 643.1	3 449.0	4 851.5	4 330.8	6 724.9
Total exports (2)	368	537	1 317	2 261	2 910	4 702	5 747	5 671	7 134	7 958	7 456.7	10 190.0
Share of manufactures in total exports (1)/(2) per cent	1.7	6.1	16.8	27.4	26.9	37.2	43.1	46.6	54.0	61.0	58.1	66.0

* SITC 5, 6, 7, 8, (excluding SITC 68).
† Excluding non-ferrous metals (SITC 68).
SOURCES UN, *Commodity Trade Statistics*, various issues; Under-Secretariat of Treasury and Foreign Trade data tapes.

TABLE 3.2   *Share of Three Most Important Product Categories in Total Manufactured Exports, 1974–87 (per cent)*

SITC Code	Product Category	1974–9	1980–5	1986	1987
65	Textiles	47.4	28.0	21.6	17.7
67	Iron and steel	3.7	13.3	17.3	11.7
84	Clothing	20.7	24.3	28.8	32.9
Total of 3 categories		71.8	65.6	67.7	62.3

SOURCES   UN, *Commodity Trade Statistics*, various issues; Under-Secretariat of Treasury and Foreign Trade data tapes.

reveals that only three categories, textiles, clothing and iron and steel, have together constituted around two-thirds of total manufactured exports (Table 3.2).

Another strong tendency in this performance was the increase in the share of Middle Eastern countries in manufactured exports, rising from 15.1 per cent in 1979 to 33.2 per cent in 1981, 40.3 per cent in 1983 and 41.9 per cent in 1985 before beginning to fall to 28.1 per cent in 1986 and 25.5 per cent in 1987.

An important sphere to probe into is the role played in the manufactured export drive by the state economic enterprises, direct foreign investment (DFI), and domestic small-scale enterprises. Although the severe lack of statistical information on the distribution of manufactured exports among these groups hinders systematic investigation, we have gathered together the little available evidence that exists to throw some light on the subject. The public sector which has traditionally played a major role in the manufacturing sector, accounting in 1980 for 40.4 per cent of total value added and 36.1 per cent of employment, seems to have shown only a flimsy response to outward-oriented policies. Our calculations indicate that total exports by the ten leading exporting state economic enterprises amounted to only TL 202.7 billion in 1984 which at the end-of-year exchange rates represented only 6.4 per cent of total exports in that year.[6] The latest figures available do not reflect any major change in this respect. The fact that, in both 1985 and 1986, the top four exporters among State Economic Enterprises (Turkish Airlines, Tüpraş, Etibank and Botaş) were active mainly in services and petroleum-related activities is rather telling of the negligible role of these enterprises in manufactured exports.[7]

The response of DFI firms seems somewhat better. The data available only for the early 1980s indicate that exports by DFI firms active in manufacturing increased from $23.0 million in 1980 to $25.2 million in 1981, and $97.7 million in 1982 (see Yıldırım, 1983, p. 13), which, on average, represented 11.3 per cent of total manufactured exports during

1980–82. Although the absence of more recent data prevents us from passing firmer judgement, it seems that there has been no major change from this early picture.[8] Even on the basis of such admittedly weak data, we may conclude that DFI firms' role in manufactured export expansion came nowhere near the role played by their counterparts in the newly-industrializing countries in South-East Asia and Latin America.

Finally, the absence of information prevents us from assessing the role of small enterprises (with less than ten workers) which in 1980 accounted for 11.5 per cent of value added and 38.3 per cent of employment in manufacturing. In view of their weak organizational ability and production structure geared more to the lower end of the domestic market, however, one does not expect their contribution to the export drive to have reached significant proportions. Even in categories like handicrafts and leather products in which these enterprises may have export potential, it is likely that exporting, if any, would be through the large (export) trading concerns. The fact that the share of the latter in total exports has increased sharply from 9.2 per cent in 1981 to 38.8 per cent in 1984, and 34.5 per cent in 1985[9] may be taken as further confirmation that the Turkish manufactured export drive was predominantly a private sector affair with only a minimal contribution from the DFI firms.

Direction of Trade

The direction of manufactured exports before 1980 was heavily concentrated on developed countries which on average accounted for 72.8 per cent of the total during 1974–79. The subsequent market diversification towards the Middle East was so rapid and so closely associated with the export drive that it was responsible for 45.5 per cent of the total increase in manufactured exports during 1980–85. Three major characteristics of this trade seem relevant for our purposes. First, exports were heavily concentrated on two countries, Iran and Iraq, which in 1985 accounted for a massive 76.6 per cent of total manufactured exports to the region. Second, disaggregation of manufactured exports by major category reveals that the share of this region reached very high proportions in all major categories, except miscellaneous manufactures, representing in most years around one-half of the total (Table 3.3). Third, the sharp fluctuations in the share of this region even before 1985 were early signs of the volatility of this trade which saw its share decline sharply during 1986–87. This in large part reflected the downward trend in world petroleum prices and the ensuing contraction of demand in the region. Although all major manufactured export categories were adversely affected by this contraction, this was least visible in chemicals. The declining role of the Middle East in manufactured exports was accompanied by a rise in the share of the EEC from 41.4 per cent in 1985 to 49.8 per cent in 1987.[10]

TABLE 3.3   *Share of Middle Eastern Countries in Manufactured Exports by Major Category, 1978–87 (per cent)*

SITC Code	Product Category	1978	1979	1980	1981	1982	1983	1984	1985	1986	1987
5	Chemicals	19.2	17.2	22.3	34.0	48.7	63.4	46.7	49.2	42.0	47.4
6	Basic manufactures*	18.6	14.0	22.7	37.7	45.5	51.3	49.1	56.4	35.5	34.0
7	Machinery and equipment	64.2	50.9	56.6	54.7	53.5	53.8	47.9	44.8	42.6	27.5
8	Miscellaneous manufactures	4.9	5.0	7.3	9.4	11.0	6.9	7.1	12.6	8.5	9.6
	Total	18.1	15.1	23.4	33.2	40.0	40.3	33.8	41.9	28.1	25.5
	Total (billion dollars)	0.5	0.6	0.8	1.7	2.5	2.6	3.8	4.9	4.3	6.7

Less SITC 68.
SOURCES   UN, *Commodity Trade Statistics*; State Institute of Statistics; Under-Secretariat of Treasury and Foreign Trade data tapes.

Factor Content of Manufactured Exports by Destination

Estimates of factor intensity of manufactured exports based on the methodology described in the Appendix are given in Table 3.4 for both 1984 and 1987. The difficulties associated with the data and our methodology notwithstanding, the Table clearly indicates that manufactured exports consist predominantly of labor-intensive categories with skill-intensive categories accounting in 1987 for nearly two-fifths of the total. The predominance of labor-intensive categories which to a large extent reflects the weight of textiles and clothing in manufactured exports, is in accordance with Turkey's comparative advantage. Closer examination of the data reveals a sharp distinction between exports to EEC, consisting predominantly of (unskilled) labor-intensive manufactures, and to the Middle East nearly one-half of which consist of capital intensive categories while skill-intensive categories account for over two-fifths of the total. A remarkable feature of the data on factor intensity is its stability over time, despite the rapid increase in exports and considerable shifts in the share of the two regions. Apart from the increase in the overall skill intensity which basically reflects the same tendency for exports to EEC, one should note the increase, albeit to a much lesser extent, of capital intensity of manufactured exports destined for EEC markets.

III   MAIN FACTORS IN MANUFACTURED EXPORT GROWTH

Previous attempts to explain manufactured export growth in the 1980s have adduced the reasons behind it to a variety of factors.[11] Here we shall

TABLE 3.4 *Factor Content of Manufactured Exports by Destination, 1984 and 1987 (per cent)*

	World 1984	World 1987	Middle East 1984	Middle East 1987	EEC* 1984	EEC* 1987
Labor intensive	72.0	72.5	49.9	52.0	93.8	91.3
Capital intensive	28.0	27.5	50.1	48.0	6.2	8.7
Total	100.0	100.0	100.0	100.0	100.0	100.0
Skill intensive	31.5	38.3	62.2	60.8	9.1	19.1

* Comprises the first 10 EEC members.
SOURCES UN *Commodity Trade Statistics*, 1984; Under-Secretariat of Treasury and Foreign Trade data tapes for 1987.

attempt a more comprehensive treatment of the subject by incorporating more recent evidence in the analysis and tie in some loose ends. Difficulties surrounding this effort which have no doubt also bedeviled previous attempts must be pointed out right from the outset. The multiplicity of factors at work some of which are traceable to Turkey's industrialization experience in the previous decades, the prevalence of some strong exogenous factors, and the lack of uniformity of these forces over time render quantitative analysis[12] and/or systematic investigation on the basis of clear-cut phases a formidable task. Although the emphasis of economic policies on exports was a major factor throughout the period, the volatility of the policy environment over time and factors like the differential effect of world petroleum price trends on each of Turkey's major export markets are cases in point. Similarly, the fact that exports to EEC and Middle East reflect export market segmentation in terms of the differences in the type of commodities exported in each direction and differences in dominant factors explaining growth of exports of each region is an element that further complicates the picture.

Despite these difficulties, we can divide the period under investigation into two major phases, the period from 1980 to 1983 when a variety of factors acted in the same direction to give a major initial boost to exports and thereafter when attempts were made to consolidate these crucial initial gains. The importance of the earlier period can be traced to a number of factors:

(i) On the policy front, export incentives through tax rebates, credits at subsidised rates, and duty-free imports reached very high proportions. The direct subsidy as a proportion of exports was estimated at 22.1 per cent in 1980, 20.5 per cent in 1981, 20.6 per cent in 1982 and 23.4 per cent in 1983, which together with the depreciation in the real exchange rate resulted in the real effective exchange rate rise (1980 first quarter=100) from 114.5 in 1980 to 123.3 in 1983 (see Milanovic, 1986). In contrast, overall direct subsidy rate decreased to 15.1 per cent in 1984,

18.6 per cent in 1985, and 16.0 per cent in 1986 (see Baysan and Blitzer, this volume), with a corresponding decline in the depreciation of the real effective exchange rate.[13]

(ii) A number of mutually reinforcing elements of the Stabilization Program, most notably restrictive monetary and fiscal policies and the sharp fall in real wages, were instrumental in restricting domestic demand which made exporting the only way out for sustaining industrial profits. With traditional export markets in EEC less than buoyant and characterized by growing protectionism also for some Turkish exports, the Middle East offered a viable alternative. Growing demand in these countries under the spurt of the sharp increase in petroleum prices in 1979, the outbreak of the Iran-Iraq War, and active role played by the government in Turkey to organize trade missions and conclude bilateral agreements envisaging Turkish exports in exchange of petroleum imports, were instrumental in generating a sharp increase in exports.

(iii) A strong, yet often neglected, factor was the link between manufactured export growth and earlier experience with import-substitution. This link was most visible at two levels. (a) Turkey's traditional import substitution industries some of which were established way back in the 1930s, like textiles, glass, iron and steel, after a long lag, reached a level of (technological) maturity to enter export markets. Learning effects and 'evolving efficiency'[14] during long periods of protection were perhaps strongest in textiles. (b) The decision to extend import-substitution into the relatively more capital-intensive and import-dependent sectors in intermediate and capital goods categories in the 1970s was instrumental in the creation of sizeable new capacities. The measurement of the contribution of these 'new' industries to export growth is surrounded, however, by a number of difficulties arising mainly from the divergent classification schemes for industrial production and exports. To overcome this difficulty industrial sectors[15] that had increased their share in total manufacturing value added by at least one percentage point during 1970–80 were classified as 'new' industries.[16] We have then, using the concordance between SITC and ISIC, allocated three-digit SITC manufactured export categories into the appropriate industrial branch. Our calculations based on this admittedly rough procedure indicate that these industries were responsible for a major portion of manufactured exports accounting for 17.9 per cent and 19.8 per cent of the total in 1983 and 1987, respectively. More significantly, exports to the Middle East accounted for slightly over one-half of total exports from these industries, accounting for 21.1 per cent and 31.3 per cent of total exports to this region in 1983 and 1987, respectively. These industries with the exception of non-metallic minerals and electrical machinary had, as expected, very high domestic resource costs (DRC)[17] and were benefitting from

relatively higher rates of export subsidy to compensate for this.[18] Another-
factor contributing to export growth during this period was the activation
of excess capacity in manufacturing for export production which resulted
in capacity utilization rates rising from 51.1 per cent in 1980 to 66.8 per
cent in 1987.[19] As can be seen, the biggest increase in these rates
occurred during this early period until 1984 and was also very rapid in
these 'new' industries. The ensuing expansion in manufactured exports
was accompanied by a strong tendency for product diversification.[20]

The foregoing discussion suggests that a set of factors in the early 1980s
facilitated penetration into nearby Middle Eastern countries with similar
development levels and domestic demand structures along the Linder
hypothesis and in some ways reminiscent of the vent-for surplus model.
This process was aided by two additional factors. First, the low absolute
value of individual exports, especially from the new industries facilitated
relatively easy entry into these markets. Second, Turkey had, before 1980,
experienced a similar pattern of manufactured export growth to the neighboring developing countries albeit on a much lower scale. A system of
export incentives using similar, if not identical devices was largely responsible for the rapid growth of exports from very low bases, despite heavy
protection in manufacturing. During 1963–70, for example, manufactured
exports increased from $4.4 million in 1962 to $52.6 million in 1970.
Although capital intensive and skill intensive manufactured exports accounted for only 26.3 per cent of manufactured exports to developed
countries in 1970 this ratio was much higher for exports to other developing
countries with 47.2 per cent.[21] The existence of such an early experience
may have served her well in replicating this pattern in the 1980s.
    It is our contention that the simultaneous presence of the variety of
factors discussed above some of which are exogenous (or even fortuitous)
in the crucial early years was instrumental in establishing an export base
and increasing exporter experience and confidence in later years. The
longer export-oriented policies remained in force, the greater was the
expectation that they will be maintained in the future. This 'snowball'
effect received a major boost with the December 1983 measures which
constituted by far the most decisive step in the direction of import liberalization and export-orientation.[22] When moves away from direct subsidies
led to a decline in exports as in 1986, however, the government was quick
to reinstate them with immediate favorable results. Likewise, when the fall
in petroleum prices began to threaten Middle Eastern markets, normalization of relations with the EEC together with the revival of demand in
OECD countries in general has enabled Turkey to revert back to her
traditional export markets.

IV PROSPECTS AND CONCLUSION

Apart from its favorable effects on the balance of payments and aggregate growth, Turkey's manufactured export drive was no doubt instrumental in generating dynamic benefits most notably in the form of substantial learning effects. Although not conducive to quantification, these were perhaps highest for entrepreneurs successfully penetrating diverse markets abroad and obtaining invaluable marketing experience in the process.

It is our contention that the future success of this experiment with outward orientation will rest increasingly on the ability to overcome obstacles in three major spheres:

(i) The volatility of external demand conditions is likely to remain as a source of uncertainty for the export drive. There is growing protectionism in world markets especially in labor intensive manufactures like textiles and clothing. The future course of relations with the EEC, the future trends in world petroleum prices, the end of hostilities between Iran and Iraq and its aftermath are among the key issues with a bearing on export performance.

(ii) The past pattern for export growth which has relied on domestic demand restraint and availability of considerable excess capacity in the manufacturing sector can not be extended into the future. As the recent experience has shown, domestic demand restraint like the one implemented in the early 1980s does not seem feasible in a pluralistic political environment in which many social groups, most notably organized labor, are likely to become increasingly vociferous in their opposition to non-stop stabilization for over eight years. The Stabilization Program's inability to cope with rampant inflation, rising unemployment, and growing inequalities in income distribution is likely to sharpen this opposition and may in fact jeopardize the continued implementation of the whole Program. The fact that exporting industrialists have not yet been able to establish as broad-based and effective a constituency as import-substituting industrialists despite considerable strides taken in import liberalization may accelerate this process.

(iii) With excess capacity and domestic demand restraining options no longer feasible, there is an urgent need to create new capacities in manufacturing through new investment. This is apparent from the sharp increase in the ratio of exports to manufacturing value added which rose from 11 per cent in 1981 to 35–36 per cent in 1987 (ISO, 1988, p. 7) Fixed capital formation in manufacturing (in constant 1983 prices) in contrast, decreased from TL 582.4 billion in 1980 to TL 444.9 billion in 1985.[23] This was due in large part to the sharp fall in public sector investments while private sector investments maintained their 1980 levels until 1985 when they too began to fall, albeit at a slower pace.

The determinants of investment in Turkey have been subject to little systematic investigation. A study covering the 1962–82 period (Öniş, 1986) has identified credit availability as the main factor for both total and private investment. A more recent study for the 1962–85 period (Conway, this volume) has identified financial liberalization and public investment as a positive and nominal depreciation of the exchange rate as a negative influence on private investment. A major survey conducted among major industrialists in 1987 has identified high interest rates, credit shortages and instability of economic policies in that order as the three most important factors negatively affecting fixed investment (TÜSİAD, 1988, p. 162). Another survey among exporters (ISO, 1988) has found that just over one-half of those interviewed claimed that they faced difficulties in investment, which they associated most closely with difficulties of investment finance. In our view, a variety of factors like high interest rates, real exchange rate depreciation, domestic inflation, and volatility of economic policies especially vis-a-vis foreign trade and payments were all part of the unfavorable domestic investment climate in the 1980s. These same factors seem also relevant for the flow of direct foreign investment (DFI) into Turkey which has shown remarkable reluctance despite substantial encouragement, especially during 1985–86.

What is even more significant for our purpose is the absence of any major sign for a major reversal in manufacturing investment trends in the near future, especially for export-oriented activities. A recent survey among exporters has shown that only one-half of those interviewed had undertaken investment in export activities the bulk of which (77.4 per cent) was, however, for the renovation, and modernization and extension of existing plants. Whether recent plans to shift the emphasis of export incentives away from the export level to the production level will stimulate export-oriented investment in manufacturing is a matter for conjecture. The prospects for DFI in manufacturing are also bleak. The stagnation in DFI flows in the world economy since 1983 especially for export-oriented activities points in the direction of stiff competition from other countries (Erdilek, 1987). In the unlikely event of DFI inflows reaching sizeable proportions, the manufacturing sector is likely to compete with the relatively more lucrative domestic activities like tourism and banking.[24]

The Turkish export drive, despite minor setbacks in 1983 and 1986, has now continued for over eight years with mid-year data for 1988 now available showing continued growth.[25] Despite its contributions to growth and more significantly to the balance of payments, there is, however, no evidence to suggest that the export drive and the radical changes in trade and industrialization policies associated with it have led to increased efficiency and competitiveness in the public and private sector enterprises.

The fact that manufactured exports are still heavily concentrated on textiles and clothing with an unduly low share of machinery and equipment, on the other hand, does not augur well for the future, given the low demand elasticity as against high supply elasticity of such exports in developed countries. Similarly, although the dominance of labor-intensive manufactures in total exports points to favorable direct employment effects, the weight of capital intensive products in recent manufactured export performance, especially with respect to exports directed to Middle Eastern markets suggests the overall impact to be small.

An optimal path for sustained export growth in the future requires progress on a broad front. First, past experience suggests that activating export-oriented investment in the private sector would require the provision of direct investment incentives. The fact that even in the heyday of strongly protectionist policies such incentives were provided points to their importance for the Turkish investment climate. This may stem, apart from the financial rewards in question, from the fact that potential investors may regard the implementation of such incentive schemes as a reflection of government's commitment, with a favorable impact on their expectations about the future course of economic policies. One may conjecture that the strong responsiveness of manufactured exports to such direct incentives in the 1980s is a manifestation of the same phenomenon for exporters. Although it would be in conflict with the privatization objective of the Stabilization Program, public sector investments in carefully selected projects may also be required to increase investments in capital goods-producing sectors and may, in the process, create a favorable environment for private sector investment. Such a process which would necessarily involve selective import substitution may also activate hitherto untapped export potential of the public sector and may in due course accelerate the process of product diversification in export markets. If supplemented by decisive steps in the direction of increasing research and development expenditure and emphasizing the extent and quality of technical education, one would expect this process to lead to a further increase in the share of skill and capital intensive products for which neighboring Middle Eastern countries along with other developing countries would offer golden opportunities. Although Turkey's EEC membership seems a remote possibility, such a strategy would guard against Turkish-EEC trade to reflect a purely inter-industry character and would instead, lead to the development of intra-industry trade especially with countries like Greece, Spain, and Portugal with relatively similar development levels and demand structures.

NOTES

1. For a review of stabilization and liberalization policies, see Şenses (1988).
2. Among the 119 countries listed in World Bank (1987), Turkey's average rate of growth of exports during 1980–85 was by far the highest.

3. According to provisional figures given in Central Bank (1988, p. 139), and TÜSİAD (1988, p. 103), Turkey's total external debt, increased from $17.6 billion in 1982 to $38.3 billion in 1987 with the share of short-term debt rising from 10.0 per cent to 22.7 per cent during the same period.
4. See Kopits (1987), Celâsun and Rodrik (forthcoming), Baysan and Blitzer (this volume), Milanovic (1986) and Akder (1987).
5. Over-invoicing of exports to OECD countries was estimated to represent 12.6 per cent of exports during 1981–85. See Celâsun and Rodrik (forthcoming, pp. 7–28).
6. High Control Board (1984). Total exports of textiles by the oldest and most important state firm in the field, Sümerbank, as given in the same source (p. 260) was $29.8 million in 1982, $36.8 million in 1983 and $27.2 million in 1984.
7. According to figures given in High Control Board (1987, p. 115), Sümerbank's total exports in 1986, for example, was only TL 29.8 billion which at the end-of-year exchange rates corresponded to only $39.4 million.
8. Interview with a high-ranking official of the Foreign Investment Department of State Planning Organization, 28 September 1988. Detailed questionnaires completed by foreign firms covering also their export performance in recent years were yet to be processed.
9. See Seyidoğlu (1986, p. 52). As of 1985, there were 24 such firms.
10. All statistical information for EEC refers to the first ten EEC members to enable us to make uniform comparisons over time. Exports to Portugal and Spain were in any case not high enough to significantly alter our main findings.
11. See in particular Celâsun and Rodrik (forthcoming), Baysan and Blitzer (this volume) and Şenses (1988).
12. For one such attempt, see Celâsun and Rodrik (forthcoming).
13. Real effective exchange rate in 1984 decreased from 123.3 in 1983 to 119.5 indicating real appreciation. According to Central Bank (1988a), real effective depreciation during 1987 was 4.3 per cent.
14. For an analysis linking manufactured export performance in Brazil and Argentina to early import substitution see Teitel and Thoumi (1986).
15. Comprising only large enterprises with ten or more workers.
16. These in descending order of the extent of structural change, included chemicals, electrical machinery, transport equipment, non-metallic minerals and rubber-plastic products. Calculations based on SIS (1987).
17. DRC rates given by Yağcı (1984) were −10.8 for chemicals, 1.7 for rubber-plastic products, 1.4 for transport equipment, 0.9 for electrical machinery and 0.6 for cement and glass.
18. With the exception of chemicals, total export subsidy rates for these industries during 1980–84 were above the average for the manufacturing sector. See Milanovic (1986).
19. TÜSİAD (1981, 1986, 1988). The figure for 1987 is an estimate given in TÜSİAD (1988).
20. The number of three-digit SITC categories appearing in United Nations *Commodity Trade Statistics* increased from 60 in 1979 to 80 in 1984.
21. Our own calculations using UN, *Commodity Trade Statistics* and Appendix Table 1.
22. For a detailed examination of these measures see Şenses (1983).
23. TÜSİAD (1986,p. 67). It seems that this downward trend has continued in more recent years. According to Central Bank (1988, p. 101) fixed investment in manufacturing (in constant 1987 prices) fell from TL 2628 billion to TL 2112 billion.

24. According to TÜSİAD (1988, p. 91), of the $536 million of DFI licensed in 1987, only slightly over one-half was in manufacturing.
25. The Summary of Monthly Foreign Trade Statistics published by the SIS shows that total exports during the first half of 1988 has increased by 30.6 per cent over the same period in 1987.

REFERENCES

Akder, H. (1987) 'Turkey's Export Expansion in the Middle East, 1980–85', *The Middle East Journal*, 41, pp. 553–67.

Celâsun, M. and D. Rodrik (forthcoming) *Debt, Adjustment, and Growth: Turkey*. Turkey.

Central Bank of Turkey (1988) *Annual Report 1987* (Ankara) in Turkish.

Central Bank of Turkey (1988a) 'Turkey, Economic Developments, Policies and Prospects' (Ankara) photocopy.

Erdilek, A. (1987) 'The Role of Foreign Investment in the Liberalization of the Turkish Economy', in T. Nas and M. Odekon (eds), *Liberalization and the Turkish Economy* (New York: Greenwood Press) pp. 141–59.

High Control Board (1984) *General Report on Public Economic Enterprises, 1984* (Ankara: Prime Ministry) in Turkish.

High Control Board (1987) *General Report on Public Economic Enterprises, 1986* (Ankara: Prime Ministry) in Turkish.

ISO (1988) *Exports and Survey Results in 1988* (Istanbul: Istanbul Chamber of Industry) August, in Turkish.

Kopits, G. (1987) 'Structural Reform, Stabilization and Growth in Turkey' (Washington DC: IMF) International Monetary Fund Occasional Paper 52.

Milanovic, B. (1986) 'Export Incentives and Turkish Manufactured Exports, 1980–84' (Washington DC: World Bank) World Bank Staff Working Paper, no. 768.

Öniş, Z. (1986) 'Stabilization and Growth in a Semi-Industrial Economy — An Evaluation of the Recent Turkish Experiment, 1977–84', *METU Studies in Development* 13 (1, 2) pp. 7–28.

Şenses, F. (1983) 'An Assesment of Turkey's Liberalization Attempts since 1980 against the Background of her Stabilization Program', *METU Studies in Development* 10 (3) pp. 271–321.

Şenses, F. (1988) 'An Overview of Recent Turkish Experience with Economic Stabilization and Liberalization', in T. Nas and M. Odekon (eds), *Liberalization and the Turkish Economy* (New York: Greenwood Press) pp. 9–28.

Şenses, F. (1989) 'The Nature of Main Characteristics of Recent Turkish Manufactured Export Growth', *The Developing Economies*.

Seyidoğlu, H. (1986) 'The Economic Effects of Export Incentives in Turkey' (Istanbul: Marmara University) in Turkish, photocopy.

SIS (1987) *Statistical Pocket Book of Turkey 1986* (Ankara: State Institute of Statistics).

Teitel, S. and F. E. Thoumi (1986) 'From Import Substitution to Exports: The Manufacturing Exports Experience of Argentina and Brazil', *Economic Development and Cultural Change* 34 (3) pp. 455–90.

TÜSİAD (1981) *The Turkish Economy 1981* (Istanbul: Turkish Industrialists' and Businessmen's Association).

TÜSİAD (1986) *Report on Foreign Trade* (Istanbul: Turkish Industrialists' and Businessmen's Association) in Turkish.

TÜSİAD (1988) *The Turkish Economy 88* (Istanbul: Turkish Industrialists' and Businessmen's Association).
World Bank (1987) *World Development Report 1987* (Washington DC).
Yıldırım, H. (1983) 'An Evaluation of Direct Foreign Investment Firms in Turkish Manufacturing from the Perspective of Value Added and Employment' (Ankara: State Planning Organization) in Turkish, unpublished thesis.

APPENDIX

In the absence of reliable disaggregated data on capital stock, we use value added per employee as a measure of capital intensity. Similarly the wage component of value added per employee is used as a measure of skill intensity. As an initial step, we classify manufacturing categories according to their capital and skill intensity, using the average for the manufacturing sector as a whole as the benchmark for classification. We then assign three-digit SITC categories to these branches by using the concordance between SITC and ISIC. The flaws of this admittedly rough procedure arise largely from the failure of (non-homogeneous) three-digit ISIC categories to take full account of the dispersion in factor intensities among activities within the same category. We have attempted to overcome this difficulty by drawing upon the 1984 Annual Manufacturing Industry Statistics, the latest available at the time of writing, and reclassifying individual exports which have been affected by this dispersion. The readjusted data incorporating this correction is presented in Appendix Table I which provides the basic data on the factor content of manufactured exports from 21 manufacturing activities which are ranked by descending order of capital intensity.

TABLE A1   *Value Added per Employee and Factor Content Distribution of Exports by Manufacturing Activity*

Manufacturing Activity	Value Added per Employee 1980 (000 TL)	Wage Value Added per Employee 1980 (000 TL)	Factor* Content	SITC Categories of Manufac. Exports	Share in Manufac. exports (1984) (per cent)
	(1)	(2)	(3)	(4)	(5)
Basic industrial chemicals	2 391.7	509.1	K,S	51,52	1.9
Rubber products	1 517.9	394.2	K,S	629[†]	1.4
Other chemicals	1 423.0	394.8	K,S	53–57, 59[†]	3.3
Electrical machinery	1 165.1	372.0	K,S	722–729	2.9
Iron and steel	1 114.5	509.3	K,S	671–679	13.8
Other non-metallic products	986.3	274.6	L,U	662, 663, 667[†]	2.4
Glass products	928.7	284.9	L,U	664–665	2.4
Paper and paper products	874.0	449.2	L,S	641–642	0.9
Transport equipment	865.5	433.7	L,S	731, 733, 735[†]	3.2
Metal products	839.3	250.0	L,U	691–698, 812	2.0
Pottery products	836.8	297.6	L,U	666	0.2
Non-electric machinery	828.6	343.2	L,S	712–719[b]	3.2
Printing and publishing	709.6	317.3	L,U	892	0.5
Textiles	706.9	239.3	L,U	651–657	26.1

TABLE A1   *continued*

Manufacturing Activity	Value Added per Employee 1980 (000 TL)	Wage Value Added per Employee 1980 (000 TL)	Factor* Content	SITC Categories of Manufac. Exports	Share in Manufac. exports (1984) (per cent)
	(1)	*(2)*	*(3)*	*(4)*	*(5)*
Miscellaneous manufacturing	686.9	210.5	L,U	862–864, 891, 893–894, 897, 899	1.2
Wood and cork	665.6	248.5	L,U	631–632	0.6
Footwear	529.6	250.0	L,U	851	0.2
Leather products	464.0	212.9	L,U	611–612, 831	0.1
Professional scientific equipment	461.0	128.6	L,U	861	–
Wearing apparel	436.4	152.9	L,U	841–842	32.9
Furniture and fixtures	376.7	118.1	L,U	821	0.8
All activities	1 047.0	321.6			100.0

* K = capital intensive, S = skill intensive, L = labor intensive, U = unskilled labor intensive.

† Denotes that certain SITC categories falling in these branches are excluded and grouped with activities with a different factor intensity. On the basis of our corrections as mentioned in the text, SITC 58 and 621 are classified as labor intensive while SITC 629, 661, 711, 732 and 895 are classified as capital intensive.

SOURCE   Columns 1 and 2 derived from SIS (1987); Column 5 from UN, Commodity Trade Statistics.

4 The Record on Private Investment in Turkey

Patrick Conway[1]

Turkey since 1980 has been immersed in an extensive price-driven restructuring of its economy. Structural adjustment to improve economic efficiency and increase trade surpluses has been stimulated by adjustments in real interest and exchange rates. Given that the stimulus to the restructuring was the severe international debt crisis of 1978–80, the yardstick of short-term success has naturally been the improvement in export performance; this has in fact been striking. As the Turkish economy consolidates its gains from this strategy and settles into a sustainable pattern of economic growth, however, the volume and pattern of private investment becomes central to long-term success.

This centrality of private investment performance is a new feature of Turkish planning. Governments beginning with the Democratic Party regime of 1950 have cited the importance of private investment, but have in fact until the 1980s relied upon government productive investment for added economic stimulus. This reliance flowed from the doctrine of Etatism, with its vision of a productive public sector of the economy complementing the private sector.[2] The price-based reforms of the 1980s, by contrast, have been designed to 'privatize' the economy. In that situation, private productive investment must expand to stimulate economic growth.

Despite this requirement, the factors that stimulate private investment in the Turkish economy have not been well identified. There is both theoretical ambiguity and conflicting empirical evidence on the impact of financial liberalization, nominal depreciation and public investment on private investment. I review briefly the theory of private investment in Section I, and the empirical evidence to date on its behavior and determinants in Section II. I then use vector autoregression (VAR) analysis over the years 1962–86 in Turkey as a general framework for identifying directly from the historical record the factors that stimulate real private investment. Section IV extends the empirical analysis to consider separately investment in agricultural, housing, manufacturing and transport sectors. Section V provides conclusions and suggests extensions to this analysis.

I make three observations from the empirical evidence. First, the data are often revised, making statistical conclusions contingent on the effects of the next revision. Second, statistical analysis of the most recent data suggests that private investment has been discouraged by the recent policies that combine high nominal interest rates, high inflation and a rapidly depreciating nominal exchange rate. Most strikingly, the increases in inflation of the 1980s have *dis*couraged private investment — contrary to most investment theories. Third, the composition of investment is as important as the level for evaluating the future growth prospects of the Turkish economy. The spurt in private investment since 1985 has been in large part due to increased housing expenditures, while agricultural and transport investment have performed very poorly. Public investment has discouraged non-housing investment on average while providing positive stimulus to housing investment.

I draw two conclusions from this evidence. High priority should be given to calculation and dissemination of an authoritative data series on private investment and its components. Present Turkish economic policy has not yet provided private investors in productive acitivity with a stable and profitable enviroment. The evidence suggests that the important components to such an environment will be greater stability and lower absolute levels of inflation and nominal interest rates and a slower rate of exchange rate depreciation. Public investment, at least as historically practised, is not a vital component of such a policy — especially when, as noted in other articles in this volume, it raises budget deficits, nominal interest rates and inflation.

I THEORETICAL DETERMINANTS OF PRIVATE INVESTMENT

The economic theory of the private firm with access to credit markets provides a general proposal on gross fixed capital formation: an entity's investment will continue to the level where the marginal cost of the investment is just equal to the marginal value product of the last addition to installed capacity.[3] Three empirical difficulties impede investigations of this condition: the 'holding period' of the investment good, the nature of the costs of capital installation, and the difficulties in obtaining reliable data.

In the extreme 'neoclassical' case there are no installation costs and a deep secondary market exists in used capital goods. Consider a production technology using both capital and variable inputs. The marginal cost of the investment good is its price P_{kt}, while the marginal benefit is the value marginal product of capital in the next period plus the resale of the investment good.

$$(1 + i_t)P_{kt} = [E_t P_{t+1} F_k(K_{t+1}, q_{t+1}) + E_t P_{kt+1}]$$

The numeraire is a consumer price index; P_t is the deflated price of the output good in this industry. If variable inputs are chosen optimally in each period t+1 for given K_{t+1}, the production technology can be written as $F(K_{t+1}, q_{t+1})$ with q_{t+1} the price vector of non-capital inputs to the production process. Investment is assumed productive only in the following period. i_t is the nominal interest rate on borrowing to cover the cost of the capital good. E_t is the expectations operator contingent on information available in period t. This simplifies to

$$P_{kt} [1 + i_t - (E_t P_{kt+1}/P_{kt})] = E_t P_{t+1} F_k(K_{t+1}, q_{t+1})$$

The left-hand side measures the costs of purchasing capital goods, with the capital-price ratio representing both the impact of depreciation on resale value and the occurrence of capital gains or losses. The right-hand side is the future value of marginal product of that addition to capital.

The secondary market for capital goods is often missing in developing countries, but its absence does not change the basics of the decision. The marginal decision now includes expectations over the productive lifetime T of the capital good.

$$P_{kt} = E_t \lambda_{t+1}$$

$$E_t \lambda_{t+1} = \sum_{i=1}^{T-t} E_t \{ P_{t+i} F_k(K_{t+i}, q_{t+i})/\Delta^{t+i} \}$$

$$\Delta^{t+i} = \prod_{s=1}^{i} (1 + i_{t+s-1})$$

Future capital-good prices become irrelevant, and the discounted value of future marginal product becomes central to the decision.

These economic rules specify an optimal stock of capital. Introducing installation and adjustment costs of investment allow definition of a continuous private investment function (I_{pt}) from these marginal conditions. Suppose, $(1/2)\Phi(I_{pt})^2$, $\Phi > 0$, represents the value of these costs (in the numeraire) at time t.[4] Then, the marginal condition sets purchase price plus installation costs equal to discounted future benefits.

$$P_{kt} + \Phi I_{pt} = E_t \lambda_{t+1}$$

This defines an investment function for each period increasing in $E_t \lambda_{t+1}$ and decreasing in P_{kt} for the no-secondary-market case.

If there is no financing available to the firm, this decision will be constrained by the availability of internally generated funds — that is, retained earnings of the firm or saving of the household. The relevant interest rate will be on deposits, while inflation will reduce investment through reducing the real value of nominal balances. Investors facing credit rationing or borrowing constraints will fall into this category, and may in addition find retained earnings insufficient to finance all investment profitable at the given deposit rate.

The government has a role in this decision both through current policy and through private expectations of future policy. Policies under government control include the nominal interest rate, the nominal exchange rate, government investment and investment subsidies. These choices will have direct effects on the private investment decision, but will also have general-equilibrium impacts that may make the policies inconsistent with financing constraints or stable price indices.[5]

The direct effects of policy on private investment behavior can be derived from the preceding equations. Increased current nominal interest rates reduce $E_t\lambda_{t+1}$ and private investment; put another way, the increase in interest rates raises the costs of financing capital goods. Expectations of future rate increases within the time horizon t have the same qualitative effect. Investment incentives will reduce P_{kt} and increase private investment. Current exchange rate depreciation will increase P_{kt} if the capital good is imported, and thus decrease desired I_{pt}. Expected future depreciation will raise P_{t+i} for tradeable goods and q_{t+i} for tradeable inputs, and thus have an ambiguous impact on I_{pt}. Public investment potentially plays two conflicting roles. Present and future infrastructural investment will enter as a technological improvement that shifts $F(.)$ out. Present and future directly productive investment, as for example in Turkish State Economic Enterprises (SEEs), will compete with these producers to drive output price down and drive input prices up, thus reducing private investment.

In the absence of specific technological, installation cost and depreciation information the theory provides little testable structure. It does, however, highlight important features of the investment decision. The decision is intertemporal in nature, with investment expenditure preceding accrual of returns. Given the stochastic nature of economic variables, the decision is also dependent on expectational forecasts of the future. These forecasts depend not only on the specific output and input markets, but also on aggregate economic conditions through inflation, interest rates and demand-stimulating income growth.

Private investment is not homogeneous; it is undertaken for quite diverse purposes, some of which are not well represented by the specification here. A basic distinction can be made between housing and non-housing investment: non-housing investment is more likely to be motivated by the factors discussed above, while housing investment may serve as a store of value in uncertain times.

II EMPIRICAL EVIDENCE: REAL PUBLIC AND PRIVATE INVESTMENT

The first difficulty in interpreting empirical evidence is choosing the most reliable data series. There have been periodic revisions of the private investment figures during the 1980s, and I found three 'authoritative' data series of real private investment dated since 1985.[6] Comparisons over the period 1972–83 indicated substantial deviations in reported aggregate real private investment in these three series. I report results based upon the most recent series from the State Planning Organisation.

It is a commonplace since Keynes' work (see for example, Keynes, 1937, p. 218) that real investment expenditure is a highly volatile component of aggregate demand. Turkish gross capital formation demonstrates this volatility.[7] As Figures 4.1 and 4.2 indicate, growth rates in both public and private real investment have fluctuated widely. Low growth in private investment occurs in transitional periods for Turkish economic policy: 1963–64 (beginning of national planning), 1971 (adoption of an outward orientation), 1974 (after the crude oil price increase) and 1977–81 (debt and political crisis management and the introduction of economic liberalization). Positive investment growth resumed in each case. Real public investment growth appears to have responded to budgetary pressures. It also became negative in 1971 as an expenditure-reducing remedy to international payments imbalances. The period 1978–84 was characterized by static real public investment as a policy to contract the government budget deficit. The pre-1970 period and 1972–77, by contrast, illustrate public investment that alternated between stimulative and very stimulative. The most recent years available indicate a resurgence of real public investment. Figure 4.3 illustrates the split in real private investment between housing and non-housing components. The recent swing in investment expenditure between these two uses is especially striking: the economic and political crises of 1978–80 led to a precipitous shift in private investment funds to the housing sector. The more stable 1980s brought that share back to its secular trend at roughly 30 per cent of total. The most recent years indicate, and investment growth statistics confirm, that housing investment is taking a growing share of total private investment. In 1986, for example, real housing investment grew at a 38 per cent annual rate while non-housing investment grew by 7 per cent annually.[8]

Recent discussions of the prospects for private investment have been quite pessimistic. World Bank (1982, p. 220) stated 'the short-term outlook for private manufacturing investment is not promising. The major constraints include low domestic demand, scarcity of funds and high interest rates. However, the private sector is more optimistic today than it has been in the past several years . . . (due to confidence) of continuity and stability of economic policies.' The Turkish Industrialists and Businessmen's As-

TURKEY

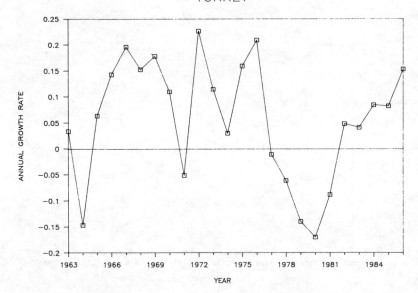

FIGURE 4.1   *Turkey: Real Private Investment Growth*

TURKEY

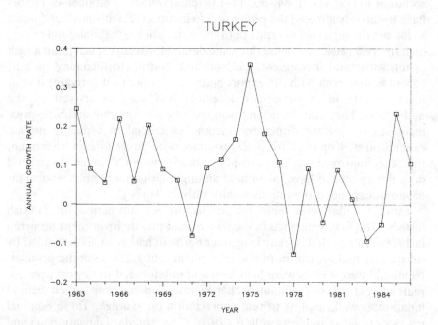

FIGURE 4.2   *Turkey: Real Public Investment Growth*

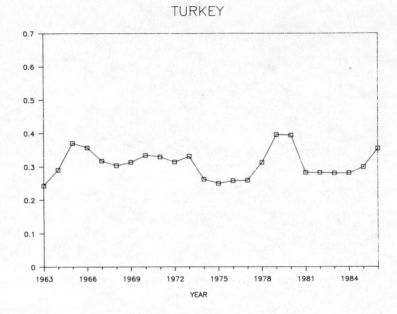

FIGURE 4.3   *Turkey: Housing as a Share of Private Investment*

sociation (TÜSİAD, 1984, pp. 11–13) remarks that 'a number of factors have negatively affected the propensity to invest in recent years', and notes as factors the high cost of crude petroleum, inflation of capital-good prices, high interest rates, restricted domestic demand, excess capacity and a lack of infrastructural investment. Celâsun and Rodrik (forthcoming, p. 5.5) conclude that even with the export boom '. . . a buoyant (private) investment climate in export-oriented sectors had not yet arrived by the mid-1980s'. They cite the negative impact of exchange-rate and SEE-price increases on private disposable income as crucial in reducing private expenditures. Kopits (1987, p. 22) comments on direct foreign investment that 'this improved market perception (of international financial markets) does not appear to have taken hold among multinational firms who so far have not expanded operations significantly in Turkey'.

Table 4.1 illustrates these various factors for sub-periods of Turkish history. The first watershed in the flow of real private investment occurred in 1978. Prior to that, steady investment growth had been accompanied by substantial real growth in public investment and gross domestic product. Nominal interest rates were held low, and inflation led to *ex post* negative real interest rates. Nominal exchange rate depreciation lagged behind inflation as well, leading to real appreciation on average. These nominal prices were fairly stable as well: for 1970–77 the standard deviation in i and π were .32 and 5.89 per cent.

TABLE 4.1 *Growth in Turkish Real Private Investment and Related Indicators**

Time Period	I_p	I_g	i	e	y	P_k/P	π
1963–69	8.9	13.8	10.5	0.1	6.5	–1.1	5.2
1970–73	10.0	4.8	12.0	12.9	7.1	–0.9	15.3
1974–77	9.7	20.4	13.6	6.3	7.6	1.9	20.0
1978–80	–12.4	–2.7	20.3	69.1	0.4	–0.2	74.6
1981–84	2.1	–1.1	41.2	48.5	4.7	2.1	36.2
1985–86	11.8	16.9	52.0	35.8	6.7	6.6	36.5

* The entries for real private (I_p) and public (I_g) investment, the nominal exchange rate (e), real gross domestic product (y) and the relative price of capital (P_k/P) are formed as simple averages of the annual percentage growth rates during the time periods cited. The nominal interest rate (i) and the inflation rate (π) are presented as simple averages of the percentage annual rates for the time periods cited.
SOURCE   World Bank report appendices.

From 1978 to 1980, the political unrest, uncertainty and debt-inspired economic austerity were reflected in stagnant real gross domestic product and real public investment. Inflation soared to 75 per cent on average, leading to further real appreciation and negative real interest rates. There was great variability in inflation and the nominal interest rate as well, with standard deviations of 23.5 and 4.7 respectively.

The period 1981–84 was one of greater political stability but relative-price variability. The nominal exchange rate and interest rate were adjusted upward to ensure real depreciation and positive real interest rates despite 36 per cent inflation. Real gross domestic product grew at moderate rates, while real public investment remained stagnant. i and π remained quite variable, with standard deviations of 6.25 and 10.02 per cent.

The most recent period 1985–86 seems to mark a second watershed with a resurgence in private investment to the growth of the 1970s. Real gross domestic product and public investment growth were quite strong. Nominal interest rate variability was eliminated while maintaining a large positive real interest rate. Inflation remained variable, with standard deviation of 7.0, and nominal depreciation just offset inflation on average to maintain a constant real exchange rate.

More elaborate statistical analyses of real investment in Turkey have highlighted many of these same determinants of investment behavior. As part of the 'Sources of Growth' project at the World Bank, Celâsun (1983) examined the difference of sectoral real investment (public plus private) behavior between the periods 1963–68 and 1968–73. Despite some sectoral differences, he concluded that changing supply-side factors during that period leading to an increasing capital intensity of production were more important than demand shocks in explaining investment growth. Recent computable general equilibrium modeling for Turkey (for example, Lewis and Urata, 1983; Celâsun, 1986) has treated private investment as equal to available saving and distributed among sectors by fixed coefficients. Thus, private investment is stimulated by variables that increases saving — including, for example, increased interest rate or real disposable income.[9]

There have been few published econometric efforts at identifying determinants of private investment behavior. Such formal decomposition of the determinants of private investment must incorporate the general theoretical features remarked above: that is, the intertemporal, expectations-dependent and general-equilibrium nature of the private investment decision. In Conway (1987, Chapters 5 and 6) I set up a structural model of decision-making by a representative consumer/investor in a small open economy with rational expectations, Cobb-Douglas production technology and quadratic installation costs. The estimated parameters were then used to simulate the general equilibrium impact of potential determinants of private investment (and other private decisions). Real investment fell with the imported-input (for example, crude oil) price increases of the 1973–80 period. It rose in real terms in response to the other exogenous and policy factors: real appreciation, real public expenditure (investment and consumption), tariff liberalization, and low real international interest rates. Conway (1988) reports a similar general-equilibrium analysis where I used a more Keynesian structure to private investment demand for the period 1963–83.

$$
\begin{aligned}
\ln P_{kt}I_{pt} = \quad &-2.13 \ + 1.27 \ln y_t \ + 0.03 \ln \varrho_t \\
&(0.38) \quad (0.08) \qquad\quad (0.20) \\
&-1.42 \ (1 + r_t^* + (\dot\varrho_t/\varrho_t)) \qquad \bar R^2 = .94, \ DW = 2.10 \\
&(0.43)
\end{aligned}
$$

ln is the natural logarithm operator. The real value of investment is the left-hand side variable; it is hypothesized to depend positively on expected real output (y_t) and the real exchange rate level (ϱ_t) and negatively on the real interest rate.[10] Standard errors are presented in parentheses, with all coefficients except that of ln ϱ_t significantly different from zero at the 95 per cent level of confidence. Overdots indicate time derivatives. Two-stage least squares were used, with y_t an endogenous variable. The expansion of real gross domestic product increases real private investment with elasticity significantly greater than unity. The real exchange rate *level* has an insignificant effect on the value of real private investment, but the *rate* of real depreciation has a negative effect through the real interest rate.[11] There is in addition a negative impact of the interest rate variable.[12] Other government policies affect I_{pt} through their impact on y_t.

The paper by Anand, Chhibber and van Wijnbergen (this volume) provides the most recent econometric study of real private investment behavior. It incorporates a number of extensions of the Keynesian specification, most notably a more precise specification of the cost of funds to the investor and proxies for credit rationing and excess capacity. The sample period 1970–86 also gives greater weight to observations from the low-investment period after 1978. The output and interest rate elasticities are significant, and close to those reported above.[13] The proxy for credit rationing also is significant and suggests a positive effect on private investment, *ceteris paribus*, from increased liquidity. It is surprising that despite the importance attributed to foreign markets in stimulating investment the specification does not include exchange rate or international interest-rate and capital-good price effects: the hypothesized behavior is of an individual in a closed economy.

Existing studies on real private investment thus provide conflicting evidence as to its recent determinants. Businessmen cite insufficient domestic demand as a rationale for postponing investment, but investment is weakest in exporting sectors with strong international demand. Reports and econometric evidence cite high domestic interest rates as discouraging investment, while the CGE models are built upon their positive effects. Real exchange rate depreciation is in theory stimulative, but econometric studies either ignore its effects (Anand, Chhibber and van Wijnbergen, this volume) or provide evidence of direct (Conway, 1987) and indirect (Conway, 1988) negative effects on real private investment.

Any solution to these conflicts must come from the empirical evidence. A common objection to the econometric modeling to date, including my own, is its imposition of technological, market and expectation-formation structure to the economy in estimation. The resulting statistical evidence provides a joint test of private investment behavior and all the imposed economic structure. The alternative is to use a technique that admits a variety of technological, market and expectations-formation assumptions in a freer, reduced-form, econometric analysis.

III PRIVATE INVESTMENT DETERMINANTS: THE VAR TECHNIQUE

The private investment decision, as noted in the theoretical discussion above, is an intertemporal optimisation decision utilising expectations of future variables. Many of these variables (for example, capacity utilization or real income) will be determined in general equilibrium. This decision can be represented by a dynamic structural model if the structure is known. If the structure is unknown, its reduced-form expression can be still estimated in vector autoregressive (VAR) form.[14]

$$X_t = \sum_{i=0}^{N} A_i X_{t-i} + \varepsilon_t$$

If there are n observations and k variables of interest, X_t is a (n×k) matrix including I_{pt} and potential determinants of the private investment decision. The evidence above suggests these should include real income (y_t), the nominal domestic borrowing rate (i_t), the nominal exchange rate (e_t), the relative price of capital goods (P_{kt}/P_t), final-good inflation (π) and public investment (I_{gt}).[15] Each A_i is a (n×n) matrix of reduced-form coefficients. ε_t is assumed to be a (n×k) matrix of normally distributed independent random errors. N, the number of lagged periods in X_{t-i}, is in theory infinite but can in practice be truncated to reflect the number of periods incorporated in expectations formation or a limit on data availability. All variables are thus treated symmetrically in the autoregressive framework, and in this sense the methodology does not impose technological or expectations-formation structure.

In practice, the interpretation of regression results through impulse response functions (defined below) imposes a theoretical structure through assignment of causality for contemporaneous covariability of the elements of ε_t. The 'stacking' of the variables for estimation assigns causality: variables higher in the vector are assumed to cause contemporaneous covariation in lower variables. The stacking used here is $X_t = [i_t \ e_t \ I_{gt} \ P_{kt}/P_t \ I_{pt} \ y_t \ \pi_t]'$, and implies contemporaneous causation flowing from government policy instruments (i_t, e_t, I_{gt}) through relative capital-good prices and the private investment decision to y_t and π_t. This stacking is important for there is substantial residual contemporaneous correlation of estimated ε_t as noted in Table A1 in the appendix.

Although the VAR methodology is less 'structured' than conventional econometric analysis, it does (as applied here) depend upon a time-invariant reduced-form relation among included variables. When the economic structure is altered, then the methodology becomes inappropriate because the elements of A_i will differ between periods. Note, however, that this would require not a change in policy variables but rather a change in technological and expectations-formation mechanisms. The insights of the VAR remain valid when the major changes have been in included government policy variables rather than policy rules.

Investment data used are series on real private and public capital formation (I_{pt}, I_{gt}), with private capital formation divided into agriculture (I_{at}), housing (I_{ht}), manufacturing (I_{mt}) and transport (I_{rt}) components.[16] Other series include the average annual domestic nominal borrowing rate for maturity of 12–18 months (i_t), real gross domestic product at market prices (y_t), the TL/$ exchange rate (e_t), the relative price of domestic capital goods (P_{kt}/P_t) and final-good price inflation (π_t).[17] All variables except i_t and π_t are introduced in logarithmic form.[18] Annual data exist for the period 1962–86 for variables except subdivisions of private investment (1963–86 available).

The initial VAR examines the response of aggregate I_{pt} to movements in those variables identified above as important in the private investment decision: the nominal borrowing rate, the exchange rate, the relative price of capital goods, the price of final goods, real government investment and real gross domestic product. The system is estimated with a one-period lag structure.[19] Coefficients and standard errors from the VAR regressions are reported in Appendix Table A2. These effects are summarised in the impulse response function results of Table 4.2. The entries in each column represent approximately the per cent growth in the variable at the head of the column due to an exogenous one standard error (σ) increase in the variable listed in the left column. These impacts are categorized by source of shock and the period of the shock. Three types of shocks are considered: contemporaneous, one period previous and two periods previous.

Table 4.2 provides a summary of empirical data on dynamic adjustment in the Turkish economy. The columns not corresponding to private investment can be interpreted as the investors' forecast of the evolution of variables important to his decision. I focus here on the actual investment decision. Consider first the contemporaneous effects of σ increases in the other variables on I_{pt}. As noted before, both π_t and y_t by assumption have no contemporaneous impact on I_{pt}. Of the others, σ increases in e_t and i_t cause decreases in I_{pt} by 4 and 1 per cent, respectively, while a σ increase in I_{gt} causes a 2 per cent increase.

Lagged σ increases have both direct effects on I_{pt} and indirect effects through contemporaneous impacts in the previous period. Given the stacking of the variables, these latter must occur either through y_t or π_t. For example, σ increases in i_{t-1} cause a 3 per cent fall in I_{pt} through their negative impact on y_{t-1} and positive impact on π_{t-1}. A σ increase in e_{t-1} yields a 7 per cent fall in I_{pt} through its negative impact on y_{t-1} and positive impact on π_{t-1}.[20] Previous-period σ shocks to the nominal interest rate, nominal exchange rate, relative price of capital and inflation rate have large negative growth effects on I_{pt}, while σ shocks to lagged real income induce positive growth.

The VAR results are useful in two ways to the investigation of private investment decision-making. First, they provide a 'best' estimate of a reduced-form model of the economy. This is useful in forecasting private investment response to candidate government policies. Second, they synthesise the empirical data that structural models of the economy must reflect. For instance, this evidence does not support the positive interest-rate effect on private investment embedded in CGE modeling. It rather is consistent with the econometric evidence cited earlier, with both concurrent and lagged effects of σ increases in i_t leading to reduced private investment. Those econometric equations also imposed a positive effect of

Private Invesment in Turkey

TABLE 4.2   *Impulse Response Functions from VAR Regressions*

To Shock in	At Lag	i_t	e_t	I_{gt}	P_{kt}/P_t	I_{pt}	y_t	π_t
				*Response of Variable**				
i	0	0.02	0.10	−0.01	−0.00	−0.01	−0.01	0.07
$\sigma=.02$	1	0.01	0.11	0.03	0.02	−0.03	−0.01	−0.01
	2	0.02	0.15	−0.01	0.03	−0.05	−0.01	−0.01
e	0	0.00	0.11	−0.02	−0.00	−0.04	−0.01	0.10
$\sigma=.11$	1	0.02	0.14	−0.02	0.01	−0.07	−0.01	0.03
	2	0.02	0.15	−0.01	0.01	−0.06	−0.01	−0.00
I_g	0	0.00	0.00	0.05	0.01	0.02	0.01	−0.00
$\sigma=.05$	1	−0.00	0.03	0.02	0.01	0.00	0.01	0.02
	2	0.00	0.06	−0.01	0.00	−0.01	0.00	0.04
P_k/P	0	0.00	0.00	0.00	0.03	−0.00	−0.00	−0.02
$\sigma=.05$	1	−0.00	0.04	−0.05	0.01	−0.03	−0.01	0.06
	2	0.01	0.06	−0.06	−0.00	−0.05	−0.01	0.06
I_p	0	0.00	0.00	0.00	0.00	0.08	0.01	−0.03
$\sigma=.08$	1	−0.01	−0.02	0.00	0.00	0.07	0.02	−0.01
	2	−0.01	−0.03	0.00	−0.00	0.06	0.02	0.02
y	0	0.00	0.00	0.00	0.00	0.00	0.02	−0.04
$\sigma=.02$	1	−0.00	−0.02	0.01	−0.02	0.03	0.02	0.01
	2	−0.00	−0.05	0.04	−0.02	0.05	0.02	−0.01
π	0	0.00	0.00	0.00	0.00	0.00	0.00	0.07
$\sigma=.07$	1	0.00	0.03	0.01	0.00	−0.02	−0.00	0.03
	2	0.01	0.05	0.00	0.01	−0.04	−0.00	0.01

* Entries in this table can be interpreted as (approximately) percentage increases in the variable at the top of each column in response to a one σ increase in the variable listed in the left margin. In the case of columns corresponding to i and π, however, the entry represents an absolute increase in response to the one σ increase in the variable listed in the left margin.
SOURCE   Author's calculations.

inflation on investment through estimating the real interest rate elasticities, but that is inconsistent as well with the VAR results. Exchange rate devaluation is both concurrently and in lagged effect negatively related to private investment as in my earlier econometric studies, perhaps because final-good price rises by less than capital-good price with devaluation. Lagged real income has the positive effect on private investment postulated by all earlier studies, while inflation's negative impact may be due to the reduced value of retained earnings or household saving from the inflation tax. Structural models of the economy that do not reflect these 'stylized facts' will not be consistent with observed private investment behavior.

These VAR results are based on historical data, but should nevertheless be treated with caution. As Table A2 indicates, a number of the coefficients in the VAR are insignificantly different from zero at the 95 per cent level of confidence. The number of these insignificant coefficients rises when first-differencing or detrending of the data is undertaken. This is in part the consequence of the short historical record. It is also due in part to the confounding of different investment decisions. We look below at the differences in sectoral private investment decision-making.

IV DECOMPOSITION OF PRIVATE INVESTMENT INTO ITS SECTORAL RECORD

As noted above, housing investment may respond quite differently than non-housing investment to policy and external stimuli. Table 4.3 presents the growth profiles of the components of private investment in the period 1963–86. Despite the obvious volatility of these figures both across time and across categories, a few general conclusions emerge. The period 1974–77 appears to have a good balance of housing and non-housing investments, with the non-housing sectors achieving 10–20 per cent growth rates and housing investment growth just exceeding the population growth rate. Thereafter, the sectoral mix of investment growth has been less attractive. The shift toward housing investment as a share of total private investment in the period 1978–80 noted in Figure 4.3 is part of an overall shift away from investment in aggregate. The 1980s have been marked by sectoral deficiencies: manufacturing and housing in 1981–84 and agriculture and transport in 1985–86.

These differences can be further quantified through a disaggregated VAR analysis. Table 4.4 presents impulse response functions for the agriculture, housing, manufacturing and transport components of real private investment in response to σ increases in the other variables.[21] The

TABLE 4.3 *Average Growth Rates of Components of Private Investment*

	I_a	I_h	I_M	I_T	$I_o{}^*$
1963–69	10.6	14.4	6.6	30.8	9.5
1970–73	11.0	11.6	10.2	10.6	2.0
1974–77	15.8	4.0	10.8	19.6	11.7
1978–80	–18.0	1.7	–18.5	–15.7	–9.5
1981–84	11.5	–4.4	1.2	16.1	9.1
1985–86	–18.3	25.8	9.6	0.6	29.7

* I_o includes other components of private investment. A major contributor to the most recent period's resurgence is tourism investment.
SOURCE Authors' calculations.

Private Invesment in Turkey

TABLE 4.4   *Impulse Response Functions: Real Private Investment*

To Shock in	At Lag	Response of Variable			
		I_{at}	I_{ht}	I_{mt}	I_{Tt}
i	0	−0.02	−0.02	−0.02	−0.02
$\sigma = .02$	1	−0.04	−0.04	−0.05	−0.02
	2	−0.02	−0.04	−0.06	−0.06
e	0	−0.09	−0.01	−0.05	−0.09
$\sigma = .12$	1	−0.06	−0.08	−0.09	−0.06
	2	−0.06	−0.07	−0.08	−0.06
I_g	0	0.02	0.02	0.02	0.02
$\sigma = .05$	1	0.00	0.02	−0.01	−0.02
	2	−0.02	0.00	−0.03	−0.03
P_k/P	0	−0.07	0.06	−0.00	−0.05
$\sigma = .04$	1	−0.08	0.06	−0.05	−0.13
	2	−0.08	0.01	−0.07	−0.10
I_a	0	0.18	–	–	–
$\sigma = .18$	1	0.09	–	–	–
	2	0.06	–	–	–
I_h	0	–	0.11	–	–
$\sigma = .11$	1	–	0.06	–	–
	2	–	0.04	–	–
I_m	0	–	–	0.13	–
$\sigma = .13$	1	–	–	0.10	–
	2	–	–	0.08	–
I_T	0	–	–	–	0.10
$\sigma = .10$	1	–	–	–	0.06
	2	–	–	–	0.04
y	0	0.00	0.00	0.00	0.00
$\sigma = .02$	1	0.03	0.04	0.03	0.04
	2	0.04	0.04	0.04	0.08
π	0	0.00	0.00	0.00	0.00
$\sigma = .06$	1	−0.02	−0.03	−0.03	−0.03
	2	−0.01	−0.04	−0.04	−0.04

SOURCE   Authors' calculations.

most striking differences are the impact of nominal devaluation on investment behavior. Contemporaneous σ increases in e_t have a negative impact
in all cases, but this impact is much larger on non-housing components (1
per cent for I_{ht} vs. 5 and 9 per cent for the others). The lagged effects are
negative, and similar in magnitude, across categories with manufacturing
investment the hardest hit by nominal devaluation.

σ increases in the nominal interest rate have similar negative effects on all sectors. Interestingly, the real price of capital has opposite effects on housing and non-housing investment. This index captures machinery costs, and thus has the expected negative effect on manufacturing, agriculture and transport investment. Housing investment, however, is increasing in these shocks.

An increase in contemporaneous public investment has a common positive effect across sectors. The lagged effects are quite different between housing and non-housing sectors, with non-housing investment being 'crowded out' by lagged public investment increases while housing investment seems to be 'crowded in'.

The income and inflation effects are quite similar across sectors and identical to those of the aggregate VAR.

V CONCLUSIONS

The present government policy of outward orientation, financial liberalization and privatization will succeed or fail in the medium term with its success in stimulating and stabilizing private investment. Despite the volatility of the historical record, statistical analysis suggests a number of interesting regularities in private investment response to external and policy shocks.

The government's relative price-based structural adjustment policies appear to have worked to reduce real private investment. The nominal interest rate increase consistent with financial liberalization has corresponded, *ceteris paribus*, to declines in aggregate investment. The nominal exchange rate depreciation has been associated with a fall in private investment both through its direct effects and the indirect effects of gross domestic product contraction and increased inflation. Aggregate private investment demonstrates a substantial positive elasticity with respect to lagged real income.

Decomposition of private investment into housing and non-housing components allows further insight. Devaluation's negative impact is shown to be much larger on the non-housing, or productive, components of private investment. The real price of capital as calculated from government statistics appears to act as the relative price of non-housing investment; as it rises, non-housing investment falls and housing investment rises. Public investment acts unambiguously to 'crowd in' private investment only for the housing sector; in other sectors an initial positive impact is reversed by lagged negative effects.

These results are suggestive, but not definitive. There are as yet too few data and too many revisions to decompose the historical record with precision. The VAR procedure may also be faulted for excluding relevant variables. Excluding concurrent firm decisions (for example, capacity utilization rates or input demands) does not bias the conclusions, for these have in effect been 'substituted out' in the reduced-form equation system of the VAR. However, other variables (real wage, relative prices of imported inputs, tariff policies, investment incentive certificates) play a role in present and future profitability and should on theoretical grounds be included in future efforts. The impact of credit rationing is also not captured here, but the evidence of Anand, Chhibber and van Wijnbergen (this volume) suggests its importance in determining investment behavior. Examination of regression residuals does not suggest strong excluded-variable bias, but the possibility remains that included variables are highly correlated with and acting as proxies of excluded variables.

I draw a cautionary conclusion from the evidence: private investment in Turkey has not yet recovered from the crisis years 1978–80. The period 1970–77 provided the private investor with an attractive and stimulative environment for productive investment, despite the budgetary and borrowing excesses of Turkish economic policy. The challenge for the Turkish government in the 1990s is to recapture that investment climate without precipitating a similar economic and social crisis. The period 1985–86 appears to do that, but its buoyant investment growth is housing-based and uneven across sectors. I conclude that productive private investment will be better encouraged in a low-inflation, low-depreciation, low nominal interest rate environment, rather than the opposite; it will also benefit from greater stability in these nominal variables.

I have heard the present Turkish policy described as 'making the playing field flat' for the exporter. For a successful medium-term strategy, Turkey must also flatten the playing field for investors. The improved competitiveness achieved through real depreciation can be maintained, but its achievement through rapid nominal depreciation and inflation must be replaced by a more stable, low-inflation environment. This will require the greater fiscal responsibility by the Turkish government discussed by other authors in this volume, and represents one of the principal gains of such a strategy.

NOTES

1. Thanks to Michael Salemi, the editors and participants at the Harvard University conference on 'The Political Economy of Turkey in the 1980s', April 1988.
2. Okyar (1965) provides an interesting description of the political and economic genesis of this concept.
3. Real investment as used hereafter refers to gross fixed capital formation, and thus excludes changes in inventories.
4. A generalized form of this installation cost function has been used by Eisner and Strotz (1963), Gould (1968), Abel (1979) and others to generate a continuous investment function. In Conway (1987) I use a similar quadratic

installation-cost function to derive an investment function for Turkey during the 1963–83 period. It is a tractable approximation but should be recognized as an *ad hoc* imposed assumption.

5. The chapter by Anand, Chhibber and van Wijnbergen in this volume provides an application of this in the discussion of sustainability of present fiscal policy for Turkey.

6. Their sources were State Planning Organization (SPO [1985] and revisions of 1988) and World Bank tables from 1988.

7. National accounting includes inventory stock changes as investment, and Keynes identified this component as well as a source of volatility. The inventory component is excluded from the figures on real investment presented hereafter.

8. The recent rise in private housing investment is in part financed through the Mass Housing Fund. As I understand this fund, contributions come from public trade taxes but expenditures are accounted for as private investment.

9. This interest rate effect on investment is consistent with a McKinnon (1973) view of financial liberalization.

10. The one plus the real interest rate enters in level form so that the coefficient 1.42 is a semi-elasticity. The real interest rate term is a proxy for $(1 + r_t^*)$ (e_{t+1}/e_t), and differs by the cross-product $r_t^*(e_{t+1}/e_t)$.

11. The dependent variable is the real *value* of private investment. If the capital good is imported, then P_k will rise one-for-one in percentage terms with the level of the real exchange rate. The volume of private investment will thus be reduced through this channel as well.

12. The domestic real lending rate $(1 + r_t)$ was insignificant when introduced independently into the estimation equation and was thus excluded.

13. The interest-rate coefficient from Conway (1988) is a semi-elasticity, while the Anand specification yields an elasticity. Adjustment for this yields almost identical elasticities in 1981: −1.69 for Anand vs. −1.56 for mine.

14. This will be an exact reduced form for linear structural models, and a linear approximation for non-linear models.

15. The real price of imported inputs (q_t) also belongs in this analysis, but was not included in an effort to constrain the number of equations estimated. I hope in future work to incorporate it.

16. There are other categories of private investment that would fall into the category of 'other'. In 1986, the shares of these categories in total private investment were: agriculture, 6 per cent; manufacturing, 33 per cent; housing, 35 per cent; transport, 14 per cent; other, 16 per cent.

17. The data used in this study are drawn from World Bank (1975), World Bank (1982), and recent Central Bank of Turkey Annual Reports.

18. I have split the sample in two, and found a non-stationarity of the covariance matrix of ε_t. First-differencing and detrending limit this non-stationarity, and yield qualitatively similar results. These results are available on request.

19. A system with regressors lagged two periods proved to provide statistically insignificant improvement in explanatory power as evaluated by an F test for each equation at the 95 per cent level of confidence.

20. Note that the σ increase in e_t reduces growth in y_t, y_{t+1} and y_{t+2} by roughly 1 per cent from both direct and indirect impacts. Conway (1987) found the contemporaneous effect as the empirical product of a model structure with imported inputs used in production. The lagged effects here appear to come through its impact on investment decisions and inflation.

21. These VAR analyses cover the period 1963–86. Each subset of investment was

introduced separately into the VAR, so there are no interactive terms between the subsets. There are insufficient data to estimate the four sectoral functions and these explanatory variables concurrently, but this would be an attractive extension. The complete impulse response tables are available on request.

REFERENCES

Abel, A. (1979) *Investment and the Value of Capital* (New York: Garland).
Celâsun, M. (1983) 'Sources of Industrial Growth and Structural Change: The Case of Turkey' (Washington DC) photocopy.
Celâsun, M. (1986) 'A General Equilibrium Model of the Turkish Economy, SIMLOG 1', *METU Studies in Development* 13, (1, 2) pp. 29–94.
Celâsun, M. and D. Rodrik (forthcoming) *Debt, Adjustment and Growth: Turkey*.
Central Bank of Turkey (various years) *Annual Report* (Ankara).
Conway, P. (1987) *Economic Shocks and Structural Adjustments: Turkey after 1973* (Amsterdam: North-Holland).
Conway, P. (1988) 'Trade Liberalization Policies in Turkey: 1980–1984', in T. Nas and M. Odekon (eds), *Liberalization and the Turkish Economy* (New York: Greenwood Press) pp. 47–67.
Eisner, R. and R. Strotz (1976) 'Determinants of Business Investment', in M. Surrey (ed.), *Macroeconomic Themes* (London: Oxford University Press) pp. 127–36. (Originally published in 1963 in *Impacts of Monetary Policy*.)
Gordon, R. and S. King (1982) 'The Output Cost of Disinflation in Traditional and Vector Autoregressive Models', *Brookings Papers on Economic Activity* 1, pp. 205–44.
Gould, J. (1968) 'Adjustment Costs in the Theory of Investment of the Firm', *Review of Economic Studies* 35, pp. 47–56.
Lewis, J. and S. Urata (1983) 'Turkey: Recent Economic Performance and Medium Term Prospects' (Washington DC: World Bank) World Bank Staff Working Paper 602.
Keynes, J. (1937) 'The General Theory of Employment', *Quarterly Journal of Economics* 51, pp. 209–23.
Kopits, G. (1987) 'Structural Reform, Stabilization and Growth in Turkey' (Washington DC: IMF) International Monetary Fund Occasional Paper 52.
McKinnon, R. (1973) *Money and Capital in Economic Development*, (Washington DC: Brookings Institution).
Okyar, O. (1965) 'The Concept of Etatism', *Economic Journal* 75, pp. 98–111.
Ott, D., A. Ott and J. Yoo (1975) *Macroeconomic Theory* (New York: McGraw-Hill).
Sims, C. (1982) 'Policy Analysis with Econometric Models', *Brookings Papers on Economic Activity* 1, pp. 107–66.
SPO (1985) *V. Beş Yıllık Plan Destek Çalışmaları*: I (Fifth Five Year Plan Supplementary Studies: I), (Ankara: State Planning Organization).
TÜSİAD (1984) *The Turkish Economy 1984* (Ankara: Turkish Industrialists' and Businessmen's Association).
van Wijnbergen, S. (1987) 'Inflation, External Debt and Financial Sector Reform: A Quantitative Approach to Consistent Fiscal Policy', (Washington DC) photocopy.
World Bank (1975) *Turkey: A Country Study* (Washington DC).
World Bank (1982) *Turkey: Industrialization and Trade Strategy* (Washington DC).

APPENDIX

TABLE A1 *Contemporaneous Correlation Coefficients: Aggregate Private Investment VAR**

	i	e	I_g	P_k/P	I_p	y	π
i	1.00	0.66	-0.20	-0.04	-0.15	-0.25	0.46
e	0.66	1.00	-0.38	-0.04	-0.42	-0.35	0.81
I_g	-0.20	-0.38	1.00	0.26	0.43	0.55	-0.33
P_k/P	-0.04	-0.04	0.26	1.00	0.07	-0.03	-0.14
I_p	-0.15	-0.42	0.43	0.07	1.00	0.59	-0.54
y	-0.25	-0.35	0.55	-0.03	0.59	1.00	-0.51
π	0.46	0.81	-0.33	-0.14	-0.54	-0.51	1.00

* These correlation coefficients are derived from the regression residuals ε_t.

TABLE A2 *Vector Autoregression in I_{pt}**

	i_t	e_t	I_{gt}	P_{kt}/P_t	I_{pt}	y_t	π_t
Intercept	0.83	-7.90	7.27†	4.08†	4.93	1.52	-13.35†
	(0.75)	(4.84)	(1.78)	(1.15)	(3.03)	(0.88)	(5.04)
i_{t-1}	-0.24	-0.01	2.01†	0.20	0.45	-0.09	-1.01
	(0.29)	(1.87)	(0.69)	(0.44)	(1.17)	(0.34)	(1.95)
e_{t-1}	0.15†	0.97†	-0.19	0.09	-0.07	0.05	-0.13
	(0.04)	(0.27)	(0.10)	(0.06)	(0.17)	(0.05)	(0.28)
I_{gt-1}	0.07	0.56	0.48†	0.33†	-0.28	-0.02	-0.35
	(0.06)	(0.40)	(0.15)	(0.09)	(0.25)	(0.07)	(0.41)
P_{kt-1}/P_{t-1}	-0.14	1.42	-1.36†	0.21	-0.95	-0.26	2.27*
	(0.14)	(0.92)	(0.34)	(0.22)	(0.58)	(0.17)	(0.96)
I_{pt-1}	-0.04	-0.04	-0.04	0.18†	0.63†	0.06	-0.16
	(0.05)	(0.34)	(0.12)	(0.08)	(0.21)	(0.06)	(0.35)
y_{t-1}	-0.13	-0.49	0.59	-0.95†	0.94	0.86†	1.54
	(0.16)	(1.06)	(0.39)	(0.25)	(0.66)	(0.19)	(1.10)
π_{t-1}	0.04	0.39	0.12	0.04	-0.36†	-0.05	0.44†
	(0.03)	(0.20)	(0.07)	(0.05)	(0.12)	(0.04)	(0.21)
SEE	0.23	0.15	0.05	0.04	0.09	0.03	0.16
$\bar{R}^2$	0.97	0.99	0.99	0.73	0.95	0.99	0.59
$Q(12)^\ddagger$	7.21	18.70	16.08	10.32	16.34	22.94†	16.11

* Standard errors in parentheses.
  Annual data: 1962–86 inclusive.
† Coefficients significantly different from zero at the 95 per cent level of confidence.
‡ The Q statistic is a measure of autocorrelation with lagged regressors, and is distributed as chi-square. Its significance in the y equation suggests that a more complex lag structure is desirable in explaining that variable.

5 Financial System and Policies in Turkey in the 1980s

Yılmaz Akyüz[1]

> *No Honour now could be content,*
> *To live and owe for what was spent,*
> *Liv'ries in Broker's shops are hung;*
> *They part with Coaches for a song;*
> *Sell stately Horses by whole sets;*
> *And Country-Houses to pay debts.*
> Mandeville, *Fable of the Bees*

It is widely held that the Turkish financial system during the years before 1980 was highly repressed. The financial repression consisted of: ceilings on deposit and lending rates and negative real interest rates; credit rationing and subsidized credits to priority sectors; excessive taxation of financial incomes and transactions; high liquidity and reserve requirements and intermediation costs; a high degree of interlocking ownership between banks and non-financial corporations; excessive reliance of corporations on credits rather than equity finance and direct security issues, and low-quality bank portfolios; undeveloped capital markets; excessive reliance of the public sector on Central Bank for deficit financing; entry barriers to foreign banks; restrictions on external financial operations, foreign asset holdings and so on. These are widely believed to have resulted in inefficiencies and distortions in resource allocation, with adverse effects on growth.[2]

The policy reforms and structural measures adopted from mid-1980 onwards, which were closely monitored by the IMF and World Bank and supported by various SALs have, in effect, aimed to reduce the degree of financial repression (Wolff, 1987, chapter 4). This paper makes an assessment of the impact of these policies on the structure and stability of the financial system and corporate finance, and the size and allocation of domestic savings. The following section will briefly review the financial policies pursued in the 1980s. Section II will examine the evolution of the financial structure in terms of the size and composition of financial assets. Section III will discuss the consequences of the policies pursued for corporate finance. The last section will examine the behavior of sectoral and aggregate savings.

I   A REVIEW OF FINANCIAL POLICIES IN THE 1980s

The first step towards financial deregulation was taken in July 1980 when the authorities lifted the ceilings on personal time deposit rates, as had been promised in the Letter of Intent to the IMF. It was considered as a 'major step in deregulation of interest rates which breaks a practice that has been in force some 50 years'.[3] However, due to the so-called gentlemen's agreement among major commercial banks, the rise in interest rates was moderate at first despite a persistent excess demand for credits in the face of a tightened monetary stance and a rapid pace of inflation, resulting in negative real rates of interest (Tables 5.1 and 5.2).[4] However, as competition from smaller banks and brokers in informal (unregulated) markets increased, interest rates started to rise rapidly. In particular, smaller banks started issuing at a discount the newly introduced certificates of deposits (CD) to brokers who, in turn, sold them to the public at substantially higher interest rates, often on a monthly basis. Brokers also bought and sold corporate bonds (which were subject to interest rate ceilings) in the same way, issued promissory notes themselves, and lent heavily to those with limited access to bank credits, particularly to high-risk businesses. Such debt often represented distress borrowing and, hence, could not be serviced regularly. Since payments to banks against CDs and interest payments to the public depended on the proceeds of new sales, this Ponzi financing could continue only as long as the flow of CDs from banks and sales to the public were growing at an accelerating pace. When banks stopped supplying CDs as a result of mounting claims on brokers and increased pressure from major banks and the authorities, the market suffered substantial loss of confidence, leading to a collapse in mid-1982 when the largest broker (Banker Kastelli) became insolvent and fled abroad. The crisis hit many enterprises and banks, necessitating substantial rescue operations and a loosening of the monetary stance. Five banks were liquidated and their liabilities transferred to public banks. It was estimated that rescue operations cost no less than TL 200 billion, or about 2.5 per cent of GNP (Artun, 1985, p. 51).

Following the financial crash, the government authorized the nine largest banks to set the deposit rates and allowed the smaller banks to pay a small premium. However, 'because the large banks were reluctant to raise interest rates to positive real levels, in December 1983 the Central Bank was authorized to determine deposit rates and to review the rates, at least every three months, on the basis of fluctuations in the inflation rate and in other economic developments' (Central Bank, 1985, p. 24). Deposit rates were raised sharply from the beginning of 1984 onwards, and have, in general, been kept above the rate of inflation. In mid-1987 interest rates on one-year deposits were once again left free for banks to determine. However, as large banks were again reluctant to raise such rates, all

Financial System and Policies in Turkey

TABLE 5.1   *Commercial Bank Interest Rates, 1980–86 (per cent per annum, end-December)*

	1980	1981	1982	1983	1984	1985	1986
Deposits							
Savings sight	5	5	5	20	5	5	10
Time/call*							
1 month	–	–	25	–	35	35	30
3–6 months	–	–	45	–	53	45	40
6–12 months	15	50	50	35	52	50	45
1 year or more	33–36	50	50	40	45	55	52
Credits							
Short-term							
General	31	36	36	32	53.5–62	53.5–64	53.5–65
Exports	22	27	31.5	26.5	45–62	53.5–64	53.5–65
Agriculture	22	22	20	20	28	30	30
Medium and long-term							
General	33–36	38–41	38–41	34	52–62	52–66	52–67
Agriculture	24	24	22	22	28	28–30	28–30
Housing	16	16	16	16	16	31	31
Memo item:							
Effective yield on							
6-month deposits[†]	11.25	37.5	37.5	28	46.75	45	40.5

* Same rates on CDs of comparable maturity.
[†] After deduction of withholding tax.
SOURCE   Central Bank of Turkcy.

deposit rates have been brought under the control of the Central Bank since the beginning of 1988 and raised substantially.

Governments also made deliberate use of the term structure of deposit rates in order to dampen inflationary expectations. From the beginning of 1984, the rates on shorter maturities were kept above those of longer maturities. However, as this policy only resulted in a greater concentration of deposits in three-month accounts (Table 5.3), it was reversed in mid-1985.

As part of adjustment measures agreed with the World Bank, reserve ratios have been unified and reduced (by more than a half between 1984 and 1988), and withholding and financial transaction taxes lowered (from 25 per cent to 10 per cent and from 25 per cent to 3 per cent respectively). The reserve requirement has been extended to foreign currency deposits and the compliance lag shortened. Interest payments on domestic currency reserves have been phased out, but continued on foreign currency reserves. The liquidity ratio was unified and initially reduced to 10 per cent, but it has been raised in subsequent years exceeding 25 per cent in 1988.

The practice of preferential loans continued and preferential credit

TABLE 5.2   *Real After-Tax Rates of Return, 1979–86 (per cent)*

	1979	1980	1981	1982	1983	1984	1985	1986
Sight deposits	−43.5	−47.0	−17.4	−17.3	−17.2	−31.9	−24.4	−14.8
Time deposits								
One year	−37.2	−37.7	9.0	9.6	−4.4	−8.5	4.9	12.7
Six months	−40.1	−42.9	5.9	12.4	−5.6	0.4	10.2	12.4
Three months	−	−	10.1	10.3	−	4.0	10.6	10.2
Public securities								
Bonds	−34.9	−38.4	10.4	10.5	−5.1	−6.9	8.4	17.0
Treasury bills	−	−33.2	7.2	−	−	5.1	18.4	20.0
Income sharing								
certs.	−	−	−	−	−	−	13.5	30.8
Corporate securities								
Bonds	−33.8	−37.1	−3.6	6.7	−4.6	−0.9	8.5	14.1
Shares	−60.2	−41.2	32.9	55.4	84.0	−59.2	1.8	23.8
Gold	46.9	9.3	−27.1	47.6	−11.9	−24.5	−1.8	27.9
US$	−22.8	31.0	18.1	11.4	8.1	3.0	−6.2	3.4
Foreign exchange deposits								
US$	−	−	−	−	−	−	2.7	11.4
Deutschmark	−	−	−	−	−	−	26.6	29.0

SOURCE   Coşan and Ersel (1987).

TABLE 5.3   *Percentage Distribution of Time Deposits, 1979–86*

	1979	1980	1981	1982	1983	1984	1985	1986
One year	96.5	94.9	50.9	21.2	45.5	4.7	6.2	20.7
Six months	2.7	4.8	37.1	63.6	45.3	7.3	44.3	34.7
Three months	0.8	0.3	12.0	15.2	9.2	88.0	49.5	44.6
Commercial	0.8	0.5	0.4	0.5	0.9	4.0	6.1	8.5
Savings	99.2	87.0	77.1	78.3	90.7	86.6	80.3	79.6
Certificates								
of deposits	0.0	12.5	22.5	21.2	8.4	9.4	13.6	11.9
Memo item								
Time deposits/								
total deposits	22.0	27.1	49.7	56.8	49.6	66.3	69.4	64.9

SOURCE   Central Bank *Quarterly Bulletins* (various issues).

schemes proliferated during the earlier part of the period. However, the contribution of non-preferential loans to the Interest Rate Rebate Fund, (IRRF, replaced by the Resource Utilization Support Fund in 1985) to finance subsidies on preferential lending has been gradually reduced. Since the beginning of 1984 banks have been allowed to set the non-preferential rates freely, and preferential rates have been raised substantially. Although the preferential treatment of export credits was phased out in 1985, it was reintroduced subsequently as export performance deteriorated in 1986.

There have been four other notable developments in the banking sector. First, to date, no less than 13 foreign banks have been allowed to open branches in Turkey, mostly using the funds under the Turkish lira options of rescheduled debt on Convertible Turkish Lira Deposits and non-guaranteed supplier arrears purchased, in some cases, at large discounts. Second, an interbank money market was created in 1986. Third the Central Bank started open market operations at the beginning of 1987. Fourth, a new banking law has been enacted requiring banks, *inter alia*, to hold part of their profits as contingency reserves, and to purchase a minimum insurance coverage for savings deposits from the Insurance Fund at the Central Bank.

Following the financial crisis a number of measures were taken concerning capital markets. A Capital Market Board (CMB) was established which is responsible for the regulation and supervision of primary and secondary markets, and is authorized to approve all public offerings of private sector securities, and to supervise joint stock companies. The Istanbul Stock Exchange was re-opened at the beginning of 1986. Until mid-1987, when private bond rates were freed, the Central Bank had been authorized to set a ceiling on such rates with a margin over the one-year time deposit rate. Investment and development banks have been allowed to issue short-term bills, and non-financial joint-stock companies commercial papers with maturities up to one year. Corporations were allowed to revalue their assets as of end-1982, and to distribute stock dividends and to make rights issues. Dividends and capital gains were exempted from personal taxation.

The public sector has become the single most important supplier of securities as the financing of its deficits has been shifted from the Central Bank to private markets. The maturity of government bonds has been shortened, and weekly auctioning of Treasury bills (largely to banks and, to a lesser extent, stock brokers) has become a major source of finance since the beginning of 1984. Government securities are exempt from withholding tax, and their yields have, on average, exceeded those on other domestic financial assets (Table 5.2). They are held against liquidity requirements by commercial banks, and used as collateral in the interbank market. Since 1984, a new instrument, income-sharing certificates, has been issued, giving entitlement to participation in profits of public enterprises. More recently plans have been made to privatize non-financial State Economic Enterprises (SEEs) in order, *inter alia*, to help revitalize capital markets.

Finally, there has been substantial liberalization of external payments since 1984. Residents have been allowed to hold foreign currency, open such accounts with commercial banks and make payments, cash with-drawals and transfers abroad. Interest rates on foreign currency accounts may be negotiated with banks, and have so far exceeded the rates in Euromarkets. Foreign exchange transactions on trade have been trans-ferred from the Central Bank to commercial banks, and the latter encour-aged to utilize short-term credits from external markets. However, as pressures developed in the foreign exchange market, and banks' foreign exchange liabilities surpassed such assets by a wide margin, restrictions were introduced in 1986, including liquidity and reserve requirements, the ratio between foreign exchange assets and liabilities, and the use of foreign currency deposits. Further pressures developed during the latter half of 1987 as inflation accelerated and the differential between curb and official exchange rates widened, reaching 25 per cent in early 1988. Banks started to make large purchases from the curb market partly to cover themselves, and partly because they expected a large devaluation, charging com-missions on sales to importers at a rate of 20 to 30 per cent over the maximum selling rate set by the Central Bank. In response to deepened instability, new measures have been introduced since the beginning of 1988, including incentives for a speedy surrender and penalties for delays. These measures, together with increased deposit rates, reserve and liquid-ity ratios, seem to aim at curbing speculations and relieving the pressure on the TL.

II THE EVOLUTION OF THE FINANCIAL STRUCTURE

Financial development is generally identified with the growth of the real size of the financial sector in absolute terms, and in relation to GNP or national wealth; that is, financial deepening. Broad money (M2) is often taken as an adequate measure of the size of the financial sector in develop-ing countries in view of the predominance of the banking system, as well as because of lack of data on other financial assets.[5] However, the role of the financial sector in the savings-investment process also depends on the structure and composition of financial assets, markets and institutions. Growth of equity *vis-à-vis* debt-finance, of long-term direct claims relative to short-term indirect securities, and of non-bank financial intermediaries relative to commercial banks are of cardinal importance for the availability of investment finance and financial stability.[6] Therefore, a broader assess-ment of the developments in the financial system will need to be under-taken than the evolution of the absolute and relative size of the financial sector.

There can be little doubt that policies pursued since 1980 have resulted in an increased depth of finance as conventionally defined. The *stock* of financial assets has continuously grown in real terms and in relation to

GNP (Table 5.4). Aggregate *new* financial issues rose in real terms almost every year, and their ratio to GNP (that is, the financial savings ratio) increased considerably (Table 5.5). Similarly, the earlier steep decline in broad real-balances was reversed, and the ratio of M2 to GNP rose and has remained relatively stable during recent years.

As for the composition of financial assets, direct securities accounted for a somewhat smaller proportion of total *stock* of financial assets in 1986 than in 1979, while claims on the banking system increased (Table 5.6). The recent upward trend in the share of direct securities in *new* issues reflects increased issues of Treasury bills and income-sharing certificates by the public sector; the share of private sector direct securities in the outstanding stock of financial assets was almost halved between 1979 and 1986.

Since a large proportion of public sector securities is absorbed by the banking system, and the private sector bond and equity issues have declined in relative terms, the share of direct securities in household portfolios has fallen substantially while claims on the banking sector increased (Table 5.7).[7] The sharp decline in the share of insurance reserves reflects, in large part, the impact of wage and employment policies; reserves of social security institutions fell, in real terms, by more than 40 per cent between 1979 and 1985. On the other hand, despite sharply increased security issues by the public sector, the share of such assets in household portfolios fell compared to the late 1970s. The recent rise in the share of such securities is due to newly-issued income-sharing certificates. Similarly, there has been no upward trend in the share of private bonds and equities. If compulsory insurance reserves and non-marketable equities are excluded, the share of claims on the banking sector, including forex deposits, in household portfolios can be estimated to be in excess of 90 per cent.

There have been significant changes in the composition of claims on the banking system in response to yield differentials. Narrow monetary assets have lost in relative importance with the substitution of time deposits for currency and sight deposits. In particular, the behavior of time and sight deposits have been extremely sensitive to interest rate differentials.[8]

Similarly, a high degree of currency substitution has been taking place during the last few years. Indeed much of the increased financial deepening has been due to the rise in forex deposits. These have increased much faster than TL deposits, reaching $5.6 billion at the end of 1987 and exceeding a third of total private sector deposits in 1987. About three-quarters of these deposits are in DM, which have brought a much higher rate of real after-tax return than TL deposits, partly because of a sharp appreciation of DM against TL and partly because of relatively high interest rates on forex deposits (Table 5.2). Even the real after-tax rate of return on US dollar deposits did not, on average, fall very much below the rates on TL deposits despite the real appreciation of TL against the US dollar between end-1984 and end-1986.

TABLE 5.4 *Indicators of Financial Deepening, 1979–86**

	1979	1980	1981	1982	1983	1984	1985	1986
Stock of financial assets (SFA) (billion TL)†								
Nominal	677	1135	2021	3159	4241	7058	11 638	17 940
At 1977 prices	271	219	285	359	366	400	471	574
M1 (billion TL)								
Nominal	445	704	972	1342	1941	2253	3209	5107
At 1977 prices	178	136	137	153	167	128	130	160
M2 (billion TL)								
Nominal	528	882	1637	2554	3288	5179	8146	11 644
At 1977 prices	211	170	231	290	283	294	330	372
SFA/GNP	30.8	25.6	30.8	36.2	36.7	39.3	41.9	45.8
M1/GNP‡	20.2	15.9	14.8	15.4	16.8	12.5	11.5	12.8
M2/GNP§	24.0	19.9	25.0	29.2	28.5	28.8	29.3	28.7

* Deposits exclude public and interbank deposits.
† Includes all assets given in Table 5.5. Calculated on the basis of initial (1978) stock figures given in Akyüz (1984b), with an adjustment for equities so as to include only those quoted on the Stock Exchange and new issues given in Table 5.5.
‡ M1 = Currency in circulation + Sight Deposits.
§ M2 = M1 + Time Deposits.
SOURCE Akyüz (1984b); Central Bank (1983–86).

TABLE 5.5   *Financial Assets — New Issues, 1979–86 (per cent distribution)**

	1979	1980	1981	1982	1983	1984	1985	1986
Banking system	85.0	77.4	85.2	80.6	81.4	81.6	78.1	74.9
Currency in circulation	21.2	16.1	7.1	11.5	12.5	6.7	6.0	6.4
Sight deposits	47.2	40.6	23.1	21.0	42.8	4.4	14.8	22.3
Time deposits[†]	16.6	20.7	55.0	48.1	12.5	56.0	43.9	20.5
Forex deposits	–	–	–	–	13.6	14.5	13.4	25.7
Direct securities	15.0	22.6	14.8	19.4	18.6	18.4	21.9	25.1
Government bonds (net)	8.2	5.2	5.7	2.9	17.2	5.3	11.2	7.6
Treasury bills (net)	1.7	8.7	4.4	5.7	–8.9	10.1	5.1	10.6
Income sharing certificates	–	–	–	–	–	0.4	3.1	3.5
Private bonds	2.1	3.9	1.8	1.2	1.5	0.4	0.8	1.8
Equities[‡]	3.0	4.8	2.9	9.6	8.8	2.2	1.7	1.6
Memo items								
Total new issues/GNP	10.7	10.3	13.5	13.0	9.4	15.7	16.5	16.1
Direct security issues/GNP	1.6	2.3	2.0	2.5	1.7	2.9	3.6	4.0
Total new issues (billion TL)								
Nominal	235	458	886	1138	1082	2817	4580	6302
At 1977 prices	94	88	125	129	93	160	186	202

* Deposits exclude public and interbank deposits.
† Includes certificates of deposits.
‡ Quoted on the Stock Exchange.
SOURCE   Central Bank (1983–86).

The increased dominance of commercial banks is also reflected by a substantial rise in their share in the total assets of financial institutions, including investment and development banks (IDB), social security institutions (SOS), private funds and insurance companies.[9] During 1980–85, commercial banks' assets grew in real terms whereas the assets of non-bank financial intermediaries declined. Similarly, commercial banks' share in total credits rose considerably whereas the share of IDB was halved (Table 5.8). Since the main function of non-bank financial institutions in Turkey is provision of investment finance, this means that there has been a tendency to move from long-term investment finance towards short-term commercial loans.

A number of factors explain the poor performance of private bond and equity markets. Given that private bonds offered, for most of the period, 10 to 15 percentage points higher interest than time deposits, but that the cost of bond finance was still lower than non-preferential loans due to high spreads between deposit and loan rates (see Section IV), the conditions would have been thought favorable, on both the demand and supply sides, for a rapid growth of bond issues. Indeed, corporate bond issues started to

Theodore Lownik Library
Illinois Benedictine College
Lisle, IL 60532*Yılmaz Akyüz*

TABLE 5.6 *Composition of the Stock of Financial Assets, 1979–86 (per cent)*

	1979	1980	1981	1982	1983	1984	1985	1986
Currency in circulation	21.2	19.2	13.9	13.1	12.9	10.4	8.7	7.9
Sight deposits	44.4	42.9	34.3	29.4	32.9	21.5	18.9	20.1
Time deposits	12.3	15.7	32.9	38.3	31.8	41.6	42.3	34.6
Forex deposits	–	–	–	–	3.4	7.9	10.0	15.6
Government bonds	13.1	9.9	8.0	6.2	9.0	7.5	9.0	8.5
Treasury bills	0.6	3.9	4.1	4.7	1.2	4.7	4.9	6.9
Income sharing certificates	–	–	–	–	–	0.1	1.3	2.1
Private bonds	1.9	2.7	2.3	1.9	1.8	1.2	1.1	1.3
Equities	6.5	5.7	4.5	6.4	7.0	5.1	3.8	3.0

SOURCE Same as Table 5.4.

TABLE 5.7 *Household Portfolios, 1978–85 (percentage distribution of domestic financial assets)*

	1978	1979	1980	1981	1982	1983	1984	1985
Currency	17.8	18.9	19.6	14.5	13.8	13.1	11.3	11.1
Sight deposits	22.8	22.4	21.1	13.8	10.9	16.0	7.6	6.6
Time deposits	9.7	12.2	18.4	39.4	47.3	38.5	51.5	51.0
Insurance reserves	28.1	26.5	22.4	17.2	14.9	14.9	13.4	13.2
Government securities*	6.1	7.0	3.8	1.6	1.4	2.7	2.4	5.0
Corporate bonds	1.5	1.6	2.9	2.5	2.2	2.0	1.3	1.1
Equities bonds[†]	14.0	11.4	11.8	11.0	9.5	12.8	12.5	12.0

* Includes bonds, bills and certificates.
[†] Paid-in capital held outside the incorporated financial and non-financial business.
SOURCE 1978–84: Akyüz (1984b), updated by TSKB for 1982–84; 1985: estimated on the basis of 1985 figures for household deposits and insurance reserves, and total currency in circulation, and 1984 stocks and 1985 issues of direct securities and the 1984 proportions of total currency and direct securities held by the household sector. It is assumed that newly-issued income-sharing certificates are held entirely by the household sector.

pick up in 1980–81 despite the maintenance of ceilings on bond rates. This was greatly facilitated by the liquidity and flexibility that the brokers provided, with repurchase guarantees on demand and monthly interest payments. However, when brokers collapsed, these elements disappeared and, with an average maturity of two years and annual interest payments in an environment of volatile inflation, bonds ceased to be competitive with bank deposits. The collapse of this market itself also had an adverse impact on demand for bonds, pushing the risk premium in comparison with 'safe' bank deposits. On the other hand, those looking for high-yield but safer assets could easily go to government securities which offered higher yields

Financial System and Policies in Turkey

TABLE 5.8 *Distribution of Bank Credits, 1979–86 (percentage)*

	1979	1980	1981	1982	1983	1984	1985	1986
Total	100.0	100.0	100.0	100.0	100.0	100.0	100.0	100.0
Public sector	50.2	48.0	40.2	34.8	31.7	25.3	27.2	27.1
Private sector	49.8	52.0	59.8	65.2	68.3	74.7	72.8	72.9
Central Bank*	26.9	27.7	24.1	19.6	17.2	13.3	12.9	10.2
Commercial banks	56.1	59.5	64.0	67.4	70.3	74.0	78.0	81.3
Public sector	9.6	11.2	7.7	6.2	6.3	4.8	9.7	12.7
Private sector	46.5	48.3	56.3	61.2	64.0	69.2	68.3	68.6
IDB	17.0	12.8	11.9	13.0	12.5	12.7	9.1	8.5
Public sector	13.7	9.2	8.4	9.0	8.2	7.1	4.6	4.1
Private sector	3.3	3.6	3.5	4.0	4.3	5.6	4.5	4.4
Memo items								
Growth rate of credits								
Nominal	51.3	66.7	55.3	29.6	28.4	23.5	68.1	73.6
Real	–12.6	–40.5	18.6	4.3	–2.2	–28.5	28.1	46.9
Public sector's share in commercial bank advances[†]	23.7	25.5	20.5	23.0	17.6	23.1	30.2	31.7

* Includes only direct credits to the public sector without intermediation of banks. The decline in 1984 is largely due to consolidation of SEE debt (not shown here); see Central Bank (1984, pp. 43–7).
[†] Includes credits, bonds and bills and other forms of advance.
SOURCE Central Bank (1982–86).

than private bonds. Moreover, firms which were large enough to undertake bond issues have continued to benefit from preferential treatment from banks due to interlocking ownership and lack of effective implementation of limits on lending by banks to a single enterprise; nor have such firms always been willing to disclose the necessary information in order to obtain authorization from the CMB for bond issues. Thus, neither the institutional arrangements nor the structure of interest rates have been conducive to the development of bond markets. Consequently, while public sector security issues increased rapidly from 1984 onwards, and more than 90 per cent of trading on the Istanbul Stock Exchange was in such securities in 1986, the private bond market remained depressed (Coşan and Ersel, 1987, pp. 60–2).

A similar development is also observed in equity markets. As a first reaction to the drastic rise in interest rates during 1981–82, equity issues picked up, accounting for 10 per cent of new financial issues by the corporate sector. However, this quickly came to an end. In 1983 the sharp rise in equity issues represented mainly the rights issues (more than 90 per cent of the increase in equities quoted on the stock exchange) in accord-

TABLE 5.9   *Net New Issues by Sectors, 1979–86 (per cent distribution)*

	1979	1980	1981	1982	1983	1984	1985	1986
Public sector	53.9	46.6	32.4	21.0	25.0	42.8	45.3	40.7
Credits*	46.4	38.9	22.1	10.9	16.7	14.7	22.5	20.7
Securities[†]	7.5	7.7	10.3	10.1	8.3	28.1	22.8	20.0
Private Sector	46.1	53.4	67.6	79.0	75.0	57.2	54.7	59.3
Credits	42.2	46.9	62.8	65.8	63.2	52.4	51.8	56.2
Bonds	1.6	2.9	1.9	1.4	1.7	0.8	0.9	1.6
Equities	2.3	3.6	2.9	11.8	10.1	4.0	2.0	1.5
Memo item								
Total new issues								
(billion TL)	305.1	618.1	862.3	926.4	949.2	1574.3	3880.7	6817.9

* Excludes accounts to be redeemed at the Central Bank.
[†] Includes bonds, bills and income-sharing certificates.
SOURCE   Central Bank (1981–86).

ance with the asset revaluation law (Central Bank, 1984, p. 59). Despite the provision of a legal and institutional framework, the market remained rudimentary, both in terms of new equity issues and the volume of trading. During 1986, only 2.5 per cent of stock exchange trading was in equities, and the turnover ratio remained at around 1 per cent, much below that observed in countries at similar or lower levels of economic development.[10] Two additional factors have also played a major role in the poor performance of equity markets. First, the reluctance of owner-families of large holding companies to broaden their share-holding base in order to retain control. Second, the practice of allowing tax deductibility of interest payments by corporations.

Thus, the other (that is, the liabilities) side of financial deepening that has taken place in Turkey since 1980 is, in effect, increased short-term indebtedness of the private sector in comparison with equity and bond finance. Between 1979 and 1986 the share of bonds and equities in new financial issues by this sector was halved (Table 5.9), while total private debt to commercial banks almost doubled in real terms and the ratio of such debt to GNP rose significantly.

This is also true for the public sector although the composition of its debt has drastically changed. The public sector borrowing requirement (PSBR) was sharply reduced from 10 per cent of GNP in 1980 to around 5 per cent in 1981, and stayed, on average, at that level during the first half of the decade.[11] The reduction of deficits of SEEs through constant increases in their prices, elimination of subsidies, and wage and employment policies played a major role. After 1985, however, PSBR rose rapidly, reaching 8.7 per cent of GNP in 1987. Although public investment rose and deficits of SEEs somewhat increased, the main reason was the sharp rise in interest payments on domestic and external debt, which together absorbed almost a quarter of budget revenues in 1987, equalling the total investment spending; the primary budget was in surplus during 1985–87.

Exchange rate and interest rate policies as well as the way in which budget deficits were financed have played a major role. Devaluations have increased the domestic currency equivalent of the government's external financial obligations in real terms, thereby aggravating the budgetary transfer problem created by net transfer of resources abroad. In the early 1980s domestic interest payments from the budget remained low (at about 0.5 per cent of GNP), in large part because the interest-bearing stock of debt was small and carried low rates (OECD, 1987, p. 59). However, as the financing of public sector deficits was largely shifted from the Central Bank,[12] new debt had to be raised in domestic markets at terms competitive with expected return on foreign exchange assets, and interest payments on domestic debt as a proportion of GNP more than tripled. This has reduced government savings, and resulted in still higher deficits which, in turn, fed into higher public debt.[13] Thus, real domestic debt of the public sector almost doubled since 1979 and, unlike original intentions, the share of the public sector in private financial markets increased considerably. Government security issues rose much faster than its credits from the banking system due to the decline in CB credits; they also increased much faster than such issues by the private sector (Table 5.9). On the other hand, while the shares of the public and private sectors in total direct credits of commercial banks remained more or less unchanged, commercial banks' advances to the public sector, including security holdings, increased much faster than advances to the private sector due to increased holding of government securities (Table 5.8).

III   COST AND AVAILABILITY OF CREDITS AND CORPORATE FINANCE

Increases in interest rates on time deposits and the rise in the share of such deposits have resulted in a rapid increase of the average cost of bank deposits, from less than 5 per cent in the late 1970s to more than 30 per cent in the 1980s, and loan rates have, in general, followed the time deposit rates. This has had a major influence on corporate finance; it has served to increase further the dependence of the corporate sector on bank credits and, hence, its vulnerability to changes in the availability and cost of credits.

It is difficult to give an accurate picture of the evolution of credit costs in the 1980s. Almost every single loan has carried a different effective rate, for a number of reasons including the persistence of a great variety of lending rates on preferential and non-preferential loans, different rates of subsidies from and contributions to the IRRF, and the practice of blocking part of loan proceeds at different rates for different borrowers as well as differential charges. For these reasons we have estimated the average cost of credits for two broad categories, namely, total and non-preferential credits, without allowing for the effect of blocked loan proceeds (Table 5.10).

Despite the liberalization of interest rates in July 1980, lending rates were raised only moderately at first, but as excess demand persisted, the limits agreed by major banks on non-preferential loans were effectively exceeded by blocking around a quarter of loan proceeds as commercial deposits.[14] In 1981 non-preferential loan rates were raised whereas pre-ferential rates were kept largely unchanged. As inflation slowed down substantially, the real cost of credits increased, exceeding 20 per cent on non-preferential loans during 1982; with part of the loan proceeds blocked, the effective real rate was probably close to 30 per cent. After 1982 real loan rates fell, partly due to an acceleration of inflation and partly to lowering of interest rates in 1983. However, from 1984 onwards both nominal and real loan rates started to rise again. In 1986, the average real cost of credits reached 22 per cent; for non-preferential loans it was about 33 per cent. Since the practice of blocking part of loan proceeds continued (though at a lower rate), the effective real rates were much higher.

The evidence suggests that the spread between the average cost of deposits and the average cost of credits rose rapidly, more than doubling between 1982 and 1986.[15] In order to identify the sources of the rise in the spread, a decomposition exercise has been carried out based on a simple balance sheet identity: total credits = total deposit — reserves — liquidity requirements + CB rediscounts and advances + net other uses (resources). It is assumed that the discrepancy between disposable deposits (that is, deposits minus reserves minus liquidity requirements) and credits are financed with CB rediscounts and advances and other resources, and the excess of disposable deposits over credits are allocated to other uses. Net costs per unit of credits of the items on the right hand side of this identity are estimated and intermediation costs (personnel and other operation expenses per unit of credits) added. The difference between spreads and these costs is taken as residual, to be discussed below.

The reserve-cost component of the spread fell between 1982 and 1984, due to substantially increased interest payments on reserves for time deposits and reduced reserve requirements. Although the latter was further reduced in 1985, interest payments on reserves were completely phased out, which, together with a tightening of supervision over com-pliance, resulted in substantially increased reserve costs in 1986. Liquidity requirements did not add to credit costs in 1984 and 1986 since a large proportion of these were held in government securities with higher yields than the average rate on deposits. In general, the cost of CB advances was

TABLE 5.10   *Credit Costs and Interest Spreads*

		1982	1984	1986
(1)	Average interest on deposits (per cent)	26.8	32.5	29.8
(2)	Average interest on credits (per cent)	32.9	45.1	51.8
(3)	Average cost of credits (per cent)	37.8	47.8	54.0
(4)	Spread (percentage points)	11.0	15.3	24.2
(5)	Fees and commissions	4.9	2.7	2.2
(6)	Reserve costs (net)	2.3	0.2	4.3
(7)	Liquidity cost (net)	0.1	–0.7	–1.8
(7a)	Cash and free dep. at CB (net)	(1.1)	(1.0)	(1.0)
(7b)	Bills and bonds (net)	(–1.0)	(–1.7)	(–2.8)
(8)	Cost of credits from CB (net)	2.4	–	0.5
(9)	Cost of other resources	–	–1.4	4.6
(10)	Personnel expenses	7.5	6.6	4.3
(11)	Other identified expenses	3.3	3.3	5.3
(12)	Total	20.5	10.7	19.4
(13)	Other unidentified costs and charges	–9.5	4.6	4.8
Memo item				
Cost of non-preferential credits* (per cent)		47.8	60.1	68.4

NOTE   (1) Average based on the composition of total deposits at the end of the year and annual average interest rates.

(2) Average based on the composition of total credits at the end of the year and annual average interest rates on credits. No allowance has been made for the IRRF contributions and subsidies, assuming, in effect, that in aggregate, these offset each other.

(3) Row (2) + row (5).

(4) Row (3) – row (1).

(5) Total fees and commissions given in the Annual Profit-and-Loss statements by BAT (1980–86). For 1986, this item is separately identifiable. For 1984, total fees and commissions are allocated between credits and banking services on the basis of the ratios observed in 1986. For 1982, the figure calculated in this way did not cover the transaction tax; thus, fees and commissions are calculated simply by taking 15 per cent of the average interest rate on credits.

(6) The cost of actual (rather than required) reserves in terms of average interest on deposits minus interest income from reserves (for 1982 and 1984) per unit of credits.

(7) In 1986, 80 per cent of liquidity requirements was required to be held in government securities and unused rediscount limits and 20 per cent in cash and free deposits at the CB. The former is assumed to be held entirely in government securities. These proportions are assumed to hold for 1982 and 1984 as well. Average interest rates on bills and bonds are used to obtain the rate of return on liquidity requirements.

(8) The excess of average costs of CB advances over average deposit rates. The former is calculated on the basis of the distribution of CB credits to banks and the rates applicable to them.

(9) Calculated on the basis of the maximum rate on deposits (when positive), and the average interest rate on credits (when negative).

(10) Personnel expenses per unit of credits.

(11) Includes depreciations, provisions for credits and other expenses.
(12) Total of rows (5) to (11).
(13) Residual: row (4) – row (12).
* Average rate on short and medium-term loans.
SOURCE   Estimated on the basis of CB and BAT statistics.

greater than the average interest on total deposits (but not on time deposits), thereby adding to the spread when credits exceeded disposable deposits, as was the case in 1982, and to a lesser extent in 1986. As for the financial intermediation cost, there was a notable improvement in personnel expenses per unit of credits. However, other expenses showed a sharp rise in 1986. An important part of this increase was due to provisions for non-performing credits which the banks were required to keep and report from the beginning of 1986.

The residual item is the difference between the spread and identified costs (other than cost of deposits) and includes, *inter alia*, profits on intermediation between depositors and creditors. In 1982 this item was negative; that is, the average interest rate plus charges on credits did not cover costs. The residual in that year was about 20 per cent of average cost of credits to *banks* (that is, row 1 plus row 14 in Table 5.10). Thus, blocking of loan proceeds at that rate would have just been sufficient to cover banks' credit costs, raising the effective spread to 20.5 percentage points. In the same year banks reported profits amounting to 2.5 per cent of total credits. However, this was entirely due to profits on foreign exchange operations. In 1984 and 1986 the residual item was positive, suggesting an improvement in the profitability of the sector. Indeed, in both years banks reported profits from non-foreign exchange operations, amounting to about 2 and 3 per cent of credits, respectively. In addition, since the practice of blocking part of loans proceeds continued, the effective mark-up on credits can be estimated to have been greater. It should, however, be added that recorded profits are poor indicators for realized profits, particularly for 1982 and 1984, prior to new legislation, when banks often treated accrued but uncollected interest as part of their income. The behavior of the spread has also been influenced by the ability of banks to pass the cost of non-performing credits onto other borrowers. There are no reliable estimates of the share of such credits in the banking system. In 1983, the top ten commercial banks reported bad debt amounting to 8 per cent of their total credits.[16] In 1986 overdue credits reported according to the new accounting system were 6 per cent of total commercial credits although a more plausible estimate would be much higher (as frequently pointed out by many bankers and businessmen). In any case, they were large enough to inflate the credit cost of other borrowers by at least 5 percentage points. Indeed banks have been able to do this since 1984 when they were authorized to set the non-preferential rates freely (Artun, 1985, pp. 64–7).

Non-performing credits have indeed been a major problem in the Turkish banking system in the 1980s. When banks pass the cost of such credits on to sound borrowers, they can also push them to the brink of collapse, thereby increasing the share of non-performing loans in their portfolios. Such banks are often left with marginal borrowers as high credit costs drive away sound customers to larger and, often, foreign banks. Moreover, liquidity problems created by such loans introduce a Ponzi element into banks' activities, leading eventually to insolvency, as has been witnessed several times during and after 1982. While the new regulatory framework provides some safeguard in this respect, the issue goes beyond the scope of bank supervision; it concerns, rather, the ability of the corporate sector to afford such levels of real lending rates.

There can be little doubt that there have been substantial variations in effective prices paid for credits by individual borrowers, depending on their relation with banks and the type of credits used. In the 1980s the degree of interlocking ownership between banks and industrial and commerical groups has strengthened. Before the 1980s there were 11 banks belonging to such groups. This number rose to 18 in the early 1980s with such banks accounting for about 36 per cent of total credits of private commercial banks. Moreover, no less than 7 major broker companies were established by industrial-commercial holdings. Although the 1982–83 financial crisis wiped out some (five) of these banks and brokers, their number and shares in the financial system have remained high (Artun, 1985, pp. 48–9). The increased interlocking ownership has resulted in a high degree of exposure for banks, and reduced the access to credits for other borrowers, pushing them to curb markets.

Two main types of credits in the corporate sector have enjoyed preferential treatment in the 1980s; namely, export and specified investment credits. There are no statistics on the size of commercial bank investment credits and their allocation among various activities. Although banks are required to place a certain proportion of their deposits in medium and long-term credits (which they often fulfil by extending them to their own economic groups), these are not identical with investment credits to the corporate sector since they include credits to other sectors as well as working capital loans. In accordance with the outward-oriented strategy, export credits rose rapidly, except in 1985 when interest subsidies were eliminated (Table 5.11); indeed, credit subsidies (together with tax rebates) have been the major stimulus behind export expansion the 1980s (Ersel and Temel, 1984). On the contrary, credits extended to manufacturing declined by almost 12 per cent in real terms between 1979 and 1986, and this sector's share in total credits dropped drastically.

The downward trend in the credits used by manufacturing is consistent with the behaviour of investment in this sector. During the 1970s about a third of private and a quarter of public investment was in manufacturing.

TABLE 5.11   *Sectoral Allocation of Credits by the Banking System,* * *1979–86*
(percentage share)

	1979	1980	1981	1982	1983	1984	1985	1986
Agriculture	13.3	15.0	16.8	14.0	16.8	14.6	15.4	16.0
Manufacturing	46.2	44.4	41.9	35.6	29.5	34.7	34.2	28.3
Construction	2.7	1.9	2.7	3.0	4.3	6.9	9.6	11.9
Domestic trade	19.2	17.9	19.1	19.6	21.4	16.4	16.7	20.2
Export	2.6	4.4	5.9	15.9	17.9	15.4	11.6	15.1
Others	16.0	16.4	13.6	11.9	10.1	12.0	12.5	8.5
Memo items								
Total credits/GNP	28.3	22.0	24.2	27.3	26.4	20.3	22.3	28.5
Share of manufacturing in total investment	25.0	27.0	26.2	23.6	23.0	22.3	20.9	18.2

* Includes deposit money banks, investment and development banks and direct credits of CB to public enterprises.
SOURCE   Calculated from Central Bank (1980–86).

In the 1980s, the public sector kept out of manufacturing and shifted its investment to infrastructure; the share of manufacturing in public sector investment fell to under 9 per cent in 1986. This has not been compensated by the private sector; the real volume of private manufacturing investment in 1985–86 was below the levels attained during the late 1970s. This disparity between manufacturing and export credits, and between manufacturing investment and export volumes lends support to the view that export expansion has taken place, in large part, by drawing on existing capacity, rather than by new capacity creation through a greater allocation of investment to export industries.[17]

Differences among firms in their activities and in the term and degree of access to bank credits have thus had a major influence on their relative performance. Nevertheless, this is difficult to quantify because of lack of data at the sectoral level. We shall, therefore, rely on some aggregate data and samples in order to examine the recent trends. Tables 5.12 and 5.13 give some indicators of cost and financial structures of two samples of firms: namely, TSKB (Industrial Development Bank of Turkey) borrowers and corporations subject to CMB supervision.[18] These samples deviate from the 'average' in certain respects. The TSKB sample includes industrial firms with a higher share of investment finance than the 'average' firm in the corporate sector. Moreover, these firms have a higher degree of export orientation: while the average ratio of exports to total sales during 1983–86 was around 10.4 per cent for the top 500 firms in Turkey, it was almost twice as high among the TSKB borrowers. The CMB sample, on the other hand, includes relatively large firms with security issues to the public.[19]

TABLE 5.12   *Corporate Sector: Distribution of Sale Revenues, 1978–86 (per cent)*

	1978	1979	1980	1981	1982	1983	1984	1985	1986
*TSKB sample**									
Raw materials	36.9	34.5	43.4	48.3	48.6	50.2	52.9	53.3	47.4
Wages and salaries	15.1	15.0	14.0	13.8	12.3	10.8	9.2	9.4	8.9
Interest	7.7	7.9	10.0	12.2	11.8	9.6	8.9	10.4	11.8
Depreciation	4.9	7.6	4.4	4.1	3.0	5.2	6.0	5.7	6.5
Net profits before taxes	12.2	11.4	5.8	3.1	5.3	7.2	8.0	6.6	8.1
Taxes	2.9	3.1	3.6	2.6	2.6	2.7	2.9	2.8	2.8
Dividends	4.1	2.8	1.6	1.8	3.5	2.3	2.7	2.7	3.1
Reserves	5.2	5.5	0.6	–1.3	–0.8	2.2	2.4	1.1	2.2
Retained gross profits after taxes[†]	10.1	13.1	5.0	2.8	2.2	7.4	8.4	6.8	8.7
Memo items									
Exports/total sales	6.0	6.3	6.8	11.6	17.4	21.0	21.4	19.6	18.6
Interest/operating surplus	30.0	35.0	52.9	83.7	72.5	57.2	53.2	64.7	60.1
CMB sample[‡]									
Interest	–	7.5	9.0	10.3	11.1	8.9	9.4	–	–
Net profits before taxes	–	9.5	8.1	6.1	4.2	5.8	5.7	–	–
Memo item Interest/operating surplus + net other income	–	44.2	52.7	62.9	72.5	60.4	62.1	–	–

* Includes 127 industrial companies for 1978–81, and about 330 industrial companies for 1982–86.
[†] Depreciation allowances plus reserves.
[‡] Includes 91 corporations; see Ersel and Sak (1987).
SOURCE   TSKB and CMB.

There are a number of clear trends in the 1980s that illustrate the consequences of the policies pursued for the cost structure and income distribution at the corporate level. First, the share of raw material costs increased considerably due, mainly, to two factors. On the one hand, since SEEs are major suppliers of intermediate inputs, elimination of subsidies and substantial increases in their prices raised the real cost of such inputs to private industry. On the other hand, the depreciation of TL in real terms increased the cost of imported intermediate inputs.

Second, there is even a faster increase in the proportion of sale revenues absorbed by interest payment. Since an important part of TSKB loans to these firms are in foreign currency (mainly to finance import components of investment), this also reflects the impact of increased cost of servicing foreign debt due to real devaluations and higher world interest rates. However, the very same factors, in particular the increased foreign exchange risk, have deterred firms from borrowing in foreign currency.

TABLE 5.13   *Financial Indicators for Non-Financial Corporations, 1978–86*
(per cent)

	1978	1979	1980	1981	1982	1983	1984	1985	1986
Debt-equity ratio									
Flow-of-funds	110	140	190	290	300	260	260	–	–
TSKB	320	380	510	590	240	200	190	210	210
CMB	–	230	300	280	150	170	150	–	–
Short-term/total bank debt*	41.0	39.4	39.3	48.7	50.4	49.1	53.0	62.7	62.8
Short-term/total liabilities†	61.8	65.9	67.0	67.4	69.4	70.4	74.1	77.5	75.3
Bonds/total liabilities									
Flow-of-funds	2.1	2.2	3.6	3.3	2.7	2.3	1.6	–	–
TSKB	3.2	3.8	5.1	5.9	2.4	2.0	1.9	2.1	2.1
CMB	–	2.9	5.2	5.1	5.8	3.5	2.4	–	–

* Excludes liabilities on current year's installment.
† Includes tax liabilities, deferred customs duties, commercial debt, shareholder loans and other payables as well as bank debt and bond liabilities.
SOURCE   TSKB and CMB. Flow-of-funds: Akyüz (1984b), updated for 1982–4 by TSKB.

Partly because of this reason, and partly because of increased needs for operating capital, the share of TSKB loans in total credits used by these firms declined from about a quarter in the late 1970s to under a fifth in the 1980s. Thus, the dominant influence on interest payments has been the increased cost of domestic finance.

The share of interest payments in total costs has risen from third to second place with the share of wages falling to third.[20] In fact the drastic decline in wage costs has been a major factor in alleviating the burden of interest payments on profits. It is reported that a World Bank study also found evidence to this effect:

the cost of credits to nonagricultural private enterprises has risen in real terms that cannot be sustained indefinitely. Few firms in Turkey can earn enough on operations to pay such high real rates on any substantial fraction of their debt. Until now the increase in real interest rates has to a large extent been offset by the decline in real wages, but this is a solution that cannot be maintained in the long run . . . Many firms will be forced to borrow from banks in order to finance part of their interest payments. For such firms, there is the danger that the debt-equity ratio will rise progressively and . . . if the lending rates to firms are not substantially reduced, the present problem — which for many firms is already one of illiquidity — may become one of insolvency.
(World Bank, 1983, p. 18; see Somel, 1986, p. 120)

This assessment refers to the early 1980s when the recession that had started in 1979 deepened as a result of liquidity and demand squeeze, and sharp adjustments in key prices. During that period, for the sample of firms in Table 5.12, real sale revenues declined while the effective cost of borrowing rose considerably. The offset from reduced wage costs was important, but did not prevent a sharp decline in profits not only in real but also in nominal terms. The proportion of operating surplus absorbed by interest payments rose to more than 80 per cent, and net corporate savings were negative. The corporate sector became unable to meet its cash outlays on operating expenses, debt service, and tax and dividend payments with sale revenues. The profit squeeze also turned into a liquidity squeeze due to a decline in the availabity of new credits.

After 1982 corporate profits and liquidity position improved due to a number of factors. Monetary policy had to be relaxed after the financial crisis, and credit supply to the private sector rose rapidly. In the manufacturing industry, new bank credits increased by five times in nominal and 2.5 times in real terms between 1982 and 1984 (ICI, 1984–86). Real credit costs increased again after 1983, but growth also picked up, raising capacity utilization and real sale revenues in industry, particularly from exports (Somel, 1986, p. 107). More importantly, wage costs per unit of sales continued to fall at a faster rate. For the sample of companies in Table 5.12, the rise in the share of corporate profits during 1983–86 was entirely due to the decline in wage costs.[21] Thus, what appears to be a rise in corporate savings since 1982 is no more than a reduction in wage costs and the consequent decline in the consumption of wage earners.

Although the redistribution from wages to profits has, in large part, accommodated the rise in the cost of finance, the corporate sector remains in a precarious situation. The cost and availability of finance continue to exert a strong influence on capacity utilization in industry, particularly among smaller firms: the percentage of firms indicating 'financial problems' as the most important reason for capacity under-utilization remained almost unchanged between 1982 and 1985 at about 25 per cent.[22]

More importantly, the structure of corporate finance has deteriorated in many respects (Table 5.13). As various estimates indicate, the debt-equity ratio rose significantly. While it is true that data based on historical values of physical assets do not reflect their 'true' values under conditions of rapid inflation, even the inflation-adjusted figures indicate a rise in the debt-equity ratio from about 1.2 in 1978–79 to 1.7 in 1981 for the TSKB sample. Such an adjustment is difficult to make for the period after 1982 since 'the adoption of new revaluation rules for 1982 resulted in a big jump in the net fixed assets and net worth accounts' (Ersel and Sak, 1987, pp. 114–15). It is, however, notable that even after the revaluation of fixed assets, the debt-equity ratio of TSKB borrowers remained very high during 1982–86, and exceeded the inflation-adjusted debt-equity ratios of similar companies in the late 1970s. Again, for a large sample of industrial firms surveyed by the ICI, the *addition* to total equity, including revaluation funds, fell relative to addition to debt, with the consequence that the incremental debt-equity ratio rose from 0.80 in 1982 to 1.18 in 1984 (ICI, 1984–86).

Even in the TSKB sample of firms, the share of short-term in total bank debt, and the share of short-term debt in total liabilities rose substantially. This is also true for the firms surveyed by the ICI where the share of *new* short-term debt rose from 72 per cent in 1982 to 82 per cent in 1984. Long-term direct securities lost in relative importance even for the CMB sample of large, bond- and equity-issuing companies. As the authors of the CMB study conclude, 'the dependence of corporations on banks is enhanced in the post-stabilization era' (Ersel and Sak, 1987, p. 109).

IV INTEREST RATES, INCOME DISTRIBUTION AND SAVINGS

The proposition that positive real interest rates are conducive to growth in developing countries rests on two assumptions.[23] First, they help raise the proportion of income saved. Second, they raise the demand for domestic interest-bearing assets, thereby increasing the availability of financial resources for investment. It is stressed that this latter effect alone improves the use of resources, since it implies a portfolio shift from such unproductive inflation hedges as commodity stocks, land, real estate, gold and foreign exchange assets. In countries with excessive financial repression, a substantial increase in interest rates (that is, a shock treatment) results in a sharp rise in financial resources available for investment, and if such incentives are maintained, there will be a continuing increase in the flow of savings as a proportion of income as the latter grows. It is also maintained that such a policy also protects small savers and improves income distribution: since small savers have limited opportunities to hold their savings in assets other than deposits, negative real interest rates tend to erode their wealth and entail a redistribution in favor of large corporations with easy access to bank credits. As noted above, a substantial degree of financial deepening has indeed taken place in Turkey since the beginning of the decade. What is less clear, however, is the origin of the portfolio shift into deposits and, to a lesser extent, government securities. There is no evidence that commodity holdings, as alternatives to financial assets, are important in the household sector. While they are important in the corporate sector as well as self-employed producers in agriculture, the evidence does not suggest any systematic relation between stock changes and the rate of interest on financial assets. Private sector stocks, as a proportion of GNP, increased by just over 0.5 per cent per annum during 1978–79 when interest rates were negative in real terms, but by more than 1 per cent during the early 1980s, and even faster after 1982.[24]

A decline in the use of household savings for the internal financing of fixed investment, particularly in housing, would also increase financial intermediation and assets. Private spending on housing investment amounted to more than 4 per cent of GNP during 1978–79. It declined sharply after 1980 and, on average, stood during 1981–85 at about half of its 1978–79 level.[25] Similarly, the share of fixed capital assets (which consist mainly of housing and, to a lesser extent, investment in machinery and tools by self-employed producers in agriculture) in the total assets of the household sector fell from about a third during the late 1970s to under a quarter during the 1980s.[26] Clearly, this experience does not conform to the McKinnon-Shaw paradigm of a portfolio shift from unproductive uses to financial resources for fixed capital formation. At best, it can represent a substitution of one type of investment for another.

A third area of unproductive use of resources is gold holding which is very widespread in Turkey. Data are not available to assess the extent of substitution that may have taken place since 1980. However, it seems that a sizeable shift from gold holdings to interest-bearing financial assets has not taken place; hence, the government is now planning to issue gold certificates in order to encourage the mobilization of gold holdings. Again, the privatization of SEEs is expected 'to channel at least a certain proportion of this capital' (OECD, 1987, p. 47).

Real interest rates are relevant in portfolio decisions not so much because commodities are alternatives to financial assets as because foreign *currency* assets are often hedges against inflation. This is true even when the official exchange rate is overvalued so long as there is an easily accessible curb-market. The sharp rise in real deposit rates in the early 1980s could not have resulted in a sizeable shift from foreign currency holdings to TL deposits in view of sharp depreciations of TL in real terms and continued yield differentials in favor of foreign currency holdings. On the contrary, the liberalization of the foreign exchange regime in 1984 certainly encouraged a shift from foreign currency holdings into forex deposits, which helped to raise aggregate financial savings at the disposal of commercial banks. However, as noted above, the experience does not simply point to a once-and-for-all shift into forex deposits from individual foreign currency holdings, but rather an ongoing currency substitution, with consequences for the stability of the domestic financial system. Indeed, this has also been causing concern to the Central Bank:

> the liberalization of the foreign exchange regime since 1984 . . . has restricted the effectiveness of interest and exchange rate policies, by rendering the control of the money supply difficult, under conditions of rapid depreciation of the Turkish lira . . . Under such circumstances, in order to prevent currency substitution from the Turkish lira to foreign

currencies, it is necessary to maintain a delicate balance between the real interest rate and the rate of real depreciation of the Turkish lira. Especially in 1987 difficulties were encountered in maintaining this balance

(Central Bank, 1986, p. 35).

Finally, increased financial asset holdings in the banking system may simply reflect the substitution of one type of financial intermediation for another. This would be the case when portfolio shift comes from informal markets which provide more financial intermediation than the banking system due to absence of reserve and liquidity requirements. It has been shown that when bank deposits are close substitutes to 'productive' assets such as loans extended in the curb-market, increases in deposit rates will be stagflationary and may give rise to 'financial shallowing' if the rise in deposit rates do not increase the savings rate sufficiently (van Wijnbergen, 1983). Increases in deposit rates will transfer financial resources to the banking system, pushing the curb rates up. It can be added that since borrowers in the curb-market often lack access to bank credits, shift of funds to the banking sector may result in increased availability of finance to large corporations at the expense of small producers, traders and peasants. Thus, the shift entails not only a redistribution of financial resources between formal and informal markets, but also the use made of them.

The rise and fall of broker markets during 1980–82 contained some elements of portfolio shifts between formal and informal markets. Initially, broker markets developed rapidly at the expense of major banks, but when the latter responded by raising deposit rates substantially, curb rates were pushed up, thereby contributing to the eventual collapse of this market. Between 1980 and 1982 the volume of CDs, as a proxy for the size of informal markets, rose by almost six times in real terms whereas time deposits by about 2.5 times. The sharp rise in CDs was partly because they had been introduced only in 1980. However, in 1983, after the collapse of the broker market, the outstanding stock of CDs fell in nominal terms while time deposits continued to rise.[27] During 1984–86 deposits continued to grow in real terms whereas the outstanding real stock of CDs was lower at the end of 1986 than at the end of 1982.

There is yet another and perhaps more important kind of transfer that tends to raise financial intermediation. When debt is about a third of GNP, a sharp rise in interest rates will transfer a substantial proportion of current incomes of debtors (that is, corporate and public sectors) to rentiers.[28] This will reduce public sector savings by a corresponding amount, given the current primary budget balance. It will also reduce current profits and savings in the corporate sector, which are largely used for the internal financing of capital accumulation rather than financial investment (Akyüz, 1984b, chapter 5). Thus, a substantial increase in interest rates will necessitate, as a counterpart to income transfers, a greater volume of financial transfers from rentiers to debtors in order for the latter to be able to undertake a given volume of fixed capital formation. In other words, they will need to borrow back the income captured by rentiers through higher interest payments. This will certainly result in increased volume of financial assets and transactions per unit of capital investment and production, as well as increased public and corporate debt.

This also means that financial deepening can take place in the context of a decline in domestic savings. As shown elsewhere (Akyüz, 1989), changes in interest rates affect aggregate savings through income distribution because different sectors have different propensities to save. When rentiers' propensity to save from real disposable income (that is, the rate of consumption that can be undertaken while leaving real wealth intact (see, for example, Sargent, 1979, pp. 17–19) is smaller than the propensity to save by profit earners, a rise in interest rates will, *ceteris paribus*, reduce private savings unless higher interest rates induce a sufficient rise in the propensity to save. Similarly, since it also reduces public sector savings, the private propensity to save will need to rise even further in order to maintain aggregate savings.

Evidence suggests that in recent years in Turkey the propensity to save of rentiers from real-interest income has been very low, if at all positive. The interest-bearing net assets of the household sector in 1984 was around 15 per cent of GNP; applying the average interest rates on assets and liabilities, this would give a net interest income of about 9 per cent of GNP.[29] To protect the real value of net interest-bearing assets, a savings rate of about 7.5 per cent of GNP was needed. In that year the entire private sector savings (as reported by the SPO) were about 9.5 per cent of GNP (Table 5.14). On the basis of the flow-of-funds data and the post-1982 recovery of corporate profits, at least 2 percentage points of this can be estimated to have belonged to the corporate sector. Thus, even if we assumed that savings from wages, dividends and self-employment incomes were zero and, hence, the entire household savings belonged to rentiers, they would have been barely enough to leave the real value of their net interest-bearing wealth intact. This was probably less so in subsequent years, particularly 1986, when inflation dropped and private savings rose.

On the contrary, in the sample of industrial firms in Table 5.12, the proportion of *current* gross profits retained never fell below 40 per cent since 1978. This suggests that, even in the absence of savings from dividends, the savings rate from *disposable* profits (that is, current gross profits plus the inflation gain on net corporate debt) is substantially greater than the rate of savings from real-interest income. Thus, a redistribution of income from corporate sector to rentiers through higher interest rates would lead to a decline in private savings unless corporate profits are protected by cuts in real wages and/or the propensity to save of the private sector, and, in particular, rentiers, is raised sufficiently by higher interest rates.

To the extent that the nominal (as well as the real) part of interest payments is treated as disposable income, and used partly for consumption, portfolio shifts by individuals from real to financial assets will imply erosion of their real wealth and decline of real savings. This was particularly true for small savers during the earlier part of the period when drastically raised interest rates encouraged liquidation of real assets (particularly real estate), as well as diversion of lump-sum receipts by retirees from their traditional use (that is, purchase of a house) to interest-bearing assets, in order to check the decline in the level of consumption in view of reduced real incomes from other sources. Thus, monthly interest payments by brokers proved very attractive for such savers despite the substantial risk involved. This also led the authorities to shorten the maturity of time deposits and introduce monthly (call) deposits as well as monthly interest payments on deposits of longer maturities (Akyüz, 1984, p. 41). Although the exact magnitude is difficult to quantify, it is well known that substantial values were lost because of a downward pressure on house prices in secondary markets, the use of nominal interest payments for consumption and the eventual collapse of brokers.

This is also reflected by the erosion of the share of small deposits in bank accounts. In 1980, household time deposits up to TL 25 000 accounted for 12.5 per cent of the total. The share of the same class of deposits (in real terms) fell to about 7 per cent in 1985.[30] Indeed, the degree of concentration of time deposits in a small number of accounts is very large, as indicated by the Lorenz curve (see Figure 5.1): in 1985, about 11 per cent of deposit holders owned 60 per cent of the total time deposits, and the Gini coefficient was close to 0.7. The degree of concentration is likely to be much greater than indicated by these figures; since deposits exceeding a certain amount are not fully protected by the insurance scheme, large deposit holders often place their deposits in several accounts in different banks. Since other types of financial asset holding such as public and private securities are expected to have an even greater degree of concentration, one can conclude that financial wealth is concentrated in a very small section of the population. On the other hand, since there is no progressive taxation of income from financial wealth, this inequality in asset distribution will be mirrored by the distribution of financial income. Furthermore, since the withholding tax rate is much lower than the average rate on wages and salaries, the size distribution of national income is also distorted.

There can be little doubt that the evolution of sectoral and aggregate savings in Turkey in the 1980s has been strongly influenced by changes in income and wealth distribution brought about by financial and other policies. It is, however, very difficult to assess the savings performance of

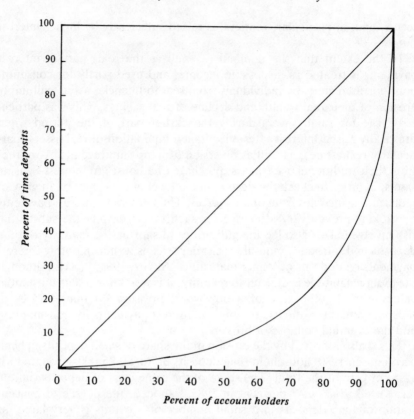

FIGURE 5.1   *The Lorenz Curve of the Distribution of Household Time Deposits:*
1985

the economy on the basis of official (SPO) data. As discussed in detail
elsewhere, there are serious shortcomings of these estimates, and they are
constantly revised by large amounts even after three to five years from
their original publication.[31] Table 5.14 contains the most recent estimates
available for 1979–86. It also contains estimates based on the flow-of-funds
data for the earlier part of the period. Although these figures may also
suffer from estimation errors, they provide another basis for the assessment of movements, if not the levels, of sectoral savings.[32]

Notwithstanding these shortcomings of the data, a number of trends can
be identified. Both sets of data show that private savings as a proportion of
GNP (and of private disposable income) fell drastically in the early 1980s
while public savings rose considerably. After 1984, according to the SPO
data, public savings kept up, before falling sharply in 1987 for the reasons
already discussed. Although the private savings rate started to rise, in 1986
it was still below the levels attained in the late 1970s. It is estimated to have

TABLE 5.14   *Savings Ratios (as a percentage of GNP)*

	1978	1979	1980	1981	1982	1983	1984	1985	1986
Flow-of-funds data									
Aggregate	23.9	20.0	20.9	20.0	18.5	–	–	–	–
Public sector*	5.4	2.7	8.4	9.0	6.6	–	–	–	–
Private sector	18.5	17.3	12.5	11.0	11.9	–	–	–	–
Household†	13.5	14.9	12.2	11.3	10.4	–	–	–	–
Corporations	5.0	2.4	0.3	–0.3	1.5	–	–	–	–
SPO data									
Aggregate	21.1	16.2	15.9	18.5	18.8	16.5	16.5	18.9	22.0
Public sector	5.3	2.7	5.3	8.7	8.9	8.8	7.1	9.6	10.3
Private sector	15.8	13.5	10.6	9.8	9.9	7.7	9.4	9.3	11.7
Memo items									
Private savings/ private disposable income	19.4	16.1	12.9	12.2	12.3	9.5	11.2	11.4	14.5
Savings in SOS‡	1.9	1.9	1.0	1.2	1.0	1.3	1.1	1.0	0.9

* Includes general and annex budgets, local administrations and non-financial SEEs.
† Also includes agricultural non-corporate business and non-profit organizations.
‡ Compulsory savings in social security institutions. These are included in household savings in the flow-of-funds data and public savings in the SPO data.
SOURCE   Flow-of-funds data: Akyüz (1984b); SPO data: Central Bank (1981–87) and SPO (1983).

risen further in 1987, reaching about 16 per cent of GNP.[33] This figure is equal to or less than the savings rate in 1978 according to whether one adopts the recently revised figure or the earlier estimate for that year. In any case, the private savings rate, although possibly rising since 1984, has not been greater during recent years than the late 1970s even though real interest rates, financial savings and per capita income have been substantially greater.

The 1979–80 recession was probably an important reason for the decline of private savings during that period. However, the decline continued during 1981–83 when real interest rates rose sharply and growth picked up. Evidence presented above suggests that the collapse of corporate profits due to increased cost of finance was an important factor. However, household savings also fell. The redistribution of household income in favor of interest earnings appears to have played a major role. In particular, attempts by small savers to maintain consumption by shifting into monthly interest-earning financial assets (often through the curb-market) served to depress household savings.

While the subsequent acceleration of growth had a positive impact, growth differentials are not sufficient to explain the sharp contrast in the behavior of private savings (as implied by the SPO data) before and after 1984. Nor can it be explained by real interest rates; although the latter rose further in recent years, the increase was much less than previously. Other influences, thus, played a major role. The savings rate from real-interest income (while remaining low or even negative as noted above) can be expected to have improved compared to the early 1980s. The erosion of real wealth of small savers in those years made it more difficult for them to continue to push consumption above the levels permitted by non-interest income. That experience may have also taught savers that high current interest income represents a rapid decline in real financial wealth. But, above all, corporate profits recovered sharply, in large part at the expense of wages.

The recovery of corporate savings (as a proportion of GNP) between 1980 and 1986 was certainly much greater than the entire increase in private savings. On the other hand, even if it is assumed that corporate savings in 1987 were only two-thirds of their 1978 levels, a *private* savings rate of 16 per cent in 1987 would barely represent an improvement in *household* savings from their drastically depressed levels during the 1979–80 recession when real GNP was smaller by a third.[34]

V   CONCLUSIONS

It is true that creating substantial 'rents' for the corporate and public sectors through 'financial repression' may not be an efficient and equitable way of mobilizing domestic resources. However, eliminating these 'rents' and increasing 'financial deepening' at the expense of incomes and consumption of working classes, erosion of small savings and greater concentration of financial wealth, and drastically increased short-term indebtedness of the public and corporate sectors without achieving a tangible improvement in the size and allocation of domestic savings, can barely constitute a sound and sustainable alternative.

While corporate profits seem to have recovered, the sector's balance sheet today is probably more distorted than in the early 1980s when the stabilization-cum-structural adjustment experiment started. The increased vulnerability of the sector to changes in the cost and availability of finance poses serious dangers in view of the fact that, with inflation approaching three digit figures, the economy now needs stabilization as much as in the early 1980s. This will certainly call for a substantial decline in PSBR. However, this is not an easy task in view of the fact that mounting interest payments account for much of the increased deficits. The scope for reducing interest rates, on the other hand, is greatly lessened by the liberalization of the capital account and foreign exchange policies, which may not

be easily reversed given the threat of potential capital flight. A rescheduling of public domestic debt, including interest capitalization as now
planned, could create very serious problems for the banking system which
already suffers from non-performing private loans. Monetization of budget
deficits (that is, CB financing) could help reduce the pace of public debt
accumulation, but it could also lead to excessive pressures on the currency
and interest rates unless its impact on domestic credit expansion is sterilized at the expense of the private sector. Thus, further sharp increases in
the prices of SEEs and cuts in civilian spending, in particular public
investment, combined with monetary tightening may be inevitable. The
consequences of these for growth, corporate finance and stability may also
be very serious, particularly if a wage-resistance develops due to changed
political circumstances.

The Turkish experience in the 1980s demonstrates once again the
potentially destabilizing nature of financial deregulation and capital-
account liberalization before permanently reducing inflation, ensuring
fiscal discipline, and eliminating the need for continuous real devaluations.
It also shows that superimposition of 'realistic' prices onto seriously distorted and inefficient structures can serve to aggravate distortions and
inefficiencies. Perhaps institutional and structural measures that directly
addressed such issues as the efficiency (rather than simply the profitability)
of SEEs, the tax system and financial intermediation, and encouraged the
corporate sector to broaden its equity base could have helped reduce the
adverse consequences of this experiment.

NOTES

1. The views expressed in this paper are personal and do not necessarily reflect
   those of the UNCTAD secretariat. I am grateful to Teoman Akgür, Hasan
   Ersel and Bilge Okay for their assistance in gathering the data, and Dani
   Rodrik, Ataman Aksoy, Detlef Kotte, Andrew Cornford and the participants
   of the Harvard Conference on 'The Political Economy of Turkey in the 1980s'
   for valuable comments and suggestions.
2. For such a characterization of the pre-1980 Turkish financial system see, for
   example Central Bank (1985, part IV); Kopits (1987); and Lanyi and Saracoğlu
   (1983, pp. 25–6).
3. Wolff (1987, p. 104). For a more detailed account of financial policies in the
   1980s see Central Bank (1981–7); Coşan and Ersel (1987); and Kopits (1987).
4. In this study real variables are measured in terms of wholesale prices.
5. On the issues and controversies concerning the meaning and determinants of
   financial deepening see Gupta (1984).
6. For a more detailed discussion of these issues see Akyüz (1984b, chapter 4).
7. Table 5.7 is based on flow-of-funds data and includes only the domestic
   currency assets since data do not allow identification of the distribution of such
   deposits between business and household sectors. Insurance reserves accumulated in provident and pension funds are included. A very large proportion of

these are in compulsory social security institutions, and as the social security system is relatively young, these reserves constitute an important part of household savings, even though they are considered as part of public sector savings in official statistics. Akyüz (1984b, p. 129). Equities in Table 5.7 represent paid-in capital rather than those quoted on the stock exchange (which represent less than a third of paid-in capital of incorporated business).

8. The largest jump in the share of time deposits took place in 1981 when interest rates were raised substantially. In 1983 when interest rates were lowered on time deposits but raised on sight deposits, a large shift occurred from the former to the latter. From 1984 onwards time deposits rose significantly relative to sight deposits, in line with substantially widened interest rate differentials in favor of the former.

9. For a detailed description of these institutions in Turkey see Akyüz (1984b), and Akyüz and Ersel (1984).

10. According to the estimates of International Finance Corporation, in 1985 this ratio was about 43 per cent in Brazil, 20 per cent in Malaysia, 15 per cent in India and 1.4 per cent in Pakistan; see Gill (1986), which contains a more detailed analysis of major impediments to the development of equity markets in Turkey.

11. On the fiscal aspects of the post-1980 adjustment process see Celâsun (this volume).

12. In 1979 more than a half of the public sector deficit was financed from the Central Bank; in 1986 the Central Bank accounted for only 13 per cent of new claims issued by the public sector.

13. For an analysis of the effects of exchange and interest rate policies on government debt accumulation see Rodrik (this volume).

14. These figures are reported to have been confirmed by World Bank (1983, p. 16); see Somel (1986, pp. 119–20).

15. It should be noted that these estimates may suffer from aggregation errors since the composition of credits is not available in required detail. Nevertheless, the movement of the spread broadly conforms to that of the differential between time deposit and loan rates in Table 5.1.

16. See Artun (1985, p. 65). When loan rates are pushed up to take care of non-performing credits, the residual item in Table 5.10 will be greater than reported profits (even in the absence of other unidentified costs), as was the case in 1984 and 1986.

17. See, for example, Boratav (1986). One reason is that only final exporters were eligible for such credits; producers did not have export incentives for the part of their value added exported as, for example, in Korea (See World Bank, 1983, p. 41).

18. It should be noted that the TSKB sample has a discontinuity in 1981–82 because the number of firms covered for 1982–86 is greater than 1979–81.

19. However, it has been argued that the 'CMB sample does not represent corporations with *extremely* biased financial structures' compared with a wider range of industrial firms surveyed; Ersel and Sak (1987), p. 93 (our italics). The survey mentioned is ICI (1984–86).

20. This proposition holds even when the data in table 12 are evaluated separately for 1978–81 and 1982–86 due to the discontinuity in the sample. During the former period interest payments rose much faster than raw material costs; between 1982 and 1986, on the other hand, interest payments absorbed the same proportion of sale revenues whereas raw material costs somewhat fell.

21. Although the increased share of exports in the total sales of these firms also

helped, real prices of inputs purchased from SEEs also increased at an accelerated pace, resulting in higher raw material costs per unit of sales.

22. See Somel (1986, Chapter 4). When percentages are weighted with production values of respondent firms, this ratio becomes smaller, indicating that 'financial problems' are more widespread among smaller firms.

23. For a statement of this McKinnon-Shaw proposition and its main assumptions see, for example, Lanyi and Saracoğlu (1983); van Wijnbergen (1983); and Coats and Khatkhate (1984).

24. The data are from SPO (1983) and Central Bank (1981–87).

25. The data are from SPO (1983) and Central Bank (1982–86).

26. See Akyüz (1984b, pp. 104–5) and the flow-of-funds tables, updated for 1982–84 by TSKB.

27. Indeed, since interest rates on sight deposits were raised substantially in that year (Table 5.1), comparison ought to be made between CDs and total deposits which increased much faster than time deposits alone.

28. This proposition holds even when debt is not entirely of the floating-interest variety, so long as it is short-term and debtors cannot rapidly reduce the stock of debt. In Turkey, interest rates on medium and long-term loans by development and commercial banks are subject to periodic adjustment. Long-term private bond rates are also adjusted on the basis of changes in time deposit rates.

29. These assets exclude transaction balances (currency and sight deposits) and reserves in compulsory insurance funds. Debt to the latter has also been excluded. Three-quarters of forex deposits is assumed to be held by the household sectors; this ratio is indeed much smaller than the share of household in total time deposits. In the calculation of net interest income account has been taken of the fact that household debt in Turkey carries a much lower interest rate than their interest-bearing assets.

30. The data are from BAT (1980–85). Time deposits up to TL 120 000 in 1985 were equivalent, in real terms, to the class of deposits up to TL 25 000 in 1980, allowing for inflation. BAT data on the distribution of savings deposits and accounts do not always allow intertemporal comparisons because they are arranged in frequency intervals that are not always comparable.

31. See Akyüz (1984b, chapter 7). For instance in 1984, figures for private savings rates for 1979 and 1980 were reduced by about 6 and 4 percentage points respectively compared to earlier estimates. Since the first draft of this paper was presented, the SPO has again revised its estimates for 1983–86: see Central Bank (1986, Table 1; 1987, Table 1).

32. The figures for 1978–81 are based on the earlier estimates of private investment by SPO, which, because of the methodology employed, affect private savings. It is difficult to estimate savings for 1983–84 (particularly for 1983) on the basis of flow of funds because of lack of data on the portion of total equity that represents asset revaluation.

33. It should be noted that the estimates for 1987 are highly tentative and likely to be revised in the future.

34. Anand, Chhibber and van Wijnbergen (this volume) state that 'rising real rates of interest have been a major contributing factor to the increase in private savings' (p. 168). While basing their argument on an econometric estimate of private consumption, they particularly emphasize the increases in real interest and savings rates between 1980 and 1987, and since 1985. Clearly, econometric results would crucially depend on the set of figures used for private savings, and, as noted, there are serious problems in this respect. The savings figures

these authors mention for the 1980s are substantially different from the recent SPO estimates although the direction of change is broadly consistent. More importantly, what these authors do not explain is the sharp drop in private savings between 1980 and 1985 when the increase in real interest rates was much greater than subsequently.

REFERENCES

Akyüz, Y. (1984a) 'Faiz ve Enflasyon Üzerine' (On Interest and Inflation), *Yapıt* 6, August–September, pp. 17–43.

Akyüz, Y. (1984b) *Financial Structure and Relations in the Turkish Economy* (Istanbul: Industrial Development Bank of Turkey [TSKB]).

Akyüz, Y. (1989) 'Interest Rates, Income Distribution and Savings in LDCs' (Geneva: UNCTAD) discussion paper.

Akyüz, Y. and H. Ersel (1984) *Türk Ekonomisinde Mali Yapı ve İlişkiler — İstatistik Ekler* (Financial Structure and Financial Relations in the Turkish Economy — Statistical Appendix) (Istanbul: Industrial Development Bank of Turkey [TSKB]).

Artun, T. (1985) 'Türk Mali Sistemi 1980–1984. Değişim ve Maliyeti' (The Turkish Financial System 1980–84: Change and Costs of Change), in B. Kuruç (ed.), *Bırakınız Yapsınlar, Bırakınız Geçsinler* (Laissez Faire, Laissez Passer), pp. 36–71 (Ankara: Bilgi Yayınevi).

BAT (1980–86) *Banks in Turkey*, Annual Reports (Ankara: Banks Association of Turkey).

Boratav, K. (1986) *Stabilization and Adjustment Policies and Programmes. Turkey* (Helsinki: WIDER).

Central Bank of Turkey (CB) (1981–87) *Annual Reports* (Ankara).

Coats, W. L. and D. R. Khatkhate (1984) 'Monetary Policy in Less Developed Countries: Main Issues', *The Developing Economies* 22, pp. 329–48.

Coşan, F. M. and H. Ersel (1987) 'Turkish Financial System: Its Evolution and Performance, 1980–1986', *Inflation and Capital Markets*, pp. 27–65 (Ankara: Capital Market Board).

Ersel, H. and A. Temel (1984) 'Türkiye'nin 1980 Sonrası Dışsatım Başarımının Değerlendirilmesi Üzerine Bir Deneme' (An Evaluation of the post–1980 Export Performance of the Turkish Economy), *Toplum ve Bilim* 27, Autumn, pp. 107–33.

Ersel, H. and G. Sak (1987) 'The Financial Structure of the Corporations Subject to CMB Supervision, 1979–1984 — Some Preliminary Findings', in *Inflation and Capital Markets: Proceedings of the OECD–CMB Conference*, pp. 89–139, Capital Market Board Publications 7 (Ankara: CMB).

Gill, D. (1986) 'Prospects for the Turkish Equity Market', Paper presented to a conference on Turkey and Europe: An Economic and Political Perspective, Sponsored by International Herald Tribune, Atlantic Institute for International Affairs and Foreign Policy Institute, 6–7 October, Istanbul.

Gupta, K. L. (1984) *Finance and Growth in Developing Countries* (London: Croom Helm).

ICI (1984–86) *Flow of Funds in Turkey and Changes in Finance Patterns* (Istanbul: Istanbul Chamber of Industry).

Kopits, G. (1987) 'Structural Reform, Stabilization and Growth in Turkey' (Washington DC: IMF) International Monetary Fund Occasional Paper 52.

Lanyi, A. and R. Saracoğlu (1983) 'Interest Rate Policies in Developing Countries' (Washington DC: IMF) International Monetary Fund Occasional Paper 22.

OECD (1987) *OECD Economic Surveys: Turkey* (Paris: Organization for Economic Co-operation and Development).

Sargent, T. (1979) *Macroeconomic Theory* (New York: Academic Press).

Somel, C. (1986) 'Miktar Kısıtlamaları Altında Üretim Kararları ve Türkiye için bir Model Denemesi' (Production Decisions Under Quantitative Restrictions, a Model for Turkey), PhD dissertation, Ankara University, SBF.

SPO (1985) *V. Beş Yıllık Plan Destek Çalışmaları: I* (Fifth Five Year Plan Supplementary Studies: I) (Ankara: State Planning Organization).

Türel, O. (1985) '1980 Sonrasında Kamu Kesimi ve Finansmanı Üzerine Gözlem ve Değerlendirmeler' (Observation and Evaluations on Public Sector Financing in the Post-1980 Period), in B. Kuruç (ed.), *Bırakınız Yapsınlar, Bırakınız Geçsinler* (Laissez Faire, Laissez Passer), pp. 94–130 (Ankara: Bilgi Yayınevi).

van Wijnbergen, S. (1983) 'Interest Rate Management in LDCs', *Journal of Monetary Economics* 12, pp. 433–52.

Wolff, P. (1987) *Stabilization Policy and Sturctural Adjustment in Turkey, 1980–1985* (Berlin: German Development Institute).

World Bank (1983) *Turkey: Special Economic Report. Policies for the Financial Sector* (Washington DC).

6 The Private Sector's Response to Financial Liberalization in Turkey: 1980–82

İzak Atiyas[1]

I INTRODUCTION AND SUMMARY

In mid-1980, economic policy makers in Turkey initiated attempts to restructure and deregulate the financial sector. The main steps taken were the removal of legal restrictions on interest rates and the allowance and encouragement of trades through new types of financial institutions and instruments. An important aspect of the deregulation attempts was that they were implemented simultaneously with and, indeed, as part of, a comprehensive stabilization/liberalization program.

Among the most important objectives of financial liberalization the following were mentioned by policy makers: (i) Deregulation was expected to increase interest rates — which were hitherto negative in real terms — and therefore increase financial savings and deposits in the banking sector, as well as introduce competition into the banking system. (ii) It was hoped that an increase in interest rates would push corporations in the private sector, which were typically highly leveraged, to reduce their indebtedness and increase their equity base. Owners of firms were advised to liquidate personal wealth and transfer it to their firms as equity capital. 'Sell your villas to finance your corporations' was the call of the day. The increase in the interest rates was expected to allocate loanable funds to most profitable users. (iii) Bankruptcy was believed to be a major regulatory force in the corporate sector. Inefficient firms, especially those in previously protected import competing sectors, were expected either to adjust to the requirements of the new economic policies, for example, by gearing production towards exports, or to leave the market.

On the macroeconomic side, the most important developments in 1980–82 were export orientation and disinflation.[2] The comprehensive stabilization/liberalization program included policies aimed at trade liberalization, real depreciation of the exchange rate and reduction of domestic absorption. Gross National Product (GNP) growth rate, which was negative in 1979 and 1980 started to pick up and reached 4.1 per cent in 1981 and 4.6

132

per cent in 1982, quite below the the 1973–77 average of 6.5 per cent (OECD, 1986, Tables 1 and A). The composition of demand changed drastically: the rate of growth of domestic absorption, averaging 8.2 per cent in 1973–77, was 1.6 and 2.8 per cent in 1981 and 1982. While the contribution of foreign trade balance to GNP growth was negative between 1973–77, it was positive in the 1980s — with the exception of 1983. Exports grew by 47 and 25 per cent in constant Turkish lira prices in 1981 and 1982 respectively. Inflation, on the other hand, was reduced from around 107 per cent in 1980 to 25 per cent in 1982. In short, 1980–82 were years of drastic realignments in major macroeconomic variables, which were bound to affect corporate performance.

The deregulation episode in the financial markets lasted two and a half years. The objective of increasing deposits and financial savings in general was met with considerable success. However, a financial crisis broke out in 1982 and several brokerage houses went bankrupt. In 1983, the Central Bank took over the administration of some 'problem' banks, put all the others under close supervision, and started to reregulate deposit interest rates. Overall, it can safely be said that the response of the financial sector to deregulation was worse than expected.

The objective of this paper is to present an overview of the events that culminated in the crisis. This will be done in two steps. First (Section II) the events in the banking sector will be summarized. In the banking sector, shocks to the corporate sector made portions of banks' assets non-performing. This was true especially for some smaller banks. Rather than forcing liquidation of their clients, these banks engaged in a fierce competition to collect funds, to raise resources both to meet their liabilities and to refinance non-performing loans. Interest rates soared. Some banks were thus able to survive even though they were insolvent, until the government finally intervened.

To get some clues about why bank loans might have become non-performing, the next section looks at the private corporate sector. Analysis of a panel data set of corporations reveals that in this period firms were subject not only to an interest rate shock, but also to a gross earnings shock (decline of sales income relative to costs). Also, while debt-to-assets ratios of profitable firms did not change much during 1980–82, those of firms under distress actually increased despite higher borrowing costs.

These observations suggest that financial liberalization may not generate desired responses if it is carried out when there are major changes in the macroeconomic environment that adversely affect the profitability of and cause financial distress in the corporate, and consequently, banking sectors. Furthermore, the market mechanism did not seem to be well equipped to carry out its most essential regulatory function in an efficient manner, that is, inducing the exit of insolvent economic units and thereby decreasing inefficiency in the allocation of financial resources.

II DEVELOPMENTS IN THE BANKING SECTOR

There were two principal sets of players in the financial crisis of 1982. On the one hand were the banks. The Turkish financial system has been dominated by commercial banks. At the end of 1979, the commercial banking system was composed of 12 state owned banks, 24 private banks and 4 foreign banks. The market was highly concentrated. The share of the largest 4 banks (one state owned and three private) in total assets was 58 per cent and 56 per cent in total deposits. Each of the 11 smallest private banks held less than 1 per cent of the total assets of the banking system.

Most private banks were owned or controlled by industrial conglomerates.[3] This pattern of ownership was the result of two trends: some of the private banks were actually established by industrial groups controlled by individual families, while smaller and provincial banks were established by local businessmen and later acquired by industrial groups and transformed into nation-wide banks. New entry into the banking system was subject to the permission of the government. Prior to deregulation, the governments had been very conservative in granting the necessary permission. As a result, the number of banks had been stable between 38–42 in the 1970s.

Another set of players that proved especially important in the events after the deregulation were the brokerage houses. Most brokerage houses were established around the year 1979, when industrial corporations started to issue bonds.[4] Some 'bankless' industrial groups, unable to enter the banking business, formed their own brokerage houses.[5] The rapid development of the — admittedly small — bond market also encouraged the establishment of independent brokerage houses.[6]

Deregulation in the banking sector was started by two important steps undertaken in July, 1980, whereby firstly, legal restrictions on deposit and loan interest rates were removed; and, secondly, banks were allowed to issue negotiable certificates of deposit (CDs).[7] Following Artun (1983), the events that followed these deregulatory steps and culminated in the financial crisis of 1982 can be summarized in two stages:[8]

Stage 1, the Initial Months

Soon after the reform program was announced, larger banks encouraged members of the banking system to form a cartel and set deposit interest rates collusively, at a rate higher than the pre-liberalization level (30 per cent on annual deposits). The monetary authorities did not seem to object to collusion, although they did think that the interest rate was low, given that the inflation rate exceeded 100 per cent in 1980. In any case, the so-called gentlemen's agreement that was drawn between the banks was not adhered to; some (mostly smaller) banks offered higher deposit rates. Initially, it seems that the breakdown of the cartel agreement was due to an attempt by smaller banks to exploit their competitive edges, which arose from their lower intermediation costs. By the end of 1980, these banks offered deposit interest rates that were 2–5 percentage points higher than the 30 per cent envisaged in the agreement. In February 1981, a new gentlemen's agreement was signed, whereby the rate of interest on one year deposits was raised to 50 per cent. Soon, this agreement was also broken by some banks.

Besides the deposit interest rate, CDs also proved to be an important tool of competition and was widely used. A substantial proportion of CDs were marketed through brokerage houses, both through those that were independent and those that were subsidiaries of banks or holding companies. A mechanism was developed whereby banks in effect used CDs and brokers to circumvent the gentlemen's agreements and tried to increase their share in the market for deposits: CDs were issued to brokerage houses in large volumes at a discount. The brokers would resell the CDs to the public at par, but they would increase the effective interest rate by attaching to the CDs parallel personal interest bearing promissory notes. The fact that the CDs originated in banks seems to have provided buyers of CDs a guarantee of their safety. The difference between the broker's buying and effective selling prices were generally lent to marginal businesses at high interest rates.[9]

Stage 2, Change in the Environment

By mid- to late-1981, the driving force behind inter-bank competition changed. Due to the poor earnings performance of the corporate sector, non-performing loans became a major problem. While meetings between banks continued and resulted in new gentlemen's agreements, smaller banks especially started to attract new deposits by increasing their interest rates basically to solve cash-flow problems created by non-performing loans, both to refinance the latter and also to meet their obligations to their claimants. In the ensuing price war for deposits some banks were known to offer as high as 65 per cent on one year deposits, when the rate of inflation was 30–35 per cent. Furthermore, two of the largest banks that previously avoided competition soon ended up joining the price war (Artun, 1985, p. 55). High cost of funds increased the cost of credit dramatically.

Sales of large amounts of CDs also continued. Some banks formed their own subsidiary brokerage houses to take advantage of the mechanism discussed above.[10] Issuing CDs through brokerage houses was not restricted to private banks and at least two state-owned banks (Vakıflar Bankası and Anadolu Bankası) participated in the practice. Realizing that things were getting out of hand, in November 1981 monetary authorities prohibited banks from marketing CDs through brokers. However, it was common knowledge among market participants that some banks went on with the practice. One of the brokerage houses that continued to market CDs after the ban was Banker Kastelli.

Banker Kastelli was the largest brokerage house in the market. The institution was mainly marketing bonds of private sector companies until the end of 1980. Finding it more and more difficult to maintain a steady supply of securities, Kastelli joined the CD business in early 1981. The evolution of Kastelli's business is a good example of financial behavior under distress: in the early stages the broker was able to exercise caution in choosing its client banks and avoided marketing the CDs of risky banks. By 1982 — after the ban on issuing CDs through bankers — illiquidity problems pushed Kastelli to market the CDs of those risky banks that the banker had earlier tried to avoid.[11] Furthermore, the owner of Banker Kastelli, Cevher Özden, started to lend large volumes of credit to several businessmen, and these loans were not repaid. Özden later rationalized this behavior in an interview as trying to maintain the survival of these businessmen so as to increase the possibility of Kastelli's own survival. In short, financial difficulties pushed Banker Kastelli to choose riskier financial strategies.

The Response of Policy Makers

Initially, policy makers had confidence in the regulatory powers of the market. As the process evolved, they seem to have been caught by surprise. In February 1981, by which time they had become regular participants in the banks' meetings, they indicated that they were going to 'make sure that banks do not offer interest rates higher than those stipulated in the gentlemen's agreement . . [such] banks will be severely punished' (Çölaşan 1984a, p. 163). Similar threats were also made to banks that were issuing CDs through brokerage houses. Policy makers thus found themselves in the contradictory position of advocating 'free' interest rates on the one hand and promoting collusion and 'responsible' behavior on the other. It was also clear that policy makers did not have at their disposal any means to measure the amount of CDs that were so marketed. These threats continued to be made throughout 1981 and 1982, but they were not carried out. The gentlemen's agreements also included statements that banks which did not comply would be punished; however, the nature of the penalties were not made explicit and no action was actually taken during that period.

The Crisis

The system exploded in 1982. In June, Hisarbank — a member of a financial-industrial-construction group — which was for a while on the verge of bankruptcy due to the bad fortunes of its affiliates, initiated a 'campaign of high interest rates' and offered as high as 80 per cent on one year deposits. The purpose of the campaign was to finance payments that were due to depositors and other holders of the bank's liabilities. The response of depositors was favorable and deposits started to be transferred to Hisarbank from other banks. Finally in the next meeting of banks two weeks later, representatives of the government forced the banks to sign a new agreement: like the previous ones, the agreement stipulated common deposit interest rates that would be observed by banks and committed them to cease marketing CDs through brokers. This time, however, the statement also included explicit measures to be taken against non-compliers. Three days after the meeting, the owner of Banker Kastelli, which had by then marketed a large portion of Hisarbank's CDs, fled the country.

It was during this meeting that monetary authorities became aware of the extent of the problem. It became clear that several banks were insolvent and unable to meet their payments on CDs they had issued. Representatives of the Central Bank found out that some banks actually had not even observed their reserve requirements. To avoid panic, the banks were initially provided liquidity from the Central Bank and started to be monitored closely. Some of the bureaucrats in charge of economic affairs resigned in July. The new team changed the policy framework. In January 1983, the Central Bank started to reregulate deposit interest rates and imposed ceilings. Later, policy makers intervened in five private banks, removed their management and declared them bankrupt. The liabilities of four of the banks (Istanbul Bankası, Hisarbank, Odibank and Bağbank) were transferred to state-owned banks; those of the fifth bank (İşçi Kredi Bankası) were taken over by the largest private bank. Each of these five bankrupt banks were owned or controlled by holding companies.[12] Three of them had formed their own brokerage houses. In addition to those banks, several major brokerage houses also went bankrupt. Needless to say financial problems were not restricted to those institutions that went bankrupt. Non-performing loans, the current estimates of which vary between 10–30 per cent of total assets in the banking system, continue to present a major policy problem.

It is worthwhile to emphasize the extent to which real interest rates increased in this period. Even if one is willing to assume that the actual deposit rates of interest that banks offered did not exceed those stipulated in the gentlemen's agreements, it turns out that the real ex-post interest rates on six-month and one-year deposits were between 14 per cent and 25 per cent between the end of 1981 and mid-1982, the period when the competition between banks was most fierce (Table 6.1). One could ask whether this increase could be primarily attributed to large forecast errors in banks' predictions of future inflation. A look at the trend in inflation during the period suggests that such was not the case: Table 6.2 shows that

TABLE 6.1   *Ex-Post Real Deposit Interest Rates* (per cent, annualized)*

	December 1981		June 1982	
	6 months	*1 year*	*6 months*	*1 year*
Nominal rate	50.0	50.0	50.0	50.0
Rate of inflation	20.1	26.2	31.8	29.5
Ex-post real rate	24.1	18.9	13.8	16.6

* Ex-post real interest rate is defined as $(1+r_t)/(1+p_{t+1})$ where
r_t = nominal interest rate at t
p_{t+1} = the rate of inflation between t and t+1.
SOURCES Inflation: State Institute of Statistics, Consumer Price Index; Nominal
rate of interest on deposits: Central Bank.

TABLE 6.2   *Annual Rates of Inflation (per cent)**

	Consumer prices	Wholesale prices
1981 Jan.	82	86
Feb.	56	47
March	45	40
April	38	34
May	30	33
June	30	38
July	33	38
August	33	37
Sept.	33	37
Oct.	29	30
Nov.	28	27
Dec.	28	26
1982 Jan.	26	25
Feb.	24	24
March	26	30
April	25	34
May	23	32
June	23	24

* Rates of change relative to the same month of the previous year.
SOURCES Consumer price index: State Institute of Statistics; wholesale prices:
Treasury.

the annual rate of increases of both the consumer and the wholesale price
indices were in a quite persistent decline since January 1981. One can
therefore conclude that interbank competition for deposits was probably a
more important determinant of high real rates.

The rise in interest rates is also apparent in the consolidated balance
sheets of banks. In the private banks, the ratios of both interest income and

TABLE 6.3 *Statistics on Private Commercial Banks*

	1977	1978	1979	1980	1981	1982	1983	1984
(1) Assets	218.6	316.3	457.5	737.5	1418.7	2148.6	2709.4	4243.9
credits	106.5	145.3	207.5	356.8	654.6	973.7	1222.0	1608.2
(2) Liabilities	218.6	316.3	457.5	737.5	1418.7	2148.6	2709.4	4243.9
deposits	151.4	204.6	310.1	518.3	1080.6	1552.6	1879.3	3208.7
(3) Average credits	95.9	124.4	173.6	272.1	483.3	798.4	1090.8	1402.0
(4) Interest income	12.9	18.0	27.7	68.1	182.9	338.0	448.0	813.4
(5) Interest expense	6.5	9.1	15.6	36.8	144.2	326.7	416.8	723.3
(6) Ave. interest inc.	3.5	14.5	16.0	25.0	37.8	42.3	41.1	58.0
(7) Ave. interest exp.	6.8	7.3	9.0	13.5	29.8	40.9	38.2	51.6
(8) Interest margin	6.7	6.2	7.0	11.5	8.0	1.4	2.9	6.4

(3): Geometric average
(6) = (4)/(3)
(7) = (5)/(3)
(8) = [(4)−(5)]/(3).
SOURCE   Turkish Bankers Association.

expenses to average stocks of credit exceeded 40 per cent in 1982 (Table 6.3). It was also clear that interest expenses rose faster than interest income: as shown in the last row of Table 6.3, interest margin (interest income minus interest expenses) as percentage in average deposits declined substantially from historical levels.[13]

What about the growth of the financial system? As Table 6.4 indicates, traditional measures of financial deepening show improvements in 1980–82: both the real money stock (M2) and the liquidity ratio (M2 expressed as a percentage of GNP) increased in 1981–82 after steep declines in 1978–80. Notice, however, that the growth rate of real M2 was reduced by more than one half between 1981 and 1982, from 34 per cent to 16 per cent. The level of real deposits showed similar increases in 1981 and 1982.

The counterpart to increase in deposits on the asset side of the banking system was a rapid increase in real indebtedness of the private sector, especially in 1981, despite both narrowing bank margins and high lending rates. Total assets of the banking system grew in real terms by 31 per cent and 18 per cent in 1981 and 1982 (Table 6.5), assets of private domestic banks grew by 35 per cent and 17 per cent. In 1981, the rate of increase in the stock of credits to the private sector was 81 per cent in nominal terms and 45 per cent in real terms. Given that in that year the interest rate on loans was very high,[14] the increase in the stock of credit meant a heavy repayment burden in the following years. In fact, 'in the second half of 1982, most of real credit expansion was absorbed by the need to refinance part of the high real interest rates charged to private enterprises' (World

Response to Financial Liberalization

TABLE 6.4   *Indicators of Financial Deepening*

	Per Cent Share in GNP*			Growth Rate[†] (per cent, constant prices)		
	M2	Deposits		M2	Deposits	
		Total	Private domestic banks		Total	Private domestic banks
1978	22.22	18.69	13.64	−9.09	−12.29	−10.19
1979	19.64	16.14	11.61	−12.23	−11.14	−19.77
1980	15.77	13.39	9.04	−16.76	−8.29	−16.37
1981	18.94	17.29	11.42	33.85	63.26	40.04
1982	23.94	23.33	14.83	16.49	26.33	12.69
1983	25.17	25.21	14.79	−9.49	−8.57	−16.40
1984	22.61	14.84	13.38	6.28	−54.19	−10.19

* Stocks expressed as geometric averages.
† Year-end stocks deflated by the December values of WPI, IFS, Supplement of Price Statistics, 1986.
SOURCE   M2 from IFS. Deposits from Turkish Bankers' Association.

Bank, 1983, pp. 11–12).[15] With an inflation rate of 25 per cent in 1982, the increase in the real stock of credit was 12 per cent between the end of 1981 and 1982, not a small rate of growth compared to historical averages. The total stock of liabilities of the private sector to the banking system increased at an even higher rate (17 per cent) in real terms. Table 6.6 shows that despite a decline in total credits from the *financial system*[16] relative to GNP, the share of the private sector in total claims of the financial system increased from 50 per cent in 1980 to 56 per cent in 1981 and 63 per cent in 1982. Of net new credits, 68 per cent went to the private sector in 1981 and 82 per cent in 1982. Notice again, however, that Table 6.5 shows that the rate of increase in both real and nominal stocks of credit to the private sector were cut by half between 1981 and 1982, mirroring the reduction in the rate of growth of M2. With high debt burdens in 1982 and reduced repayment capacity due to lower corporate gross earnings, these reductions probably exacerbated widespread illiquidity in the private sector in 1982.

How does one try to make some sense out of all this? Deferring the issue of what kind of a shock created financial distress in the corporate — and consequently in the banking — sector to the next section, let us concentrate on how banks reacted to financial distress. It is clear that once banks were hit and problems of insolvency arose, they tried their best to avoid bankruptcy. Given high probable costs to bankruptcy, legal barriers to establish new banks and other sunk costs that need to be borne to re-enter the market after bankruptcy, possible reputational problems and high rents

TABLE 6.5 Assets of the Banking System

	per cent of GNP*			per cent Annual Growth (current prices)†			per cent Annual Growth (constant prices)‡		
	Total Assets	Credit to Private Sector	Total Claims on Private Sector	Total Assets	Credit to Private Sector	Total Claims on Private Sector	Total Assets	Credit to Private Sector	Total Claims on Private Sector
1977	51.3	20.4	20.9	37.8	27.3	27.4	1.1	-6.6	-6.6
1978	47.6	17.5	17.9	36.8	26.0	26.6	-8.1	-15.4	-15.0
1979	41.2	14.1	14.5	54.9	46.3	46.1	-14.7	-19.4	-19.5
1980	36.1	11.0	11.3	106.4	73.1	73.4	6.1	-11.0	-10.9
1981	44.8	13.1	13.8	63.4	80.7	86.5	30.7	44.6	49.2
1982	52.3	15.7	17.1	48.1	41.0	47.3	18.1	12.4	17.4
1983	57.7	16.4	19.2	43.7	34.3	49.3	2.0	-4.7	6.0
1984	55.5	13.8	17.1	62.2	33.6	33.9	9.4	-10.0	-9.8

* Stocks expressed as geometric averages.

† End of year.

‡ End of year stocks deflated by WPI (December) in IMF, IFS Supplement of Price Statistics, 1986.

SOURCE Central Bank, Quarterly Bulletin.

Excludes investment and development banks.

Total claims = Credits + Participations + Bonds + Other

TABLE 6.6   *Private Sector's Share in Total Credit*

	1977	1978	1979	1980	1981	1982	1983	1984
Total credit/GNP	47.5	40.8	36.7	29.9	31.4	30.5	29.7	23.1
Share of private sector credit in total	50.7	50.9	49.8	52.0	59.8	65.1	68.2	74.8
Share of private sector in new credit	39.4	51.7	47.6	55.3	73.9	83.3	79.2	102.5

SOURCE   Central Bank, Quarterly Bulletin.

of bank ownership, this quest for survival is not very surprising. The more interesting question, however, was the mechanism. Once hit by an earnings shock, which makes a bank unable to meet, say, its interest payments to depositors, the bank will try to raise additional resources to meet these payments and to avoid bankruptcy. The obvious way to raise these resources is to attract new deposits. This was done in Turkey, both by raising deposit interest rates and by issuing CDs. However, higher promised interest payments mean a higher stock of liabilities in the future. To assure positive value for the bank and to avoid bankruptcy in the future, the bank has to charge higher interest rates on its loans.

What kind of borrowers would be willing to accept higher lending rates? Holders of its non-performing assets may be one possibility. Analogous to the bank, a borrowing firm which is on the verge of bankruptcy will be willing to accept higher lending rates if they provide a possibility for survival. The bank may be able to charge high interest rates also to borrowers that cannot borrow from other banks because of their risk characteristics — as did, for example, Kastelli, once financial distress occurred. Clearly the bank is limited by competition from other banks in the interest rate it can charge to safe borrowers. Unavoidably, then, the portfolio of the bank has to become more risky. The bank will typically be willing to take additional risks since it is protected by limited liability.[17] But this is clearly inefficient: at a time when loanable funds are most needed to solve temporary liquidity problems of good firms, a sizeable portion of the funds may end up being used to finance bad firms. This is exactly what happened in Turkey, especially in the case of smaller insolvent banks. Furthermore, what where essentially Ponzi schemes could not be prevented by the functioning of the market mechanism, and apparently required intervention by the state. The welfare question that needs to be addressed, then, relates to *additional expected losses* that were incurred after the banks became insolvent. Why was the market unsuccessful in driving insolvent banks out of the system?

The preceding question may be asked much more concretely: why did depositors respond favorably to the interest rate 'campaign' of Hisarbank?

It is well known that return to depositors is not monotonically increasing in the nominal promised interest rate because higher interest rates mean the probability that they will be repaid is smaller; when interest rates are very high relative to the earnings potential of the bank, this negative effect becomes dominant and expected return to depositors starts to decline.[18] Clearly, when the nominal interest rate that Hisarbank offered was 80 per cent, with a very high probability of bankruptcy, the expected interest rate was much lower. Why did depositors not withhold their deposits?

One can develop various hypotheses to explain the observed behavior of depositors. One explanation could be that because information about banks' asset structures and balance sheets was so scarce, depositors could not tell good banks from bad banks, that is, there was a problem of adverse selection. If the problem was just one of adverse selection, however, one could also argue that the level of interest rates offered by Hisarbank — during a period when corporate earnings were distressed, illiquidity was widespread and therefore expected bank profitability was low — should have acted as a signal revealing that the high interest rates reflected not a higher profitability potential but Hisarbank's insolvency.

There are two other potential explanations, which, interestingly, are based on completely different assumptions about depositors' 'rationality' but imply very similar behavior and market outcomes. The first hypothesis is simple and can be dubbed 'interest rate illusion': depositors in Turkey were simply not used to a liberalized financial system, and the developments were too fast for them to learn. Therefore depositors confused promised interest rates with expected interest repayments and did not adequately take into consideration the riskiness of banks. The second hypothesis maintains that depositors are on the contrary quite rational: they are well aware of potential costs of bank bankruptcies when depositors are not protected — bank runs, increased illiquidity, disruptions in payment mechanisms and production,[19] let alone political costs. Therefore, they — correctly — foresee that if a bank goes bankrupt the government will intervene and provide ex-post deposit guarantees — even if an explicit insurance scheme does not exist — in order to maintain the stability of and confidence in the banking system, and to avoid bank runs and the adverse political consequences of letting depositors suffer. The implication of this hypothesis also is that depositors respond to promised rates of interest, believing that in the case of incomplete repayment, the difference will be covered by the government. This argument was put forward in accounts of financial crisis in Chile.[20]

What happens when depositors are responsive to promised rather than expected interest rates, for whatever reason? The basic point to be made is that markets can prevent the kind of Ponzi schemes that have developed in Turkey and induce the exit of unprofitable banks and firms through bankruptcies only if depositors withhold their funds from insolvent banks.

Discounting the risk element in interest rate offers prevents exactly that. In the absence of self-regulatory mechanisms in the market, efficiency requires that a supervisory institution monitor banks and be ready to intervene and liquidate them whenever they become insolvent. Such a regulatory framework was clearly absent in the 1980–82 period. When the government did finally intervene in 1982, it was too late.

III ADJUSTMENT IN THE CORPORATE SECTOR

It was seen in the previous section that the problems in the banking sector began when an important portion of the loan portfolios of the banks became non-performing. In this Section I would like to look at the other side of the coin and review the performance of the corporate sector — major borrowers of banks, especially in 1981 and 1982 — and try to provide answers to the following types of questions: (i) did the shocks to the corporate sector simply consist of increased interest expenses or did adverse cost/demand conditions also play a role? (ii) how did firms react to these shocks financially? Is there any indication that distressed firms actually increased their indebtedness during this period?

To answer these questions, a panel data set of firm-level financial statements will be analyzed. The source of data is the income statements and balance sheets of a sample of 91 firms registered at the Capital Markets Board (CMB) of Turkey. The same data set has been used by Ersel and Sak (1986) in a similar study. The data is available for the period 1979–84.

It should be noted at the outset that the sample is not representative of all private sector firms in Turkey. First, all of the firms are issuers of either stocks and/or bonds to the public or have at least 100 shareholders. Second, the average scale of the corporations in the sample is large, so that the firms in the data set can be taken as representative of large corporate sector only. The following table, taken from Ersel and Sak (1986, p. 93), compares the average total assets of firms in the CMB sample and those in samples compiled by the Istanbul Chamber of Commerce (ICI)[21]:

	1981		1982		1983	
	CMB	*ICI*	*CMB*	*ICI*	*CMB*	*ICI*
Average assets (Million TL)	3264	222	5079	347	6848	487

Besides possible selectivity bias, the reader should also be cautioned that additional biases exist since the data are not corrected for inflation.

The section will proceed as follows. First profitability will be defined. It will then be decomposed into standard financial ratios that capture real and financial factors that affect profitability as well as the firm's financial response to movements in these factors. After summarizing the movements in the ratios over time, a simple analysis of variance model will be used to statistically compare average values of the ratios across time and groups of firms.[22]

I define profitability (PR) as the ratio of pre-tax income (Y) to the book value of equity (E):

$$PR = Y/E.^{23}$$

Then, PR can be decomposed in the following way:

$$PR = [(EBIT \cdot AU) - (FC \cdot GR)] / (1-GR) \tag{1}$$

where
EBIT = EBIT margin, earnings before interest and taxes divided by net sales income.
AU = asset utilization ratio; net sales income over total assets.
FC = financial costs ratio; interest expenses over total debt.
GR = gearing ratio; total debt divided by total assets.

The decomposition in equation (1) is useful because it helps one identify the real and financial factors affecting profitability. Real factors are captured by EBIT and AU. Movements in EBIT are primarily determined by movements in sales and non-interest costs. EBIT can be further divided into sub-components, the most important of which is gross margin (GM, net sales income minus cost of goods sold divided by net sales income).[24] Changes in GM reflect changes in the price of output relative to input prices and therefore is expected to be closely influenced by such economic variables as demand, wages, exchange rate and policies that affect these variables. The asset utilization ratio, AU, reflects the rate at which assets of the firm generate sales income. It is generally interpreted as a proxy for capacity utilization.

Financial factors are captured by FC and GR. FC is influenced by interest rate and monetary/credit policies. The importance of financial costs for a firm's profits is directly proportional to the firm's level of indebtedness. Gearing ratio (or leverage) is an indicator of the firm's indebtedness. In general GR will be interpreted as firms' response to changes in the other variables. Everything else equal, profitability is affected positively by increases in EBIT, GM, AU and decreases in FC. The effect of a change in leverage will be discussed below.

Once these variables were calculated, each of them were statistically compared across time and groups of firms through a simple analysis of variance (ANOVA) model. Let T stand for the number of observations for each firm and N of the number of firms in the data set (assuming, for the moment that the data is balanced). Total variation in each of the variables was decomposed into three effects:

$$r = D_F\beta_F + D_Y\beta_Y + D_L\beta_L + e$$

where

r   = the financial variable analyzed.

D_F = NT×N matrix of firm effect dummy variables. The j'th column of this matrix consists of ones for firm j and zeroes otherwise.

D_Y = NT×T matrix of year effect dummy variables. The t'th column of this matrix consists of ones for year t and zeroes otherwise.

D_L = NT×T matrix of nested year/loss effect dummy variables. The t'th column of this matrix consists of ones for observations that have made negative profits in year t, and zeroes otherwise.

β_F, β_Y, and β_L are vectors of regression coefficients (of dimensions N×1, T×1 and T×1, respectively) and e is an NT×1 (column) vector of independently and identically distributed disturbances.

The firm effects are assumed to capture the individual characteristics of firms that stay constant across time. The year effects capture the influence of macroeconomic variables that affect all firms equally within a year but which change over time. Finally, the matrix of 'year/loss effects' was used to statistically compare, in each year, the performance of the variables across firms that recorded non-negative and negative profits. The year/loss effects were used as a proxy to measure the (marginal) effect of falling into a state of financial distress.[25]

Since, as they stand, the D matrices are not linearly independent, I have normalized[26] the system so that the regression coefficients are expressed as differences from the 1979 year effects. Let the coefficients of the new model be given by B_F, B_Y and B_L. These coefficients should be interpreted in the following manner: (i) the (T–1) elements of B_Y reflect the average differences of the dependent variable relative to its average value in 1979, for the observations that correspond to non-negative profits; (ii) the (T) elements of B_L reflect the average differences of the dependent variable for observations with negative profits, relative to those with non-negative profits. The (N–1) elements of B_F will not be reported.

There were strong outliers for all the financial ratios. Since in the presence of strong outliers the estimated coefficients do not adequately reflect the bulk of the sample, observations for which the estimated error term was at least three times the standard error of regression were deleted from the sample and the model was re-estimated. The largest number of observations deleted in this manner was 7. The results reported below belong to this second round of estimation.[27]

The following hypotheses were tested for each of the dependent variables:

H1: Differences across firms are not statistically significant (all elements of B_F are 0).

H2: Differences across years are not statistically significant (all elements of B_Y are 0).

H3: Differences across observations with non-negative and negative profits are not significant (all elements of B_L are 0).

H4: Differences between observations with non-negative and negative profits are the same across years (all elements of B_L are equal).

Whereas H3 is used to test whether the values of the dependent variable are on average different between the two groups of firms, H4 is used to test whether the magnitude of this difference itself changes over time.

Before turning to the statistical results, it will be useful to take a look at how the (unweighted) averages of financial ratios evolved over time. These are summarised in Table 6.7.[28] First of all, we see in the first row of that table that profitability declined substantially, from 42 per cent in 1980 to −5 per cent in 1982, and started to pick up in 1983 and 1984. Several factors have contributed to the decline. The first is the decline in gross margins. Between 1980 and 1982 gross margins declined from 26 per cent to 19 per cent and continued to decrease in 1983. The movements in GM clearly indicate that sales prices increased less rapidly than the prices of inputs used in production during these years. EBIT margin has also declined during that period.

How can one account for the reduction in GM and EBIT? One explanation may be demand; increase in domestic absorption was still quite weak in 1981 and 1982. However, total sales of firms in the data set did increase in real terms during these years. Increase in costs was probably more important. Using consolidated figures from another data set, Akyüz (this volume) shows that raw material costs increased substantially during these years, reflecting the impact of two stabilization policies on corporate income statements: (i) the impact of large devaluations on the cost of imported inputs, and (ii) increases in the prices of state economic enterprises which produce intermediate inputs.[29]

The fluctuations in the asset utilization ratio are less pronounced — except for the decline in 1981. It should be noted at this point that capacity utilization was already at very low levels in the late 1970s, mainly due to a foreign exchange crisis that prevented the use of necessary imported inputs.

Moving down Table 6.7, financial costs have increased between 1980 and 1982, from 13 per cent to 18 per cent.[30] The increase in FC reflects the effect of money and credit policies on the cost of firms' borrowing.

However, contrary to the expectations of policy makers, the increase in the cost of borrowing did not induce firms to decrease their leverage in the period 1980–82. In fact, simultaneous with the increase in financial costs, the gearing ratio also increased from 69 per cent to 73 per cent during these years.

TABLE 6.7 *Annual Non-Weighted Averages of Financial Ratios*

	1979	1980	1981	1982	1983	1984
Profitability		0.424	0.240	−0.046	0.185	0.358
Gross margin	0.233	0.262	0.223	0.193	0.183	0.218
EBIT	0.172	0.179	0.171	0.142	0.131	0.172
Asset utilization		1.525	1.440	1.513	1.549	1.846
Average financial costs		0.132	0.154	0.183	0.168	0.189
Gearing ratio		0.686	0.703	0.727	0.682	0.626

SOURCE CMB data set.

How significant were these changes? To answer this question, we can now have a look at the statistical results. These are displayed in Table 6.8. Each block in Table 6.8 first displays the values of B_Y and B_L, the estimated coefficients of the year and loss effects, respectively. After that, each block displays the results of four F tests mentioned above: the values P1 — P4 are the levels of significance at which the hypotheses H1 — H4 can be rejected, respectively. For example a value of 0.012 for P4 in the block for the variable GR indicates that the hypothesis H4 can be rejected at 1.2 per cent level of significance. Finally, the stars on the values of the coefficients indicate the results of individual t-tests.

Starting with profitability in the first block, once loss making observations are controlled for, the drop in the profitability of firms with positive profits is much less pronounced and statistically insignificant. The significance of the loss effect, on the other hand, is very high. Furthermore, the value of P4 shows that the changes in the difference between the profitability of firms making positive profits on the one hand, and losses on the other, is also significant. Another surprising result is that firm effects turn out to be insignificant: P1 has a value of 1.0. In all other ratios, the individual characteristics of firms turn out to be quite significant in explaining the variations of the dependent variables.

In the second block in Table 6.8, one sees that the decline in gross margins is significant, and average GM ratio of loss-making observations is significantly lower: the values of both P2 and P3 are close to zero. However, the hypothesis that the difference between the two groups of firms is constant cannot be rejected at 10 per cent level of significance. Therefore, the increasing differential between the profitability of the two groups of firms cannot be explained solely by the performance of the GM ratios.

The reduction in EBIT is very small and not significant for profit making observations. Loss making observations have persistently lower EBIT margins. The absolute value of the difference between the EBIT margins

TABLE 6.8   *ANOVA Results*

Dep. Var.: Profitability (PR)

	1979	1980	1981	1982	1983	1984
B_Y			−0.033	−0.123	−0.125	−0.027
B_L		−0.678*	−0.832*	−1.698*	−0.907*	−0.815*
F-test	P1: 1.000	P2: 0.815		P3: 0.000		P4: 0.004

Dep. Var.: Gross Margin (GM)

	1979	1980	1981	1982	1983	1984
B_Y		0.019	−0.016	−0.069*	−0.047*	−0.015
B_L	−0.161*	−0.090*	−0.088*	−0.125*	−0.159*	−0.055*
F-test	P1: 0.000	P2: 0.000		P3: 0.000		P4: 0.123

Dep. Var.: EBIT Margin (EBIT)

	1979	1980	1981	1982	1983	1984
B_Y		0.015	−0.002	−0.004	−0.030	−0.010
B_L	−0.266*	−0.172*	−0.108*	−0.195*	−0.204*	−0.019*
F-test	P1: 0.000	P2: 0.330		P3: 0.000		P4: 0.000

Dep. Var.: Asset Utilization (AU)

	1979	1980	1981	1982	1983	1984
B_Y			−0.018	0.002	−0.040	0.141[†]
B_L		−0.441*	−0.456*	−0.293*	−0.107	−0.015
F-test	P1: 0.000	P2: 0.166		P3: 0.000		P4: 0.069

Dep. Var.: Average Financial Cost (FC)

	1979	1980	1981	1982	1983	1984
B_Y			0.029*	0.046*	0.037*	0.063*
B_L		0.022	−0.017	0.034	0.022[‡]	−0.028
F-test	P1: 0.000	P2: 0.000		P3: 0.134		P4: 0.100

Dep. Var.: Gearing Ratio (GR)

	1979	1980	1981	1982	1983	1984
B_Y			0.015	0.017	−0.010	−0.028
B_L		0.064[‡]	0.054[†]	0.159*	0.116*	0.147*
F-test	P1: 0.000	P2: 0.119		P3: 0.000		P4: 0.012

* Significant at 1% level.
† Significant at 5% level.
‡ Significant at 10% level.
SOURCE   Authors' calculations.

of the two groups has declined from 0.27 to 0.20 between 1979–82 with fluctuations in the intervening years.

The changes in the ratio of asset utilization are not significant for observations with positive profits: H2 cannot be rejected at traditional levels of significance. Firms making losses have significantly lower AU ratios (low P3). Again, the difference between the two groups of firms significantly narrow over time: the value of B_L increases from −0.441 in 1980 to −0.015 in 1984, with a P4 value of 6.9 per cent.

The increase in average financial costs between the years 1980–82 is significant, as expected. The interesting point is that the FC ratios of observations with losses do not seem to be significantly higher than those with profits: the hypothesis that all the elements of B_L are zero cannot be rejected at the 10 per cent level of significance. Notice that the t-statistics of the coefficients B_L are also low. Hence financial costs are not important in explaining the difference in the profitability of the two groups of firms.

The results obtained so far can be summarized as follows: in the 1980–82 period there has been a decrease in the profitability of firms in the CMB data set. Although financial costs have increased considerably during those years, that component of profitability does not explain the poorer performance of firms with losses. On the other hand, loss making observations have significantly lower GM, EBIT and AU ratios.

If this interpretation is correct, then it can safely be said that firms were hit by two shocks in 1980–82: the interest rate shock took place almost simultaneously with the demand shock, as reflected in the decline in gross margins. A look at the movements in leverage can now give us an idea about how firms adjusted financially to these shocks. Also, the lower levels of GM, EBIT and AU explain only the existence of the profitability gap between the two groups of observations; why the gap has increased between 1980–82 requires further explanation.

To prepare the stage, let us think about the ways in which a firm can finance a loss. It would have basically three options, or a combination thereof: sell assets (or reduce liquid assets), increase equity or increase debt. If the rate of growth of assets is positive, as in the CMB sample for both groups of firms, then a loss with a contemporaneous increase in leverage would suggest that the loss has been financed by more debt than equity.

Table 6.8 shows that the increase in the debt to asset ratios of profit-making firms was statistically insignificant (P value of 12 per cent). The movements in the leverage of loss making firms, on the other hand, is significant. In 1980, the leverage of observations with losses was on average 6 percentage points higher than that of the firms in the other group, and the difference increased to 16 percentage points in 1982 and 15 percentage points in 1984. Furthermore, this increase in the difference was significant. Since the rate of growth of assets was positive in this period for both groups of firms, these results suggest that firms financed their losses by borrowing relatively more, *in exactly the same period when cost of borrowing increased substantially*. These results also lead to the following rather surprising conclusion: the gap in the average profitability between the two groups of observations is primarily to be explained by the increases in the leverage of loss-making observations during a period of higher financial cost.

Everything else constant, an increase in the cost of borrowing is expected to induce firms to hold less debt. The apparent higher borrowing in the present sample must have occurred due to a shift in the demand curve for loans rather than a movement along it.

What might have caused such a shift in the demand for loans is a question that requires further research. One variable that the present analysis suggests is the drop in earnings. There are at least two ways in which a decrease in gross earnings could induce firms to use relatively more debt than equity. The first one has to do with liquidity constraints. A drop in earnings decreases the ability of firms to finance current expenditures, including expenditures on interest. Therefore firms with low earnings have to rely more heavily on debt. What about the expectations of policy makers that owners of corporations would liquidate their personal wealth and use it to finance their corporations? This leads to the second explanation. On the one hand, one might argue that the personal wealth of firm owners was simply not enough to finance the gap produced by the reduction in earnings and increases in interest costs. On the other hand, one might go one step further and argue that even if personal wealth was sufficient, the owners might not have had the incentive to allocate it to finance their firms. The idea is that if the perception of owner/managers about the near future is bleak, in the sense that the perceived probability of bankruptcy is high, then they will prefer to borrow rather than jeopardize their personal wealth by advancing it towards a risky activity.[31] The two explanations are not mutually exclusive and possibly both carry an element of truth. The implications of these explanations are consistent with the comparative performance of firms in the years 1980–82 and 1984. In the 1980–82 period, debt to asset ratios increased because lower asset returns dominated the effects of increased financial costs. In 1984, however, both rates of return on assets and financial costs were high, and firms responded by lowering their indebtedness.

IV CONCLUSION

There were, basically, two somewhat related stories laid out in this paper. The first one was about the response of the banking system to deregulation. It was argued that the complete absence of a regulatory framework allowed insolvent banks to avoid bankruptcy by offering high rates to depositors, using funds thus collected to finance their obligations and refinance non-performing loans. The second one was related to the response of firms. Contrary to the expectations of policy makers, firms that made losses were shown to increase their debt to asset ratios even though cost of borrowing had increased. It is not possible to clearly demonstrate the correspondence between these two stories. Although in the CMB data set there were some observations with negative book values of net worth, it is not clear how many firms that had low earnings were actually insolvent.

However, there is a unifying theme between the two stories: the unexpected consequences of deregulation and increases in the level of indebtedness of firms seemed to be generated by a drop in the earnings of the corporate sector that resulted from stabilization policies and the radical changes in the economic environment. Once firms and banks are hit by financial distress, and if bankruptcy entails private costs, then they should be expected to implement risky survival strategies. These strategies may even involve financing of firms or banks with negative net present values, as long as the *equity* values of these projects are positive. Furthermore, there does not seem to exist in the market a mechanism to ensure the *exit* of these firms or banks. What the Turkish experience points out is a potential inconsistency between macroeconomic stabilization policies, that do involve radical changes in the economic environment, and financial liberalization, especially when the latter is implemented without an adequate regulatory framework.

This last qualification is important. Given the liquidity problems that arose in the corporate sector, continuing to suppress deposit interest rates at negative real levels would probably have made things worse. There was a clear need to mobilize additional financial resources. We have seen that interest rates were quite effective in mobilizing financial resources. What was questionable however was the allocative efficiency of interest rates: once mobilized, substantial resources were used to prolong survival rather than to alleviate temporary liquidity problems or finance investment. Presumably, this additional loss could have been prevented by active supervision of the banking system and/or by setting interest rate ceilings at some maximum positive sustainable level.

NOTES

1. The views expressed in this paper are those of the author and do not necessarily represent the views and policies of the World Bank or of its executive directors or the countries they represent. This paper is a product of my dissertation work. I am grateful to Charles A. Wilson, my advisor, and, Tosun Arıcanlı, Ishac Diwan and Dani Rodrik for helpful comments and encouragement. The

paper benefited greatly from discussions in the conference on 'The Political Economy of Turkey in the 1980s', especially from comments by Ataman Aksoy, Tercan Baysan and Merih Celâsun. I thank research teams at the Capital Markets Board and the Central Bank of Turkey for their help and support in obtaining the data. Financial support from Uluslararası Endüstri ve Ticaret Bankasi, 100. Yıl Fonu and the Institute for the Study of World Politics is gratefully acknowledged. All errors and omissions are mine.

2. For a detailed overview of macroeconomic policies and performance in the 1970s and 1980s, see Celâsun and Rodrik (forthcoming).
3. One important exception is Türkiye İş Bankası, the largest private bank in Turkey.
4. Artun (1983, pp. 70, 77) argues that bond issues resulted from new financing requirements due to the impact of devaluations of 1978–9 on corporations.
5. Examples are Meban of Transtürk Holding, Eczacıbaşı Yatırım of Eczacıbaşı Holding and Oyak Yatırım of Oyak Holding.
6. One has to make a distinction between the brokerage houses discussed in the text, which traded, at least in the initial stages of the process, in securities of *industrial firms and banks* and other unorganized money market institutions that collected funds solely against *personal* cheques and IOUs. The latter type of institutions (dubbed 'market bankers' in Turkey) mushroomed following the deregulation and were the actors of another crisis that unfolded at the end of 1981. These institutions and their evolution will not be addressed in this study.
7. For a more comprehensive overview of financial reform, see Akyüz (this volume).
8. The following summary is primarily based on accounts given in Çölaşan (1983, 1984a, 1984b), Ulagay (1987), and Artun (1983, 1985).
9. Corporate bond issues were limited by capital adequacy requirements. According to Artun (1983, p. 70) and Çölaşan (1984b, p. 73) these requirements became binding in 1981 for major bond issuers and the resulting reduction in new supply of securities was one of the reasons that drove brokerage houses into the CD business.
10. For example, Istanbul Bankası, Hisarbank and Bağbank established Fintaş, Eko-Yatırım and Fiban, respectively. All three of these banks were intervened in and liquidated in 1983, see below.
11. For example, those of Hisarbank, Odibank, Istanbul Bankası (Çölaşan, 1984b, p. 241).
12. See Artun (1985, p. 48, 53). Hisarbank and Odibank were members of the same group, Kozanoğlu-Çavuşoğlu.
13. An official report prepared at the time claimed that the interest margin of credits was negative in 1981 and the first quarter of 1982 (Çölaşan 1984b, p. 477). The standard practice of banks in Turkey was to capitalise interest payments when they were due and thus increase the principal amount outstanding. In the meantime, interest payments that were not collected were recorded as income. Therefore it is highly likely that income statements, on which figures in Table 6.3 are based, overstated interest income.
14. Data on average lending rates on non-preferential loans does not exist. Hanson and Neal (1985) estimate the nominal rate of interest on non-preferential loans as 65 per cent. Other informed estimates go as high as 80 per cent.
15. The same observation is made in the aforementioned report: '. . . the banks' inability to collect interest payments has seriously affected their liquidity. In spite of this, the banks have refinanced borrowers' outstanding interest payments and thereby have further jeopardized their cash positions' (Çölaşan,

1984b, p. 448, my translation). Similarly, Celâsun and Rodrik (forthcoming, p. 4–17) state: 'A significant part (guesstimates running around 40 to 60 per cent) of the nominal credit expansion in this period was directed to refinancing of the interest payments connected with non-performing loans'.
16. 'Financial system' comprises all banks and the monetary authority.
17. That is, additional risks may increase the equity value of the bank while decreasing the value of other claims on the bank.
18. This non-monotonicity of expected returns in contractual interest rates forms the basis of the credit-rationing literature: see, for example Stiglitz and Weiss (1983, 1985).
19. See Diamond and Dybvig (1983) for a formal treatment of these ideas.
20. See for example, Diaz-Alejandro (1985, p. 8) and Harberger (1985). Hinds (1987, n. 22) cites several instances of such 'ex-post deposit guarantees' in Chile, Colombia and the United States. In Turkey, a precedent was established in 1960 when, following the failure of several banks, a Bank Liquidation Fund was established to pay off the deposit holders of these banks. All liabilities of the banks were covered. A deposit insurance scheme was formally introduced in Turkey in 1983. The transfer of insolvent banks' assets and liabilities to state-owned banks in 1983 constituted another example of ex-post deposit guarantees.
21. The ICI samples comprise more than 1200 firms.
22. The approach adopted here is similar to Petrei and Tybout (1984).
23. The variables are defined in the Appendix.
24. Other components of EBIT, namely overhead and other net income (see Appendix for definitions) are small in the CMB data set. Furthermore, relatively large recording errors have been detected in these variables. See Ersel and Sak (1986, Appendix A2). Therefore, these components will not be treated individually.
25. The number of observations with negative profits are 11 in 1979 and 1980 (12 per cent of all observations), 24 (26 per cent) in 1981, 22 (24 per cent) in 1982, 14 (22 per cent) in 1983 and 8 (15 per cent) in 1984.
26. Here normalization simply means to delete just enough columns from the D matrices such that the resulting system is linearly independent, to avoid a typical 'dummy variable trap.'
27. Furthermore, some corrections had to be made on the data to eliminate discontinuities and inconsistencies that were created by the adoption of an inflation accounting scheme in 1983. These corrections required additional information on firms. Ersel and Sak (1986, Appendix A2) discuss the problem and the additional information necessary to correct it. Such additional information could not be found for some firms. As a result, 27 observations in 1983 and 37 observations in 1984 had to be deleted.
28. Stocks such as total assets, total debt and equity in year t are expressed as averages of years t–1 and t. Therefore, the 1979 values of ratios that involved stocks were not calculated. The total number of observations that did not involve stocks was 482, whereas the total number of observations for ratios that did involve stocks was 391.
29. Part of the increase in costs may be due to the fact that some interest expenses are recorded under Cost of Goods Sold. See the note below.
30. Interest expense figures in income statements probably underestimate true interest expenses because firstly, some interest payments are recorded under the Cost of Goods Sold account and cannot be retrieved, and secondly, firms that borrowed from Islamic banks do not record their payments as interest expenses.

31. What is at play here is again the effect of limited liability. Although an increase in debt relative to equity would probably decrease the *total* (debt plus equity) value of the firm when the cost of borrowing is high, it may increase the expected wealth of the owner, where wealth consists of personal wealth plus the *equity* value of the firm. With a high probability of bankruptcy, even if the nominal cost of debt is high, *expected* cost of debt may still be lower than the cost of equity.

REFERENCES

Artun, T. (1983) *Türkiye'de 'Serbest' Faiz Politikasi* ('Free' interest rate policy in Turkey) (Istanbul: Tekin Yayınevi).

Artun, T. (1985) 'Türk Mali Sistemi 1980–84: Degişim ve Maliyeti' (The Turkish financial system 1980–84: Change and Costs of Change), in B. Kuruç (ed.), *Bırakınız Yapsınlar, Bırakınız Geçsinler* (Laissez Faire, Laissez Passer), pp. 36–71 (Ankara: Bilgi Yayınevi).

Celâsun, M. and D. Rodrik (forthcoming) *Debt, Adjustment and Growth in Turkey*.

Çölaşan, E. (1983) *24 Ocak: Bir Dönemin Perde Arkası* (Behind the Scenes of the [programme of] 24 January) (Istanbul: Milliyet Yayınları).

Çölaşan, E. (1984a) *12 Eylül: Özal Ekonomisinin Perde Arkası* (12 September: Behind the Scenes of Özal's Economics) (Istanbul: Milliyet Yayınları).

Çölaşan, E. (1984b) *Banker Skandalının Perde Arkası* (Behind the Scenes of the Bankers' Scandal) (Istanbul: Milliyet Yayınları).

Diamond, D. W. and P. H. Dybvig (1983) 'Bank Runs, Deposit Insurance and Liquidity', *Journal of Political Economy* 91, pp. 401–19.

Diaz-Alejandro, C. (1985) 'Good-bye Financial Repression, Hello Financial Crash', *Journal of Development Economics* 19, pp. 1–24.

Ersel, H. and G. Sak (1986) 'The Financial Structure of the Corporations Subject to CMB Supervision: 1979–1984 — Some Preliminary Findings', in *Inflation and Capital Markets: Proceedings of the OECD-CMB Conference*, pp. 89–139, Capital Market Board Publications 7 (Ankara: CMB).

Hanson, J. A. and C. R. Neal (1985) 'Interest Rate Policies in Selected Developing Countries' (Washington DC: World Bank) World Bank Staff Working Paper 753.

Harberger, A. C. (1985) 'Observations on the Chilean Economy, 1973–1983,' *Economic Development and Cultural Change* 33, pp. 452–62.

Hinds, M. (1987) 'Draft Paper on Financial Crises in Developing Countries', photocopy.

OECD (1986) *OECD Economic Surveys: Turkey* (Paris: Organization for Economic Co-operation and Development).

Petrei, A. H. and J. Tybout (1984) 'How the Financial Statements of Argentine Firms Reflected Stabilization and Reform Attempts during 1976–81' (Washington DC: World Bank) World Bank Staff Working Paper 706.

Stiglitz, J. and A. Weiss (1983) 'Incentive Effects of Terminations: Applications to the Credit and Labor Markets', *American Economic Review* 73, pp. 912–27.

Stiglitz, J. (1985) 'Credit Rationing with Collateral', Bell Communications Research Economics Discussion Paper 12 (New Jersey: Bell Communications).

Ulagay, O. (1987) *Kim Kazandı, Kim Kaybetti?* (Who Won, Who Lost?) (Ankara: Bilgi Yayınevi).

World Bank (1983) *Turkey: Special Economic Report for the Financial Sector* 4459-TU (Washington DC).

APPENDIX

Format of Financial Statements of Firms in the CMB Data Set

Balance Sheet

Assets		*Liabilities*	
Cash and equivalents	A1	Short term bank loans	L1
Securities	A2	Other current liabilities	L2
Accounts receivable	A3	Current liabilities	L3
Inventories	A4	Outstanding bonds	L4
Other current assets	A5	Long term bank loans	L5
Current assets	A6	Other long term liabilities	L6
Long term receivables	A7	Long term liabilities	L7
Participations	A8	Total debt	D
Net fixed assets	A9	Paid-in-capital	E1
Investments in progress	A10	Reserves	E2
Other fixed assets	A11	Allowances	E3
Non-current assets	A12	Revaluation fund	E4
		Losses from previous years	E5
		Pre-tax income	E6
		Net worth	E
Total assets	A	Total liabilities	L

Income Statement

$Y1$ = Net sales income   (1)
$Y2$ = Cost of goods sold   (2)
$Y3$ = Gross profit   (3 = 1–2)
$Y4$ = Operating expenses   (4)
$Y5$ = Operating income   (5 = 3–4)
$Y6$ = Other income   (6)
$Y7$ = Other expenses   (7)
$Y8$ = Interest expenses   (8)
$Y9$ = Pre-tax income   (9 = 5+6–7–8)

Financial Ratios

$GM = Y3/Y1$ Gross margin
$AU = Y1/A$ Asset utilization
$FC = Y8/D$ Average financial costs
$GR = D/A$ Gearing ratio
$PR = Y9/E$ Rate of return on equity
$EBIT = (Y5+Y6-Y7)/Y1$ EBIT (earnings before interest and taxes) Margin
$EMAU = (Y5+Y6-Y7)/A$ Rate of return on assets before interest and taxes

7 External Balance and Growth in Turkey: Can They Be Reconciled?

Ritu Anand, Ajay Chhibber and Sweder van Wijnbergen[1]

I INTRODUCTION

Turkey has, alone among the high-debt countries, managed to maintain a high growth rate after rescheduling its debt. Its real GNP grew by 5 per cent on average since 1980. By comparison, countries with recent debt-servicing problems, grew at only 1.2 per cent since 1981,[2] almost a four percentage point difference on average. At the same time, Turkey's debt-output ratio increased by an amount roughly similar to the increase in the debt-output ratio of the high-debt countries, from 28 per cent at the end of 1980 to 56 per cent at the end of 1986 (see Table 7.1).

In fact, it is surprising that Turkey's debt-output ratio did not increase a great deal more than it did in the high-debt countries. As a percentage of GNP, Turkey ran a much lower non-interest current account surplus than the high-debt countries did on average after their debt-crisis: –0.25 per cent of GNP for Turkey over the period 1980–86 versus +2.6 per cent over 1982–86 for the high-debt countries. This apparent inconsistency is explained by the higher growth rate that Turkey managed to sustain. Turkey's debt-output ratio followed a path similar to that of the high-debt countries, not so much because of large trade surpluses, but because of its high output growth coupled with continued access to foreign financing.

This paper discusses two issues this experience raises. One, how did Turkey translate the extra breathing space continued access to foreign financing gave it into sustained high real growth? In particular, what was the public sector's role in this process? Second, what are the prospects for a repeat performance? Can Turkey, in the years to come, reconcile external balance and sustained output growth?

To this end, we develop and apply to Turkey an econometric model designed to shed light on the public sector's role in the internal adjustment to external transfer targets. The central issue is, how to bring about a private savings over investment surplus that will reconcile external targets and fiscal deficits without jeopardizing output growth. In what follows we first present the analytical structure of the model (Section II). The results

TABLE 7.1 *Measures of the Overall Debt Burden*

	1980	1981	1982	1983	1984	1985	1986	1987 (Est.)
Turkey*								
Debt (US$ billion)	16.3	16.9	17.6	18.2	20.8	25.5	32.5	37.3
Medium/long-term	13.8	14.7	15.9	16.0	17.6	20.8	25.6	28.8
Short-term	2.5	2.2	1.8	2.3	3.2	4.8	6.9	8.5
Debt/GNP	28.0	28.6	32.8	35.6	41.5	47.9	55.9	57.6
Debt/exports[†]	284.1	198.3	175.0	192.9	180.5	194.5	260.5	227.2
Current account Surplus/GNP	−5.0	−2.8	−1.6	−3.6	−2.8	−1.9	−2.6	−1.5
Non-interest current account surplus/GNP	−3.9	−0.8	1.2	−0.4	0.4	1.4	1.0	2.2
Countries with recent debt-servicing problems[‡] Debt/GDP	32.5	37.6	43.7	47.6	47.6	49.1	51.3	53.9
Debt/exports[†]	151.5	186.1	240.9	254.6	246.3	266.8	309.5	313.4
Current account surplus/GNP	−3.6	−5.9	−5.5	−2.0	−0.9	−0.5	−1.8	−1.5
Non-interest current account surplus/GDP	−0.5	−1.7	−0.5	2.8	4.1	4.2	2.5	2.6

[*] For comparability the debt figures reported here for Turkey refer to gross debt. In the rest of the chapter net debt is used.

[†] The debt-export ratio refers to year-end debt to exports of goods and services (and for Turkey also workers' remittances) during the year.

[‡] Countries with recent debt-servicing problems are defined as those which incurred external payment arrears in 1985 or rescheduled their debt during the period from end-1983 to end-1986.

SOURCES Undersecretariat of Treasury and Foreign Trade, Central Bank; *World Economic Outlook* (IMF, October 1987).

of empirical estimation of the behavioral equations in that model are presented in the latter part of Section II, which first deals with the impact of real interest rates on private consumption; a subsequent subsection links private investment to capacity utilization, real interest rates, the volume of credit to the private sector and variables relating to the size and composition of public investment expenditure. At the very end of Section II we establish econometrically the link between private and public investment and the growth rate of real GNP.

This model is then used in Section III to assess the public sector's role in Turkey's macroeconomic achievements since 1980. In Section IV the focus is on the future. We first assess Turkey's leeway on the current account if creditworthiness is to be maintained. We use a pragmatic approach due to Daniel Cohen (1985, 1988) to quantify this issue. The model developed in this paper is then used to explore whether sustainability restrictions on fiscal deficits and the creditworthiness constraints on external borrowing leave enough room for satisfactory output growth. Finally we highlight the importance of continued access to foreign financing by presenting scenarios where such access is denied.

II EXTERNAL DEBT, INVESTMENT AND THE PUBLIC SECTOR

Analytical Framework

The model presented here has been designed to shed light on the key question raised in this paper: can the objectives of external balance and satisfactory output growth be reconciled? Several channels are highlighted. First of all, the relation between interest rates, fiscal deficits and external balance. High real interest rates, by depressing private investment and consumption, create more room for fiscal deficits for any given external balance target. At the same time, high real interest rates complicate fiscal management, since they raise the cost of servicing the domestic public debt. Crucial parameters are the sensitivity of private savings and investment with respect to the real interest rate; these receive detailed econometric attention later in this Section.

A second channel relies not so much on the interrelation between aggregate fiscal deficits, real interest rates and the current account, but more on the composition of government expenditure programs. A substantial part of total investment in Turkey is undertaken by the public sector. As a consequence, the allocation of government expenditure over consumption and investment is an important determinant of output growth for any given expenditure level. But not all public sector investment projects are as effective in promoting growth. The model highlights, in addition to the amount of public investment, the importance of its composition. Evidence is provided that public investment in manufacturing actually depresses private investment. Thus the composition of public investment is an important determinant of its impact on private investment and hence on aggregate investment and output growth.

Final channels incorporated in the model are the effect of capacity utilization on private investment and, in addition to the impact of investment on output growth, a reverse impact of output growth on private savings and investment. These channels have been important in the past few years as Section III demonstrates and are therefore incorporated in the model.

Real Interest Rates, Fiscal Policy, Output Growth: The Way the Model Works

If there is imperfect arbitrage between foreign and domestic interest-bearing assets, either because of imperfect substitutability or explicit capital controls, the link between foreign and domestic interest rates is severed. External targets can then be maintained even if fiscal deficits increase, as interest rate policy can be used to generate a matching higher net private savings surplus. If, alternatively, arbitrage causes domestic interest rates to closely follow foreign interest rates corrected for exchange rate depreciation, macroeconomic policy faces much tighter constraints: interest rates can no longer be used as an instrument.[3]

As long as domestic interest rates are not linked to foreign interest rates (that is foreign rates plus exchange rate depreciation) there is an additional degree of freedom in macroeconomic policy. Then changes in domestic real interest rates can resolve potential discrepancies between fiscal deficits and external targets through their impact on the net private savings surplus.[4] In the process, private investment and hence output growth will be affected. This is an important link between fiscal policy and output growth. The relevant identity is:

$$CAS = FS + NPS(r) \qquad (1)$$
$$= FS + Sp(r) - Ip(r)$$

where CAS is the current account surplus, FS is the fiscal surplus, Sp is private savings, Ip is private investment and r is the real interest rate.

The analysis so far is not enough to tie the link between fiscal deficits and output growth. It has focused on the impact of the fiscal deficit on private investment; output growth depends on total investment, however, not just on private investment. Clearly, the impact of changes in fiscal deficits on output growth depends on whether the underlying adjustment is made out of public investment or out of public consumption. The model therefore distinguishes between public consumption and investment. Output growth depends on the sum of public and private investment, a relation that is verified econometrically below:

$$\log(y) - \log(y(-1)) = fct((Ig+Ipr(r))/y). \qquad (2)$$

For given public sector investment and fiscal deficit, equations (1) and (2) yield a negative link between output growth and improvements on the current account of the balance of payments. This can also be read from Figure 7.1. In the bottom quadrant, we represent graphically the relation summarized in equation (2). The top quadrant shows how higher real interest rates are necessary for a current account improvement for given fiscal deficit; the bottom quadrant then shows how these higher real interest rates slow down output growth through their impact on private

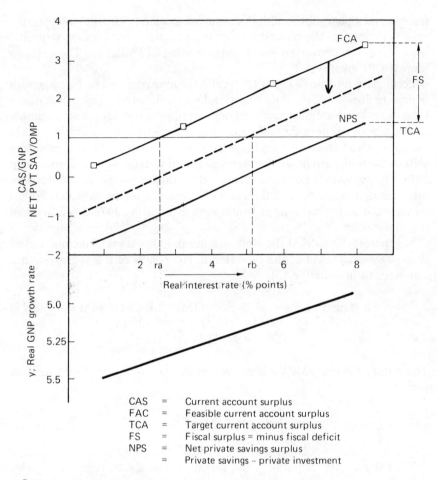

CAS = Current account surplus
FAC = Feasible current account surplus
TCA = Target current account surplus
FS = Fiscal surplus = minus fiscal deficit
NPS = Net private savings surplus
= Private savings – private investment

SOURCE   Authors' calculations.

FIGURE 7.1   *Fiscal Deficits, Real Output Growth and Real Interest Rates for Given Current Account Targets*

investment. This conflict between external balance and output growth is of course at the core of the macroeconomic problems caused by the debt crisis.

Application to Turkey: Empirical Preliminaries

This Section presents the estimation of the parameters in the behavioral equations of the model.

Private Consumption

Private consumption (CONKP, nominal consumption deflated by the CPI) depends on the real interest rate, the real exchange rate, inflation, current

income and a proxy for wealth ('permanent income'). The real interest rate
used is defined as the highest (compound) interest rate on time deposits,
net of taxes and converted into a real rate using CPI inflation. The inflation
term is CPI inflation.

Permanent income (a proxy for wealth) is approximated by trend growth
in private disposable income. This trend is calculated by a regression of the
logarithm of private disposable income on time, a constant, and a dummy
to distinguish the period before and after 1978. The dummy variable takes
the value zero before 1978 and one from 1978 onwards. It captures a level
shift in the time path of real income associated with the severe downturn in
1978. Output growth has since recovered to roughly similar growth rates as
the ones that characterized the pre-1978 period. Clearly, no catch-up has
taken place with what output would have been if the 1978 downturn had
not taken place.

We therefore modeled the shift as a break in the level of income rather
than in the coefficient of the time trend. The results of this regression are
summarized in equation (3):

$$\log(\text{PERYP}) = 4.47 + .058\ \text{TIME} - 0.10\ \text{DUMMY} \qquad (3)$$
$$(16.4)\quad (13.5)\qquad\qquad (2.01)$$
$$R2 = 0.97,\ D.W.=0.47$$

Temporary income TMPYP is defined as the excess of actual income over
trend:

$$\text{TMPYP} = \text{YP/PERYP}$$

YP is actual disposable income and PERYP the permanent component.

With these data definitions, the private consumption regression yields
the following estimates:

$$\log(\text{CONKP}) = -1.54 - 0.82\ \text{LOG}(1 + \text{RDEP}) - 0.77\ \text{CPIinf} \quad (4)$$
$$(1.92)\quad (2.12)\qquad\qquad\qquad (2.37)$$
$$+ 1.35\ \log(\text{PERYP}) - 0.19\ \log(\text{TMPYP})$$
$$(7.91)\qquad\qquad (0.32)$$
$$R2 = 0.96,\ DW = 1.72,\ \text{Sample Period 1970–86, TSLS}$$

The impact of the real after-tax deposit rate RDEP on private consumption is negative and significantly so. In addition, private consumption
depends negatively on inflation, with an almost equal coefficient. This has
also been found in consumption analysis for some developed countries: in
particular see Bean (1986) for similar evidence on the UK. Finally, the
effect of permanent income on consumption is strongly positive, as expected, with a coefficient close to one. The coefficient on temporary

income is low and insignificant (a t-statistic of only 0.32; significance requires a value of 2 or more). All these results fit in well with accepted theory of consumer behavior.

Private Investment

The investment equation is based on an eclectic 'accelerator' model. Private fixed capital formation (that is investment net of stock changes) depends on, first of all, anticipated future sales, proxied here by lagged output ($Y(-1)$; clearly data on current output are not available when investment decisions are taken). In addition, the real after-tax lending rate (RLEND), converted into a real rate using the GNP deflator, is used to capture the cost of funds.[5] However, prevalence of credit rationing and the use of credit subsidies suggest that quantities, in addition to prices, are likely to be important. This effect was captured, in an admittedly crude way, by including the ratio of credit to the private sector over output (CRD/Y) as an explanatory variable. In addition, capacity utilization in manufacturing (CPUTL) was included as a proxy of the ratio between expected sales and output capacity. The final explanatory variable is less conventional. The (lagged) share of infrastructure investment in total public investment, SHINF, is included in an attempt to assess the impact of allocation of public sector investment on private investment. The econometric results are remarkably good:

$$\log(\text{INFKP}) = -15.68 + 1.24 \log(\text{CRD/Y}) \qquad (5)$$
$$(4.20) \qquad (2.52)$$
$$+ 1.21 \log(Y(-1)) - 1.69 \log(1 + \text{LREND})$$
$$(6.49) \qquad\qquad (4.17)$$
$$+ 1.45 \log(\text{CPUTL}) + 0.35 \log(\text{SHINF}(-3))$$
$$(1.40) \qquad\qquad (1.15)$$

$R2 = 0.79$, $DW = 1.66$, Sample Period 1970–86, TSLS

The regression results show that both the quantity and the cost of credit have a strong and significant impact on private sector capital formation. The real after-tax lending rate has a negative sign and is significantly different from zero: the t-statistic equals 4.17. The credit variable too is highly significant. The precision of the coefficients on capacity utilization and on the share of infrastructure investment in total public sector investment is low, although they have the right sign.

Investment and Output Growth

The relation between investment and output growth is based on a simple production function approach. First, a measure of capacity output was derived by combining actual real GNP with the measure of capacity utilization used in the investment equation:

$$YKA = Y/CPUTL$$

This is an imperfect measure, since CPUTL applies to manufacturing only, and it is used to derive aggregate capacity, not just capacity output in manufacturing. No better measure was available however. Also, reliable data on labor use are not available. So in the end the equation estimated simply links capacity output to last period's capacity output and the share of total fixed capital formation in GNP:

$$\log(YKA) = 0.016 + 0.45\ (INFT(-1)/Y(-1)) \qquad (6a)$$
$$(0.20)\ (1.20)$$
$$+ 0.94\ \log(YKA(-1))$$
$$(28.3)$$
$$R2 = 0.98,\ DW = 1.67,\ \text{Sample Period 1970–86, OLS}$$

This can be rewritten to yield an expression linking investment shares with the rate of output growth:

$$\log(YKA) - \log(YKA(-1)) = \qquad (6b)$$
$$0.016 + 0.45\ (INFT(-1)/Y(-1))$$
$$(0.20)\ \ (1.20)$$
$$- 0.06\ \log(YKA(-1))$$
$$(1.70)$$

In the actual model used for the simulations, (6b) was used, with the coefficient for $\log(YKA(-1))$ on the right-hand-side set equal to zero.

III   FISCAL POLICY, PRIVATE SAVINGS AND INVESTMENT AND OUTPUT GROWTH

The Role of Fiscal Policy: an Outline

The introduction argued that Turkey has adopted a growth-oriented debt strategy rather than rely on sustained high surpluses on the non-interest current account to keep the debt-output ratio on check. The key factor determining success or failure of such a strategy is an internal adjustment program that relies sufficiently on reduced consumption rather than re- duced investment to generate the internal surplus that is required. If consumption does not fall, either external targets or output growth will need to be sacrificed; the former if investment is not reduced and the latter

TABLE 7.2 *Key Macroeconomic Indicators (percentage share of GNP)*

	1980	1981	1982	1983	1984	1985	1986	(1st Est.) 1987	(Rev. Est.) 1987
Total consumption	84.1	82.0	81.8	83.7	83.3	80.9	77.7	77.9	76.5
Private	71.9	71.3	71.1	73.5	74.5	72.5	68.9	68.9	67.0
Government	12.3	10.7	10.8	10.2	8.8	8.4	8.8	9.0	9.5
Fixed investment	19.5	18.9	18.9	18.8	18.0	20.1	23.6	23.7	24.9
Public	10.9	11.7	11.5	10.6	9.9	11.7	14.0	14.0	13.6
Private	8.5	7.2	7.3	8.2	8.2	8.4	9.6	9.7	11.3
Stock changes	1.9	2.6	1.5	1.1	1.4	0.9	1.4	0.1	0.1
Public	0.5	1.5	0.5	–0.4	0.0	–0.2	0.1	–0.5	–0.1
Private	1.4	1.1	1.0	1.5	1.4	1.0	1.3	0.6	0.2
Current account	–5.5	–3.5	–2.2	–3.5	–2.8	–1.9	–2.6	–1.7	–1.5
Imports of goods and NFS	15.0	16.5	17.9	19.6	23.1	23.5	20.7	21.0	n.a.
Exports of goods and NFS	7.2	10.9	14.5	15.7	19.5	20.7	18.0	19.3	n.a.
Memo items (in %)									
GNP growth	–1.1	4.1	4.5	3.3	5.9	5.1	8.0	6.8	
Inflation rate: CPI (year average)	110.9	36.8	23.1	31.4	48.4	45.0	34.6	38.8	

SOURCE SPO; SIS.

if it is. In this Section, it is shown how Turkey has by and large succeeded in doing so, and how fiscal policy has contributed to this achievement. However, the analysis also brings out that continued success of this strategy is being jeopardized by a deterioration in fiscal deficits and the ensuing reliance on the issue of high cost internal debt.

An obvious part of the adjustment process is to shift government expenditure away from consumption towards investment. Table 7.2 shows the extent to which this was achieved in Turkey. As a consequence, the public sector savings rate (revenue minus current expenditure as a percentage of revenue) increased substantially over the period, in fact to levels not reached at any time since 1967 (see Figure 7.2). However, not much is gained by such a strategy if, in the end, additional public sector investment simply substitutes for reduced private sector investment. This was probably avoided in Turkey; private investment did not decline as a share of GNP between 1981 and 1985, and actually increased after that (Table 7.2).[6] It is now in fact slightly higher than the level it reached during the period 1972–80.

Finally, it is possible that government consumption cannot be cut sufficiently to make room for public sector investment and still reduce the fiscal deficit sufficiently to effect the external transfer. Table 7.2 shows that

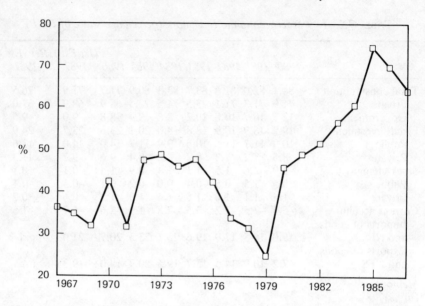

FIGURE 7.2   *Public Savings Rate: 1967–87. Share of Public Disposable Income*
SOURCE   SPO.

government consumption was reduced substantially from 12.3 per cent in 1980 to 8.4 per cent in 1985 and 8.8 per cent in 1986; but public sector investment rose by almost the same amount. If, in that case, private investment should not suffer, sufficient private savings need to be generated to complete the internal adjustment effort. However, if interest rate policy is used to stimulate private saving, private investment will be reduced; hence the need to complement such a strategy with measures to promote private investment to ensure that the adjustment effort comes mostly out of private consumption rather than out of private investment.

   In Turkey, fiscal deficits and the deficit on current account of the balance of payments have more or less moved in tandem during most of the 1970s and 1980s. This pattern was broken in 1986–87, however, when fiscal deficits deteriorated, but the current account deficit improved. At the same time, real interest rates went up significantly. This suggests that high real interest rates were necessary to induce a higher net private savings surplus; this prevented the increase in fiscal deficits from spilling over into the current account. The importance of this mechanism for Turkey is demonstrated below. If high real interest rates created the room for higher fiscal deficits without a matching current account deterioration, how was Turkish output growth so high? High real interest rates presumably slow down at least private investment, thus slowing down output growth. To understand why this did not happen in Turkey, one needs to analyze more closely various mechanisms other than real interest rates and the size of fiscal deficits through which fiscal policy influences private investment.

Fiscal Policy and Capital Accumulation: Crowding-Out or Crowding-In?

Aggregate investment has recovered from the sharp cutbacks made during the macroeconomic turmoil of the 1978–80 period. The share of total fixed investment in GNP is currently (1986–87) 5.8 percentage points above the average over the five-year period between 1967 and 1971.

By far the largest part of the increase in investment is due to higher public sector investment. The ratio of public sector capital expenditure to GNP increased from 11 per cent to 14 per cent between 1980 and 1987. This shift in government expenditure towards investment is the main explanation of why output growth has not suffered from the mismatch between fiscal deficits and external targets and the resulting high real interest rates.

Private fixed investment, while increasing from the low point (7.2 per cent of GNP) reached in 1981, has not recovered significantly beyond the levels reached in the early 1970s. Empirical analysis shows that the high real interest rates have been an important factor behind the somewhat lackluster performance of private sector investment.[7]

Several factors have worked against this negative impact of high real interest rates, and explain why private investment has in fact been rising at all over the past five or six years. First, the Government has consistently provided generous investment incentives over this period. Second, except for 1984, the growth rate of credit extended to the private sector has consistently exceeded the rate of output growth, in most years by a substantial margin. Third, capacity utilization increased over this period. The final factor is more directly related to fiscal policy. At issue is the composition of public investment. Since 1980, the Government has shifted the composition of its public sector investment program heavily towards sectors where it complements rather than competes with private sector investment.

A counterfactual analysis of private investment (see Chhibber and van Wijnbergen, 1988) shows that the negative impact of the high rates of interest dominated early on, but that their negative impact was gradually offset by the other measures discussed. From 1984 onwards, the impact of the positive measures more than offset the negative impact of real interest rates. By 1986, the net positive impact of the measures mentioned exceeded the negative impact of the high real interest rates by a full percentage point of GNP. This analysis therefore supports the view that the overall impact of fiscal policy and improved capacity utilization on private investment has been positive, the high real lending rates notwithstanding.

Real Interest Rates, Income Growth and Private Savings

Public investment increased substantially, while other measures helped to avoid the potential negative impact on private investment over the 1980–87 period. At the same time, fiscal deficits deteriorated, but the deficit on the current account of the balance of payments was in fact reduced as a percentage of GNP. What made these apparently disparate developments consistent was a substantial increase in private savings over the 1980–87 period. Private saving reached a low point in 1983 at 5.9 per cent of GNP, down from 7.8 per cent in 1980; but it has been improving since 1985, to reach 11 per cent in 1987. This section explores some of the reasons behind this improved savings performance and assesses its likely continuation in the future.

Rising real rates of interest have been a major contributing factor to the increase in private savings. The after-tax real rate of interest on one-year time deposits has risen from −3.5 per cent in 1980 to almost 6 per cent in 1984, and up to about 13 per cent in 1987.

The sharp rise in interest rates since 1985 explains a substantial part of the even sharper rise in the private savings rate that has taken place since 1985. The econometric results summarized in Section II suggest that a 2.5 percentage point rise in the real interest rate increases NPS by 1 percentage point of GNP. Without the increase in real rates that took place since 1985, the econometric analysis suggests that savings would have been lower by around 0.8 per cent of GNP in 1985 and by almost 2 percentage points of GNP by the end of 1986.

While interest rate developments explain much of the improved savings performance, the rise in savings since 1985 cannot be fully attributed to the increase in real interest rates that also took place since then. The econometric analysis suggests that of the 5 percentage points increase since 1985, only 2 percentage points can be attributed to the simultaneous rise in the real rate of interest.

Another important factor, especially in the past couple of years, may be that the higher than average growth in the economy and in private disposable income is perceived as only a temporary increase in income. In Section II it is shown that the propensity to consume out of temporary income is negligible. The perception that an increase in disposable income is temporary, rather than permanent, would therefore have a smaller effect on consumption, or alternatively, a larger effect on savings. This factor alone would account for an increase in the savings of about 1.5 — 2.0 percentage points in 1986 and 1987.

Fiscal Deficits, Interest Rates and Growth

Large fiscal deficits have not prevented a satisfactory current account performance. The price for this has been the need to maintain increasingly high real rates of interest. The empirical analysis presented shows that in Turkey such a policy is effective by restraining private consumption, and, to a lesser extent, private investment expenditure. Deleterious effects on output growth have until now been avoided. The analysis in the preceding sections identified high public sector investment as the most important explanation of why output growth did not slow down. This section uses the econometric model of Section II to quantify this link.

Figure 7.3 shows the results of simulation runs made with that econometric model. Interest rates were varied, but fiscal deficits were adjusted so as to maintain external balance targets. First, the fiscal cutbacks necessary to sustain external balance as interest rates are lowered were assumed to come entirely from government consumption. Public sector investment remains constant by assumption. The figure shows that a five percentage cut in interest rates will cause a drop in the private sector's surplus of savings over investment of 2.1 percentage points of GNP (see Figure 7.3A, upper right).[8] A substantial part of the decline in net private savings comes from increased investment by the private sector in response to the lower real interest rates. Since public sector investment was fixed by assumption, output growth goes up, by 0.5 percentage point of GNP on average over the five-year period the model was run (see Figure 7.3A, upper left; the base run simulates the period between 1981 and 1986).

The results are very different when the fiscal cutbacks are assumed, perhaps more realistically, to come also from public sector investment rather than from consumption. Assuming that all government expenditure would be cut back proportionally implies that 60 per cent of the cut comes from reductions in the public sector's investment program. The results are summarized in Figure 7.3B. Now while the lower interest rates stimulate private investment, the cut in public sector investment more than offsets this: as a result, output growth actually declines by an average 0.5 percentage point of GNP over the five-year simulation period. Shifting from no cut in public sector investment to letting 60 per cent of the fiscal adjustment come out of cutbacks in public investment therefore causes a full percentage point drop in GNP growth for the five years over which the model was run.

There is, moreover, a vicious circle aspect to this policy experiment. Cutting public sector investment reduces output growth, which in turn will lead to less of a private sector's savings surplus. As a consequence, fiscal deficits and hence public sector investment need to be cut further to maintain external balance, growth slows down more and so on. As a result, a five percentage points cutback in real interest rates requires a cut in the fiscal deficit of 2.1 percentage points of GNP if external balance is to be maintained through reduced government consumption. However, with 60 per cent of the cuts coming from public sector investment, deficits need to be reduced by 2.8 percentage points of GNP, a full 0.7 percentage point of GNP more.

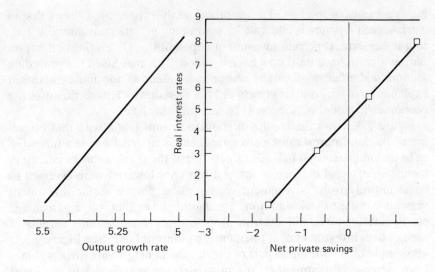

FIGURE 7.3A   *Entire Fiscal Cut from Government Consumption*

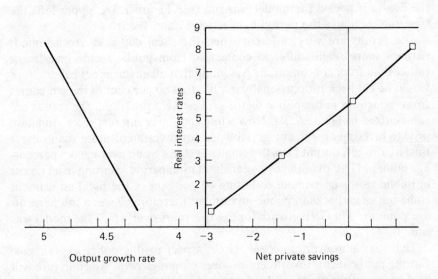

FIGURE 7.3B   *60 Percent of Fiscal Cut from Public Sector Investment*
SOURCE   Based on results generated by the econometric model.

FIGURE 7.3   *The Effect of Changes in Fiscal Deficit on Interest Rates and Output Growth*

The arguments presented here do not imply a blanket endorsement of ever-increasing public sector investment; public sector investment of course does come at a cost.[9] They do highlight, however, that public sector investment has played an important role in Turkey's strong growth performance over the last few years. Moreover, they show that stabilization programs relying on reductions in public sector investment will have high and permanent negative output effects through the mechanisms demonstrated. These are in addition to any output effects that may arise because of short-run macroeconomic problems, which are not covered here.

IV   OUTPUT GROWTH AND EXTERNAL BALANCE: CAN THEY BE RECONCILED?

Looking Ahead: External Constraints, Fiscal Consistency and the Prospects for Sustainable Growth

The main issue now is, of course, can the successful performance of the past six years be repeated in the future? Can Turkey sustain a reasonable growth rate within the limits set by creditworthiness constraints? If so, what should the public sector do to bring this about?

Exports, Output Growth and External Borrowing

Creditworthiness and Foreign Debt

Assessing the precise limits imposed by creditworthiness constraints is difficult for several reasons. First of all, while debt-export ratios are important, they are a biased estimate of the ratio of a country's debt to its output of tradable goods. Some domestically produced tradables are likely to be sold at home rather than exported. So the true measure lies somewhere between the debt-output ratio (which also counts non-tradables) and the debt-export ratio, which excludes tradable goods produced and sold at home. This section follows an approach pioneered by D. Cohen (1985, 1988). This approach chooses the ratio in between the debt-output (D/Y) and the debt-export (D/X) ratios in such a way that there are no incentives to overvalue or undervalue the exchange rate simply to mechanically improve creditworthiness indicators. The precise way in which this ratio is derived is presented in Cohen (1988); it is influenced by the price elasticity of export demand and output supply. The outcome for Turkey places a 60 per cent weight on debt-export ratio and a 40 per cent weight on the ratio of debt to GNP. This construct is referred to as the debt-resource ratio, D/R.

A second, more fundamental problem, involves not so much the choice of any particular creditworthiness indicator, but how to assess whether the value of the indicator chosen is too high or not (high values indicate low creditworthiness). An indicator is too high (creditworthiness too low) if at that value the burden of servicing the debt exceeds the likely penalty on non-compliance to repayment terms. The problem with this definition is that nobody really knows how high that penalty is. This section follows Cohen in a very simple but forceful approach to this issue. The cost of default is not known, but if a country has not defaulted at the current value of its debt-resource ratio, that value is, by implication, not yet too high. Otherwise the country would have defaulted already. A cautious borrowing policy then is a policy that will prevent a rising debt-resource ratio.

One important caveat: it does not follow from this analysis that a borrowing policy designed to rapidly lower debt-resource ratios is necessarily a good idea. While it is true that lower debt-resource ratios indicate higher creditworthiness, the transitional costs of reaching that lower ratio clearly raise the cost of servicing the existing debt. Since creditworthiness involves comparing the cost of default with the cost of servicing the current debt, such a strategy, which has been imposed on many high-debt countries, would lower rather than increase current creditworthiness.

Sustainable Current Account Deficits

How much foreign borrowing is compatible with maintaining the debt-resource ratio at its current value, and hence maintaining the level of creditworthiness? Since the debt-resource ratio is a weighted average of the debt-output and the debt-export ratio, it will depend on the growth rate of the borrowing country and of its trading partners. The growth rate of its trading partners is one of the determinants of a country's likely export growth. The other determinant is the elasticity of demand for the borrowing country's exports with respect to income in the countries to which it exports.

Empirical analysis[10] suggests that the income elasticity of demand for Turkey's exports is high: 1.6 with respect to the OECD and 4 with respect to the oil-exporting countries in the Gulf region. This results in a weighted value of 2. Thus, if the weighted output in Turkey's trading partners[11] grows by 4 per cent, Turkey's exports are likely to grow by 8 per cent. The real exchange rate has no impact on the amount of feasible borrowing, as a consequence of its construction.

The results are presented in Table 7.3. The table gives the maximum increase in foreign debt that will avoid a rising debt-resource ratio, for different growth rates at home and abroad. The table lists increases in debt and hence gives the feasible current account deficit. The table lists on its vertical axis various alternative growth rates for Turkey, ranging from 3 to 7 per cent. On the horizontal axis, the top row lists potential growth rates

TABLE 7.3   *Allowable Foreign Borrowing: Sustainable Current Account Deficits (per cent of GNP)*

Output growth of Turkey	Potential Growth Rates for Turkey's Trading Partners					
%	0	1	2	3	3.5	4
3	1.12	1.21	1.29	1.38	1.42	1.46
4	1.49	1.58	1.66	1.75	1.79	1.83
5	1.87	1.95	2.04	2.12	2.17	2.21
6	2.24	2.33	2.41	2.50	2.54	2.58
7	2.61	2.70	2.78	2.87	2.91	2.95

SOURCE   Authors' calculations.

for Turkey's trading partners, aggregated using their respective shares in Turkey's exports. The numbers indicate, as expected, that lower growth rates, whether at home or abroad, allow for less debt accumulation. In fact for zero growth rate at home and abroad, the formula indicates that no further borrowing is possible (this possibility is outside the range of the table). Raising the domestic output growth rate by 4 percentage points allows an extra current account deficit of 1.5 per cent of GNP for given foreign output growth rate. A slump abroad lowers borrowing potential: if growth in trading partner countries falls from, say, 4 per cent to zero, the amount of feasible debt accumulation goes down by 0.3 percentage points of GNP.

In Section IV it is argued that a 6 per cent output growth rate is feasible for Turkey if some policy adjustments are implemented. Also, the IMF and the World Bank project growth rates in the world economy that yield a combined weighted growth rate for Turkey's trading partners of 3.5 per cent for the next five years. The table suggests that this implies a feasible current account deficit of 2.5 per cent of GNP for Turkey. This is about the same level as in 1986 (2.6 per cent of GNP) and substantially larger than the current account deficit of 1987. The consequences of alternative levels are pursued at the end of Section IV.

Macroeconomic Consistency, Foreign Borrowing and the Public Sector Deficit

Macroeconomic consistency requires more than keeping external deficits within the limits set by creditworthiness. Domestic output growth, inflation targets and internal debt management all have implications for the financing of public expenditure. In van Wijnbergen, Anand and Rocha (1988) a quantitative framework was developed to derive what these targets imply for the size of the financeable deficit. This was defined as the deficit that does not require more financing than is compatible with sustainable external borrowing, existing targets for inflation and output growth, and a sustainable internal debt policy.[12] This Section explores the sensitivity of the outcome of that exercise to the assumptions made on debt management and output growth.

In the 'base case' derived in the aforementioned paper, a number of assumptions were made about what can roughly be summarized as debt management. Internal debt issue was targeted at maintaining a constant debt-output ratio; external debt issue at maintaining a constant debt-resource ratio, in line with the analysis presented in the last part; finally, the assumption of a constant real exchange rate from 1988 onwards precluded any capital losses on foreign debt. All this adds up to a required deficit reduction of 1.2 per cent of GNP compared to the deficit the government ran in 1986, if at least a target of 20 per cent inflation is to be met.[13] Changes in these assumptions, in particular concerning debt management and output growth, are discussed in this Section.

Fiscal Implications of Debt Management

What would have happened if Turkey had not followed its policy of a relaxed external deficit and only moderate internal debt issue? In particular, what are the fiscal consequences of a debt substitution policy followed in many debtor countries? Many of them in effect paid off relatively cheap external debt from revenue raised by issuing much more expensive domestic debt.

Assume that Turkey had not increased its external debt at all between 1980 and 1986, other than what was caused by capital losses due to exchange rate depreciation, but instead had issued internal debt. In Anand, Chhibber, Rocha and van Wijnbergen (1988) it was shown that after correction for cross-currency exchange rate fluctuations and real depreciation of the TL, Turkey's debt-output ratio went up by only 13.8 percentage points of GNP. The rest was due to capital losses. What would have happened if Turkey, instead of increasing its external debt-output ratio by 13.8 per cent of GNP, had issued an equivalent amount of internal debt instead?

First the results of a mechanical debt swap: a one-off sale of domestic debt to retire an equivalent amount of external debt. This effectively amounts to a debt-buy-back scheme. This experiment considers only the budgetary consequences of changing one type of debt instrument for another. It does not consider the transfer problem associated with effecting any transfer of resources to foreigners; this issue is taken up below.

Such a scheme becomes problematic when domestic real interest rates are substantially higher than the average real interest cost of foreign debt. In that case the budgetary situation deteriorates. This would also be an issue in Turkey: over the 1988–92 period, real rates at home are projected to be 6 percentage points above the average real cost of foreign debt. As a consequence, the increased interest burden caused by such a debt swap would raise the actual fiscal deficit by 0.8 per cent of GNP in each subsequent year, and the required deficit reduction for consistency with 20 per cent inflation rises to 2.1 per cent of GNP, up from 1.2 per cent of GNP in the base case. Alternatively, the equilibrium inflation rate would jump to 85 per cent per year, up from 50 per cent, if no fiscal adjustment would be undertaken.

A straight asset swap was, however, not the form in which this debt substitution was implemented in most high-debt countries. In order to effect the implied transfer to foreigners, the government needs to find a way to increase either its own surplus or the net private savings surplus by a matching amount. Typically, the domestic counterpart of the increased external transfer was a gradual increase in domestic debt issue, absorbed through an increase in the private net savings surplus. This in turn required higher real interest rates. Such a strategy would be much worse from a budgetary point of view. The reason is that this scheme would in fact raise the cost of the internal debt beyond its already high level and thus worsen the impact on the budget further. Assume that such a debt substitution strategy would be implemented over the next five years, the time horizon taken in this chapter. Since over that period real interest cost of foreign debt is assumed to equal the real output growth rate, the entire adjustment would need to come out of the non-interest current account. To achieve the target reduction of 13.8 percentage points of GNP over a five-year period thus requires a substantial positive shift (2.7 per cent of GNP, 13.8 divided by 5) in the non-interest current account in each year.

Inducing an increase in net private savings requires a rise in the real interest rate. The empirical analysis in Section II suggests that such a large increase requires an increase in domestic real interest rates of almost 7 percentage points. This would not only raise the servicing costs of the additional domestic debt created during such a policy, but also the cost of debt incurred earlier as it gets refinanced. This is important because by now most of Turkey's internal debt has a short maturity (by December 1986, 76 per cent of the internal debt had a maturity of one year or less). The impact on the budget would be large. To sustain consistency with a 20 per cent inflation target after such a debt substitution policy would now require a reduction in the fiscal deficit of 3.6 per cent of GNP. This is almost double the adjustment necessary after a straight asset swap. The budget deterioration would in fact be so large, that covering it through monetization would no longer be feasible. Increased debt issue would be even worse because of the high real interest rates. Finally, external debt would not be available by the very design of the scheme, which was to reduce external debt. A fiscal cutback would thus be unavoidable and would have to be substantial. This raises the issue of whether output growth could in fact be sustained. This is explored further below, but the numbers presented here should already indicate that it is highly unlikely.

Fiscal Implications of Different Rates of Output Growth

Higher growth allows more internal debt issue, since the target is a constant debt-output ratio; it will also increase demand for real money balances by both banks and the private sector, thus increasing the scope for revenue from monetization for any given inflation rate. Hence more growth allows a larger deficit and less need for fiscal adjustment. This is at the core of the conflict between stabilization policy and growth: if stabilization policies cut output growth, further fiscal adjustment is needed for macroeconomic consistency. This adjusment may, in turn, slow growth further.

Table 7.4 indicates the extent of the trade-off. A 4 per cent growth target instead of 6 per cent reduces financing room by about one percentage point of GNP: for a 20 per cent inflation target, the required deficit reduction for consistency with a 20 per cent inflation target (RDR) becomes 2.3 per cent of GNP at per 4 per cent real growth instead of 1.2 per cent at 6 per cent real output growth. A major recession brings it out more starkly: a sustained period of only 2 per cent growth in real income would raise the required adjustment necessary for consistency with a 20 per cent inflation target to no less than 3.3 per cent of GNP. Numbers this large raise the specter of self-fulfilling prophecies: a deficit reduction this severe could easily validate the low growth rate on which it was premised.

External Borrowing and the Potential for Continued Output Growth

The analysis has until now focused on the revenue the government can expect from various sources of financing given its macroeconomic targets. Reducing the fiscal deficit to what is financeable given those macroeconomic targets makes sure that the fiscal policy is at least sustainable. If this adjustment is made, achieving the stated macroeconomic targets will not be jeopardized by fiscal crises, high inflation or escalating payments. However, it does not guarantee that those macroeconomic targets can or will be achieved; only that the fiscal deficit is not inconsistent with them. Whether the targets can be achieved is taken up in this Section.

The central question is whether external restraint and consistency requirements for fiscal deficits leave enough room for public and private investment and satisfactory output growth. Can external balance and growth be reconciled, or is there an inherent conflict between these two objectives? This Section provides projections generated with the models developed in Section II and in van Wijnbergen, Anand and Rocha (1988) that should allow an answer to this question.

TABLE 7.4 *Fiscal Implications of Output Growth*

Output Growth (per cent)	Required Deficit Reduction for a 20% Inflation Target (per cent of GNP)
2	3.3
4	2.2
6	1.2

The Base Case: Creditworthiness and Sustainable Growth

The projections incorporate the restrictions on the current account that creditworthiness implies (see Section IV). Thus, the external borrowing limit is 2.5 per cent of GNP. This is in fact a more liberal target than the low current account deficit of 1987. Besides more leeway on the external account, it is also assumed that the fiscal corrections necessary for macro-economic consistency will in fact be implemented. This means a reduction in the fiscal deficit of 1.2 per cent of GNP with respect to 1986. Compared with 1987 the cut in the fiscal deficit should be substantially larger. Public sector investment was assumed constant in real terms in 1987, and, by assumption, grows at 5 per cent in real terms thereafter. This implies a slow gradual reduction in the share of public sector investment in GNP.

A lower fiscal deficit combined with a more liberal current account target allows for a fall in the surplus of private savings over investment. This is exactly what lower real interest rates will bring about. The decline in the fiscal deficit, if implemented, allows a gradual fall in real interest rates of 3 percentage points over the period 1988–92. Private saving falls from the high levels achieved in 1987 to a still respectable 11.8 per cent of GNP at the end of the period. Lower real interest rates also lead to an increase in the share of private investment in GNP, which rises by one percentage point of GNP over the period. This is just enough to offset the assumed gradual slowdown in the rise of public sector investment. As a result private investment increases its share in total investment by 4 percentage points. The share of total capital formation remains at around 20 to 21 per cent of GNP. The most important result follows from this: output growth is maintained at an average growth rate of 6 per cent throughout the period. This is a respectable growth rate by comparison to the 1980–85 average, although below the performance in 1986 and 1987. Accelerating inflation and falling inventories strongly suggest, however, that the average growth rate of almost 7.5 per cent over 1986 and 1987 was caused by unsustainable aggregate demand pressure. Continuation of such a high growth rate is therefore probably incompatible with stable macroeconomic performance unless much higher investment rates would bring aggregate supply in line with aggregate demand.

Real interest rates on foreign debt were projected to average 6 per cent over the planning horizon; this implies that with a 6 per cent real growth rate, real interest payments do not by themselves lead to further increases in the debt-output ratio. As a consequence, the ratio of net debt to output stays roughly constant at around 53 per cent of GNP. This suggests the main conclusion: if fiscal restraint measures are implemented to restore consistency with other macroeconomic targets, sustained output growth is possible without escalating foreign debt.

Four caveats should be stressed at this point. First of all, the scenario depends heavily on the actual implementation of substantial fiscal correction. There is no accurate information on fiscal deficits in 1987 yet, but indications are that the deficit has increased substantially beyond what it was in 1986. The corrective measures necessary for the base case scenario to be feasible are commensurately larger.

Second, the scenario assumes that the bulk of the fiscal correction will come from current expenditure, subsidy cuts or tax increases. Public sector investment was assumed constant in real terms in 1987, and increasing at slightly below the growth rate of the economy after that year (5 per cent instead of 6 per cent). If the fiscal adjustment comes from public sector investment in addition to the small decline with respect to GNP assumed here, growth performance will fall short of the base case projections.

Third, no further real depreciation of the exchange rate is projected beyond 1988. Exports are predicted to grow at 7 per cent in real terms in this case.[14] If instead a policy of real exchange rate depreciation would be followed, the debt-output ratio would increase faster due to the capital losses incurred after a real depreciation.[15]

Fourth, the scenario assumes that the foreign financing necessary to cover a current account deficit of 2.5 per cent of GNP will indeed be forthcoming. This will require additional financing, since Turkey has just entered a period of substantially increased repayment obligations. The implicit assumption is that these can be refinanced, and that additional funds will be available to allow a current account deficit of 2.5 per cent of GNP. Of course, in the current external environment it is conceivable that additional funds cannot be raised. The next Section therefore considers what will happen if this additional financing will in fact not materialize.

What Happens to Growth if Foreign Financing is Cut Back?

The results are dramatically different if a cutback in the current account deficit is imposed. This alternative assumes a zero current account deficit throughout the simulation period.[16] The internal adjusment is brought about by a matching cut in public sector investment. The impact on output growth is severe: by 1992, the growth rate has fallen by two full percentage points. Output growth falls by 1.5 percentage points on average over the five-year period.

Both private savings and investments fall under the impact of slower growth, but savings by much more than investment: the latter declines by 0.5 per cent of GNP at the end of the simulation period, while private saving falls by 1.8 percentage points of GNP. Net private saving therefore declines by 1.3 per cent of GNP over the simulation period. This has further adverse effects on fiscal policy: to still maintain external balance, a further round of fiscal cutbacks is needed. By the end of the period, fiscal deficits need to be cut back by 4 percentage points of GNP instead of just 2.5, the initial current account cutback. This is a vicious circle many high-debt countries that follow such orthodox policies encounter. Fiscal retrenchment to achieve external balance causes a slump at home, which necessitates more of the same measures that triggered the slump to begin with. By the time this destabilizing process has worked itself out, output growth has declined a full 2 percentage points per year.

The 'stabilization program' does yield benefits on the external account. The debt-output ratio falls, although by less than the cumulative current account cutback: 8.9 percentage points of GNP versus a cumulative current account improvement of 12.7 percentage points. The almost four percentage points shortfall is due to the slowdown in output growth: the fall in output growth reduces the beneficial effects of the current account cutback on the debt-ouput ratio by almost a third.

A second mode of response would be for the public sector to shift the burden of adjustment to the private sector. It could do so by covering the external transfer through increased issue of internal debt instead of by adjusting its fiscal deficit. This would create a situation that is very similar to the second debt-substitution scenario discussed in the last Section. The outcome would be an almost six percentage point increase in real interest rates, which the government would have to match when issuing its own securities. This would rapidly deteriorate the fiscal situation even without much further debt issue because of rising interest payments on existing debt. The analysis in the previous Section demonstrated that the resulting deficit would be too large for financing through monetization. However, debt issue at interest rates so far above the real growth rate of the economy would lead to rapid escalation of debt service obligations.

This scenario is in many ways the worst case scenario: no external funds forthcoming, and a failure of the public sector to adjust to this situation. Macroeconomic stability would be in doubt in such circumstances. It is by no means a likely scenario, but serves a useful purpose. It demonstrates the need for additional foreign financing, coupled with fiscal policy adjustments to restore consistency with a growth-oriented debt strategy. The alternatives are either a slowdown in output growth if the public sector does adjust to reduced external financing, or macroeconomic instability if it does not.

V CONCLUSIONS

To summarize the results of this analysis, external restraint comes at a high cost in terms of lost output growth. This will happen in a direct manner if the internal adjustment relies on a cut in public sector invesment. Cuts in public sector consumption, in addition to what is already assumed in the base case, are probably no longer really possible on a large scale; public sector saving has already increased a great deal over the last few years. Alternatively, if the government relies on debt issue, private sector investment would fall substantially because of the necessity to raise interest rates. In addition, the interest rate would have to rise to levels that would make further internal debt issue highly destabilizing. The conclusion should be clear. The secondary market quotation of Turkey's debt suggests that external debt is not threatening Turkey's creditworthiness at current levels and anticipated future increases. Internal adjustment is necessary for consistency with inflation targets, but pushing for tighter external policies seems both unnecessary and potentially highly damaging to Turkey's growth prospects and internal balance.

The model simulations developed and presented here are illustrative of the trade-offs involved under structural adjustment. Undoubtedly, the financing needs commensurate with larger public sector deficits generated high medium term inflation and real interest rates. But the thrust of the program was growth-oriented centering around export performance through real devaluations and the ability to keep savings and investment rates up. Fiscal policy played a key role in the process through an increase in a well-directed public expenditure program which supported the private sector through necessary infrastructure investments and special incentives and credit for export and investment. A key factor, of course, was the substantial excess capacity inherited from the heavy investments made in the 1970's which allowed for a quick improvement in output and exports once the exchange rate was aligned.

NOTES

1. This paper draws on joint work at the World Bank with Roberto Rocha, to whom we are indebted for helpful discussions and to John Brondolo for research assistance. In addition, we would like to thank Rüşdü Saracoğlu, Teoman Akgür, Hasan Ersel and Halûk Tükel of the Central Bank, Gazi Ercel of the Treasury and Yavuz Ege of the State Planning Organization in Turkey, Javad Khalilzadeh-Shirazi at the Bank and Dani Rodrik for comments and assistance at various stages of this project. The findings, interpretations, and conclusions do not represent official policy of the World Bank.
2. Turkey's rescheduling exercise took place over the period 1978-80, before other debtor countries rescheduled their debt. Hence the shift of comparison

period. The data for the high debt countries are taken from the IMF World Economic Outlook, October 1987. The WEO refers to this group as 'Countries that experienced recent debt servicing problems'. For brevity's sake, we refer to the same group as 'high-debt' countries in this paper.

3. In the case of Turkey there is no arbitrage between domestic and foreign interest rates: for empirical verification see Anand, Chhibber, Rocha and van Wijnbergen (1988). There is no competition in Turkey between foreign and domestic banks for business loans; domestic banks enjoy what amounts to a monopoly position.

4. Changes in deficits will only require changes in real interest rates to induce private savings surplus if private savings would not rise automatically in response to tax cuts. Such an automatic offset may take place if the private sector recognized that a cut in taxes without a matching cut in expenditure simply raises the taxes they will need to pay in the future. Then a tax cut would have no impact on private consumption. Thus deficits would have a one-for-one impact on private savings and no impact on either real interest rates or external balance. This is known as 'debt neutrality' in the economic literature. Empirical tests strongly reject this assumption of 'debt neutrality' for Turkey.

5. See Chhibber and van Wijnbergen (1988) for documentation of the interest rates and various tax wedges that have been incorporated in the derivation of the lending rate figures, as well as for the theoretical basis and data to estimate the private investment equation.

6. Although almost the entire increase was due to increased housing investment.

7. The various channels through which public policy affects private investment are explained more fully in Chhibber and van Wijnbergen (1988).

8. In the run, the spread between lending rates and deposit rates was kept constant. A five percentage points cut in the borrowing rate thus implies a five percentage points cut in the lending rate too.

9. Other expenditure components need to be cut or alternative means of financing need to be found; each carries its own cost.

10. See Anand and van Wijnbergen (1988) for documentation.

11. Weighted by their share in Turkey's exports.

12. A simple version of this framework was first used in Anand and van Wijnbergen (1987). The current version incorporates external debt considerations and implications of the financial structure for inflation tax revenues. It is presented in van Wijnbergen, Anand and Rocha (1988).

13. The deficit has increased substantially since, by almost 4 percentage points of GNP; consistency with the targets mentioned therefore will require a commensurately larger cut back in fiscal deficits.

14. Output in Turkey's trading partners is projected at 3.5 per cent. This is an export-weighted average of growth rates assumed in the World Development Report for the OECD and the Middle East. Econometric evidence presented in Anand and van Wijnbergen (1988) shows an income elasticity of Turkish exports of about 2, which explains the 7 per cent real growth rate for exports.

15. Of course, by virtue of its design, the debt-resource ratio would not increase after such a policy. The debt-export ratio would decrease enough to exactly offset, at the weights chosen, the increasing debt-output ratio.

16. The current account deficit concept used includes only real interest payments; a zero current account deficit thus corresponds to a deficit at positive world inflation rates and positive foreign debt. World inflation is the rate of change in the dollar-based foreign price index used in the real exchange rate calculations.

REFERENCES

Anand, R. and S. van Wijnbergen (1987) 'Inflation and the Financing of Government Expenditure in Turkey: An Empirical Analysis' (Washington DC: World Bank) photocopy.

Anand, R. and S. van Wijnbergen (1988) 'Export Incentives, Exchange Rate Policy and Export Growth in Turkey' (Washington DC: World Bank) in process.

Anand, R., A. Chhibber, R. Rocha and S. van Wijnbergen (1988) 'External Debt, Fiscal Policy and Sustainable Growth in Turkey: An Empirical Analysis' (Washington DC: World Bank) photocopy.

Bean, C. (1986) 'The Estimation of "Surprise" Models and the "Surprise" Consumption Function', *Review of Economic Studies* 53, pp. 497–516.

Chhibber, A. and S. van Wijnbergen (1988) 'Public Policy and Private Investment in Turkey' (Washington DC: World Bank) photocopy.

Cohen, D. (1985) 'How to Evaluate the Solvency of an Indebted Nation', *Economic Policy* 1, pp. 139–67.

Cohen, D. (1988) 'The Management of the Developing Countries' Debt: Guidelines and Applications to Brazil', *World Bank Economic Review* 2 (1), pp. 77–103.

van Wijnbergen, S., R. Anand and R. Rocha (1988) 'Inflation, External Debt and Financial Sector Reform in Turkey: a Quantitative Approach to consistent Fiscal Policy' (Washington DC: World Bank) photocopy.

8 Some Policy Dilemmas In Turkish Macroeconomic Management

Dani Rodrik

I INTRODUCTION

It has been more than eight years since the Turkish economy first embarked on a strategy of outward orientation. The Özal era has been characterized by reforms, quite radical by Turkish standards, aimed at eliminating once and for all the macroeconomic stop-go cycles and associated balance-of-payments crises to which the Turkish economy had been prone in the previous three decades. In its broad outlines, Özal's program has undeniably been successful in extricating the economy from the depths of a debt crisis (in 1978–80) and in re-igniting economic growth. Yet, it is hard to avoid the feeling that the light at the end of tunnel recedes almost as fast as the Özal engine advances: inflation remains untamed, debt service exerts a growing pressure on public finances and real wages continue on their downward trend. In late 1988, the annual inflation rate stood close to 100 per cent, and the public-sector deficit around 8 per cent of GNP. This has led to two sets of equally plausible responses. The critics warn about a debt crisis around the corner; the sympathizers worry that the international financial community does not appreciate enough the adjustment already undertaken.

In the initial phases of the Turkish adjustment, the retrenchment on the current account was significantly cushioned thanks to a combination of debt relief-cum-reschedulings with fresh capital inflows. But since 1984, the economy has had to generate a net resource transfer abroad of around one per cent of GNP. Since foreign debt is predominantly the liability of the public sector, this reverse transfer must have as its counterpart a corrresponding level of resource mobilization by the government. In fact, as the private sector has increased its net foreign liabilities in the aftermath of the partial liberalization of the capital account, the public sector net resource transfer abroad has been several times higher than that for the economy as a whole.

In an economy where foreign exchange is generated by the private sector, but debt has to be serviced by the public sector, policy has to address both requirements simultaneously. The external transfer can take place only if there is a corresponding *internal* transfer from the private to the public sector. The maximum level of debt service is determined by whichever of the two transfers is the smaller one *ex ante*. A straightforward implication is that an export boom, as in Turkey, is on its own insufficient for prompt and adequate debt service. The public sector has to extract the excess supply of foreign exchange thus generated, and it can do so in only one of three ways: by reducing its primary deficit, by increased domestic borrowing or by seignorage. To a varying extent, the Turkish government has resorted to all three.

The purpose of this paper is to highlight three areas where the policies pursued so far have had conflicting effects when viewed from the above perspective of fiscal crisis. The first area is export-promotion policy. While the almost continuous real depreciation of the Turkish lira since 1980 has no doubt played a key role in alleviating the foreign exchange bottleneck, I will argue that this policy is now increasingly working at cross-purposes with respect to the fiscal constraint. Second, a similar logic prevails with policies with respect to financial markets. Financial liberalization and the opening of the capital account may have contributed to a rationalization of asset markets, but they have created severe dilemmas with respect to the management of the government's domestic debt. Third, I will argue that the privatization effort currently under way also undermines in subtle ways the fiscal discipline necessary to maintain external debt service.

The bulk of this paper deals with these policy dilemmas, and probes potential ways out. At the outset, however, it is important to stress that Turkish policy choices and outcomes have been conditioned in part by a rather unfavorable external environment. To some extent, Turkey had benefited in 1977–81 from being the only major LDC debtor undergoing a debt crisis: the inflows coming under the auspices of the OECD at the time did not threaten contagion. But after 1982, commercial banks were in no mood to expand their exposure to developing countries, even to those like Turkey which seemed to be doing all the right things. To put the Turkish experience in perspective, then, I start in the next section with a comparative look at Turkish macroeconomic performance and debt indicators.

II   A COMPARATIVE LOOK

Critics of Turkish economic performance in the 1980s typically pay little attention to the fact that the international environment of the 1980s has been decidely more hostile to growth than that of the previous two decades. With much of the developing world engulfed in a debt crisis, a sharply reduced willingness on the part of foreign lenders to extend resources, and increasing levels of trade protection fostered by the current account imbalances among the main OECD countries, the world conjuncture has not been conducive to fast growth, especially for countries relying on exports as an important source of demand. Hence, while Turkish growth has been slower than in the 1960s and 1970s, much of the blame for this must attach to circumstances outside the control of the Turkish authorities.

When viewed in the comparative perspective of other developing countries, the Turkish growth performance in fact looks quite respectable. As Table 8.1 shows, the average annual rate of growth of 4.8 per cent is higher by a half than the respective figure for (capital-importing) developing countries as a group (3.1 per cent). With respect to inflation, Turkey's average rate of 36.9 per cent would be considered a virtuous performance when compared to the hyper-inflationary cases in Latin America. But this figure is virtually indistinguishable from the average for the developing countries as a whole (see Table 8.1).

Perhaps more surprising is the discovery that the Turkish recovery has not been accompanied by a resurgence in investment. This comes across clearly in the comparative figures: in Turkey, the share of investment in GDP has been consistently lower by two to three percentage points than in the other countries, except in 1986 which saw a boom in public investment. This undistinguished investment performance has gone alongside more moderate fiscal deficits. These facts bring to the fore an important puzzle:

TABLE 8.1 *Macroeconomic Performance in Comparative Perspective*

	1969–78	1981–86	1981	1982	1983	1984	1985	1986
GDP growth (%)								
LDCs*	5.7	3.1	3.0	2.0	1.7	4.7	4.0	3.1
Turkey	6.2	4.8	3.6	4.5	3.9	6.0	4.2	7.3
Inflation[†] (%)								
LDCs*	17.6	36.3	28.9	28.0	39.1	46.2	48.2	32.7
Turkey	19.0	36.9	37.6	32.7	28.8	45.6	45.0	34.6
Investment/GDP (%)								
LDCs*		23.3	26.0	24.5	22.5	22.3	22.1	22.2
Turkey		20.8	21.5	20.3	19.6	19.6	20.5	23.2
Central govt. deficit (% of GDP)								
LDCs*		4.6	4.0	5.4	5.1	4.0	4.1	4.6
Turkey		2.8	1.3	2.1	2.1	5.2	2.8	3.2
Export volume (% annual change)								
LDCs*	5.0	5.0	1.5	−0.9	8.0	11.0	3.9	7.0
Turkey	4.3	21.6	68.7	24.1	13.9	23.1	10.0	0.1

* Capital-importing developing countries.
[†] Consumer prices.
SOURCES IMF (1987) and IMF, *International Financial Statistics*; OECD (1987); Celâsun and Rodrik (forthcoming).

if neither investment spending nor public expenditure has been a comparatively important source of demand, where has all this growth come from?
The last row in Table 8.1 provides the answer: exports. During the 1981–86
period, Turkish exports have grown at an average annual rate of 21.6 per
cent in volume terms, a phenomenal performance compared to the 5.0 per
cent growth rate for other countries. These numbers can be put into
perspective by considering that world trade grew at a paltry rate of 3.0 per
cent in this period, and that the corresponding Turkish figure in 1969–78
had been only 4.3 per cent. This, then, is the real Turkish success story.
Even when the so-called fictitious component of exports is eliminated, the
Turkish export boom looks quite astonishing (see estimates in Celâsun and
Rodrik, forthcoming, Chapter 7).

More than anything else, it was the rise in exports that allowed Turkey to
regain her creditworthiness. The export boom of the early 1980s halved the
debt-exports ratio from 507 per cent in 1978 to 222 per cent in 1982. But as
Table 8.2 shows, the traditional debt indicators took a turn for the worse
after 1984. There were several reasons for this. First, the real depreciations
of the lira continued to deteriorate the debt-output ratio. Second, the rate
of export expansion slowed down somewhat after this date. Third, the
depreciation of the dollar beginning in early 1985 inflated the dollar value
of the portion of debt denominated in other currencies (mainly DM and
Japanese yen). Fourth, debt relief was phased out and the rescheduled
liabilities started to come due. Finally, and perhaps most ominously, there
was an increased reliance on short-term debt (which shows up in Table 8.2
as an increase in the debt-service requirement).

Table 8.2 compares the trends in the principal debt indicators for Turkey
with those for the developing countries as a group. Since Turkey was
coming out of a debt crisis in 1981, the group of 'countries with recent
debt-servicing problems' (in IMF parlance) is also included as a compara-
tor. Notice that the Turkish debt-GDP ratio, which stood at 53.1 per cent
in 1986, is now significantly higher than the average for all developing
countries, and only slightly better than in the 'problem' countries. Of
course, the economic significance of this is questionable, as much of the
increase is due to the real depreciation of the Turkish lira. But, as I will
argue in the next section, the implied capital losses deteriorate the underlying fiscal balance and impose a genuine economic burden.

A particularly noteworthy aspect of Table 8.2 is the contrasting trends in
the debt-service ratios of Turkey and of the 'problem' countries. Since
1983, the highly-indebted countries have managed to bring down their
debt-service (as a share of exports) from more than 90 per cent to 74 per
cent. This is due partly to the reduction in world interest rates, and partly
to the rescheduling arrangements undertaken since 1982. The spreads over
LIBOR in these restructurings have progressively declined from more than
2 percentage points to less than 1 point, and grace periods and maturities

TABLE 8.2   *Principal Debt Indicators (%)*

	1981	1982	1983	1984	1985	1986
Debt-GDP ratio						
LDCs*	30.7	35.4	37.8	38.9	41.2	43.1
CWRDSP†	38.5	45.5	50.0	51.1	52.2	54.8
Turkey	28.6	32.8	36.1	42.4	47.8	53.1
Debt-exports ratio						
LDCs*	128.4	155.8	164.2	158.1	171.2	182.9
CWRDSP†	185.8	241.5	254.3	247.2	263.9	302.4
Turkey	280.2	222.2	231.4	218.2	223.3	278.8
Debt-service ratio‡						
LDCs*	44.2	54.2	56.4	50.2	48.8	48.9
CWRDSP†	65.6	86.4	90.9	76.4	78.1	74.1
Turkey	71.1	58.1	53.9	51.0	67.2	84.1
Share of short term debt in total						
LDCs*	21.1	21.2	17.6	17.4	14.5	13.2
CWRDSP†	22.1	22.6	17.3	17.1	12.8	11.7
Turkey	13.0	10.0	12.4	15.0	18.8	22.1

* Capital-importing developing countries.
† Countries with recent debt servicing problems.
‡ Includes previous year's stock of short-term debt in the numerator; denominator is exports of goods and services.
SOURCES   Author's calculations from IMF (1987); Celâsun and Rodrik (forth-coming).

have become more advantageous to the debtor countries (see Sachs and Huisinga, 1987, p. 562). As Table 8.2 shows, the relative importance of *short-term* debt has fallen quite drastically in these countries, from 22.6 per cent of total debt in 1982 to 11.7 per cent in 1986. In Turkey, the trend has been in the opposite direction. In 1984, roughly fifty cents of every dollar of export earnings[1] went to service Turkey's foreign debt; this number has now risen to more than eighty cents, despite the respectable export performance.[2] This is due to two fundamental reasons: the grace periods on practically all of the debt rescheduled in 1978–80 have now run out; and secondly, the share of short-term debt has more than doubled since 1982.

The second point is especially important. Since short-term debt has to be amortised within a year, the appropriate measure of debt service in year t must include the stock of short-term debt at the end of year t–1, as is done in Table 8.2. By considering only interest payments and amortisation on medium- and long-term debt, the official debt-service indicators tell a rather misleading story. To be sure, the maturity structure of debt would be of no importance in a world with no uncertainty, where only solvency matters and liquidity crises never occur. Barring doubts about solvency, in such a world short-term debt can always be rolled over and the distinction between long-term and short-term debt disappears. The experience with the convertible Turkish lira deposits (see Celâsun and Rodrik, forthcoming, Chapter 2) in 1975–77 makes it amply clear that this is not the world we inhabit. What is worse is that much of this short-term debt has been contracted at almost usurious rates, with some of the Dresdner deposits paying spreads of over 5 percentage points over LIBOR.

Paradoxically, then, Turkey, a 'model' debtor, has been forced to amortise her long-term and cheap debt by converting it into short-term and expensive debt, while the problem debtors have managed to refinance their liabilities at increasingly advantageous terms. The latter strategy is, of course, hardly desirable given the background of acrimony and disastrous economic performance against which it has become operative. But the Turkish strategy is also rather disturbing in that it tends to undermine the very creditworthiness which uninterrupted debt service seeks to achieve.

III   EXCHANGE RATE POLICY

The exchange rate has been one of the key policy tools in the Turkish adjustment of the 1980s. Prior to 1980, periodic devaluations in the wake of foreign exchange crises would be systematically undone in the course of the following years, as Turkish inflation outstripped foreign inflation. Since 1980, the authorities have not only resisted creeping appreciation of the real lira (with only few temporary exceptions), but have maintained a downward bias. While the precise figures differ according to the index and weights used in the construction of an effective exchange rate, the real exchange rate has depreciated by at least another 20 per cent since the initial devaluations in 1980. The cumulative depreciation between the end of 1979 and mid-1987 amounts to 50–98 per cent, depending on whether the exchange rate is stated as the value of the lira per unit of foreign currency (50 per cent) or as the inverse (98 per cent).[3]

The objective of this policy has been the standard one: switching expenditure out of, and resources into, tradable sectors. Judging from the performance of exports, exchange rate policy appears to have been quite successful. But it is worth remembering that exchange rates are only one determinant of export performance. The behavior of exporters in the 1980s has also been shaped by the presence of generous export subsidies, advantageous market conditions in the Middle East, and (initially) depressed domestic demand. To ascertain the quantitative role played by exchange rate policy, we need to sort out the influence of these various effects. The relatively crude attempts at doing so contained in Celâsun and Rodrik (forthcoming) and Rodrik (1988a) suggest that at most 35–40 per cent of the increase in exports between 1979 and 1984 is due to exchange rate policy — both the reduction in exchange rate instability and the downward trend in the real rate. Given the vast depreciation that has taken place, this is somewhat disappointing and reflects the fact that the estimated export supply elasticity is rather small.[4]

Whatever the success of exchange-rate policy on the trade front, it is becoming clear that continuous real depreciations impose a great burden on the fiscal balance. By now, the authorities realize all too well that depreciation of the lira raises the domestic currency costs of debt service. But the real problem is greater, and analytically a bit more complex.

To see what is involved here, consider the public-sector fiscal balance identity (ignoring domestic debt and seignorage for simplicity):

$$D - ei^*B^* = -e\Delta B^* \tag{1}$$

where D is the primary budget surplus, e is the (nominal) exchange rate (foreign currency per lira), i^* is the foreign interest rate, B^* is the stock of foreign debt (in foreign currency), and Δ is the first-difference operator. The left-hand side is the public sector surplus, which can be used to amortise foreign debt. Rewriting (1):

$$d = (r^* + \hat{s})b^* - \Delta b^* \tag{3}$$

we get the equality between the primary surplus of the public sector and the public net resource transfer abroad. As long as this transfer is positive (as it currently is in Turkey), nominal devaluations must be accompanied by *increases* in the domestic currency value of the primary surplus to keep the transfer abroad unchanged in foreign currency. But this is a bit misleading in that increases in e matched by equivalent domestic inflation will not in general impose any burden on the public sector balance, as D will rise alongside e. To express the identity in real terms, we deflate all stocks by the domestic price level, and define b^* as the real value of foreign debt in terms of domestic goods. Then (2) becomes:

$$d = (r^* + \hat{s})b^* - \Delta b^* \tag{3}$$

where d is the real primary surplus, r^* is the foreign real interest rate, and $\hat{s}$ is the proportional change in the *real* exchange rate.[5] This shows that holding the real value of foreign debt constant ($\Delta b^* = 0$) requires a corresponding rise in the real primary surplus whenever the real exchange rate depreciates ($\hat{s} > 0$).

In Turkey, the foreign debt-output ratio is presently close to 0.60. Consequently, equation (3) indicates that a 10 per cent permanent real depreciation has to be accompanied by an increase in the primary surplus of the public sector by no less than 6 percentage points of GNP in order to neutralize the capital loss. Notice that the correct measure of the real income loss is the change in the real exchange rate multiplied by the *total* stock of debt, and not just that part of debt which is serviced in the current period. If the fiscal adjustment turns out to be less than this amount, the public sector's real indebtedness must rise. Alternatively, there must be increased resort to the inflation tax. In the past, both have taken place.

In part, the real depreciation is self-financing to the extent that the increase in the relative price of traded goods generates additional revenues for the public sector. The intake from trade taxes, for example, would be expected to increase with the depreciation, as long as the import-demand elasticity falls short of unity. Similarly, the export revenues of public enterprises would be enhanced. But on the whole, it seems clear that the public sector suffers a net revenue loss when the real exchange rate depreciates. Trade tax revenues have risen only by about 1 per cent of GNP in the 1980s (see World Bank, 1987, Figure 2.5), despite the massive real depreciations. As for public enterprises, few of them are important net exporters (see Şenses in this volume).

Another way of stating the problem is that the public sector suffers a terms-of-trade deterioration against the private sector whenever the real exchange rate depreciates, provided that non-traded goods are a net source of revenue for the government. Income moves from the public to the private sector. This is the reverse of what is needed for debt service. Paradoxically, the real depreciation may make it harder for debt service to continue, even though its initial effect is to generate additional foreign exchange for the economy. The problem is that the foreign exchange ends up in the private sector, while the ability of the public sector to extract it is crippled by the depreciation.[6]

Hence there is a fundamental dilemma in exchange rate management. The private sector has now come to expect that the authorities will not only devalue the lira in line with domestic inflation, but that they will also build in a margin of enhanced competitiveness, a real depreciation of, say, around 5 per cent annually. This kind of active exchange rate policy, more than anything else, acts as a signal that the government is serious about its outward-orientation. On the other hand, such real depreciations deteriorate the underlying real public-sector budget, necessitating recourse to increasing domestic borrowing, inflation and ad hoc revenue-raising measures such as price hikes for SEE products.

After seven years of adjustment, it is hard to make a good case as to why the real exchange rate has to be maintained on a downward path. From now on, it might make more sense to target a *constant* real exchange rate, barring external or internal shocks and to communicate the policy openly to the public. To do so, a suitable nominal anchor must be provided by prudent monetary management, which may in fact become easier once the additional public finance gap due to real depreciations is eliminated. As for trade performance, there is a continued role for tariffs and some export subsidies on 'marginal' exports. Tariffs set at moderate levels have two desirable effects: first, they raise revenue for the government; second, they substitute for costly devaluations. Export subsidies on 'marginal' exports — that is commodities presently not exported in significant quantities, but with presumably large supply elasticities — make sense for the second reason as well. Provided that subsidization is limited to a narrow range of exports,[7] they can also be less costly on the public budget than real depreciations which increase the cost to the government of buying foreign currency across the board.

In the final analysis, a sound export performance must rely on structural change and adequate investment in exportable sectors. Both of these require a stable macroeconomic environment and a climate of steady, predictable economic policy-making that derives from fiscal prudence. Continued real depreciations now work at cross-purposes with these goals.

IV FINANCIAL LIBERALIZATION

The Özal program has laid heavy emphasis on reform of financial markets from the very beginning. The domestic component of financial liberalization started in July 1980 with the decontrol of bank deposit rates. Following the financial crash of 1982 deposit ceilings were re-introduced, but the government has aimed at maintaining the rates for time deposits at positive levels in real terms. After 1984, the capital account was also liberalized in part, and domestic residents were allowed to open foreign-currency deposit accounts. Such accounts have quickly risen in volume, and now constitute more than a quarter of all bank deposits.

It appears that the government initially viewed high interest rates as being desirable from the perspective of inflation-control. The present Central Bank governor has argued that interest rate policy 'was perhaps the single most important factor in lowering the rate of inflation' (Saracoğlu, 1987, p. 8). More recently, the ease with which domestic residents can switch into foreign assets has forced the authorities to use the interest rate as a means of easing pressure on the value of the Turkish lira. In early 1988, for example, time deposit rates were raised to 65 per cent (on one-year deposits) to check the growing black market premium on foreign currencies. Further pressure on the currency led to more increases in interest rates later in the year. As this switch in emphasis demonstrates, capital-account liberalization means that the main competitor with domestic money is no longer physical assets, but foreign assets.

From the perspective of the public-sector budget, financial liberalization has had a number of undesirable and unforeseen consequences. The objective of the liberalization is to enrich the menu of financial assets available to the private sector, and to enhance their yields. While unobjectionable in principle, this clashes in practice with the need to finance public sector deficits at low cost. Remember that, barring foreign borrowing, public deficits can be covered only by issuing domestic debt or base money. As the menu of assets broadens, private demand for these public-sector liabilities is naturally reduced. Consequently, any net increase in public liabilities becomes more costly at the margin. Government bonds and treasury bills have to offer a higher yield. A given amount of seignorage revenue can be raised only at the cost of higher inflation, as the 'base' of the inflation tax — the monetary base — has shrunk. Alternatively, a given inflation target becomes compatible with a *lower* level of seignorage revenues than before.

Calculations undertaken by Yılmaz Akyüz (this volume) are suggestive of the portfolio shifts which have taken place as a result of financial liberalization. Table 8.3 presents his data in a slightly re-arranged form. The important point is that the share of public sector liabilities (including base money) in the total stock of financial assets has fallen from 43.8 per cent in 1979 to 29.4 per cent in 1986. This is a large reduction in view of the vigorous borrowing drive of the government in recent years. Despite the substantial financial deepening in this period, the ratio of government liabilities to GNP was no higher in 1986 than its level in 1979 (13.5 per cent). What this reflects, of course, is the explosion in time deposits and foreign exchange deposits — the result of interest-rate policy and capital-account liberalization. Interest-bearing government liabilities (including income sharing certificates) have increased their share in total financial assets, but this increase is small compared to the leap in time and foreign-currency deposits.

The competition from alternative assets forces the government to increase the yields on its liabilities. This is a clue as to why the after-tax return on government securities is presently so high. The realized *real* rates of return on public-sector liabilities ranged from 17 per cent (treasury bonds) to 31 per cent (income sharing certificates) in 1986, compared to 10–13 per cent for time deposits (See Akyüz, this volume, Table 8.2). That these returns are in fact higher than the corresponding rates on time deposits and foreign currency deposits perhaps reflects the increasing strain put by a rising public debt in an environment where households are diversifying their portfolios in other directions. In other words, the outward shift in the supply curve for government liabilities may have coincided with an inward shift in the demand curve, increasing the equilibrium interest rate on both accounts.

The fact that government securities compete with foreign assets also implies that exchange-rate policy feeds into domestic interest rates. This is because households make their portfolio allocation decisions on the basis of anticipated returns on domestic and foreign assets, and the rate of

TABLE 8.3   *Composition of the Stock of Financial Assets (%)*

	1979	1986
Currency in circulation	21.2	7.9
Required reserves*	8.9	4.0
Monetary base	30.1	11.9
Government bonds	13.1	8.5
Treasury bills	0.6	6.9
Income sharing certificates	–	2.1
Government debt	13.7	17.5
Total public sector liabilities	43.8	29.4
Sight deposits†	35.5	16.1
Time deposits	12.3	34.7
Foreign currency deposits	–	15.6
Commercial bank liabilities†	47.8	66.4
Private bonds	1.9	1.3
Equities	6.5	3.0
Corporate liabilities	8.4	4.3
Total	100.0	100.0

* Calculated as 20 per cent of the stock of sight deposits.
† Net of required reserves.
SOURCE   Calculated from Akyüz (this volume, Table 5.6).

depreciation of the lira is a capital gain on the latter. Let us denote by i and i* the domestic and foreign (nominal) interest rates, and by Eê the expected rate of depreciation of the lira. Portfolio equilibrium then requires:

$$i = i^* + E\hat{e} + \varrho \qquad (4)$$

where ϱ is the risk-premium on Turkish assets. This can also be expressed in real terms:

$$r = r^* + E\hat{s} + \varrho \qquad (5)$$

where r and r* are the real rates of interest and Eŝ is the expected depreciation of the real exchange rate. As discussed in the previous section, government policy has maintained the real exchange rate on a downward path. After seven years, it is safe to assume that the private sector fully anticipates a margin of real depreciation, and that since 1984 has built it into the domestic interest rates. As expression (5) makes clear, the anticipation of continuous real depreciation raises the domestic real interest rates above the foreign real rates. Moreover, the non-negligible short-run variability in the real exchange rate may add to the risk premium on domestic assets. It would then increase the margin between domestic and foreign rates further. During 1985–86, the Turkish real interest rates (on time deposits) have exceeded real dollar rates by 10 percentage points or more, reflecting both the risk premium and the anticipated real depreciations of the lira.

To conclude, financial and capital-account liberalization has raised the cost to the government of domestic borrowing and of reliance on seignorage. The continuing real depreciation of the lira has added insult to injury by raising the entire structure of domestic real interest rates relative to world rates. When the fiscal house has not yet been put in order, such liberalization proves to be a costly luxury.

The consequences can be observed in the domestic debt trap that the government currently finds itself in. To see this, observe that the evolution of the domestic debt-output ratio, denoted b, is governed by the following equation:

$$\Delta b = (r - n)b - \delta \tag{6}$$

where n is the real growth rate of GDP and δ is the primary surplus of the public sector as a share of GDP. (I am ignoring foreign borrowing and seignorage.) Presently, the high cost of domestic borrowing implies that r exceeds n by a margin of at least 5 percentage points. Hence, domestic debt is on an unsustainable course, and will feed on itself in the absence of a sufficiently large increase in the primary surplus.[8] The magnitude of the requisite fiscal adjustment can be gauged through a simple exercise. The domestic debt-output ratio is presently around 0.3. Assuming conservatively that $r - n = 0.05$, the primary budget has to be in surplus by 1.5 per cent of GDP just to keep the domestic debt-output ratio from exploding.

Even if one concludes, as I have, that financial liberalization has been on balance undesirable, it is not clear what prescription one draws for the immediate future. Once the public has tasted the rewards of portfolio diversification, high-yield securities, and access to foreign assets, it is likely to be counterproductive to attempt to go back. Restrictions on foreign currency deposits, for example, would probably lead to capital flight and expanded black market activity. So the government has to resign itself to live with the consequences of having let the genie out of the bottle too early. But free-market ideology should not obscure the fact that 'throwing some sand in the wheels' of capital account transactions (as James Tobin once suggested for a country whose capital markets are considerably more developed — the US) may be inherently desirable in a context of continued fiscal weakness.

V PRIVATIZATION

The sale of public enterprises to the private sector has long been a major objective of the Özal administration. After a long period of preparation,[9] the first such sale took place recently with Teletaş, a telecommunications firm. The shares were over-subscribed, an indicator of success. This initial privatization has paved the way for others.

The economic case for privatization is frequently presented as being self-evident. The arguments made in its favor in Turkey broadly mirror those made elsewhere. According to these arguments, privatization will be conducive to increased efficiency in enterprises which have long been a drain on public finances. The sale of these enterprises will not only raise resources for the government, but it will also eliminate the need for future subsidies to cover their losses. None of these arguments is self-evident. There is little systematic evidence from developing countries that would suggest that private enterprises are more efficient than public enterprises.[10] In any case, privatization will typically involve the more profitable state enterprises — and therefore presumably the efficient ones — so that broad comparisons across categories of private and public firms are meaningless. As for the fiscal impact of privatization, the arguments are frequently confused. Since my emphasis here is on the public sector balance, I will concentrate on these arguments and leave efficiency issues aside.

The first point to note is that the revenues from the sale of public enterprises cannot be generally considered a net increase in government resources. This is because the private sector is unlikely to pay more for an enterprise than its value, that is its present discounted stream of profits. Since these profits would have accrued to the government without the sale, privatization simply brings forward in time the revenues that would have been generated down the line, without increasing the net discounted present value of government income. Hence, the proceeds from privatization should not be considered current income for the public sector. A reduction in the public sector borrowing requirement that comes via privatization is a pure accounting trick.

Now, since privatization is a means of bringing future income into the present, it is no different from borrowing through the issue of government securities. It would be preferable to the latter if it came on cheaper terms. That, in turn, would be the case if there was a generalized belief that the enterprise would be operated more efficiently under private auspices; then, the firm would be more valuable to the buyers than to the seller, the share price could be set at a higher level than that which capitalizes future profits under public ownership, and there would be a net gain to the government. But several factors mitigate this favorable scenario. First, it is well to recognize that the public does not have an unbounded appetite for absorbing assets. This results in a hidden cost to privatization. Equity in privatized enterprises will likely displace some other assets in private portfolios, and government securities in particular. Wholesale privatization will therefore tend to increase the cost of government borrowing and exacerbate the problems discussed in the previous section.

More fundamentally, in order to make the privatization look 'successful', the government will typically be tempted to *under*-price the shares.[11] This has happened in Britain and elsewhere. The vast over-subscription for the shares of Teletaş strongly suggests that it is happening in Turkey as well. The government then ends up transferring future income to the present at highly disadvantageous terms. An appropriately discounted measure of government wealth would show a *decline* as a result of the sale.

Also less recognized is that public enterprises have long ceased being a drain on the public budget. Thanks to a policy of frequent price hikes on SEE products, the financial profitability of these enterprises has improved greatly. In fact, SEE profits have been a major factor in the reduction of public-sector deficits since 1980: of the cut in the PSBR from 11.6 per cent (of GNP) in 1980 to 5.6 per cent in 1986, 4.2 percentage points (70 per cent) was due to the reduction in SEE deficits and only 1.8 percentage points (30 per cent) to the reduction in central government deficits (See Celâsun and Rodrik, forthcoming, Table 8.3). In 1986, savings of non-financial SEEs made up 38.1 per cent of total public savings, up from −24.7 per cent in 1979 (Ibid., Table 8.6). As to the source of this increased profitability, it does not appear that improved efficiency and resource utilization are likely candidates. These profits mostly reflect a straight-forward exploitation of monopoly power. It is hard to be sanguine about privatization if these monopoly profits will be simply handed over to the private sector. If monopoly practices are going to be curbed, on the other hand, share prices will reflect it and privatization proceeds will be reduced. Given the overall fiscal imbalance, there is a clear second-best case for keeping the source of monopoly profits within the public sector.

VI CONCLUDING REMARKS

The fiscal imbalance remains the weakest aspect of Turkish macroeconomic management in the 1980s. I have tried to indicate here a number of areas in which the pursuit of other objectives has interfered with the fiscal goal. Barring another series of debt restructurings, whether the Turkish experience will be looked on favorably in the years to come depends crucially on the extent to which public sector resource mobilization will be adequate to service external debt. Moreover, debt service will have to be undertaken simultaneously with sound investments in infrastructure, health and education. This puts a heavy premium in the on-going liberalization on a policy mix which does not effect the public budget adversely.

NOTES

1. Including earnings on factor and non-factor services.
2. My estimate of the debt-service ratio for 1987, based on balance-of-payments data for the first three quarters of 1987, is 84.3 per cent, virtually indistinguishable from the number for 1986. This suggests that the temporary dip in Turkish exports in 1986 is not the sole reason for the rise in the debt-service ratio.
3. These numbers are based on World Bank calculations. (See Baysan and Blitzer, this volume, Table 1.1).
4. The estimated elasticity of export volume with respect to the previous quarter's real exchange rate is 0.47 (Celâsun and Rodrik, forthcoming). More recent econometric work by Kumcu (1988) finds evidence of a structural change after 1980, with the long-run export supply elasticity being higher after 1980 (1.15) than before (0.85).
5. Let π and π^* stand for the domestic and foreign inflation rates. Then equation (3) follows from the following relations:

$$\Delta b^* = e\Delta B^*/p + (\hat{e}-\pi)b^*, \; r^* = i^* - \pi^*, \text{ and } \hat{s} = \hat{e} + \pi^* - \pi$$

6. For a theoretical analysis of these issues, see Rodrik (1988b).
7. The widespread habit of over-invoicing and fictitious exports suggests that it might be quite difficult to accomplish this in practice.
8. This sustainability issue with regard to domestic debt has been highlighted in a recent World Bank report evaluating the five structural adjustment loans (SALs) extended to Turkey.
9. See Leeds (1988) for a detailed account.
10. For a balanced review of the evidence, see Vernon (1987).
11. This point has been stressed by Raymond Vernon.

REFERENCES

Celâsun, M. and D. Rodrik (forthcoming) *Debt, Adjustment and Growth: Turkey*.
IMF (various years) *International Financial Statistics* (Washington DC: International Monetary Fund).
IMF (1987) *World Economic Outlook* April (Washington DC: International Monetary Fund).
Kumcu, E. (1988) 'Economic Liberalization and Changing Structure of Foreign Trade', photocopy.
Leeds, R. (1988) 'Turkey: Implementation of a Privatization Strategy', in R. Vernon (ed.), *The Promise of Privatization: The Challenge for American Foreign Policy*, (New York: Council on Foreign Relations) pp. 149–78.
OECD (1987) *Economic Surveys: Turkey* June (Paris: Organization for Economic Co-operation and Development).
Rodrik, D. (1988a) 'External Debt and Economic Performance in Turkey', in T. Nas and M. Odekon (eds), *Liberalization and the Turkish Economy* (New York: Greenwood Press) pp. 161–83.
Rodrik, D. (1988b) 'The Welfare Economics of Debt Service', National Bureau of Economic Research Working Paper 2655, (Cambridge Massachusetts: NBER).
Sachs, J. and H. Huisinga (1987) 'US Commercial Banks and the Developing-Country Debt Crisis', *Brookings Papers on Economic Activity* 2, pp. 555–601.
Saracoğlu, R. (1987) Economic Stabilization and Structural Adjustment: The Case

of Turkey', paper presented at the World Bank-IMF Symposium on Growth-Adjustment Programs, 25–27 February, Washington, DC.

Vernon, R. (1987) 'Economic Aspects of Privatization Programs' (The Economic Development Institute Washington DC: World Bank).

World Bank (1987) *Fiscal Policy and Tax Reform in Turkey* (Washington DC).

9 Inter-Class and Intra-Class Relations of Distribution under 'Structural Adjustment': Turkey during the 1980s

Korkut Boratav

I INTRODUCTION

This paper attempts to survey and analyze changes in income distribution between (and, partly, within) social classes in Turkey during the 1980s. The justification of the choice of 1980 as the starting point of the investigation must be evident to observers of the Turkish scene. It was in January of that year that an orthodox stabilization program was launched in Turkey — a program which soon evolved into a structural adjustment model signifying a clear-cut rupture with the policies of the preceding decades. There are also good grounds for treating the 1980s as a whole from the viewpoint of economic policies: the parliamentary, military, semi-military and, once again, parliamentary regimes which followed each other during these years represented striking continuities with respect to the basic economic policy orientations. And it is no less a personality than the present prime minister Turgut Özal who symbolizes this continuity as the 'overlord' in economic matters during the whole of this period except for an interval of sixteen months in 1982–83.

The components of the new policy model dominating the economy during the 1980s have been studied at length and need not be repeated here. To summarize the model in a few words, apart from the *traditional stabilization* package which shifted to the background particularly since 1984, its structural reorientation has been towards more *liberalization* both internally and externally, *less state involvement in productive activities* — including steps towards privatization — and *export orientation* as the primary priority in resource allocation. But more importantly within the context of the present paper, it has been the contention of the present writer that *changing and redefining the policy parameters regulating and shaping income distribution against labor in general* was a major goal of the structural adjustment program of the 1980s. Admittedly this was not one of

199

the stated objectives of the program. However, once goals with sensitive and adverse political implications become part of a major policy reorientation, we can substantiate their existence — as we have done throughout this paper — by observing the changes in those policy tools evidently aimed at realizing the unstated objective and by an analysis of their final impact. The main preoccupation of this paper is to investigate how far this last structural goal was realized.

A clear-cut conceptual framework appropriate for understanding the dynamics of relations of distribution in Turkey is required to pursue our objective. This is done in Section II. This framework, as it will be shown, distinguishes between primary and secondary relations of distribution and the three sections which follow will investigate the distributional changes which have taken place at two different domains of *surplus extraction* (Section III on 'wage labor versus capital' and Section IV on 'peasants versus merchants and moneylenders') and *surplus redistribution* (Section V). Changes in *inter-class* relations of distribution are thus investigated in Section III and IV; and *intra-class* changes — with respect to the bourgeoisie — are covered in the fifth section. A set of empirical *indicators of distribution* will be constructed in each section by means of which changes in the relevant relations of distribution will be followed. These indicators are to be based on the conceptual framework of Section II. The policy variables and policy changes which have a direct bearing on distributional changes will be set forth in each section. Direct linkages between policy components and distributional changes are elaborated in non-formal fashion. Hence, for those interested in analyzing income distribution within formalized macro — or general equilibrium — models, the findings in our paper can serve as a starting point. Finally, the present writer is convinced that the distributional changes in Turkey during the period under investigation have a number of deep-going non-economic implications as well and Section VI concludes the paper by discussing some of these issues. A few controversial reflections are made there with respect to the *ideological* and *political* incidence of what has happened at the level of relations of distribution.

II CONCEPTUAL FRAMEWORK[1]

Unlike neoclassical investigations of distribution in which two different concepts of income distribution are used — one for analysis (functional distribution) and the other for evaluation (size distribution) — this paper will utilize a single concept for both purposes, namely income shares of *social classes* and of major *socio-economic sub-groups thereof* or of *intermediate social strata*. Such an approach naturally requires a conceptual framework on the basis of which our groupings, and in particular *social classes* can be defined.

It is the Marxian concept of *relations of production* which will serve as the basis of such a definition. Particular relations of production in class societies — according to alternative interpretations — are either *defined by* or *correspond to* particular mechanisms of *surplus extraction* from direct producers. This initial extraction/appropriation of the surplus constitutes the *primary relations of distribution*. In each case primary relations of distribution confront a particular class of *surplus extractors* to another particular class of *direct producers* from which surplus is appropriated. And it is the unique and particular *mechanisms of surplus extraction* — or, once again particular *relations of production* — through which the specific duality of social classes is defined. In other words, a social class can only be defined with respect to its dialectical opposite within a particular mode of surplus extraction.

Secondary relations of distribution, on the other hand, refer mainly to the redistribution of the surplus between *sub-groups* of economically dominant classes; between *intermediate social strata*; and between sectors, industries, economic activities and agents. Surplus reallocation or value transfers through the intermediation of the market or of the state, in which *relative price movements*, *financial* and *fiscal systems* play the dominant role, are crucial in this respect. It is through these mechanisms that the initial appropriation of the surplus is modified.[2]

The practical and methodological implication of this approach with respect to investigations on income distribution is that it shifts the focus of attention from the distribution of *national income* to particular (and primary) relations of distribution within the national economy and tries to depict, measure and analyze the *distributional trade-offs which occur in each particular area*. Wage labor versus capital; tenant versus landlord; petty (simple) commodity producer versus merchant/moneylender are some of the dialectical dualities and focal points which should serve as the *starting point* of studies on income distribution. It is at the level of secondary relations of distribution that the analysis should encompass the totality of the national economy. The distribution of national income, albeit between income types which may correspond to the remuneration of social classes and strata, is the *end result* of the processes which take place within primary and secondary relations of distribution and, hence, should not serve as the *starting point* of analysis.

If we shift our attention to the Turkish scene, Table 9.1 is proposed to serve as the social matrix for Turkey on the basis of which relations of distribution will be discussed and analyzed in this paper. Three relations of production (capitalist mode, semi-feudal mode and petty commodity production) are defined by primary relations of distribution (that is, particular mechanisms of surplus extraction) and they produce three pairs of social classes: working class versus capitalists; dependent peasant/tenants versus landlords; independent peasantry versus merchants/moneylenders. At the level of abstraction used in the construction of the social matrix, petty commodity production is taken in its 'pure' form — that is, excluding the auxiliary existence of wage labor and tenancy within that mode; the multitude of forms, some of them akin to petty commodity production, in the urban economy are disregarded[3] and merchant/moneylending capital confronting the peasantry is considered to exist in its precapitalist form and hence, *not* as a sub-group of the capitalist class to be covered within secondary relations of production.[4] (This last distinction loses its practical relevance when we start to analyze the changes in the quantitative indicators of distribution with respect to petty commodity production.)

In the empirical estimation of changes taking place in Turkey within the sphere of primary relations of distribution, quantitative indicators summarized in Table 9.1 — and to be further elaborated in Sections III and IV — will be constructed and changes in these indicators will be interpreted as reflecting distributional changes between conflicting social classes. However indicators on ground rent proposed for semi-feudal relations of distribution cannot be constructed for Turkey due to the lack of reliable and continuous data.

Secondary relations of distribution as depicted in the second part of Table 9.1 define seven groups. Three of them are the industrial/farming, commercial and financial sub-groups of the capitalist class who engage in an intra-class bargaining/competition/struggle to share the surplus initially extracted within primary relations of distribution. Rentiers, a stratum with an ambiguous social composition and origin, is a fourth group engaged in the same struggle. The remaining three groups, that is, bureaucracy/military, professionals and 'urban marginals' can be considered to constitute the intermediate social strata.

It is through the financial and fiscal systems strictly controlled or dominated by the state, through the characteristics of specialized markets for specific services — with respect to the professionals and some categories of 'urban marginals' as well — and through changes in relative prices that secondary relations of distribution operate. It should be pointed out that some relative price movements have direct impacts on those indicators reflecting primary relations of distribution: terms of trade and commercial margins for agricultural commodities are concepts essentially based on relative prices. Real wages, if calculated on the basis of price indices of wage goods, embody the distributional effects of relative price movements affecting these goods and the share of wages in value added are influenced by differential price movements of inputs and outputs for those products whose value added is being calculated. However, the relative price movements which fall within the scope of *secondary* relations of distribution, as defined here, reflect a *further* transfer of value; and for the sake of

TABLE 9.1   *The 'Social Matrix' for Analysing Relations of Distribution in Turkey*

Primary Relations of Distribution

Relations of Production	Social Classes	Indicators	Further Distinctions
Capitalist	Worker versus capitalist	Wages/value added in current prices, real wages (together with output/employment data)	Private and state industry, capitalist farming to be distinguished
Simple commodity production	Peasant versus commercial (merchant) capital	Relative margin of final prices over prices received by farmer, terms of trade for agriculture	Market for loanable funds (moneylending)
Semi-feudal	Small tenant versus landlord	Ground rents/value added, ground rent per unit of land in real terms	Other types of tenancy between smallholders to be distinguished

Secondary Relations of Distribution

Relevant Socio-economic Groups	Mechanisms and Categories of Secondary Distribution
Industrial and farming capital	Relative prices (of output with respect to cost elements), direct taxes, non-price subsidies and incentive schemes, loan rates of interest
Commercial capital	Commercial margins (can also be integrated into an analysis of relative prices), direct taxes, incentive schemes, loan interest rates
Financial capital	Relative margins between rates of return on financial liabilities and assets, parameters of the financial system, direct taxes, taxes on financial operations
Bureaucracy and military	Civil service salaries, non-salarial material benefits
Rentiers (non-agricultural)	House-rents, interest rates on savings (time) deposits and on other financial assets in nominal and real terms
Professional (non-salaried) groups	Markets for specialized and qualified services. Scarcity rents due to entry barriers
'Urban marginals'	Undefined

conceptual clarity, it is useful to stick to the distinction between primary and secondary levels of the distribution process.[5]

The distributional impact of relative price movements is an area of great confusion in economic policy debates in Turkey, particularly around the concept of the so-called 'rents' of protection, or of government intervention in general. In an economy like Turkey where different rates of return between industries and activities due to market imperfections and due to various forms of government intervention are the rule; and where pricing behavior differs in different activities, price changes may reflect not only changes in production conditions and costs, but also changes in mark-ups over costs. It is this second type of relative price movements which reflects modifications in income distribution and it is here that a good understanding of market anatomy and of pricing behavior in various spheres of the economy becomes crucial.

Table 9.2 provides a simplified picture of marketing channels and price relations referring to major commodity groups based upon the structural characteristics of the Turkish economy. There are nine groups of commodities (column 1) and eight groups of supplying and demanding agents (columns 3 and 4). Imports of consumer goods, local production of capital goods and private production of industrial intermediate goods are excluded from the table. For some commodity groups (numbered 1, 2, 4, 5 and 9) two different stages at the circulation process, hence two different market levels with different agents are considered whereas local non-agricultural supplies for the internal market are assumed to be marketed directly by producers (commodity groups 3, 6–8, therefore manifest a single market level).

The distributional consequences of any change in the economy which has a bearing on any one of the markets in Table 9.2 depend on the type of pricing behavior which the relevant agents follow. Mark-up pricing,[6] flexible pricing independent of short-run changes in cost elements, administrative pricing by public authorities and world prices translated into import/export prices via the effective exchange rates are the pricing variants prevailing in the Turkish economy. The so-called theory of 'rents of protection' is implicitly based upon a pure flexible pricing behavior on the part of importers. An overvalued exchange rate leading to 'cheap' imports of intermediate goods (4a in Table 9.2), combined with flexible pricing for these scarce commodities is at the source of these so-called 'rents'. A more realistic picture including industrialists and the state directly as importers (column 4 of 4a) and the prevalence of administrative or mark-up pricing would seriously undermine the conclusions of this particular 'rent' theory.

In short, the framework presented in Table 9.2 enables us to encompass relative price changes of final goods and of those (imported/domestic or agricultural/industrial) cost elements so as to distinguish price movements solely reflecting costs from those due to changing price/cost margins — two cases with different distributional consequences. Some of the post-1980 economic policy changes can be analyzed within this context.

TABLE 9.2 *Marketing Channels, Agents and Pricing Behavior in the Turkish Economy*

Commodity Groups	Nature of Prices and Pricing Behavior*	Supplied and Marketed by	Demanded and Purchased by
1a. Agricultural consumption goods[†]	Prices received by farmers (FP)	Farmers	Merchants
1b. Agricultural consumption goods	Final prices (FP)	Merchants	Consumers
2a. Agricultural raw materials	Prices received by farmers (ADP, FP)	Farmers	Merchants, state[‡]
2b. Agricultural raw materials	Factory purchase prices (FP, ADP, MKP)	Merchants, state[‡]	Private industry, state[§]
3. Domestic intermediate goods	Factory selling prices (ADP)	State[§]	Private industry, state,[§] farmers
4a. Imported intermediate goods	Import price in TL (WP)	External world	Importers, private industry, state[§]
4b. Imported intermediate goods	Internal selling price (ADP, FP, MKP)	Importers	Private industry, state,[§] farmers
5a. Imported capital goods	Import price in TL (WP)	External world	Importers, private industry
5b. Imported capital goods	Internal selling price (FP, MKP)	Importers	Private industry, state,[¶] farmers
6. Wage-goods (industrial)	Final prices (MKP, ADP)	Private industry, state[§]	Consumers
7. Consumer durables	Final prices (MKP)	Private industry	Consumers
8. Non-tradable services	Final prices (ADP, FP)	Private sector, state[¶]	Consumers
9a. Exported goods	Prices received by farmer or by industrialist (FP, MKP)	Farmer, industry	Exporter
9b. Exported goods	Unit export value in TL (WP)	Exporters, state[‡]	External world

* FP: flexible pricing; MKP: mark-up pricing; ADP: administrative price fixing by the state or public agencies; WP: world prices exchange rate.
[†] Mainly vegetables and fruits, excluding wheat.
[‡] Public marketing boards.
[§] State industry.
[¶] State sector in the broad sense.
SOURCE Author's tabulation.

III   WAGE LABOR VERSUS CAPITAL

Primary relations of distribution with respect to the capitalist mode correspond to the conflicting relationship between wage labor and capital. The most appropriate indicator of distribution representing this relationship is the *share of wages within value added*. In cases when data on value added are lacking, but time series on wage rates are available, one can use real wages as an alternative indicator together with complementary data on employment and output.[7]

Table 9.3 presents our findings on the wage indicators referred to above. It should be noted that in our calculations of real wages, wholesale price indices are used as deflators and, hence, wage movements in the table should be interpreted as referring to *wage costs* instead of *wage earnings*. The table depicts the picture of a substantial decline in wages — both in absolute and relative terms — during the 1980s. Between the highest level in the 1970s (1977 or 1979 for the two series) and 1985, the decline in real wages is 52.1 per cent and 28.6 per cent for all employees and for manufacturing workers respectively. There are modest, but positive rates of growth in labor productivity in the manufacturing industry as a whole during this period of real wage declines which inevitably result in significant regressions in wages/value added ratios.[8] This tautological outcome does not provide an analytical explanation. A step in that direction can be taken if we consider the effect of mark-up rates on wage shares.

Wages/value added ratio, by definition, declines (i) if real wages decline — or, what is essentially the same thing, if the share of wages in variable costs falls with an unchanging technology — with a non-declining mark-up rate; or (ii) if the mark-up rate increases when real wages are not increasing; or (iii) if real wages decline together with an increase in mark-up rate at the same time.[9] If there is an inverse functional relationship between real wages and the mark-up rate, or a wage/profit trade-off in the classical sense, the outcome would be much more predictable.

Table 9.4 divides the 1963–85 years into a number of sub-periods and provides the average mark-up rates of the state and private sectors of the manufacturing industry and compares them with average growth rates of real wages for the same sub-periods or years. On the basis of the findings of the table two observations can be made with particular reference to private industry.

Firstly, although no direct causality can be claimed, the table gives a strong impression that in 'normal' years mark-up rates on variable costs have an inverse relationship with the rates of change of real wages. The only exception is observed in 1978/9 — two years of acute production and supply bottlenecks and, hence, of erratic 'jumps' in mark-up rates for certain industries within the private sector, possibly reflecting a temporary transition to flexible pricing.

TABLE 9.3 Wage Indicators, 1976–86

	Indices of Real Wages				Wages/Value Added in Manuf. (%)			Manuf. Industry Indices			
	All employees	Manufacturing Industry						Labor Productivity*		Employment	
		State	Private	Total	State	Private	Total	State	Private	State	Private
Years	1	2	3	4	5	6	7	8	9	10	11
1976	100.0	100.0	100.0	100.0	27.5	34.8	31.7	100.0	100.0	100.0	100.0
1977	102.4	130.7	112.7	120.1	40.4	34.6	36.9	87.4	111.1	112.2	99.0
1978	95.2	136.2	110.9	120.6	46.3	33.1	37.7	73.1	105.1	112.8	108.9
1979	82.3	142.4	117.0	127.4	51.8	32.2	38.7	59.8	99.7	114.9	103.0
1980	57.6	123.6	88.1	101.8	35.3	27.6	30.7	73.0	84.2	112.2	106.4
1981	53.6	133.1	103.9	106.9	22.9	27.7	25.3	126.8	91.7	106.2	112.0
1982	54.4	127.5	95.8	106.2	20.3	26.3	23.5	131.5	96.2	104.0	119.5
1983	56.9	117.4	100.4†	106.5	23.3	26.0†	25.6	101.8	98.2†	109.0	108.7†
1984	51.8	95.4	89.2	91.0	23.7	23.8	23.8	87.0	102.2	106.0	115.4
1985	49.1	90.8	91.7	90.9	19.2	24.7	22.4	100.7	98.5	104.8	119.2

* Labor productivity in manufacturing is measured by value added per worker in constant prices where the industrial commodity group of the wholesale price index is used as deflator.

† Coverage narrowed in 1983.

SOURCES Column 1 is based on the wage series of Social Security Organization published by State Institute of Statistics (SIS). The 1985 figure of this column is taken from an estimate by the *1986 Yearbook* of the Trade Union of Petroleum Workers. Columns 2–11 are based on manufacturing industry surveys and censuses for various years as published by SIS. Daily (column 1) or annual (columns 2–4) nominal wages per worker are deflated by the wholesale price index of the Undersecretariat of Treasury and Foreign Trade (formerly of the Ministry of Commerce).

TABLE 9.4   *Mark-up Rates and Real Wages in Manufacturing Industry*

Years	Average Rate of Change in Real Wages (%)		Mark-up Rate (%)*	
	State	*Private*	*State*	*Private*
1963–66	6.3[†]	4.7[†]	48.1	27.0
1967–70	5.4	6.5	86.1	19.4
1971–74	−1.1	−0.7	71.8	29.0
1975–77	14.9	15.4	41.5	26.5
1978–79	4.4	1.9	27.1	34.3
1980	−13.2	−24.7	20.5	35.3
1981	7.7	17.9	22.5	32.2
1982	−4.2	−7.8	31.0	31.9
1983[‡]	−7.9	4.8	36.5	32.3
1984	−18.4	−11.2	30.0	32.0
1985	−4.8	2.8	36.5	28.6
1980–85	−7.2	−3.8[§]	29.5	32.1

* Mark-up rates are obtained by dividing gross production value of the relevant industry to variable costs including wages minus one.
† 1964–6.
‡ Coverage for private industry narrowed.
§ Average of annual changes for the 1980s except 1983.
SOURCES   Table 9.3 for columns 1 and 2. Özmucur (1987) for columns 3 and 4 except for 1985 which is calculated by the author.

Secondly, if once again we exclude 1978/9, there is a distinct increase in the mark-up rate during the 1980s in comparison with the preceding periods. This has a direct bearing on the changes in wages/value added ratios. The decline in real wages during these years — or, alternatively, the decline in the share of wages in variable costs — reinforces the direct adverse effect of mark-up increases on the wage share; and, hence, results in a definite regression in wages/value added ratios.

Evidently primary relations of distribution have shifted dramatically in favor of capital and against labor during the 1980s — a result on which all researchers agree.[10] If we now shift our attention to the requirements of 'accumulation on a world scale', wage movements in Turkey have to be 'translated' into international currencies; and such 'translated magnitudes' — together with labor productivity levels and trends — will be perceived and assessed by international capital in a comparative context. Table 9.5 presents hourly wages in $ terms and indicators of labor productivity in manufacturing and compares them with South Korea, Spain, Greece and Portugal.

The effect of real currency depreciation in Turkey during the 1980s comes out strikingly in Table 9.5. Wages in US$ terms regress much more

TABLE 9.5 *Hourly Wages in Dollar Terms and Labor Productivity Comparisons in Manufacturing Industries*

	Turkey		South Korea		Spain		Greece		Portugal	
Years	Wages	L.Prod.	Wages	L.Prod.	Wages	L.Prod.	Wages	L.Prod.	Wages	L.Prod.
1976	1.21	100.0*	0.47	100.0	1.75	100.0	1.23	100.0	1.35	100.0
1977	1.61	103.7	0.62	110.9	2.03	105.3	1.47	94.9	1.24	98.0
1978	1.82	95.9	0.84	124.7	2.53	130.9	1.82	96.4	1.26	88.7
1979	2.46	74.7	1.09	129.1	3.55	140.2	2.17	96.7	1.35	94.7
1980	1.67	72.8	1.04	123.8	3.94	143.3	2.40	92.8	1.62	108.7
1981	1.64	89.0	1.11	127.2	3.64	149.8	2.35	88.5	1.59	
1982	1.40	92.4	1.19	127.5	3.58	155.6	2.60	88.9	1.47	
1983	1.36	83.4	1.24	130.0	3.15	161.8	2.36	89.4	1.23	
1984	1.12	79.3	1.23	142.0	3.17		2.33	89.3	1.18	
1985	1.11	82.0	1.33		3.27		2.27			

* 1974–76.
SOURCES See Boratav (1987a) for main sources and methods. (The monthly wage and productivity findings in that source are transformed into hourly data by using weekly working hours for the relevant countries as given in ILO Yearbooks except for Turkey where legal working hours were used.) Column 2 is taken from Türel (1987) except for the 1985 figure which is calculated by the present author by using industrial wholesale prices as deflator.

than wages in constant local prices when we compare column 1 of Table 9.5 with column 4 of Table 9.3. Thus from the viewpoint of international capital, currency depreciation strengthens the effect of the deterioration in real wages. However, in a comparative framework, changes in the 'degree of attraction' of Turkey for international capital also depends on trends of labor productivity and, in this respect, the stagnant nature of the Turkish industry — in contrast with South Korea and Spain — partially neutralizes the positive effect of wage regression. Drawing up a balance sheet of the net result of these conflicting factors requires a separate analysis.[11]

These adverse distributional changes from the viewpoint of the Turkish working class have, in our view, been definitely determined by the incomes policy model of the 1980s which, in its turn, had been shaped by the reactionary/authoritarian ideology dominating the official circles during the same period. A full balance sheet of the anti-labor and anti-union components of the economic policies of the period and the official justification for this orientation would require too much space and is beyond the scope of the present paper. An extremely condensed summary of these measures would be as follows.

The martial law measures immediately following the 1980 coup severely restricted union activities and collective bargaining, banned strikes and closed DISK, the militant trade union confederation. Wage settlements were taken over by the government-controlled High Board of Arbitration which, for four years, allowed for nominal wage increases systematically and consistently below annual inflation rates. Legislation by the Junta curtailed heavily the various indemnities linked to redundancy, dismissal and retirement even when these were parts of existing collective agreements. Finally, as the ultimate stage in the institutionalization of the new model with respect to labor relations, the 1982 Constitution defined and drastically curtailed the activities and areas where unionization and collective bargaining were to be allowed. The new constitution was immediately followed by legislation on trade unions, collective bargaining strikes and lockouts which detailed and further extended the restrictions of the constitution. It was on the basis of these new institutional parameters that the gradual transition to a parliamentary regime took place. A novelty which Özal governments in the post-1984 years brought to labor relations is the gradual extension of 'contractual employee' status — a status without unionization rights and without any guarantees against layoffs — to workers in state enterprises.

The mere listing of the new orientations in labor relations makes obsolete, in our view, any further search for causality to explain the drastic regression of labor incomes during the 1980s. The whole operation at the labor front seems to have had as its objective *to cause a significant decline in value of labor power* — or, in more conventional terms, to lead to an overall downward shift of the supply curve of labor. And it is evident that this objective was attained.

Once such a structural shift at the labor market takes place, further operations of the same nature and magnitude become both unnecessary and unfeasible. Indexation of nominal wages to the inflation rate, or even allowing for productivity-linked wage settlements, may become tolerable from the perspectives of the employers since these methods would signify freezing either real wage levels or wages/value added ratios at the already depressed magnitudes and, moreover, would be desirable for sustaining 'social peace'. The relatively soft and flexible business reaction to the widespread demands for wage increases early in 1988 following an acceleration of the inflation rate may be interpreted as a movement towards the adoption of such a strategy.

IV PEASANTS VERSUS MERCHANTS AND MONEYLENDERS

What is the most appropriate scheme of income distribution corresponding to primary relations of distribution in an agrarian structure where petty commodity production is widespread? Under a 'pure' form of petty commodity production where wage labor and tenancy are non-existent, the division of the *net output* produced by the peasantry between *merchants' (commercial) profit, moneylenders' (banks) interest* and *net producer's income* would provide the relevant framework. Prices at the final destination of agricultural commodities would constitute the starting point.

Transportation-storage costs and — in cases of further processing — elements of value added would have to be deducted from the final price so that the 'pure' commercial margin over and above farm prices reflecting merchants' profits could be arrived at. Unit production costs for each crop and the interest charge per unit of net output are other necessary elements of the calculation.[12]

Although monographs at village level may provide the necessary data for a calculation on the lines suggested above, they cannot produce national time series for following distributional changes at the agrarian front. Conventional statistics, with the necessary corrections and adjustments, can provide us with appropriate quantitative indicators which may reflect the direction and magnitude of changes occurring at the primary relations of distribution with respect to petty commodity production. It should be stated that the following analysis making use of such indicators for Turkey is relevant for small and medium-scale market-oriented family farming which is the most widespread form in the Turkish countryside.[13]

The two quantitative indicators which we shall use are (i) terms of trade for agriculture and (ii) commercial margins for agricultural (or agriculture-based) commodities. If the two price indices used in the calculation of agriculture's terms of trade represent *prices received by farmers* and *prices paid by farmers for non-agricultural inputs*, changes in this indicator would reflect the changes in the degree of the 'squeeze' of the peasant through backward market linkages. To be more specific, movements in agriculture's terms of trade would represent changes in the margin between the gross production value received by the farmer and the production costs corresponding to non-agricultural inputs paid by the farmer per unit of marketed output. If, following Table 9.2, we assume that marketing of inputs to agriculture is controlled by industry, movements in agriculture's terms of trade would represent changes in *surplus extraction of industrial capital* (local or international) in its *commercial functions* from *peasant farming*.

Changes in the second indicator, that is, in commercial margins, are calculated on the basis of another pair of price scissors. The relevant price indices in this case are *prices paid by final users* (that is, importers abroad or consumers) of agricultural (or predominantly agriculture-based) commodities and *prices received by farmers*. Movements in commercial margins of agricultural commodities as defined represent changes in the relative size (share) of gross value of agricultural produce received by farmers within gross value of production paid by the final user. Hence, it is representative of surplus extraction of *merchant's (commercial) capital* from *peasant producers* through forward market linkages. Surplus extraction in the form of interest charges should be estimated independently.

Neither of these indicators can encompass the internal division of net output produced by the peasant fully; but they reflect parts of the whole picture and they also possess the advantage that they can be calculated on the basis of conventional statistics. It should also be clear that these indicators provide a set of tools for estimating the distributional impact of relative price changes (that is, covering groups 1–5 and 9 in Table 9.2 where farmers are either suppliers or purchasers of the relevant commodities), but they still refer to *primary* relations of distribution because market relations and relative price movements are the main mechanisms through which surplus is extracted from this particular class of direct producers — that is, petty commodity producers.

For an investigation of changes in our indicators of distribution with respect to the Turkish peasantry, Table 9.6 will serve as our starting point.

The most striking observation is the dramatic decline in agriculture's terms of trade from 1976/7 to 1986. This deterioration amounts to 53 per cent in the implicit GDP deflator from 1977 to 1986 and to 40 per cent according to the relevant commodity groups of the wholesale price index. It is interesting to note that during the 63 years of the Republican period, the Turkish farmers have witnessed only one other period of comparable relative price collapse — the Great Depression years of the early 1930s when from 1928–29 onwards terms of trade deterioration according to the implicit GDP sector deflators was 26.6 per cent in seven years and 43.9 per cent in five years in terms of the wholesale price index (see Boratav, 1987b).

A market-oriented peasantry facing such a dramatic price collapse would be expected either to withdraw from the market or to move in the opposite direction and attempt to preserve real income *levels* by increasing marketed quantities of crops at lower real prices. Increased self-exploitation of household labor and sustaining the real level of productive inputs by depressing consumption levels and by increased indebtedness are the means at the disposal of peasant farmers. The degree of market integration of the Turkish peasantry during this period made the 'withdrawal option' an unfeasible alternative and, hence, we observe a definite movement in the direction of increased marketed output as reflected by the 25 per cent increase in real agricultural GDP per active person between 1976 and 1985 (column 2, Table 9.7).

Can we construct indicators which can reflect the final incidence of both relative price deterioration and of increased output on farmers' real incomes? Table 9.7 is an attempt in that direction. Columns 4 and 8 of the table are based on two interrelated indicators constructed to reflect the combined effects of price and output movements on per capita farmers' incomes. Changes in agricultural GDP per active person — in constant or current prices — are translated into their purchasing power equivalents in terms of *industrial* price movements. Agriculture/industry terms of trade and GDP's implicit deflator for industry are used in the construction of purchasing power indicators in columns 4 and 8 respectively. It comes out

TABLE 9.6 *Terms of Trade and Commercial Margins for Agriculture*

| | Terms of Trade | | | | Commercial Margins | | | |
Years	GDP Deflator 1	Wholesale Prices 2	Bread/ Wheat 3	Sugar/ S. Beet 4	Cloth/ Cotton* 5	Margarine/ Sunflower 6	Tobacco(x)/ Tobacco(f) 7	Cotton(x)*/ Cotton(f) 8
1976	100.0	100.0	100.0	100.0	100.0	100.0	100.0	100.0
1977	102.6	97.2	105.7	91.7	88.3	87.6	79.2	120.1
1978	85.1	85.0	110.7	93.8	81.6	99.5	100.2	134.2
1979	69.3	67.5	118.2	99.2	68.0	92.6	84.7	155.2
1980	59.8	62.7	122.1	190.1	67.8	118.2	182.4	107.6
1981	59.8	67.7	106.8	135.1	186.0	133.5	183.6	164.4
1982	53.7	63.0	118.6	121.9	72.5	126.7	199.1	183.5
1983	51.9	58.8	130.0	118.7	95.9	113.4	243.6	203.3
1984	52.7	66.8	121.9	118.7	93.1	188.1	250.5	222.4
1985	49.7	63.3	120.2	112.3	114.8	141.1		
1986	48.2	60.1	116.5	115.9	102.4	124.9		

* With respect to cotton prices received by farmers, they refer to raw cotton in column 5 and lint cotton in column 8.

SOURCES SIS Yearbooks for 1983 and 1987 for all columns. Column 1 is based on the ratios between the implicit deflators for agriculture and industry in GDP (factor price) series. Column 2 is based on the ratios between the agricultural and industrial components of the wholesale price index used in the preceding tables. Columns 3–6 are the index numbers based on the ratios between the indices of Istanbul retail prices and prices received by the farmers. Columns 7–8 are the index numbers based on the ratios between the indices of unit export prices in TL and prices received by farmers.

TABLE 9.7 *Price and Output Effects on Per Capita Farmer Incomes*

Years	Agric. GDP per Active Person; TL in 1968 Prices	Index of (1)	Agric. Terms of Trade	Pur. Power (TOT) Index of Rural per Capita GDP = (2x3)/100	Agric. GDP per Active Person; TL in Current Prices	GDP's Deflator for Industry	Pur. Power (indus.) in Constant TL of Rural Per Capita GDP = (5/6)	Index of (7)
	1	2	3	4	5	6	7	8
1976	3 708	100.0	100.0	100.0	15 279	1 000	15 279	100.0
1977	3 706	100.0	102.6	102.6	19 250	1 203	16 002	105.4
1978	3 846	103.7	85.1	88.2	26 650	1 936	13 765	90.7
1979	3 995	107.7	69.3	74.6	41 597	3 572	11 645	76.7
1980	4 105	110.7	59.8	66.2	83 521	8 091	10 323	68.0
1981	4 144	111.8	59.8	66.9	120 975	11 599	10 430	68.7
1982	4 399	118.6	53.7	63.7	152 900	15 376	9 944	65.5
1983	4 387	118.3	51.9	61.4	192 692	20 141	9 567	63.0
1984	4 534	122.3	52.7	64.5	308 863	30 451	10 143	66.8
1985	4 636	125.0	49.7	61.6	432 008	44 935	9 614	63.3

SOURCES AND METHODS Column 3 from Table 6; the agricultural GDP data is taken from SIS Yearbooks for 1983 and 1987; column 6 is calculated from the same source. Active agricultural population for 1980 is taken from SIS 1980 population census data; and for 1985 — a year for which *rural* population figures are given, but no figures for active population are provided — active population is estimated on the basis of rural population as follows: the average of active agricultural/rural population ratios for the 1965, 1970, 1975 and 1980 censuses (47.06 per cent) is assumed to be valid for 1985 which produces an agricultural active population estimate of 11 119 000. Active agricultural populations for 1976–79 and 1981–84 are estimated through interpolation based on the figures for 1975, 1980 and 1985. For the 'purchasing power' calculation of real per capita incomes in columns 4 and 7, see the explanations in the main text.

that the significant per capita increase in agricultural output during the difficult period of 1976–85 has not overcome the deterioration in relative prices and that in terms of its purchasing power equivalent, per capita real incomes for farmers have regressed by 38.4 per cent or 36.7 per cent during the same period.[14]

If we now shift to our second indicator of distribution, that is, commercial margins, Table 9.6 provides the outcome of relative price movements — that is, prices paid by final users of agricultural (or mainly agricultural) commodities and prices received by the producers of the same commodities — which constitute this indicator. These price movements correspond to commodity groups 1a, 1b, 2a, 2b, and 6 in Table 9.2. From the columns 3–8 of Table 9.6 we observe that relative prices have generally deteriorated from 1976 (and, as a rule, more distinctly from 1978–79) to 1986 against the peasantry.

The widening of the commercial margins in the internal market (columns 3–6) during the 1980s is partly a reflection of the elimination of subsidies and of price controls in those wage-goods covered in Table 9.6. Hence, the distributional outcome of such an operation affects both the peasantry and the urban consumer masses adversely and benefits commercial capital subjected to price controls in the preceding period as well as the Treasury which used to subsidize some of the basic consumer goods. The final incidence of the elimination of consumer subsidies on these goods should be considered an area of separate inquiry.

Of greater interest not only from a distributional perspective, but also from the view of commercial policies, are those price scissors involving unit export prices versus prices received by farmers with respect to the two major export crops, cotton and tobacco. It is significant to observe that for these two commodities, the rapid depreciation of the Turkish lira during the 1980s has been beneficial to the exporters, but not to the farmer and that the price deterioration for the producers of these crops is not directly related to adverse *external* terms of trade movements. An institutional and structural analysis of market relations with respect to these crops before and after 1980 would be illuminating in this respect.

The factors leading to the deterioration of relative prices against farmers — both in terms of agriculture's terms of trade and of widening commercial margins — are without doubt extremely complex and could best be analyzed within the framework of a formalized macro-model — something which is beyond the scope of the present paper. It is, nevertheless, interesting to note that these changes had taken place during a period when protectionist and interventionist policy tools were being scrapped in favor of liberalization and of market-orientation and the outcome in relative prices for agriculture was completely counter to the expectations of the advocates' orthodox stabilization/adjustment programs. It must also be noted that whereas the widening of commercial margins occurs mostly in the 1980s, the crisis years of 1978–79 were the years when most of the decline in agriculture's terms of trade took place for the period covered in Table 9.6. This deterioration of the late 1970s was probably beyond the control and design of the policy makers of those years; and as the crisis conditions and the galloping inflation of 1978–80 were overcome, a gradual return to the preceding price relations could be expected and, in that case, the 1980s should have emerged as years of recuperation in terms of trade for agriculture. As *one* explanation of why this did not take place, we can examine the scope and content of government support policies directed towards agriculture during this period.

Tables 9.8A and 9.8B are constructed with a view to shedding light on this problem. First of all, it can be observed from Table 9.8A, column 1 that the relative magnitude of support purchases by public agencies within agricultural GDP has declined significantly from 1976 to 1986 and that this decline has been particularly pronounced during the 1980s. (The ratio stands at 10.1 per cent for 1985–6).

TABLE 9.8A *Relative Magnitude of Support Purchases and Relative Support Prices (Support Prices/Wholesale Prices)*

Years	Sup. purc.*/ agr.v. ad. (%)[†] 1	Weighted sp.[‡]/whole -sale p. [§] 2	Wheat sp./ whs. p. 3	Cotton sp./ whs. p. 4	Tobacco sp./ whs. p. 5	Tea sp./ whs. p. 6	Sug. beet sp./ whs. p. 7	Sunflower sp./ whs. p. 8
1976	20.4	100.0	100.0	100.0	100.0	100.0	100.0	100.0
1977–9	18.0	73.5	75.8	77.4	69.7	74.8	70.8	86.0
1980–7	12.0**	64.4	75.8	73.2	46.2**	53.9	60.2	77.4

TABLE 9.8B *Relative Support Prices (Support Prices/Agricultural prices)*

Years	Weighted sp.[¶]/ agric. p. [‖] 1	Wheat sp./ agric. p. 2	Cotton sp./ agric. p. 3	Tobacco sp./ agric. p. 4	Tea sp./ agric. p. 5	Sug. beet sp./ agric. p. 6	Sunflower sp./ agric. p. 7
1976	100.0	100.0	100.0	100.0	100.0	100.0	100.0
1977–9	78.8	77.7	82.6	74.2	79.7	75.8	93.0
1980–7	78.0	91.7	88.6	55.8**	65.2	72.9	93.6

**1980–86.

* *Sup. purc.*: Value of support purchases by public agencies in current prices.

[‡] *Sp.*: Index numbers of average support prices paid calculated by dividing the total value of support purchases to the quantity bought by public agencies for each of the relevant crops except for 1987 for which the price data provided by ANKA (see below) is directly used.

[†] *Agr.v.ad.*: Agriculture's contribution to GDP (factor price) in current prices.

[§] *Wholesale p. (whs. p.)*: wholesale price index used in the previous tables.

[¶] *Weighted sp.*: Index numbers of weighted support prices for the crops covered in the table. Each year's weight is based on the relative magnitude of support purchases for that year except for 1987 for which the same weights as for 1986 are used.

[‖] *Agric. p.*: Index numbers of agricultural commodities component of whs. p.

SOURCES For sup. purc. and sp.: State Planning Organization (SPO) *Annual Programs for 1976–86*: for sp. data on 1987, *ANKA Economic Bulletin*, 5 October 1987; for all other data SIS Yearbooks for 1983, 1985 and 1987.

If market relations had generally improved in favor of farmers during this period, this decline in the scope of support policies could have been interpreted as the gradual scrapping of a redundant policy tool. But we know that no such improvement has taken place during the 1980s. In this case a further question should be posed on whether the deterioration in relative prices for farmers has taken place despite government attempts to arrest this decline through *high support prices* within the limits of a *narrower scope* of support policies resulting from fiscal austerity. The findings on relative support prices (with respect to overall wholesale prices or the agricultural group of wholesale prices) do not give support to this hypothesis either. There has been no attempt during the 1980s to correct the effective collapse of relative support prices during the crisis years of 1978–79. Support prices during the 1980s have moved significantly behind wholesale price movements during the 1980s. The weighted support price index with respect to wholesale prices declines from 73.5 to 64.4 from the late 1970s to the 1980s and the same tendency is observed for all individual crops except for wheat which reflects relative price stability between the two periods.

But more significant from the viewpoint of policy intentions is the comparison between the movements in support prices and those for average prices for all agricultural commodities. The findings in Table 9.8B suggest that during the 1980s support prices in general have moved somewhat behind price movements affecting agriculture in general (for example, witness the slight decline in the index representing weighted support price/agricultural price ratios) and that for some crops (tobacco, tea and sugar beet) there may have been a deliberate policy in this direction.

It could be concluded that government policies towards agricultural prices have, at best, aimed to keep intact the adverse price structure which had emerged during the crisis years; and, at worst, been deliberately used to depress them even further. The contraction in the scope of support purchases and the new practice of setting support prices behind the general (and, in certain cases, agricultural) price movements have been the relevant mechanisms in this respect.

As for the surplus extracted in the form of interest by moneylending/ financial capital from the peasantry, systematic data and suitable time series do not exist. A field study in the Çukurova region in 1984, however, produced findings which show that farmers with holdings below 250 decares cover around 47 per cent of their current production costs through loans and that nearly 85 per cent of these loans are obtained from the 'unorganized credit market', that is, from merchants or specialized moneylenders. The same study establishes that — in a year with 52 per cent annual inflation — 60 per cent interest rates are charged for loans with 3–6 months of maturity. Although these findings for a single year do not give a picture of the *changes* in the same farming region during the 1980s, one can conjecture that under conditions of declining real prices and increased supplies to the market, peasant farmers should be expected to run into increased and even extreme indebtedness to cover current costs. If the financial and cost structures for Çukurova agriculture had prevailed for the Turkish agriculture as a whole — naturally an unjustified assumption — 7.7 per cent of agricultural GDP would have been extracted in the form of interest by moneylenders.[15]

As for the future, it can be conjectured that government support policies will no longer be a significant factor in the formation of agricultural prices and that spontaneous market forces will gradually dominate the evolution of peasant incomes. Theoretical analysis (for example, Boratav, 1980) strongly suggests that a market-oriented peasant agriculture *vis a vis* a capitalist urban (and international) economy is inherently and structurally at a disadvantage unless active government policies are used to arrest or reverse the deep-rooted tendencies towards unequal exchange. We tend to interpret what happened during the 1980s as a premeditated withdrawal of the government from being an active agent within the Turkish agrarian structure and increased rates of surplus extraction by industrial, commercial and money-lending capital as the natural outcome of this structural change. In our view, the indicators of distribution and the supporting findings on support policies presented in this section corroborate such a scenario.

V   INTERNAL DIVISIONS WITHIN THE BOURGEOISIE

The surplus initially extracted from direct producers is redistributed among various sub-groups of the bourgeoisie. Rates of return on financial liabilities and assets and the margins between the two, changes in non-agricultural commercial margins reflecting the movements in relative prices and the tax, subsidy, transfer components of the fiscal system are the major factors affecting secondary relations of distribution in this context. Major government policies which contribute to the modification of the structure of relative prices include exchange rates (affecting commodity groups 4a/4b, 5a/5b, 9a/9b in Table 9.2), parastatal prices (group 3) and export subsidies (group 4a/4b). Public policies on interest rates and on the financial system in general were, during most of the period covered, dominant in the determination of rates of return on financial assets/liabilities. The sub-groups of the bourgeoisie who occupy different and conflicting positions within the secondary relations of distribution are represented by industrial, commercial, financial capital and rentiers.

Although the functional and, hence, conceptual distinctions between these groups are unambiguous, under the concrete conditions of the Turkish economy, there exists overlapping between them which may even extend — through rentiers — to other segments of the social matrix. The most significant case of such overlapping refers to the large holdings in which production, marketing (including export and import activities) and banking functions are combined vertically and operated in a coordinated manner. In such cases the actual distinctions between industrial, financial and commercial capital may become superfluous from a distributional viewpoint. With respect to the rentiers, this is evidently a heterogenous group in which intermediate social strata, in particular professionals and upper echelons of the bureaucracy as well as the ('consuming') household members of the entrepreneurial bourgeoisie should be well represented. However, as we shall discuss later on, the economically significant segments of the rentiers are probably a relatively small and compact group.

Despite these observations, the extent of such overlapping (particularly with respect to vertical integration of holding-type business groups) should not be exaggerated. As an example one can refer to the relationship between private banks and holdings in Turkey. In 1987, there existed 26 private national banks and about 15 of them were controlled by 12 holdings (Akgüç, 1987, pp. 60–1). Although this pattern of integration reflects a high degree of control of financial capital by industrial/commercial business interests, it also shows that a very large segment of the business community confronts a banking system over which it has no direct control. A similar observation is valid for the typical Turkish industrialist whose imported input requirements are usually provided by specialist importers and whose exports — under a pattern which, as we shall see, emerged during the 1980s — have to be channelled through large and specialized export corporations. Another factor which complicates the picture in this context is the degree of flexibility which business groups can manifest in changing their activity from, for example, productive to commercial or financial areas in response to policy changes unfavorable to one but favorable to the other. In this regard, once again, one can conjecture that the largest and holding-type groups have a higher degree of flexibility than medium-sized specialized businesses.

These considerations lead us to conclude that an in-depth investigation of the socio-economic anatomy of the Turkish bourgeoisie would be a pre-condition of fully understanding the distributional trade-offs between its major sub-groups. Lacking such an investigation, we shall limit ourselves with providing a few quantitative indicators reflecting changes in the relative economic positions of industrial, financial, commercial capital and rentiers. Table 9.9 summarizes these indicators.

Columns 1–4 demonstrate that with respect to the internal division of the industrial surplus, a dramatic progression of interest income has taken place against the decline of (before-tax) industrial profits during the 1980s. The former now occupy 40–60 per cent of the surplus in the two groups of enterprises covered by the table; and it seems that larger firms having easier access to the banking system are under a heavier interest burden than the medium-sized firms represented by the provincial Eskişehir industry.

The policy element which has led to such an outcome is the decision to offer positive real interest rates to rentiers and the high margin — esti- mated to be at least 50 per cent of time deposit rates — between borrowing and lending rates. It is also significant that this policy element has been the

TABLE 9.9 Indicators on Internal Division of the Surplus

| | Internal Division of Industrial Surplus (%) | | | | Trade and Finance in GDP | | | | Indicator of Rentiers' Incomes | | |
| | 500 Largest Firms | | Eskişehir Industry | | | | | | | | |
Years	Interest and Rentals 1	Industrial Profits 2	Interest 3	Industrial Profits 4	Finance/GDP (%) 5	Trade/GDP (%) 6	Index of Real Bank Profits 7	GDP Trade Deflator/Wholesale Prices 8	Time & Forex Deposit Interests/GDP (%) 9	Index of Real Interest Income 10	Real Interest Rate (%) 11
1979	–	–	13.3	86.7	1.8	15.3	100.0	100.0	0.7	100.0	–47.9
1980	–	–	22.2	77.8	1.8	16.3	247.3	108.4	1.2	170.0	–80.9
1981	–	–	36.3	63.7	2.2	17.2	429.4	112.8	4.9	779.2	+0.7
1982	60.2	39.8	39.2	60.8	2.0	17.3	437.5	116.5	5.6	960.4	+12.3
1983	65.8	34.2	53.7	46.3	1.9	18.0	329.0	116.2	4.5	787.1	+5.4
1984	42.2	57.8	42.0	58.0	2.7	18.4	636.7	116.8	9.5	1756.0	+3.7
1985	42.1	57.9	46.0	54.0	2.9	17.6	617.6	111.9	9.8	1907.2	+10.1
1986	61.8	38.2	39.0	61.0	2.9	17.5	968.8	112.0	10.0	2129.0	+25.6

SOURCES Columns 1 and 2 are based on Özötün (1987), columns 3 and 4 on ECI (1985, 1987), columns 5–8 on SIS Yearbooks for 1983, 1985 and 1987. Columns 9–11: the interest income in columns 9 and 10 is the sum of interests on time deposits and foreign exchange (forex) deposits in banks. Data on time deposits are from SIS Yearbooks 1985, 1987 and Monthly Bulletin VIII–IX for 1987. Data on forex deposits are from Central Bank Annual Report for 1986. For annual interest rates on time deposits, Coşan (1985) for the years 1985–86 and for interest on forex deposits oral communication from Central Bank experts.

main issue under criticism by the industrial segment of the bourgeoisie which has supported the post-1980 policies strongly otherwise. Thus, it was rentiers and financial capital which actually reaped the benefits of the successful repression of wages by industrial capital. The following lamentations by the president of the İzmir Chamber of Industry is an eloquent statement of this indirect trade-off between wages and interest in the Turkish economy:

> Within the structure of costs, labor's share should come next to the share of raw materials. This is the natural state of things . . . However, under the present circumstances in the Turkish enterprises, the share of interest charges has reached almost twice that of the wage share. If the value of labor has declined to one-half of the cost of finance in an enterprise, there must be an imbalance there. In order to survive, we industrialists are repressing wages and transferring the resulting savings to the increased cost of money. We can bargain only with our workers; but we have no bargaining power *vis a vis* interest, energy and raw material costs.
>
> *Milliyet*, 10 December 1987

Which groups have been the major beneficiaries of the huge rise in gross interests during the 1980s? Columns 5–7 and 9–11 provide some indicators with respect to this question. The share of finance in GDP has increased by more than 50 per cent from 1979 to 1986, and it is evident that it has been exclusively the profits of the banking sector which have gained from this relative progression.[16]

On the other hand, if we compare the interest income accruing to the rentiers with the profits of the financial/banking sector, we observe that its relative and absolute progression is far beyond that of financial capital *per se*. Interest income on time deposits and on foreign currency deposits of Turkish residents reaches the astonishingly high ratio of 10 per cent of GDP in 1986 and rises by 21 times in real terms from 1979 to 1986. It should also be noted that a significant portion of other types of rentier incomes — interest from shares, government and private sector bonds and from the informal money market, real estate rentals, aside from various kinds of capital gains realized in real estate, gold and foreign exchange markets — are not covered in this estimate. The picture which comes out suggests strongly that *rentiers* have been the major beneficiaries of the economic environment of the 1980s.

But who are the rentiers? What is their social composition? In one sense they are the 'savers' at large and, hence, represent the general public; or even, 'the people' as the official ideology of the 1980s has been taking pains to depict them. The only indirect indicator of their size, the number of time deposit accounts in the Turkish banking system amounting to roughly 8 million in 1986 (TUB, 1987) can be shown as evidence supporting the myth of the identification of 'savers' with 'the people'. But on the other hand, closer inspection of the same data shows that time deposit accounts of less than TL 3 million (roughly \$4000 in 1986 rates) comprise 94.3 per cent of all accounts, but incorporate only 45 per cent of the total value of time deposits. And 460 000 accounts (5.7 per cent of the total) account for 55 per cent of all deposits. If we also consider the fact that it is usual for a single 'saver' to spread out his or her funds among different banks and accounts and make the reasonable assumption that those who invest in financial assets outside time deposits should be sought within the ranks of deposit holders who exceed the TL 3 million limit, we can roughly conclude that the economically significant rentier group probably consists of no more than a few hundred thousand people.

With respect to the relative economic position of commercial capital within secondary relations of distribution, the relevant indicators in Table 9.9 reflect definite, but undramatic improvements. The share of trade in GDP and the indicator of overall commercial margins (represented in column 8 by the index of the ratio between two price indices, that is, GDP implicit deflator for trade and wholesale prices) show progressions during the 1980s, particulary between 1979 and 1984. However, certain categories of surplus accruing to the exporting segment of commercial capital are probably not covered by these indicators. The ratio of the total value of tax rebates on exports to the total value of industrial exports have risen from 6 per cent to 19 per cent between 1980 and 1984 (Ersel and Temel, 1984). The magnitude of this particular type of subsidy would amount to roughly 2 per cent of GDP.[17] If we also consider the negative real interest rates on export credits and the gains from foreign currency holdings allowed to exporters, we can conclude that the indicators in Table 9.9 underestimate the relative progression of external-oriented commercial capital in the 1980s. In this context, it should be recalled that most export incentives during this period were bestowed upon exporters, particularly through the large export corporations, and not to the industrial or agricultural producers *per se*.

The relative price structure outlined by Table 9.2 as it affects commercial margins was based on the assumption that merchant's (commercial) capital occupies a distinct place with respect to the marketing of agricultural commodities and as importers or exporters. Agricultural support policies, exchange rate policies, price controls on imported commodities, the role of public agencies as being directly involved in foreign trade and subsidy systems for exports differentiated between the exporter and producer are the relevant policy elements affecting the relative economic position of commercial capital *vis-à-vis* other segments of the bourgeoisie. A bird's eye view of the policies during the 1980s demonstrates clearly that almost in all these areas the new economic measures have favored commerce *vis-à-vis* industry and agriculture. A word of caution may be necessary, however, with respect to the price controls of 1978–79 when under conditions of supply bottlenecks and acute scarcity, administrative pricing had largely become ineffective and high windfalls were realized by inventory holders in parallel markets. Nevertheless we believe that the exceptional conditions of these two years cannot be generalized for the whole period of the 1960s and 1970s; and that the so-called 'rents' theory as a particular and partial way of looking into commercial profits has been based on a distorted and exaggerated perception of economic realities of those decades in Turkey. Our indicators suggest that, even when compared with the exceptional crisis year of 1979 and disregarding major subsidy elements and so forth, the 1980s show a distinct improvement in the relative economic position of commercial capital in Turkey.

As for the three intermediate strata covered in our social matrix — that is, the bureaucracy, the professionals and the 'urban marginals' — we have reliable information with respect to one of them only, namely on civil servant salaries. National accounts series suggest a drastic decline in the share of these salaries within non-agricultural GDP from 15.8 per cent in 1976 to 15.3 per cent in 1979 and to an astonishingly low level of 7.2 per cent in 1986. A rough estimate of per capital civil servants' salaries shows a real decline of 50 per cent during the same period.[18]

VI CONCLUDING OBSERVATIONS AND UNRESOLVED QUESTIONS

The preceding sections of this paper have attempted to show the magnitude of the changes in income distribution which took place during the 1980s. These changes, as we have tried to show, go beyond mere quantitative movements. The *model of regulation* of the economy has been modified radically and relations of distribution were one of the major components of this qualitative transformation. In this context the period should clearly be distinguished from the crisis years of the late 1970s when certain (that is, agrarian) indicators of distribution had started to deteriorate but the process was not due to policy design. A comparable period in the history of Republican Turkey when such deep-going changes had been concentrated into such a short span of time is probably non-existent.[19] By the nature of things, transformations of this nature and of comparable magnitude taking place at the level of relations of distribution should be expected to produce equally deep-going impacts on resource allocation, on patterns of accumulation and of growth in the economy. An economic analysis of these broader questions — which has partly been undertaken by the author elsewhere (Boratav, 1986) — is beyond the scope of the present paper.

Of equal relevance and interest would be an investigation of the 'social' (more specifically 'sociological'), political and ideological repercussion of these deep-going distributional changes. If our empirical findings are reliable, they demonstrate that the past decade has witnessed primarily to a fundamental deterioration in the relative economic position of *labor in general* against *capital in general*; and, secondly, to important changes in the balance of forces within the sub-groups of the dominant classes in the Turkish society. Evidently transformations of this nature can no longer be grasped by economic investigation only. Adaptation and defence mechanisms on the part of workers and peasants whose incomes are being squeezed are a case in point. Some of these mechanisms can be considered 'economic' in the narrow sense like the 'positive output response of the peasant against terms of trade deterioration' — something which we discussed earlier. But other and more complicated mechanisms are also observed which can no longer be perceived and grasped by the conventional tools of the economists. New linkages take place between urban and rural branches of the same kinship group. Labor, earnings and wealth are reallocated within these groups or merely within the family. Domestic production expands in scope within the urban household. The younger generation is withdrawn much earlier from formal education and movements into the informal sector increase significantly. A number of deliberate policy elements aimed at the 'urban poor', particularly during the last three years complicate the picture even further. Municipal services to shanty towns and to the working-class quarters of the cities have been expanding significantly. Partial property rights are granted to former squatters and municipal restrictions on new buildings are relaxed which lead to dramatic increases in capital gains to certain residents of shanty towns located near city centers.[20] Hence lower wages may lose their significance in a social atmosphere where *the wage* as such starts to become a secondary element determining the welfare of the family.

The cultural and ideological implications of these changes would be expected to contrast sharply with the 1970s when a new urban culture was starting to emerge within the working class. This was a period when in the daily lives of the urban masses the working place and the trade union were becoming more and more central compared with the 'residential quarters' and the shanty town; when 'working in a factory' and 'having the status of a regular worker, belonging to the workers' insurance scheme' had significantly higher prestige than survival in informal activities; and when increased inflow from the ranks of worker and peasant families into university campuses was taking place. The striking reversal in these tendencies should be, in our view, related to the distinct shift into religious obscurantism, de-politization and the emergence of hooliganism in urban centers as widespread new phenomena of the recent years.

The incidence of these changes into the political domain is also extremely complicated. International financial circles are taking pride in the Turkish case in which the ruling party has won elections on an IMF/World Bank platform. In fact, the 'political success story' implied here is an exaggeration, since the dominant theme of the 1987 election campaign was indeed economic and social policy issues which resulted in only 36 per cent of the votes for the ruling party. However, this should not deflect the observer from the fact that there was no landslide of worker and peasant votes against the government. And it seems that the ideological offensive of the official circles and of the bourgeoisie during the last eight years has made significant inroads into the 'minds and hearts' of the popular classes. The ideological and political incidence of the distributional changes and of the above-mentioned adaptation mechanisms within these classes remain a challenging area of investigation for the social scientist. And another closely related theme for investigation is the factors behind the commitment of the military to the economic program of the bourgeoisie and the role it played in the 'ideological offensive' mentioned after the 1980 coup.

In this particular context, the 1980s have, in our view, witnessed the evolution of a distinct maturity within the bourgeoisie whose *class* interests have prevailed over the sectional and conflicting interests of its various sub-groups. In other words, the overall *anti-labor and pro-capital* orientation of the economic policies of the period has been the unifying force behind the bourgeoisie and resulted in the mobilization of massive moral, ideological and material support provided by all segments of the business community first to the Junta, and, later, to the Motherland Party. The internal divisions between for example, financial, industrial and commercial segments of capital have always been secondary to the essential class position during this period. This, in our view, also corresponds to a definite degree of maturity in the nature and content of class rule in Turkish society.

A particular brand of bourgeois ideology — with respect to economic policy issues — in its 'consumerist' as opposed to 'entrepreneurial' form has been strikingly widespread within the ranks of the educated professional groups aspiring to Western life styles and consumption norms and thereby repudiating vehemently any economic model and political alternative in which protectionism and etatism are likely to play significant roles. The emergence of a 'liberal and anti-etatist' discourse within the Turkish left around the theme of 'civil society versus the State' should be seen as an outgrowth of this particular ideological position. These new 'waves' have penetrated the Social Democratic movement strongly, contributed to a striking intellectual paralysis and a sense of helplessness *vis a vis* 'the economics of Turgut Özal' and prevented the emergence of viable 'left' alternatives from the Social Democratic platforms.

These observations point to the existence of a vast unexplored area where the specialized approach of the economist, or even of the *political* economist is no longer sufficient and only interdisciplinary approaches are likely to bear fruit. During the past decade or so, the transmission of the unstable conditions in the world economy to the Third World has partly been through the kind of externally-imposed economic policy models experienced by Turkey during the last decade and its distributional conse-quences have been broadly parallel in countries which have passed through the same experience. Hence designing a correct methodological approach to the investigation of the ideological, political and social dimensions of these distributional changes should probably be seen as a priority agenda item for social scientists of different disciplines not only in Turkey, but also in other areas in the developing world as well.

NOTES

1. This section draws heavily from Boratav (1986).
2. Our conceptual framework which distinguishes *social classes* from *social strata* on the basis of the distinction between surplus extraction and surplus redistri-bution is clearly parallel with the approach in Gibson, Lustig and Taylor (1986) where, however, the writers prefer to use the terms *fundamental versus subsumed classes* on the basis of the same criterion. For differences in the interpretation of these concepts between this paper and Gibson, Lustig and Taylor see below, notes 4 and 5.
3. The Turkish Confederation of Petty Merchants ('Esnaf') and Artisans claims a membership of 1.4 million, almost all of it in the urban economy and covers an extremely wide area from taxi operators to shopkeepers and from traditional artisanal producers to street peddlers. Within the context of Table 9.1, lack of reliable information on this extremely amorphous group leads us to consider them belonging to 'urban marginals', being fully aware that indicators of distribution for *commercial capital* may also reflect the relative economic position of certain elements within this group and that most of the productive activities in the group fall into *petty commodity production within the urban economy*.
4. Our conception of primary relations of distribution for petty commodity production refers to the distribution of net output between the market-oriented peasant (as the direct producer in this mode) and merchant/moneylending capital. The latter extracts the surplus from the former through the markets for commodities and loanable funds. This approach differs clearly from the analysis of Gibson, Lustig and Taylor (1986) where petty commodity producers are considered a 'subsumed' (instead of a 'fundamental') class because 'campesinos (that is, peasants) absorb a share of aggregate demand that would otherwise be satisfied by the agrarian capitalists and thus it can be said that they sustain themselves by way of transfers from fundamental classes' (ibid.). The difficulty with this formulation is that, if we change the place of the two terms 'campesi-nos' and 'agrarian capitalists' in it, the sentence makes equally good sense, but the role of the two classes are reversed. More substantively, once we consider the peasantry as a class which *shares* the surplus through transfers instead of a

class *producing a surplus* which is appropriated by other classes, the dynamics of predominantly peasant economies becomes inexplicable. Whose surplus do the peasants share in these societies?

5. It is not the existence of the distributional impact of relative price movements which distinguishes secondary from primary relations of distribution; it is the distinction between surplus redistribution and surplus extraction which is crucial in this respect. This is another methodological discrepancy between Gibson, Lustig and Taylor (1986) and the present paper.

6. One can also distinguish two alternative patterns of mark-up pricing: stable mark-up coefficients versus mark-up rates having an inverse relationship with real wage rates. This distinction — which corresponds to the Keynes/Kalecki versus Marx/Sraffa closures in Gibson, Lustig and Taylor (1986) — has significant distributional implications to which we shall come back in the next section.

7. Recall that wage share (W/Y) equals wage rates (W/L) divided by labor productivity (Y/L). If we assume that changes in gross output reflect movements in value added, we can infer changes in W/Y on the basis of real wage, employment and gross output time series data.

8. The very few individual annual discrepancies in this respect — that is, private industry in 1978 — are probably due to the different deflators used in calculating labor productivities and real wages. Note that between 1979 and 1985 labor productivity declines by 1.2 per cent in private industry, but rises by 68.4 per cent in state industry resulting in an overall progression of 19.8 per cent in manufacturing industry as a whole in six years. On the other hand, the choice of the year with highest real wages (1977) as the basis for comparison with the 1980s makes good sense because the 1960s and 1970s were characterized by *almost* uninterrupted annual progressions in real wages and, hence, 1977 was no year of exception on this score.

9. Özmucur (1987, p. 86) states similar conditions formally without, however, showing that an increase in his 'non-wage costs'/'wages' ratio corresponds to a decline in real wages under non-changing production techniques. However if a full correspondence between Özmucur's ratio and real wages is to hold true, the price deflator used in calculating real wages should not diverge from the implicit deflator for manufacturing industry's inputs.

10. Özmucur's (1987) estimate of the share of wages and salaries in non-agricultural factor incomes shows a decline from 51.9 per cent in 1977 to 21.6 per cent in 1986. Eskişehir Chamber of Industry (ECI, 1987) in a sample survey of industrial firms in the region comes out with wages/value added ratios of 62.7 per cent in 1979 and 43.9 per cent in 1986. In another study prepared for the Istanbul Chamber of Commerce, Özötün (1987) finds out that the share of wages in value added of 500 largest industrial firms in Turkey had declined from 52.6 per cent in 1982 to 37.9 per cent in 1986. Celâsun's (1986) estimates on size distribution of income for 1978–83 are also based on changes in income types which are similar to our findings and those referred to in this note.

11. In Boratav (1987a), by distinguishing between two forms of foreign investments, that is, those directed towards the internal market and those directed towards production for export, two different indicators measuring changes in the 'degree of attraction' of Turkey from the viewpoint of foreign investors are constructed and an international comparison on the basis of changes in those indicators is undertaken.

12. For a formal presentation of this scheme and a discussion of the theoretical and methodological issues involved, see Boratav (1972, 1980).

13. The Turkish debate in the late 1960s and early 1970s on relations of production

in Turkish agriculture concentrating mainly on the nature and the degree of prevalence of petty commodity production to which the present writer was one of the contributors is surveyed by Seddon and Margulies (1984). For a recent survey on land tenure in Turkey once again showing the widespread prevalence of petty commodity production, see Altan (1987).

14. Keyder (1970) uses the same indicator as that in column 4 of Table 9.8 with a somewhat different interpretation in her paper. It should be pointed out that except starting originally from different base years, the two indicators of columns 4 and 8 are constructed on the same kind of quantitative information and should produce the same results. Celâsun (1986) arrives at similar conclusions through a different calculation.

15. For Çukurova findings, see Doğruel and Doğruel (1987). The rough estimate of the interest share in agricultural GDP is done as follows: the ratio of non-labor costs of production to value added was 28.9 per cent according to the basic data used in GDP estimates for agriculture in 1971 (SIS, 1972). Taking 47 per cent as the ratio of costs financed through loans and 56.7 per cent as the average (weighted between moneylenders' and banks' rates) rate of interest on the basis of the Doğruels' findings — without annualizing the moneylenders' rate — total interest payments by farmers would amount to 7.7 per cent of agricultural GDP ($0.289 \times 0.47 \times 0.567 = 0.077$). Since we use medium or small farmers' coefficients in this calculation, the estimate should be considered somewhat on the high side.

16. Salaries of bank employees numbering 67 000 in 1986 (TUB, 1987) must have moved more or less parallel with average wage movements in the economy during the 1980s. Banking is one of the activities where strikes were banned and unionization restricted by the post-1980 labor legislation.

17. With industrial exports accounting for 72.1 per cent of total exports and with an export/GDP ratio of 14.3 per cent, an average tax rebate ratio of 19 per cent on the value of industrial exports would amount to roughly 2 per cent of GDP in 1984.

18. In estimating the change in per capita real salaries, the 'government sector' in GDP series is divided into the 'number of civil service posts' as given in the 1985 and 1987 Budget Laws for various years. This gives us estimates for per capita annual civil servant salary figures in current prices which are then deflated by index numbers of wholesale prices.

19. For a survey of the major indicators of distribution during the Turkish economy since 1923, see Boratav (1987b).

20. 'Don't increase your workers' wages; bring municipal services to shanty towns and distribute property titles to them'. This is the directive which Prime Minister Özal is reputed to have given to mayors of large cities.

REFERENCES

Akgüç, A. (1987) *100 Soruda Türkiye'de Bankacılık* (Banking in Turkey) (Istanbul: Gerçek Yayınevi).

Altan, F. (1987) 'Tarımsal İşletmelerin Yeniden Tabakalandırılması Üzerine Bir Deneme' (An Essay on the Re-Stratification of Farm Holdings), *11. Tez* (November) 7, pp. 35–45.

Boratav, K. (1972) 'Küçük Üreticilikte Bölüşüm Kategorileri' (Categories of Distribution in Small Scale Farming), *SBF Dergisi* 27 (4) pp. 771–814.

Boratav, K. (1980) *Tarımsal Yapılar ve Kapitalizm* (Agrarian Structures and Capitalism) (Ankara: SBF Yayınları).

Boratav, K. (1986) 'Distribution, External Linkages and Growth under Orthodox Policies: The Turkish Economy in the Early 1980s', photocopy.

Boratav, K. (1987a) 'Türkiye'de İmalat Sanayiinin AET'deki Geleceği Açısından Uluslararası Ücret ve Emek Verimi Karşılaştırmaları' (International Comparison of Wages and Labor Productivities and Prospects for Turkish Manufacturing Industry Within EEC), in *1987 Sanayi Kongresi Bildirileri*, pp. 189–209, (Ankara: Makine Mühendisleri Odası).

Boratav, K. (1987b) 'Birikim Biçimleri ve Tarım' (Patterns of Accumulation and Agriculture), *11. Tez* (November) 7, pp. 84–105.

Celâsun, M. (1986) 'Income Distribution and Domestic Terms of Trade in Turkey, 1978–1983', *METU Studies in Development* 13 (1, 2) pp. 193–216.

Coşan, M. F. (1985) 'Mali Kıymetlerin Tahmini' (An Estimation of Financial Assets) (Ankara: Sermaye Piyasası Kurulu) photocopy.

Doğruel, F. and A. S. Doğruel (1987) 'Çukurova Bölgesinde Tarımsal Üretimin Finansmanı ve Küçük Üreticilik' (Financing Agricultural Production and Small Scale Farming in the Çukurova Region), photocopy.

ECI (Eskişehir Chamber of Industry) (1985, 1987) 'Finansman Anketi Sonuçları' (Results of Financial Survey), *ESO Bülteni* (1985) 1 and 2; (1987) November, passim.

Ersel, H. and A. Temel (1984) 'Türkiye'nin 1980 Sonrası Dışsatım Başarımının Değerlendirilmesi Üzerine Bir Deneme' (An Evaluation of the Post-1980 Export Performance of the Turkish Economy), *Toplum ve Bilim* 27, Autumn, pp. 107–133.

Gibson, B., N. Lustig and L. Taylor (1986) 'Terms of Trade and Class Conflict in a Computable General Equilibrium Model for Mexico,' *Journal of Development Studies* 23 (1) pp. 40–59.

Keyder, N. (1970) 'Türkiye'de Tarımsal Reel Gelir ve Köylünün Refah Seviyesi' (Agricultural Real Income and the Welfare Level of Peasantry in Turkey), *METU Studies in Development* 1 (1) pp. 33–57.

Özmucur, S. (1987) *Milli Gelirin Üç Aylık Dönemler İtibariyle Tahmini, Dolarla İfadesi ve Gelir Yolu ile Hesaplanması* (Quarterly National Income Estimates, in US Dollars and by Income Types) (Istanbul: Istanbul Ticaret Odası Yayınları).

Özötün, E. (1987) '1986 Yılında 500 Büyük Sanayi Kuruluşunun Ulke Ekonomisinde Yarattıkları Katma Değer ve Dağılımı' (The Level and Distribution of Value Added Created by the 500 Largest Industrial Firms in the National Economy) *Istanbul Sanayi Odası Dergisi* (October) 260, pp. 162–73.

Seddon, D. and R. Margulies (1984) 'The Politics of Agrarian Question in Turkey', *The Journal of Peasant Studies* 11 (3) pp. 28–59.

SIS (State Institute of Statistics) (1972) *Türkiye Milli Geliri, Kaynak ve Yöntemler, 1962–1971* (National Income of Turkey, Sources and Methods, 1962–1971) (Ankara: DIE Yayınları).

TUB (1987 and various years) *Bankalarımız* (Our Banks) (Ankara: Turkish Union of Banks).

Türel, O. (1987) 'Turkiye'de Sanayinin Gelişimine Genel Bir Bakış' (An overview of industrial development in Turkey), in *1987 Sanayi Kongresi Bildirileri* (Ankara: Makina Mühendisleri Odası) pp. 1–22.

10 The Political Economy of Turkey's External Debt: The Bearing of Exogenous Factors

Tosun Arıcanlı

I THE TURKISH ECONOMY AND EXOGENOUS FACTORS

Turkey is frequently represented as an exemplar of the process of structural adjustment through economic liberalization. This conclusion is based mainly on the export performance of the economy. Since 1980, Turkish exports have been increasing at an unprecedented rate, and that is interpreted to be a consequence of the economic policy applied during the 1980s.

The Turkish government's economic policy in the present decade has been more liberal than any since the early republic. But this is not the only reason for Turkey's success in coping with the debt crisis. It is common knowledge now that the war between Iran and Iraq was behind the initial surge in Turkish exports. In addition, Turkey's economic comeback has been influenced by the favorable cycle of international politics in the Middle East, which is independent of economic performance alone. Without a full accounting of the non-economic variables, as well as the external economic shocks, it is almost impossible to make a realistic assessment of developments in the Turkish economy during the past two decades. Factors falling outside a strictly economic analysis have been causing major shifts in the pattern of government spending and balance of payments.

It is clear that what helped Turkey get out of its debt crisis were the huge capital inflows of the 1980s. Whether these inflows were the cause or the effect of Turkish economic performance is a question that needs to be considered explicitly. It is obvious that non-economic factors have been instrumental for the beginning and continuation of these flows.[1]

A review of the major turning points in Turkey's economy shows the correspondence between autonomous factors and economic performance in general. As Table 10.1 demonstrates, the effectiveness of past economic policy packages needs to be discounted according to the extent of impact of the non-economic variables.

A few major external shocks set the general course of the Turkish

230

TABLE 10.1 *Exogenous Factors of Major Significance for the Performance of the Turkish Economy*

Time Period	Developments Exogenous to the Turkish Economy	Impact of the Exogenous Factor on the Economy
1960s to 1973	Fast growth of European economies create a large demand for Turkish labor	Remittances of Turkish migrant laborers increasingly ease foreign exchange shortage and alleviate balance of payments deficit. This translates into a period of fast growth and high employment.
1974 to 1980	Oil price shocks and stagnation in the industrialized world	Balance of payments adversely affected. Short-term borrowing to finance a fast-growing economy results in the debt crisis.
1974 to 1980	Military intervention in Cyprus and dispute with Greece on the continental shelf in the Aegean sea	Turkish military intervention in Cyprus eventually turns against Turkey due to human rights issues relating to dislocated populations. Consequent disputes with Greece on the rights to exploration of oil in the Aegean further aggravate Turkey's position in international politics due to armed conflict between two Nato allies. As a consequence, international pressure and sanctions on Turkey are aggravated.
1970s	Detente	In this period of cooling off between the US and USSR, US strategic interests in Turkey not as important. No special place for Turkey in great power politics. Consequence: diplomatic impasse with Greece heightened.
1979 and 1980	Iranian Revolution and the end of detente	Loss of Iran results in a heightened interest in the strategic location of Turkey. The US change of administration enhances interest in Turkey. Election of a socialist government in Greece in 1981 enhances US and European interest in Turkey. Consequence: a very favorable attitude to Turkey and its economic problems. Economic aid follows the resumption of military aid at a heightened level.
1980	Iran-Iraq war begins	An automatic export market for Turkey, especially for industrial commodities.
1985–	Decline and crash of oil prices	This development directly diminishes the import bill but Middle East export markets are also adversely affected.

TABLE 10.1   *continued*

Time Period	Developments Exogenous to the Turkish Economy	Impact of the Exogenous Factor on the Economy
1986–	Normalization of US–USSR relations	Has direct implication on the advantage Turkey enjoys as a recipient of foreign aid and preferential treatment.
1988–	End of the Iran–Iraq war	Lesser emphasis on Turkey's 'exceptional' place in the Middle East. Greater competition for Turkey in its exports to Iran and Iraq.

economy in the post-1973 period. For a decade beginning in the 1960s European economic growth was transmitted to Turkey through migrant Turkish workers' remittances flowing from Germany. For Turkey, the oil price shock was enhanced through a labor surplus component consequent to the termination of labor migration due to European austerity programs. The proper economic adjustment of the Turkish economy implied the accommodation of the political consequences of both domestic and European austerity programs. No politician was willing to pay this price. Consequently, the political choice led Turkey in a counter-cyclical growth path that was unsustainable.

The next major external shock was the Iranian revolution which facilitated huge resource transfers to Turkey for an extended period, however, failing to achieve a sustainable adjustment. The route of the Turkish economy during the past decade can be summarized as a series of political and economic disequilibria which are sustained mainly be exogenous factors.

II   1960S AND EARLY 1970S: IMPACT OF EUROPEAN ECONOMIC GROWTH

International Labor Migration, Industrialization and Employment Policy

During the 1960s and the early 1970s the Turkish economy was experiencing a textbook case of Import Substituting Industrialization. Workers' remittances from labor emigration to Europe, which absorbed nearly 100 000 workers a year by the early 1970s, provided the foreign exchange to fuel a high rate of industrial growth without any bottlenecks. The steady rise in workers' remittances produced a current account surplus in Turkey for a brief period. The only problem was that the steady rise in workers' remittances was viewed by policy-makers as a fact of life rather than a

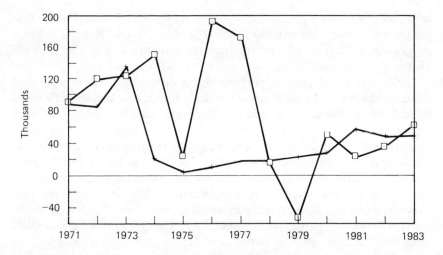

FIGURE 10.1   *Migration and Change in Insured Employment*

+   Annual labor migration.

□   Annual growth in insured employment.

SOURCES   Migration: World Bank (1982) Ministry of Labor Continuous
Reporting System on Migration (SOPEMI) (Paris: OECD).
Employment: ILO.

passing phenomenon. Despite the backward state of Turkish industry in
comparison with its trading partners, prospects for a continuing foreign
exchange surplus paved the way for a more liberal trade policy. The competitive quality of industry was not the issue so long as the surplus existed.

The political significance of the employment policy for this period is
more profound than is generally appreciated. External labor migration was
a much bigger gift to the Turkish economy than the remittances as foreign
exchange earnings represented. It opened up employment channels to
urban migrants easing the problem of unemployment — see Figure 10.1.
Since the 1950s rural-urban migration had been a major problem for
Turkish policy-makers. The agricultural sector, which had been saturated
with labor since the 1950s was the source of this migration. The economically active population in Turkish agriculture remained almost unchanged
at over nine million since the mid-1950s. Hence, the growth in the rural
population added to the urban population, already concentrated in a few
metropolitan areas. The new urban 'crowd' baffled the 'westernized' elite
and affected political jargon.[2] These urban migrants were being incorporated increasingly into the new multiparty political structure through the use
of cultural, and especially religious, concepts that had been unacceptable
in the single party period before 1950. Beginning in the early 1960s labor

migration to Germany took care of this uneasy social issue for Turkish politicians. It was obviously no solution to the problem. Rather, it was a geographic relocation of Turkish squatter settlements into the German ghetto.

The ease in social and geographic mobility during the 1960s also allowed accommodation of the new urban population reducing social conflict and radicalization. Polarization and conflict were mostly confined to elite institutions, with universities leading the way. Compared to the later period, both political debate and political violence were confined to parliament and educational institutions. The left was strong in elite educational institutions and organized labor, and increasingly its agenda was focused on more abstract issues of organization. The right had some hold over labor and was diffused in the informal sectors of small industry, where the smaller radical parties were based. Thus, the radical right was situated closest to the faster growing population. At the same time their objectives were defined more simply in terms of nationalism and primary forms of solidarity. Their activism was defined in terms of eradicating the left which was represented as the enemy of the nation and the fundamental values.

During 1971–73, the years of military intervention and slower growth, prospects for a major change in overall economic policy did not surface. The course of economic policy, however, would change drastically immediately after the elections in 1973.

Shocks on Employment and Remittances

During 1973–74 the Turkish economy received a double shock. The first was the impact of the oil price shock on the import bill. While the general structure of trade remained the same, in 1977 oil imports equalled 80 per cent of export earnings.[3] The second was the new economic policy of the EEC countries, a response to the first oil price shock. This was an austerity program that directly affected the absorption of non-EEC guest workers.[4] Turkish labor migration came to an abrupt halt. The growth of remittances by Turkish workers first stopped and then began to decline.[5]

The impact of the European austerity programs on Turkish labor migration was drastic. In terms of the capacity of the Turkish economy, annual rate of international migration had equalled to over 50 per cent of annual domestic employment creation. During the early 1970s annual change in more privileged domestic employment with social insurance[6] roughly equalled to annual labor emigration. Now about 100 000 potential migrants per year joined the domestic labor force.[7]

The response of Turkey's governments in this period, irrespective of their political makeup, was diametrically opposed to the policies of the European governments. Investment and employment increased to a level that absorbed what would have been potential migrants. With declining remittances and a trade deficit, this was maintained through a drain on foreign exchange reserves. Later they had to be supplemented with borrowing in the short-term credit market that proved to be unsustainable (Celâsun and Rodrik, Chapter 2).

Unresponsiveness of Turkish economic policy to world economic developments in this period is an overstated fact. One of the more blatant examples was the declining real consumer price of heating oil until the late 1970s.[8] Employment policy can be classified here along with other practices of pricing and management. However, the political and social significance of the employment policy was qualitatively different. Accommodation of the urban masses became a part of the political game. Figure 10.2 is a reflection of economic policies of the period on employment structure. Unemployment was contained to a large degree, despite the end to labor migration.

III DOMESTIC POLITICS DURING THE YEARS OF GROWTH AND CRISIS: 1973–80

The Makeup of the Governments

1973–80 was a period of coalition governments which were compelled to be committed to high rates of growth and employment. In this period not a single political party managed to come to power without coalition partners. Two relatively new political parties (which together accounted for about 20 per cent of the popular vote) became indispensable for coalition governments. These were a nationalist party (the Nationalist Action Party) and a religious party (the National Salvation Party). The Republican People's Party (the social democrats) perceived these smaller parties as posing ideological threats to the existing liberal order. The other major actor on the political scene was the Justice Party (AP), representing the conservative wing. Both of the two new parties attempted to preserve their popular base through high expenditure while they had a share in coalition governments. Thanks to their indispensability for coalitions, and the high competition for political power between the larger parties, they controlled an undue share of ministries, which translated into investment, employment and, consequently, patronage.[9] The larger political parties, responding to the radical mobilization of the smaller parties, joined the race to create employment and patronage. State economic enterprises, which were later blamed for inefficiencies and other economic ills, served the crucial function of job creation while encouraging growth and private investment in down-stream activities.

In terms of clients, the conservatives favored employers and the liberals favored the wage earners and the salaried. The constituencies of smaller

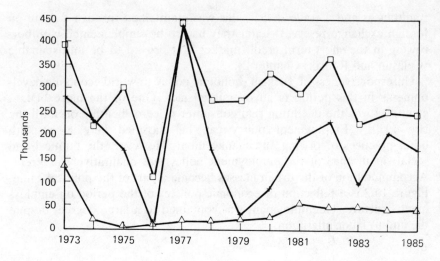

FIGURE 10.2   *Growth of National Labor Force, Unemployment and Migration*

□   Annual growth in national labor force.

+   Annual growth in national labor−annual growth in unemployment.

△   Annual labor migration.

SOURCES   Migration: see previous figure. Labor Force and Unemployment:
World Bank (1982); SPO.

parties were composed of marginal groups that formed part of the urban
masses. As to the peasantry, the agrarian policy of the larger parties was by
and large the same. Client groups were mainly formed in terms of their
regional party loyalty from past experience.

It was obvious that growth of employment was contrary to current
economic 'rationality'. But economic prospects that depended on exogenous
factors, that is, OPEC and OECD policies, were not all that clear, and
domestic prospects were quite transparent. Any government that applied
an austerity program for that period would have been digging its own
grave. The big choices that the political parties faced were between
immediate economic austerity — following the lead of the EEC economies
— or maintenance of their political base through high public expenditure.
With short-run built into the system due to the nature of coalitions, the
second was the natural political choice.[10]

Hence, until 1978 all the coalition governments, regardless of political
denomination, had practically the same employment and incomes policy
for similar reasons. The overarching factor was the 'multi-partisan' platform of economic growth. In their own personal styles each political leader

had an investment agenda. The Republicans drummed up the employment policy and consolidated their hold on the labor unions. The Justice Party and the Salvationists emphasized technological aspects of investments and were busy in promising a rosier future due to their leaders' technical credentials; both were engineers. Regardless of how each program was packaged, the immediate goal was to nurture a voter base. In an era of eternal coalition governments this was a policy of last resort that led to high rates of growth for a restricted period.

The Volatile Issue of Urban Masses in the Late 1970s

The period of 1974–77 was one of intense struggle among political factions to capture the new urban masses. Activities of radical groups were ever more visible. Institutionalized channels were doing well in their function of recruitment. Despite the high level of economic activity, the numbers of unemployed increased drastically between 1973 and 1978 due to the end of external migration.[11] This meant that to the extent that political groups in the center lost their channels of organization through institutional means, the radical right gained potential recruits. For the first time, there was a very active and volatile organized movement among the urban masses, exactly where the right wing was best organized. In this polarization and recruitment process the main players were the social democrats and the radical right. The left having been crushed after the military coup of 1971, became politically irrelevant, especially while it engaged in obscure, theoretical and elitist deliberations. The center right, represented by the Justice Party, had to give up its public recruitment activities due to its incompetence in this area of organization and public appeal. Instead, it capitulated to the nationalists in recruitment policy and had to rely on their political cooperation in the long run. The nationalists' organizing principle was to eradicate the left, which was defined to include the social democrats.

The resulting violence turned into a conflict between leftist students and their nationalist foes. Soon afterwards, by 1978, urban violence turned into a phenomenon totally outside the universities, under the franchise of the marginals. The number of armed assaults increased drastically. By 1979 the daily death toll reached twenty. The increasing intensity of urban unrest and the recruitment activity of the radical political groups went hand in hand. But economic conditions were a factor as well. There was a close correlation between the intensity of unrest and worsening economic conditions — be it declining wages or higher unemployment.

There was an explicit effort to increase the number of higher-quality insured jobs during the early part of the period, but the drive was too short-lived. By 1978 when the social democrats came to power foreign reserves had run out and short term borrowing proved unsustainable.

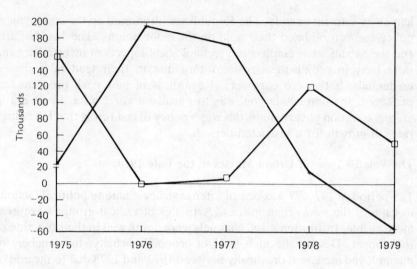

FIGURE 10.3   *Growth in Insured and Uninsured Employment in the 1970s*
*Uninsured employment is the difference between domestic employment and insured employment.

□ Annual growth in uninsured employment.

+ Annual growth in insured employment.

SOURCES   Domestic Employment: World Bank 1982, and SPO. Insured
Employment: ILO.

Thus, when they had to apply a 'mandatory' austerity program, they had to cut where it hurt their own constituency most: salaried, organized labor and peasants. Interestingly, the only sector they tried to support was small industries where the marginals concentrated. Figure 10.3 shows the remarkable rise in the employment of the uninsured in 1978, while insured employment was suffering. Small scale industries are the main employers of uninsured urban workers.

Looking at this scenario from the vantage point of a decade of hindsight, given the choices available to policy-makers, the alternative route of earlier austerity would not have been less disruptive to Turkish political life. European austerity policies forced Turkey to face its own economic accommodation problems with great urgency. The trade-off was between economic and political stability without an intermediate solution due to the nature of coalition governments. It can then be argued that under the political constraints the economically 'irresponsible' policies were not too much off the mark. They bought valuable 'time'. Time, however, was bought on short-term credit and thus was very limited.

IV THE FACTOR OF INTERNATIONAL POLITICS

Economic accommodation of internal political pressures in Turkey worked through external borrowing. In the sphere of international politics there was no mechanism of accommodation. In fact the diplomatic impasse that Turkey entered after 1974 adversely influenced Turkey's ability to get a favorable response for its economic and military wishes.

Detente and the Cyprus Crisis

Both of these exogenous factors directly influenced the Turkish government's capacity to accommodate at least the initial shock of the imminent economic crisis through official capital inflows. Detente worked against Turkey's political interests. The country's geo-political importance, a significant part of cold-war politics, was substantially played down. Both the US and USSR were entering a period of 'low-profile'. At the same time, the Turkish government's unquestionable loyalty to the US had turned into a liability in domestic politics.[12] Closer relations with the EEC provided a new orientation which helped de-emphasize the United States' indispensability. In the general tone set in the 1970s Turkey's relations with the Soviets were also being normalized.

From the US point of view, Turkey was now one of three allies in the south-west flank of the USSR whose importance was diluted as a consequence of lower intensity in East-West tensions. Secondly, Turkey's position in the Middle East had become marginal after the 1967 war. US relations with the Muslim Middle East now centered on the 'twin pillars' of Iran and Saudi Arabia. The major problem in the region from the US standpoint was to deal with Arab radicalism, or containment of Egypt's leadership.[13] An Arab ally would be much better for that purpose than Turkey.

Petro-dollars increasingly strengthened this new US policy. The cost of security in the Middle East could now be paid for by Iran and Saudi Arabia. Naturally, attention shifted more towards Iran than ever before. In light of the shifting focus of Middle Eastern politics, Turkey now moved toward Europe, where the Turkish elite considered itself to be a natural member — that is the Council of Europe, NATO, OECD and, in future, the EEC.

However, detente marginalized Turkey from both sides by placing it outside Middle Eastern politics and in direct competition with Greece in terms of geo-political advantages. Improved economic relations with Germany was Turkey's only antidote for this situation. It seemed for a time that the civility of economic integration that began with labor migration would gradually overshadow the politically volatile security alliances, which had been frequently disrupted by regional and global politics.

But the future of economic cooperation was doomed with the first oil price shock. The Cyprus crisis of 1974 that immediately followed, rocked the basis of Turkey's foreign relations. Unexpectedly and in an extremely short period of time, graduation from Middle East to Europe put Turkey at a disadvantage. By 1975 Turkey was demoted from a progressive nation of the Middle East to an unfit member of the European community.

The Impact of the Cyprus Crisis

In July 1974, when Greek forces in Cyprus engineered a coup against the Cypriot government, Turkey intervened on the basis of its treaty rights in the foundation of the Republic of Cyprus and made a successful military landing on the island. The coup collapsed immediately. Soon after the Greek junta in Athens fell and was replaced with a civilian government. At this point, international public opinion was on Turkey's side. Its government wanted a quick settlement based on partition of the island, but this was unacceptable to the new civilian government in Greece. Turkey reacted by enlarging its military operation and occupying 40 per cent of the island, presumably with the intention of returning part of it in a negotiated settlement. A quick peace settlement would have been a great windfall for the major partner in Turkey's coalition government — the Republicans. But extended negotiations would not be in Turkey's interest because the government believed that Greece had far greater advantages in the international diplomatic arena. Incorporation of a greater part of the island would have made it possible for Turkey to extend a part of the occupied area for a political settlement. It was believed that Greece could not refuse such an offer. Thus what could have otherwise been an international quagmire would be resolved quickly.

The second military operation was not a popular move anywhere except in Turkey. The Greek response was one of indignation and refusal to negotiate under the existing circumstances. The new civilian government in Greece was not at all ready to start its new life with an admitted political defeat. The fears of the Turkish government were realized. Negotiations were going to be difficult. Moreover, the Greek Cypriot refugees from the Turkish occupied north, who numbered in excess of 150 000, turned into a major international human rights issue.

By October 1974 the US Congress had suspended military assistance to Turkey. The following June the Turkish government (this time under the leadership of the Justice Party) retaliated by closing US military facilities in Turkey.[14] Tension with Greece intensified soon afterwards over the issue of rights on prospective oil fields in the Aegean sea. The issue of oil exploration and definition of the continental shelf became one of military clout over the Aegean. In this context, international public opinion held that Turkey was the aggressor.

The process of shaky short-term debt structure that pushed Turkey into the debt crisis of 1977–78, looks much different within this broader political context. Official sources of long-term debt could not have been tapped within the context of multilateral international sanctions. Turkey had neither its earlier position of political advantage in the region nor the ability to solicit favors for its internal economic policies. Its domestic economic policies were not synchronized with the world cycle and hence had no economic merit on their own. It was because of this international political conjuncture that Turkey turned to the faster solution of securing loans in the private banking sector based on the economy's previous accumulation of foreign exchange reserves. Soon, however, foreign reserves were depleted and the foreign debt could not be sustained. In 1977 Turkey turned to the IMF.

The Prospects for a Solution

During 1977 and 1978 negotiations with the IMF and the World Bank were indicative of imminent financial relief for the Turkish economy. For the Turkish government access to private capital markets was critical for urgent foreign exchange requirements. The bureaucracy believed that under the circumstances this could only be possible as a consequence of an IMF 'green light'.[15] The main problem was negotiation of terms with the government. IMF's austerity program was not acceptable.

Despite the economic quagmire that the social democrats found themselves in when they returned to power, through a 1978, coalition government with independents, their mood was one of self-confidence in attempting once again to borrow from the private banks. Now that they were in power, the mismanagement of the previous years could be corrected. The only thing they needed was the confidence and financial support of the 'Western community'. But the negotiators were not impressed with the enthusiasm of the new government. From the tone and speed of the negotiations it was clear that relief would not reach the administration fast enough to help the political problems that all the governments of the period encountered. While the immediate economic problem was speedy access to foreign exchange, the political-military dimension of the crisis was no less urgent. The US arms embargo had an unsettling influence on the armed forces as well as the political structure.[16]

Yet, not everything was quite against Turkey. The US State Department and the White House had been seeking a compromise with the Congress and in the meantime managed to find clauses and amendments so that arms shipments to Turkey would continue, albeit at a reduced level. Knowledge that the administration was sympathetic to the Turkish cause was not enough to change the nature of the crisis with the armed forces. During the discussions and hearings in the Congress there was always a pro-Turkish voice on the floor. It emphasized the strategic importance and the indispensability of Turkey, the southern flank of NATO. On the other hand, the pro-Greek voice stressed the human rights issue relating to Cyprus and the use of US weapons in an aggressive military action. The latter argument won out. The response of the Turkish government to the impasse created by the US congress was to turn to the USSR as an alternative source for arms. At times, the social democrats who had expected instant US cooperation when their coalition government was formed, blamed the US administration for the impasse.

Turkish-US relations in this period went beyond the issues of arms sales and credits. Turkey's international role was being judged in the US. While anti-Turkish sentiments relating to the Cyprus issue could be diffused around Europe, they were explicitly expressed and relevant to policy-making in Washington. The Turkish government felt 'betrayed'. The conviction was such that a favorable decision on arms would have turned everything around, even the internal stability of the country.

The arms embargo was finally lifted at the end of the summer of 1978. By early 1979 the good news arrived that the US planned to provide Turkey with an aid package of $300 million in 1980, $50 million more than the amount agreed upon in 1976 (but one which had never materialized). In the meantime, 'Ankara had recently asked the . . . [EEC for an] . . . $8 billion subsidy over the next five years and projected its total requirement for foreign credits during that period at $15 billion. . . . [O]fficials [said] that foreign credit on that scale is unthinkable'.[17]

Enter the Iranian Connection

Explicit mention of the Iranian instability as it affected Turkish relations did not appear to shift the balance in favor of Turkey until 1979.[18] The US State Department did not suspect that Iran would fall until it was too late, despite social protest and even violence. The downfall of a regime that was assumed to be very sound and the active Muslim force that brought about the downfall created a state of affairs in Western governments that was closer to panic than reflective re-evaluation.

This state of panic was the reason why Turkey ended up as an excellent candidate in terms of alternatives to 'security' options in the region. From now on the nature of the argument was to change drastically from one of the 'prospective costs of Turkish-Soviet relations' to a serious concern about the fate of the southern flank in defense pacts. Earlier arguments about Turkey's indispensability on the southern flank of NATO were merely the acknowledgement of Turkey's strategic position. After 1979 there was a *fear* (whether well-founded or not) that the ramparts were falling and that Turkey could tumble too. Until the end of the arms embargo the tone of US's attitude was effective accomodation of a disgruntled ally due to the inconvenience of Congress's foreign policy intervention. By 1979 the story was one of the domino theory in action. The US could end up going from a position of having several choices in security matters to having no choice whatsoever.

The revolutionary factor — 'religious fundamentalism' — that brought Iran down was not yet identified in the analyses of the region. It was not obvious whether it also existed in Turkey or not. Indications that it might were strong. First, both countries were Muslim and in the Middle East. Second, Turkey had a radical political party organized on religious lines. Third, Turkey was in crisis. Turkey had to be denied the fate of Iran!

Looking back, from the Turkish point of view, that was the best time to have a major economic crisis without a practical solution. Economic and social roots of the question did not receive much attention. All the emphasis turned to the nature of aid and ready-made policy packages. As a result the Turkish economy received an unforeseen boost through official capital flows. Meanwhile the political structure suffered first through political violence and instability of governments, and second through the military intervention of 1980. In turn, the initial reason for the international attention and support to the Turkish economy was to 'save' the regime. Later the economic success story of 1980s fueled further capital flows.

The Manifestation of the new Political Approach to Turkey

The transformation in the tone of new commentary on Turkey in this period is remarkable. A few headlines from early 1979 are illustrative: 'The Next Iran?' (*Washington Post*, 14 January); 'From Turkey to Pakistan, America Confronts an "Arc of Crisis"' (*Los Angeles Times*, 25 February); 'U.S. Intelligence Facilities in Turkey Get New Attention after Iran Turmoil' (*Washington Post*, 9 February).[19] General Alexander Haig, then US Army Commander in Chief of the US European Command, told the Senate's Committee on Armed Services on 22 February 1979 that 'Turkey is absolutely irreplaceable' as a consequence of recent events in Iran (US Congress, Senate, 1979).[20] In the House of Representatives on 20 March 1979 Paul Findley said:

What is needed now if Turkey is to remain a viable ally of the Western world is an international rescue operation whose scope has not been equalled since 1945. How much would it take? By all accounts, perhaps $10 billion to $15 billion over a five-year period, mostly in loans and credits . . . And what is to be gained? Well, our overall losses in the Iranian debacle are sure to run many times the amount Turkey now needs . . . We cannot afford to temporize until Turkey, like so many of our erstwhile allies, lies prostrate and dismembered.[21]

The potential for possible crisis in Turkey was interpreted in many different ways. 'Informed observers in Jerusalem' predicted on 14 February 1979, that 'Turkey might be the next country in the Middle East to undergo a violent anti-Western upheaval, like that in Iran.' Furthermore, if Khomeini stayed in power for a longer period, 'Iranian soldiers would probably be on Israel's eastern border in two or three years'. These predictions were probably motivated by upcoming Camp David peace talks.[22]

The Turkish government saw many possibilities for the future. Now that the embargo days were over and Iran had fallen, there were demands for more aid. Turkey's ambassador designate to Washington, Şükrü Elekdağ, told Warren Christopher that 'Defense cannot be separated from economic issues', while the 'US made no bones about the reason for military assistance. . . . [that is] the operation of valuable US intelligence and communications facilities.'[23]

The other sticking point in the negotiations had been the terms of the aid package with respect to the degree of austerity programs. Given political circumstances in Turkey at that time, the policy package that was presented as a precondition was not acceptable, though by this time, with no access to international capital markets the austerity package was being applied by default. In this respect, the financial sector was more cautious about Turkey's situation. The *New York Times* reported on 7 March 1979:

> Apart from the sticking point of conditions several other obstacles have arisen. . . . According to one ranking monetary official, who has been following the developments closely, there is great apathy in parliaments of creditor countries about help for Turkey. . . . [Referring to the Iranian experience] 'It is coming to be realized' he said, 'that large amounts of money are not the only requirement for political stability. The money can simply end up down the drain'.[24]

Recapitulation: Favorable Political Shocks

Qualitatively, by 1979 Turkey was in a much different position in international politics. It was no longer a marginal Middle East player. Its economic difficulties were acknowledged with a specific price tag. Furthermore, its internal instability was now a US liability. Economic aid was seen as one of the vehicles for alleviating social instability. The international financial organizations were a major stumbling block on this issue, but the protraction of decision-making was already achieving the biggest factor of dispute: austerity. By the end of 1979 a major transformation had taken place in the distribution of income. It was the Republicans that had to apply austerity measures to their own constituency.

The Cyprus issue, the major factor in stalling financial cooperation of the OECD countries until the summer of 1978, suddenly dropped out of sight

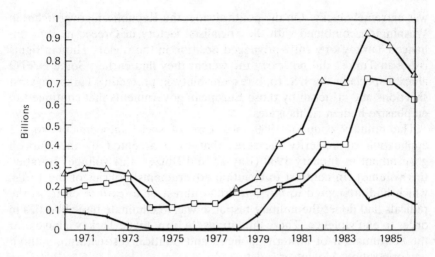

FIGURE 10.4   *US Military and Economic Aid to Turkey (Grants and Loans)**
Data compiled in MUFTI (1987).

+   Economic.

☐   Military.

△   Total.

SOURCES   Laipson (1983); *Congressional Quarterly* 17 January 1987 (US
Department of State).

(Kuniholm, 1986a, 1986b, 1985). Again, it was the Iranian revolution that
was responsible for this outcome, as the following news analysis states:

> Western concern about the state of the Turkish economy and the
> effectiveness of Turkey's armed forces was a second severe shock for the
> Greek Cypriots in the last five and a half months. . . . The strategic
> importance of Turkey has been underlined by the unrest sweeping
> neighboring Iran. To the Greek Cypriots the situation points to the end
> of Turkey's international isolation. . . .[25]

As figure 10.4 shows, US military aid that resumed in 1978 flowed in
increasing amounts to Turkey with an added economic component. Its
course follows a path similar to that of other official capital flows begun in
this period (Mufti, 1987). By the summer of 1980 'IMF commitments to
Turkey [were] 870 per cent of quota, the largest multiple awarded by the
IMF until then. Indeed many executive directors of the Fund felt uneasy
about the special flexibility shown to Turkey' (Celâsun and Rodrik, forthcoming, p. 9.10).

As for the future course of international political relations, again Turkey was extremely lucky. On the political side, the Republican government in Washington combined with the Socialists' victory in Greece in 1981 enhanced Turkey's recently privileged position in the region. Human rights issues in Turkey did not carry the weight they had earlier. Some NATO allies, especially the US, took responsibility in protecting Turkey against sanctions and criticism by those European governments that continued to emphasize human rights issues.

The military coup of 1980 took care of social impediments to the application of austerity measures that were accepted by the Turkish government in January 1980 (Baysan and Blitzer, this volume; Boratav, this volume). In contrast to coalition governments' policies of the 1970s, which had attempted to *buy out* urban unrest or to *cash in* on it, as the radicals had done, the military response was to eliminate basic liberties in order to end violence. These limitations, in turn, made Turkey a haven for the continuation of austerity policies and political restructuring without any opposition, violent or sedate.

V   EXOGENOUS FACTORS AND ECONOMIC POLICIES OF THE 1980S: AN OVERVIEW

The achievement of Turkey's economic policy since 1980 is evaluated on the basis of its remarkable record in export promotion and liberalization. Both of these can be interpreted as demonstrations of the effectiveness of market adjustment in fundamental problem areas. In other areas the liberal period has proven to be ineffective. Foreign investment did not even approach the expectations of policy-makers despite an impressive opening up of the economy (Erdilek, 1988. pp. 141–59). Private domestic investment did not respond to the export push (Conway, this volume). This was partly due to financial liberalization and the consequent interest rate structure. Income distribution was another problem that the liberal policy period failed to solve while unemployment reached record levels.

Factors that led to Turkey's successful export performance were domestic austerity together with exogenous shocks. Hefty subsidies also helped as they had done earlier during the crisis of 1977–80. Attempts to encourage exports through a reorientation of the Turkish industrial sector began at the height of the crisis in 1978. By 1979 teams of businessmen were criss-crossing the Middle East and Africa in an attempt to market their wares in collaboration with the Turkish Foreign Service. New markets did not provide much of an incentive, with severe shortages in imported intermediate inputs in the domestic industry.

During the post-1980 period the supply problem of intermediate inputs was solved through liberalization and generous capital inflows. But what made exports flow were partly factors that lay outside economic policies of the period. In the first place, the crisis of 1977–9 had depressed industrial ouput, creating a huge excess capacity. In private industry the capacity utilization rate stood at 51 per cent in 1980.

Austerity measures kept home demand from growing (Boratav, this volume, Tables 9.3, 9.4 and 9.5; also Celâsun, this volume, Section II). Potential export markets were the only alternative for the industrial sector. This route, however, did not develop along the lines of earlier expeditions into likely markets. Rather, it was the war between Iran and Iraq that opened up a new alternative. The conflict practically created a captive market for Turkey.

Both Iran and Iraq initially refused to trade with the other's trading partners. This could not apply to Turkey due to its strategic importance for the trade of both countries. Turkey could supply basic industrial products to both with relative ease. This developed into a symbiotic relationship between Turkey and its new trading partners. But, this commercial associ-ation did not have the promise of long term stability. It was primarily a series of barter deals exchanging Turkish manufactures for crude oil in a period of short-term crisis (Baysan and Blitzer, this volume). In times of peace Turkey could face serious competition from industrial countries along this new line of trade in the region. In the period of depressed demand in the OECD countries, the new Middle East market, including other oil exporters of the region, was a great windfall for the Turkish economy. However, with the sharp downturn in oil prices after 1985, the market had reached its limits.

And yet, exports to industrial countries started picking up after 1984 — Figure 10.5 (see also Baysan and Blitzer, this volume, Table 1.6). Com-pared to the composition of exports to the Middle East, manufactured exports going to OECD countries have a lower skill content (Şenses, this volume). But the change was encouraging beyond expectations. What accounts for this successful transition and what is the role of the post-1980 economic policy in this episode? Since 1980 Turkish exports have been entering a very tough market, restricted by rigid quotas in OECD coun-tries, and beset by foreign relations problems with the EEC over textile exports. So the recent success can be attributed to Turkey's ability to overcome quota restrictions in textile imports set by its trading partners in Europe and America. 'Learning' on the part of Turkish exporters and organizing by the Foreign Service have been responsible for this achieve-ment.

Credit is also due to the industrial protection of the earlier period which has made the industrial capacity possible that was exploited in the 1980s. Especially under the present conditions of sluggish investment, no growth would have been possible without prior accumulation.

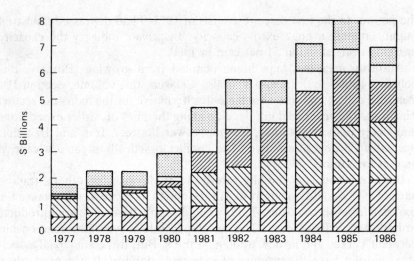

FIGURE 10.5 *Destination of Exports*

Rest of the world.
Other oil exporters.
Iran and Iraq.
US and Germany.
Other industrial economies.

SOURCE   IMF, (various years) *Direction of Trade Statistics*.

The Role of Middle East Politics and Prospects

Between 1980 and 1985 Turkey's net borrowing was in the order of $10 billion. Long-term (gross) capital flows in this period amounted to about $11 billion. Out of this, $9 billion was official capital. An overall evaluation of the economy as presented in this volume does not warrant enthusiastic support for the Turkish economy on the basis of the success of its economic policies. Causality in this matter may also go the other way; it is the flow of official capital that has made the Turkish economy buoyant. Since 1983 net resource transfer to Turkey has been negative. But, large current account deficits are now accommodated through short term commercial credit leading to a highly volatile situation reminiscent of the mid-1970s. This turnaround in Turkey's credit structure and economic prospects suggests that Turkey's success depends on its association with official financial organizations! A major part of this capital flow has been due to the security interests of its NATO allies. As more than the southern flank of the treaty organization, Turkey came to play a vital role in the Middle East. Pamela Harriman, a member of the Atlantic Council delegation, notes: 'As a secular state with a largely Moslem population, Turkey can be a forceful example of democracy in the Middle East. For it to play that role in its own interest and ours, it needs the steady American interest and support. On both counts, we now deliver less than we should' (*New York Times*, 20 February 1988, p. 27). While this comment refers directly to US Government loans and grants, it is clear tha the official US attitude set the tone for capital flows from the other OECD countries.

If the remarkable magnitude of capital infusion in the Turkish economy was to achieve what was the declared goal of the structural adjustment process, the policy should have been revised long ago. Definitely, continued loans and grants did not help realize the desired economic adjustment. However, its healthy persistence can be explained by the political goal of buying 'democracy' and cooperation in a strategically important country. In 1985, Assistant Secretary of State for European Affairs, Richard R. Burt elucidated Turkey's value in a Senate Foreign Relations Committee hearing:

Turkey has become a vital strategic bridge . . . both in a geographical sense and in a cultural sense between Western Europe . . . and the Middle East . . . The Turks . . . have insights and wisdom and experience that can be very helpful and very useful, particularly as NATO as an alliance has to look beyond its existing boundaries and worry about the extent to which Western interests are at stake in so-called third areas, like the Middle East, like the Indian Ocean, and like the Persian Gulf. . . . The Turks have given us the most valuable insights on the thinking in both Baghdad and Teheran, . . . they can have access to these capitals which we, for one reason or other, lack (US Congress, 1985).

Turkey had come around from acquiring emergency aid in a panic situation in 1979 to establishing itself as an important instrument in Middle East politics. This was primarily due to the extension of conflict and the disqualification of competing candidates for the same function. It was the crisis in the Middle East that paid off for Turkey. During this period, the economy has been unable to achieve the structural renovation to maintain required growth for the future.

At this juncture the end to the conflict between Iran and Iraq and progress toward normalization of relations between the US and USSR are factors that will divert attention from Turkey's strategic position to its economic accomplishments. In this period of a major shift from official to private capital infusion, scrutiny of economic performance will become paramount.

NOTES

1. In the current literature on Turkey the impact of autonomous factors on economic performance is commonly measured and incorporated into the analysis. Oil price shocks and their impact on the Turkish economy is considered in the study by Celâsun and Rodrik (forthcoming). See also Lewis (1986). Lewis analyses the effect of external shocks on the Turkish economy in a CGE model. The significance of external shocks are generally acknowledged even if studies are not concerned with them. See also Baysan and Blitzer (this volume).

2. The preoccupation of the urban elite with the *gecekondu* (urban squatter) issue during the 1950s and 1960s is representative of the dilemma they faced: the new urban structure did not appear as 'modern' as they perceived themselves to be. Under the guise of concern (social or academic) for the urban migrants of 'traditional' origins there lay the fear of this foreign population in the cities. The agenda then was the transformation of this new urban population into modern society. Contemporary studies approach the issue not as an anomaly, but as a form of self-adaptation by the new migrants.

3. Between 1972 and 1977 imports of crude oil and oil products increased from $155 million to $1468 million. During the same period total imports increased from $1562 million to $5796 million and total exports from $855 million to $1753 million (World Bank, 1982, pp. 414–415).

4. Lewis (1986) considers the impact of the oil price shock on the economy. Although he measures different types of external shocks, interrelationships between the external shocks are not fully accounted for due to limitations of modeling and the nature of his assumptions. For example, Lewis's assumption in fixing remittances at their historic levels through 1978 (p. 62) is unrealistic because historic remittances between 1974–78 reflect a severe curtailment in the flow of labor to EEC countries due to the oil price shock itself. The result is that the best scenario is not good enough when the full impact of external factors is considered. Celâsun and Rodrik in their favorable scenario assume that in the absence of a reduction in foreign activity, remittances would have continued to grow at the trend rate observed during 1972–74. 'This brings the effect of the external shock to a level of severity higher than Balassa's average' (forthcoming, pp. 2.5).

    Neither Celâsun and Rodrik nor Lewis consider other exogenous variables which are not classified as external shocks — such as international sanctions as a consequence of Turkish intervention in Cyprus and the consequent diplomatic conflict with Greece. These resulted in major repercussions in terms of the flow and source of foreign capital to Turkey. Unsound borrowing techniques that Celâsun and Rodrik study in their second chapter are partly the result of Turkey not having access to more favorable credit. Such shocks, due to their non-economic nature, are not regularly included in models of economic analysis.

5. From a peak of $1426 million in 1974, workers' remittances fell to $982 million in 1977. The migrant labor population was unchanged in this period. The decline was due to the overvalued exchanged rate (World Bank, 1982).

6. Providing retirement and health insurance. For data and definitions see ILO (various years).

7. Between 1972 and 1977 domestic employment accommodated part of the frustrated candidates for out-migration.

	1971	*72*	*73*	*74*	*75*	*76*	*77*
Annual change in insured* employment	91[†]	120	124	151	23	195	173
Annual emigration	88	85	136	20	4	10	19

* Retirement and health insurance provided by the 'social insurance program'.
[†] In thousands.
SOURCES Employment figures from ILO, *Yearbook of Labour Statistics*, various years; emigration figures from World Bank, 1982, p. 405.

8. Sugar, bread, white cotton cloth also head the list of basics the price of which had been controlled as a republican tradition. But, in the period of oil price shocks oil prices stood out as the most dramatic example.
9. The smaller parties held a key role in the establishment of coalitions and bargained for a disproportionate share in the cabinet positions that they were to control. According to the leader of the religious party, Necmettin Erbakan, the key in the party's emblem signified that the party held the key to the deadlocks in the Turkish political system.
10. With the wisdom of hindsight it is obvious that the policies of the Turkish governments in this period could not continue. Some writers go so far as to call them irrational (Baysan and Blitzer, this volume). To be fair in the historical evaluation of the 1970s, we need to observe that no critique of economic policies was made contemporaneously. Turkish economists did not understand then what was happening in world markets and foreign observers were not interested in studying the problem until it developed into a grave issue. The harbinger of crisis was the depletion of foreign exchange reserves and the end of short-term credit. On this account, open reflection of politicians and bankers of the period would be most revealing.
11. The increase was over threefold for those looking for a job (job search) — from 44 000 to over 150 000 (ILO). The figure represents about 50 per cent according to the estimates of the Ministry of Labor, from under a million to about 1.5 million.
12. In 1964 US interference in Turkey's use of NATO weapons marked by the 'Johnson Letter' during an earlier phase of the Cyprus crisis, became the watershed in Turkey-US relations.
13. For an unconventional interpretation of the US's Middle East policy during the detente period see Schurmann (1987, pp. 247–313).
14. For recent accounts of the episode see Rustow (1987, pp. 97–105), and Harris (1985, pp. 192–6). For a more complete account see Laipson (1981). In Laipson's account (and also Rustow's) there is considerable emphasis on the crisis in the US executive branch following the Watergate episode. They argue that if it was not for the abnormal state of affairs in the United States at that time, US military aid to Turkey would not have been discontinued. On the other hand, the European reaction to the Cyprus crisis was similar to that of the United States.
15. Between mid-1977 and 1982 the Turkish economy was virtually cut off from private capital markets.
16. On the arms embargo and the course it took in US foreign relations see Laipson (1981) and Laipson (1983).

17. 'US Informing Turkey About Plan to Provide $300 Million Aid in '80,' *New York Times*, 10 January 1979.
18. See, for example, Barbara Slavin and Rosanne Klass, 'Help for Turkey now Looms Larger', *New York Times*, 14 January 1979: 'The question mark of Iran has punctuated Turkey's strategic and political importance to the United States with a new exclamation point'.
19. *Washington Post*, 14 January 1979, p. G6; *Los Angeles Times*, 25 February 1979, pp. 2 and 6; *Washington Post*, 9 February 1979, p. A15.
20. In the words of US Deputy Secretary of State Warren Christopher, Turkey's importance in the region went far beyond the Iran question. Rather it was a broader regional issue involving the issue in the broadest sense. 'This Turbulence — in Iran, Afghanistan, Yemen, and elsewhere — affects fundamental US economic and security interests . . . the importance of a stable, democratic and pro-Western Turkey has never been clearer' (US Congress, House, 1979). Statements by Alexander Haig and Warren Christopher are from Mufti (1987).
21. *Congressional Record*, House, 21 March 1979, pp. 5633–4.
22. 'Israeli Says Turkey May Face Upheaval,' *New York Times*, 16 February 1979, p. 11.
23. 'Turkey Demands More US Aid for Use of Bases', by John Lawton, *Washington Post*, 9 May 1979, pp. Al, Al8.
24. 'Creditor Nations Delay Financial Aid to Turkey,' *New York Times*, 7 March 1979, pp. Dl, D13. And this did not help relations at all as the *New York Times* reports on 19 March 1979: 'Turkey's Relations with US still Tense: Despite Lifting of Arms Embargo, Ecevit is Bitter at NATO and Economic aid Conditions'. Following are some excerpts from the news story: 'This hostile attitude comes at a delicate time for Turkish American relations. Turkey has never been so important to American interests; with the closing of monitoring stations in Iran, the facilities in Turkey are the closest to the Soviet Union . . . Ecevit said recently that he would like the United States to use its influence with the IMF to ease its demand for Austerity measures in Turkey'.
25. 'Aid to Turkey Stirs Greek Cypriot Fear', *New York Times*, 28 January 1979, p. 8.

REFERENCES

Celâsun, M. and D. Rodrik (forthcoming) *Debt, Adjustment and Growth: Turkey*.
Erdilek, A. (1988) 'The Role of Foreign Investment in the Liberalization of the Turkish Economy', in (eds), T. F. Nas and M. Odekon, *Liberalization and the Turkish Economy* (New York: Greenwood Press) pp. 141–60.
Harris G. (1985) *Turkey: Coping with Crisis* (Boulder Colorado: Westview Press).
ILO (various years) *Yearbook of Labour Statistics* (Geneva: International Labor Organization).
Laipson, Ellen (1981) *Congressional-Executive Relations and the Turkish Arms Embargo*, report prepared for the House Committee on Foreign Affairs, Congress and Foreign Policy Series 3 (Washington DC).
Laipson, Ellen (1983) *US Interests in the Eastern Mediterranean: Turkey, Greece and Cyprus*, report prepared for the Subcommittee on Europe and The Middle East of the House Committee on Foreign Affairs, 98th Congress, 1st Session (Washington DC: Government Printing Office, 13 June 1983) Committee Print 1607.

Kuniholm, B. (1986a) 'Rhetoric and Reality in the Aegean: US Policy Options toward Greece and Turkey', *SAIS Review* 6, 1, pp. 137–57.

Kuniholm, B. (1986b) 'The Carter Doctrine, the Reagan Corollary, and Prospects for United States Policy in Southwest Asia', *International Journal* 41, Spring, pp. 342–61.

Kuniholm, B. (1985) 'Turkey in the World', in (ed.) G. Harris, *The Middle East in Turkish American Relations* (Washington DC: The Heritage Foundation) pp. 9–16.

Lewis, J. (1986) 'Coping With Adjustment: Turkey 1973–81', Development Discussion Paper 233, Harvard Institute of International Development, (Harvard University, Cambridge Massachusetts).

Mufti, M. (1987) 'Turkish American Relations and the Turkish Economy', unpublished, Cambridge Massachusetts.

Rustow, D. (1987) *Turkey: America's Forgetten Ally* (New York: Council of Foreign Relations).

Schurmann, F. (1987) *The Foreign Politics of Richard Nixon*, (Berkeley California: University of California, Institute of International Relations).

US Congress, House, Hearings Before the Subcommittee on Europe and the Middle East of the Committee on Foreign Affairs, Supplemental Aid Requests for Fiscal Years 1979 and 1980 for Turkey and Oman, 96th Congress, 15 May 1979. 79: H381-31 (Y4. F76/1: T84/3), pp. 7–8.

US Congress, Senate, Committee on Armed Services, Department of Defense Authorization for Appropriations for Fiscal Year 1980, 22 February 1979. 79: S 201–12.5 (Y4. Ar5/3: D36/7/980/Pt.2) p. 785.

US Congress, *Senate Foreign Relations Committee, Security and Development Assistance Hearings*, Microfilm, S381–28.8, March 22, 1985, CIS/MF/12, pp. 794–5.

World Bank (1982) *Turkey: Industrialization and Trade Strategy*, a World Bank country study (Washington DC).

11 Turkish Debt and Conditionality In Historical Perspective: A Comparison of the 1980s with the 1860s[1]

Emine Kıray

After the mid 1950s Turkey embarked on a industrialization strategy which relied heavily on foreign capital inflows to finance its intermediate and capital goods imports. Associated with this strategy were regular balance of payments crises, often leading to exogenously imposed stabilization measures. Such stabilization measures were negotiated with the IMF in 1958, 1970, 1978–79 and finally in 1980. Of these, the 1980 programme stands out as the most radical in terms of the extent of structural change it seeks to achieve. The implementation of the 1980 programme which liberalized and opened the Turkish economy to world markets has been accompanied by unprecedented levels of foreign capital inflows. The performance of private investment, however, has not matched expectations and the debt burden of the economy has steadily increased. There are a number of useful comparative analyses of the 20th-century stabilization programmes (see Schick and Tonak, 1987; Ekzen, 1984). The purpose of this paper is to widen the historical context of the comparative analysis by looking at the period of the Ottoman debt and the stabilization programme of the 1860 British mission.

The first section discusses the reform recommendations of the 1860 mission and compares them to the recommendations of the IMF and the World Bank today. Strikingly, all the programmes recommend the government to reduce budget deficits, restrict monetary growth, and ensure real devaluation for short-term stability; and to deregulate markets, curtail the role of the state, and liberalize foreign trade and foreign capital inflows for long-term growth. The second section discusses the outcomes of proposed reforms, concentrating on a comparison of the 1860s with the 1980s. Again the similarities are striking. Regardless of economic performance or improvement in repayment capacity, based on official approval alone, there are extensive capital inflows into the economy. In both cases investment fails to revive and the economy sinks deeper into debt. The last two sections review the differences between the 19th- and 20th-century economic structures and offer some lessons from history.

I CONDITIONALITY

The Ottoman state incurred a large foreign debt in the 1854–1914 period. Between 1854 and 1875, 15 loans totalling 220 million British pounds were issued, primarily to finance budget deficits, convert internal liabilities to external liabilities and pay back old loans. From 1860s onward the burden of the debt increased rapidly. In the early 1860s the annual service charges were 10 per cent of total government revenues; in the late 1860s this figure was 33 per cent and in 1874, 67 per cent. In 1875 the state defaulted and in 1881 the Public Debt Administration (PDA) was established whereby Europeans directly administered and collected some of the tax revenues to service the debt. Between 1886 and 1914, 26 more loans totalling 93 million British pounds were issued for the consolidation, conversion, and repayment of old loans and for financing railroads. All but four of these were administered by the PDA. The PDA was not formally abolished until 1928. The final payment on the Ottoman debt of the 1854–1914 period was made by Turkey in 1954 — exactly a century after the first loan.

Repayment problems surfaced very early on in this process. When in 1860 the attempt to raise a loan in Paris failed and the state could not meet its obligations to the European mercantile houses, it turned to Britain for help. The British, in turn, sent two members of the Board of Trade, Lord Hobart and Mr Foster, to investigate finances. Their 'Report on the Financial Condition of Turkey' was submitted to the British Houses of Parliament in 1862 and the British Ambassador to Istanbul, Sir Henry Bulwer, was charged with presenting the contents of the Report to the Sultan and pressing for the recommended reforms (for more details, see Kıray, 1987).

Short-term Stabilization

Similarities between the diagnoses and recommendations of the IMF and the World Bank today and those of the Hobart-Foster mission in 1860 are quite striking. In Hobart and Foster's report the problems of the Ottoman economy are classified into short-term and structural aspects. As in the missions of today, the two issues they concentrate on with respect to short-term stabilization are excessive monetary growth and budget deficits. The Report identifies the root cause of the short-term problems faced by the economy as the persistent budget deficits. The argument is that the Ottoman state has run large budget deficits and financed these by issuing *kaime*, inconvertible paper currency. This has produced an excess demand for goods, created inflationary pressure, and resulted in balance of payments deficits, leading to gold outflow. The recommendation is very familiar: top priority must be given to the withdrawal of paper currency and the reestablishment of the international monetary rules of the game, in this case the gold standard.

The Report does not explicitly discuss the implications of contractionary monetary policy for the balance of payments. Nevertheless, international monetary theory of the classical school indicates that external adjustment was expected to occur through real depreciation of the Ottoman currency. According to the quantity theory of money, the reduction in the money supply would reduce the price level, leaving the level of output unchanged. The price-specie flow mechanism, in turn, would improve the balance of trade while at the same time allowing the nominal exchange rate to appreciate enough to stop the gold outflow. In other words, balance of payments adjustment would come not through a real depreciation based primarily on nominal depreciation as in the IMF sponsored programmes, but through a real depreciation based solely on a fall in the domestic price level.

The second item in the Report's agenda for short-term stability, as for the missions of today, is the reduction of the budget deficit. Here the recommendation is tax reform on the revenue side and a rearrangement of priorities on the expenditure side. The argument is that the Ottoman economy can sustain budget surpluses and repay the debt without significantly increasing the tax burden and without reducing expenditures. On the expenditure side the recommendation is to reduce the salaries of the higher officials and officers and to reduce the number of lower officials and officers. The savings obtained from these measures, according to the Report, need to be applied to infrastructure, military spending, and judicial reform. On the revenue side the most important reform recommendation is to abolish tax farming (*iltizam*), institute direct collection and thus get a portion of the revenues the tax farmers appropriated illegally. By redistributing the illegal gains of the tax farmers, the Report argues, the state can increase revenues while reducing the tax burden of the peasantry. In addition to direct collection, they recommend some tax increases — raising the tobacco tax rates, widening the coverage of the stamp tax, the conversion of some *waqf* (religious foundation) property to freehold upon the payment of a lump sum fee, and instituting a new residential tax in Istanbul and a per capita tax on male servants — to eliminate the budget deficit. If these measures are undertaken, the Report argues, the Ottomans will be in a position to repay the existing debt as well as get access to more foreign loans.

Despite a hundred years of change in the institutional structure of the global as well as the domestic economy, the thrust of the 20th-century short-term stabilization plans is very much the same. In all of the IMF missions the diagnosis of the short-term problems regarding the balance of payments and inflation is that large and persistent budget deficits financed by domestic credit creation have led to excess demand, inflation, overvaluation of the real exchange rate and thus to balance of payment deficits. The general recipe in all four of the 20th-century missions to Turkey is also for reduction of the budget deficit, ceilings on domestic credit creation and devaluation of the exchange rate.

With respect to exchange rate policy, the recommendation under the Bretton Woods system (1958 and 1970 missions) is a once and for all devaluation of the nominal exchange rate. Under the new international system where most industrial countries have flexible exchange rates the recommendation is a crawling peg, as in the 1978–79 negotiations, or flexible exchange rates, as in the 1980 programme which, since May 1981 has instituted daily specifications of the exchange rate. The analysis in all is that the reduction of the budget deficit would allow for contractionary monetary policy by reducing the state's demand for credit. Both policies would reduce domestic absorbtion and rein in inflation. While these contractionary monetary and fiscal policies put downward pressure on prices, the nominal devaluation would allow further real depreciation of the currency, improving the trade balance and reducing the pressure on the balance of payments. Moreover, since in the IMF's analyses the net impact of devaluation is expansionary, the level of output would be maintained. Achieving short-term stability, in turn, would allow the economy to repay the existing foreign debt as well as get access to more private foreign credit.

Structural Adjustment

For long-term structural adjusment, again much like the analyses of the IMF and World Bank, the recommendations of the 1860 mission concentrate on three aspects: get the prices right, reduce and redefine the role of the state in the economy, and liberalize both foreign direct invesment and foreign trade.

The mission's overall recommendation is to allow markets to determine prices; to 'remove interferences with the free course of supply and demand' — end all government monopolies, abolish the system of guilds, remove price controls, and stop prohibiting the peasantry from leaving the estates of the landholders — for 'any attempt to artificially regulate labor and production by government control can only result in injury to the state and to the people' (Hobart and Foster, 1862, p. 33).

In addition, the mission finds the presence of the state in the economy to be much too extensive. The Report argues that in the longest run increases in revenue and productivity must come from the sale of properties belonging to the state — real estate, fisheries, forests, mines and land. Best results will be obtained if the state abolishes the exclusion of foreigners from landownership rights, or, in other words, liberalizes foreign direct investment. The recommendation is to:

> lay aside all jealousy of private enterprise, whether national or foreign and throw doors open to free competition, . . . [in fact] it is by foreign capital that the land would be made most valuable both to the government which would receive a higher price for the property and to the community which would profit by the development of its productive power.
>
> (Hobart and Foster, 1862, p. 15.)

The proper role for the state, Hobart and Foster reiterate, is to provide defense for security of property, justice to ensure the fulfillment of contracts and infrastructure to stimulate trade.

With respect to the liberalization of trade, the Report endorses the Trade Agreement of 1860. This agreement reduced the 12 per cent duty on exports to 8 per cent, and provided for a further percentage point reduction each year thereafter until it reached 1 per cent. In return, the 5 per cent duty on imports was increased to 8 per cent, but the 4 per cent duty on transit trade was reduced to 2 per cent. Hobart and Foster acknowledge that this agreement would reduce customs revenues in the short run, but assert their optimism that trade liberalization as well as the abolition of tax farming which was to reduce the tax burden of the peasantry would 'on the whole . . . contribute in a very important degree to increase [revenues] indirectly by the relief which it will give to the cultivators of the soil and the consequent stimulus to production and trade throughout the Empire' (Hobart and Foster, 1862, p. 7).

In essence the mission argues that in the long run, higher investment and growth would be achieved by giving full rein to competition between private domestic and foreign captial, within the context of the allocative mechanism of free markets and a curtailed role for the state. These policies of getting the prices right, reducing and redefining the role of the state, and liberalizing foreign trade and foreign capital flows are all also an integral part of the 20th-century missions to Turkey. The 1980 programme, however, stands out as the most far reaching in this respect.

In all of the earlier 20th-century missions, despite formal recommendations for liberalization and structural change, the emphasis was on balance of payments adjustment through short-term macroeconomic policies. The explicit overriding objective of the 1980 programme, in contrast, is the liberalization and structural transformation of the economy. In this respect, the vision of the policy makers in the 1980s is essentially the vision of Hobart and Foster in the 1860s.

As the other papers in this volume discuss in detail, in the 1980s, in order to establish the allocative mechanism of free markets, the state has decontrolled the prices of all goods in the private as well as the public sector, with the exception of a few basic goods. Similarly, the state attempted to remove all interest rate regulations in July 1980, though it has been forced to reinstitute some regulatory guidelines following the financial panic of 1982 (see Akyüz, this volume).

In order to reduce the role of the state in the economy, policy makers have taken steps to overhaul the public sector, with the longer term goal of privatizing the State Economic Enterprises (SEEs). During the initial stage, the government took measures to subject the SEEs to market forces by removing price subsidies and cancelling almost all preferences given to SEEs with respect to taxes, tariffs and credits. As part of the second stage, the government passed legislation authorizing the sale of SEEs to the private sector in 1986 (Kopits, 1987).

In order to liberalize trade, the state initially reduced import quotas and gave subsidies to exports in an attempt to achieve broad neutrality in the foreign trade regulatory structure. Since 1983, policy measures have been taken to further liberalize trade through reductions in import tariffs as well as export subsidies (see Baysan and Blitzer, this volume). In order to liberalize foreign capital flows, the state has authorised convertible Turkish lira deposits, has allowed banks and local authorities to borrow in international financial markets, and has set up a new incentive structure for foreign direct investment, including plans for free trade zones. Although liber lization is by no means complete, for the policy makers of the 1980s, as for Hobart and Foster, the ideal appears to be a laissez faire, laissez passer system.

One major difference between the 19th-century programme and the 20th-century programmes is in incomes policies. The 20th century programmes have sought to limit the rate of growth of nominal wages to a rate below inflation rate, worsening the income distribution. In contrast, the recommendations of the 1860 Report would have led to an improvement of the income distribution, redistributing income from tax farmers and high level bureaucrats to peasants through the institution of direct tax collection, the reshuffling of expenditure priorities and reduced tariffs. The rationale behind this was a supply-side reasoning that higher disposable income for peasants would increase the production of exportables. The explicit purpose of the 20th-century policy is to reduce inflation, partly because the wage-price spiral is seen to be a main link between excess demand and inflation and partly because devaluations, removal of price subsidies and interest rate increases already put much cost-push pressure on prices, threatening the integrity of the overall programme. In practice this policy helps to reduce domestic absorbtion, reduce imports and free up domestic production for export. Again, implementation has been most drastic during the 1980 programme. Between 1979 and 1985 there was a 40 per cent reduction in real wages and a 17 per cent reduction in real agricultural incomes as nominal wages and the rate of increase of agricultural support prices fell below the rate of inflation (see Boratav, this volume).

Despite this difference, however, the overall policy recommendations of the 19th century and the 20th century are very similar: reduce budget deficits, restrict monetary growth and ensure real devaluation for short-term macro stability; free markets, curtail the role of the state, and liberalize foreign investment and trade for long-term growth.

II OUTCOMES

Although the degree of implementation of the recommendations as well as the success or failure of the missions by their own criteria vary through time, the essential outcome also seems to be very similar. Following each of the missions there are significant capital inflows and debt rescheduling easing the balance of payments crisis. At times, after the 1980 mission, as after the 1860 mission, for example, the country is held up as an exemplary debtor triggering even more capital inflows. Initially there is an improvement in export performance, but ultimately imports rise faster than exports and the country goes further into debt. Meanwhile there appears to be little or no change in the productive or the repayment capacity of the economy.

In 1862 Hobart and Foster concluded their Report optimistically by stating that: 'The case with which [the government] has to deal is . . . simply of financial disorder, caused chiefly by inattention to the ordinary rules of political economy and fiscal administration', and that if the state implemented the reforms they recommended financial stability would be restored (Hobart and Foster, 1862, pp. 41–2). The Report, in turn, was received very favorably in the British parliament and in the British capital markets. In Parliament, undersecretary of State for Foreign Affairs, Mr Layard, noted the 'gratifying feature of the Report' that 'there was nothing fundamentally rotten or bad in the state of Turkish finance' and reminded his audience that the Ottoman state had 'never failed to pay her debts with the greatest of punctuality'. Prime Minister Lord Palmerston followed with an eulogy on the virtues of Sultan Abdul Aziz. This optimism and the willingness of the Ottoman state to undertake almost all of the short-term recommendations and most of the long-term recommendations triggered extensive capital inflows in the period following the mission.

Soon after the Report became public, the Ottoman government communicated its desire to raise a loan to withdraw the paper money. The 1862 loan for 8 million British pounds was a phenomenal success in the European money markets, being five times over-subscribed. As *The London*

Times noted on 1 April 1862: 'Hundreds of the wisest, the shrewdest, and the richest of Englishmen have been rushing to declare in a language which cannot be doubted their conviction that the the "sick man" is convalescent'. Another loan for 8 million British pounds in 1863 was used to retire some of the short-term debt and a loan for 32.9 million in 1865 was used to convert the remaining short-term debt. In 1865 and 1869 two additional loans were contracted for 6 million and 22 million pounds, respectively, to cover budget deficits and pay back old loans. Thus, while during the eight years between 1854 and 1861 the Ottoman state had borrowed a total of 15 million British pounds, during the seven years after the mission it was able to borrow a total of 76.9 million pounds. Neither foreign loans, nor the reforms the Ottoman state undertook, however, helped the productive capacity of the Ottoman economy. Liberalization of the economy undermined the existing manufacturing sector, there was no outburst of private investment in agriculture, and the repayment capacity of the economy did not improve (for details, see Kıray, 1987, chapter 7). The debt service burden increased steadily from 15 per cent of exports in the early 1860s to 40 per cent in the late 1860s and to 66 per cent in 1874.

Similarly, after the announcement of the 24 January 1980 reform programme, Turkey was able to renegotiate more than $6.5 billion of outstanding debt and OECD countries provided emergency loans totalling $1.3 billion. Between 1980 and 1984 Turkey received SDR 3.5 billion in stand-by agreements with the IMF and $1.56 million in five structural adjustment loans from the World Bank. Total foreign debt, including short-term debt, has increased from $16.5 billion in 1980 to $20.8 billion in 1984 and to $38 billion in 1987. One of the major achievements of the programme has been the growth of exports, averaging 25 per cent per year between 1980 and 1985. Despite this record export growth, however, medium- and long-term debt service as a percentage of exports has increased from 26 per cent in 1984 to 37 per cent in 1986, and is expected to exceed 60 per cent in 1988.[2] At the same time, as all the papers in this volume point out, private investment has been lagging and growth of the productive capacity of the economy has not matched expectations. Public investment in infrastructure, financed by foreign loans, has sustained growth rates, but net private investment in manufacturing, the target sector of the export push, remains negligible (see Conway [this volume] and Anand, Chhibber and van Wijnbergen [this volume]). In spite of all the structural reforms, repayment capacity of the economy has not improved. The impressive growth in exports has been sustained by an increase in capacity utilisation and a reduction in domestic absorbtion, but has not produced an outburst of private investment activity.

It is clear that in the 19th century, the official approval the British parliament gave to the Ottoman state and the consequent inflow of foreign capital had to do with the Near Eastern policy of Britain. By 1850 the

Ottoman economy was the third largest importer of British goods, behind the Hanse Towns and Holland, and thus important to British interests. At the same time, with the advent of railroads, the Ottoman Empire gained political importance as the critical link for the overland route to India. In addition, the British wanted a strong ally in the region to stem the expansionist policies of the Russian Empire. Thus, regardless of the performance of the Ottoman economy, the British were willing to fund the fiscal crisis of the Ottoman state. Indeed, after the opening of the Suez Canal in 1869, the political focus switched to Egypt, the British government withdrew official approval, and the inflow of British loans decreased.[3]

Similarly, the loans to Turkey without close scrutiny of economic performance, seem to do both with US foreign policy in the region and the need to find an exemplary debtor. Turkey gained political importance in the region after the Iranian revolution. This was reinforced after the Soviet invasion of Afghanistan and the outbreak of the Iran-Iraq war. Turkey was seen as a stabilizing influence during a period in which the turmoil in the Middle East intensified. The thawing of relations between the Soviet Union and the United States, withdrawal of Soviet forces from Afghanistan, and defusion of the tensions in the Gulf indicate a less optimistic scenario for the future rate of capital inflow (see Arıcanlı, this volume). At the same time, these unprecedented levels of capital inflows have allowed Turkey to be cited along with South Korea and Thailand as a 'successfully adjusting debtor', legitimizing IMF and World Bank prescriptions. Turkey's growth performance, averaging 4.9 per cent per year between 1980 and 1986, is indeed impressive when compared to the average annual growth rates of 0.7 per cent in the 17 highly indebted countries over the same period (World Bank, 1988, p. 65). What is problematic, however, is the way the economy will react as the rate of foreign capital inflow slows down, since the performance of the Turkish economy has been critically dependent on foreign capital inflows that have financed public investment (see Anand, Chhibber and van Wijnbergen, this volume).

III   HISTORICAL ANALYSIS

One possible interpretation of these similarities in policy prescriptions and outcomes is that nothing fundamental has changed over the past 130 years. Orthodox economic wisdom as well as the national and international structural parameters remain the same, so that we observe a regular cyclical process.[4]

As should be clear by the analysis of this paper, there is in fact much truth to the proposition that economic orthodoxy has not changed. Despite persuasive arguments by structuralist and institutionalist economists who point out that the impact of the policy prescriptions may in fact be perverse due to the structural specificities of the LDCs (see, for example, Taylor, 1983), no alternative policy package has been found that also satisfies the interests of the international and domestic elites. The upshot of all the stabilization and structural adjustment programmes has been to let markets rule and open up the economy to international economic stimuli. There are, however, subtle but important differences between the various programmes in their insistence on certain policies.

The second proposition, that the structural parameters have not changed significantly over the past 130 years, is much harder to maintain. This is, in fact, where broad historical analyses are most useful — in helping to identify systemic turning points, qualitative rather than quantitative differences between periods. A historical approach also underlines the importance of the nature of relations with the global economy in determining the domestic economic structure. In this context three different periods emerge with respect to national and international economic structures as well as the ways the two interact: 1860s, 1950–80, and post–1980.[5]

During the 19th century, as the Europeans began to consolidate a worldwide economic system, it is clear that they perceived both the markets and the primary resources of the Ottoman economy to be very important for their own growth. They visualized a free market system whereby the Ottomans would utilize their comparative advantage and become producers and exporters of primary goods and importers of manufactures.[6] They found, instead, a pre-capitalist world empire. Throughout this period the Ottoman state borrowed and the Europeans lent expressly to finance structural reforms.

The task of the 1860 mission was to ensure a structural transformation that accommodated the European vision. Thus, in addition to short-term stabilization measures forcing the state to play by the rules of the international monetary system, there were recommendations for extensive internal and external liberalization. Peasants as the producers of the agricultural output were given priority, liberalization of foreign direct investment was naturally couched in terms of 'landownership rights', and much emphasis was put on building roads explicitly in order to facilitate the inflow of manufactured imports and the outflow of primary exports.

The outcome of the liberalization and structural transformation attempt, however, was a socio-economic structure that could not sustain investment and growth. While industry, unable to compete with imported manufactures, disappeared, there was little domestic or foreign investment in the agricultural sector. The Ottoman economy became an exporter of primary goods and an importer of manufactures, but in essence exported its existing agricultural surplus in return for imports of military and luxury goods. The result was stagnation and default in 1875. In contrast to the outward orientation and laissez faire laissez passer vision of the 19th century, the post-World War II (or, post-Great Depression) period was a period of relative inward orientation throughout much of the world. In the West investment and growth was sustained largely by domestic demand through the establishment of the welfare-warfare state, the labor-capital accord which passed productivity increases onto real wages, and Keynesian economic policies. The counterpart of this in most less developed countries and in Turkey was the Import Substitution Industrialization (ISI) policy.

After 1954, and more systematically after 1962 Turkey followed a deliberate industrialization policy which also depended on domestic demand for growth, but did not emphasise the domestic production of capital goods. In terms of international economic relations, the strategy relied on import regulation: encouragement of imports of capital goods, raw materials and semi-finished goods; limitations on imports of luxury goods; and protection against competing imports. At the same time Turkey continued to rely on exports of primary goods and, after the 1960s, export of labor power to provide it with the necessary foreign exchange to fuel this mode of accumulation. The resulting structure of accumulation was an inward oriented one where oligopolistic firms were protected from international competition, growth and investment were sustained by internal markets and thus relatively high real wages were accommodated within the system. The weak link, of course, was foreign exchange. While rapid industrialization and growth increased the demand for imports of capital and intermediate goods, the emphasis on manufactures for domestic consumption did not generate an equivalent export and foreign exchange earning capacity. Periodic crises, then, were manifest as balance of payments crises, leading to foreign debt. During this period, in other words, foreign debt helped finance a rapid, though lopsided, industrialization process. Whereas best estimates for the Ottoman economy in the 19th century indicate an annual growth rate of no more than 1–1.5 per cent, the annual growth rate of the Turkish economy between 1962 and 1976 was 6.9 per cent (Boratav, 1988, p. 140).

In this global environment of relative autonomy, the Bretton Woods institutions, however grudgingly, accepted the legitimacy of planning, regulation and the general ISI framework. In the 1958, 1970, and the 1978–79 negotiations the emphasis was on national and international macro stabilization. Structural adjustment recommendations were for gradual liberalization and there was not much insistence. They implicitly acknowledged the importance of regulating the interest rate structure, foreign exchange regimes, and pricing practices to meet internal policy goals (Ekzen, 1984, pp. 181–4).

Such of course is no longer the case. In the 1980s, with the insistence or blessing of the IMF and the World Bank, Turkey has once again started to borrow to finance a structural transformation. More importantly, once again the ultimate goal seems to be to establish some sort of a laissez faire, laissez passer system with the aim of utilizing static comparative advantage and pushing out exports. Although a more detailed study of the Bretton Woods institutions is needed to understand this intellectual shift, the severity of the Third World debt crisis and orthodox analyses of why the NICs have been successful in avoiding balance of payments difficulties — essentially giving free rein to markets — seem to have been instrumental.

The difference between the current situation and the 19th century is that the ISI period has allowed Turkey to build an industrial base, enabling it to export high value added manufactures. The difference with respect to the earlier 20th century period is that in the 1980s Turkey has switched from a mode of accumulation which relied on the growth of domestic demand to one which relies on the growth of world demand. In other words, once again the policy makers have given the power of determination of outcomes to world markets. This raises serious issues with regards to what Turkey's comparative advantage will be in the long term, since it cannot be independent of how various economies adjust to the recent strains in the world economy.[7]

The short-term prospects of the new strategy, however, may prove to be even more problematic. The sustainability of the ISI strategy was called into question with the three debt crises Turkey experienced over a period of twenty years. The weak performance of private investment and the rapid expansion of foreign debt during the past eight years, however, do not bode well for the sustainability of the open economy strategy either. As Rodrik points out in this volume, the continual real depreciation of the Turkish lira, the liberalization of interest rates and the capital account, as well as the privatization plans of the government already put an undue burden on the internal transfer from the private sector to the public sector which is necessary to service the debt. While reductions in public investment to increase the primary budget surplus will lower the growth rate and dampen private investment, domestic financing of budget deficits in liberalized financial markets is likely to create macro-instability, again discouraging private investment. Meanwhile it is clear that neither debt service nor import liberalization can be sustained unless there is investment in the export sectors.

IV CONCLUSION

In 1881, six years after the default, the Ottoman state and the representatives of the European bondholders reached an agreement. The Decree of *Muharrem* reduced the outstanding Ottoman debt by 40 per cent and the annual service charges by 80 per cent. In return, the administration of approximately 20 per cent of the Ottoman tax revenues was turned over to the Public Debt Administration (PDA) which serviced the debt. While the Hobart-Foster mission had recommended the liberalization of the Ottoman economy and a reduction in the role of the state, the PDA accomplished its mission through increased control, planning and regulation.

The PDA, for example, continued to administer salt revenues as a state monopoly, retained the prohibition on imports of salt, and managed to double revenues and increase exports by six-fold between 1892 and 1909. It turned over the administration of tobacco revenues to the *Regie*, giving it monopoly control over cultivation, processing, purchase and sale of all tobacco products. The *Regie* in turn doubled both production and exports between 1900 and 1911. The PDA lobbied European governments to allow an increase in customs duties and managed to institute a 3 per cent surcharge in 1907. Similarly, in opposition to the capitulations, it managed to extend the incidence of the stamp tax to foreigners and foreign nationals in 1894, leading to a 60 per cent increase in revenues by 1902. At the same time, the PDA acted as an agent of foreign firms, negotiating the privileges and concessions they required from the Ottoman state before they would undertake direct investment (Blaisdell, 1929, pp. 109–13, 133–46, 154–73, 222–35). It was with these extra-market incentives that investment in railroads, harborworks, municipal services, industry and mining increased from a negligible amount in the 1860s and 1870s to 74 million British pounds in 1914 (Pamuk, 1984, pp. 63–5).

Whereas between 1854 and 1881 there was a net inflow of 34 million British pounds due to the public debt, between 1882 and 1913 there was a net outflow of 49 million pounds, as the PDA accomplished its mission. It was, moreover, a successful repayment plan by economists' criteria: balance of payments calculations by Pamuk indicate that there was no net transfer of resources to Europe between 1882 and 1913. The Ottoman economy continued to run average annual trade deficits of 2.2 million British pounds, financed by net capital inflows due to direct investment and short-term mercantile credit.

The casualty of the PDA era, of course, was the freedom to undertake the necessary measures with an eye to domestic development and industrialization objectives. The problems of a largely stagnant agricultural economy like the Ottoman economy are very different than those faced by a semi-industrialized country like Turkey. The lesson of history, however, may well be that Turkey needs to put aside various ideological imperatives and tackle the debt issue with realism and resolve according to its own priorities, before the creditors do so on their own terms.

NOTES

1. I would like to thank Tosun Arıcanlı and Marcellus Andrews for their comments on earlier drafts of this paper; Elizabeth Bernatowicz and Michelle Geoffrion for valuable research assistance; and Ford Foundation's Senior Fellows and

Dana Foundation's internship programmes at Wellesley College for providing funding for research assistance.
2. TÜSİAD (1987, p. 2); see also Baysan and Blitzer (this volume). As Rodrik (this volume) points out, when short term debt is included, the debt service-export ratio becomes 51 per cent in 1984 and 84.1 per cent in 1986.
3. For details on the relative importance of Britain, France and Germany as lenders, see Kıray (1987, chapter 2).
4. For the 20th century, Schick and Tonak (1987) describe a cyclical process in which an experiment in free trade and free markets supported by economic orthodoxy leads to balance of payments crises; these are funded by short-term foreign debt and accompanied by quota-tariff-tax restrictions on foreign trade which fail to alleviate the crisis; a short-term solution is offered by familiar IMF prescriptions which provide the needed capital inflows but start the process over again by instituting liberalization.
5. A fuller understanding of history would, of course, require the periodization of the interwar period as well as a discussion of the evolution of the world economy and Turkey's relations with it. This, however, is well beyond scope of this paper. For a discussion on Turkey since 1908, see Boratav (1988).
6. The vision of the West is nicely summarized by David Urquhart in his book on Turkey published in 1833:

> It is established that our cottons, muslins, chintzes, etc., are if not better, infinitely cheaper than those of the East. Taste is gradually directing itself to our manufactures . . . We may calculate, at no remote period, if, indeed, political troubles are arrested, on supplying the necessaries as well as the luxuries of the whole of the Eastern population, whose energies will thus be exclusively directed to agriculture and the furnishing of raw produce . . .
>
> (Cited in Issawi, 1966, p. 442.)

7. Today the world economy as a whole has a much less nationally oriented structure. With the world recession of the early 1980s international competition has intensified, excess capacity has appeared in many sectors, profit margins have fallen, there is financial instability, and the international monetary system is under strain. How countries will adjust, what type of an international division of labor will emerge is not at all clear. Two international trends are discernible. One trend is the intensification of price competition though successive reductions in production costs. In this case the comparative advantage of Turkey would be the new, disciplined industrial labor force, provided wages are kept low and political stability is maintained. The second trend, the social democratic trend if you will, is international Keynesianism to boost global effective demand. In this case Turkey may be able to follow a strategy of exporting manufactures, while also sustaining a relatively good income distribution which provides domestic as well as international demand.

REFERENCES

Boratav, K. (1988) *Türkiye İktisat Tarihi, 1908–1985* (Turkish Economic History, 1908–1985) (Istanbul: Gerçek Yayınevi).

Blaisdell, D. C. (1929) *European Financial Control in the Ottoman Empire* (New York: Columbia University Press).

Ekzen, N. (1984) '1980 Stabilizasyon Paketinin 1958, 1970, ve 1978–79 Paketleri ile Karşılaştırmalı Analizi' (A Comparative Analysis of the 1980 Stabilization Package with the 1958, 1970 and 1978–79 Packages), in İ. Tekeli *et al.*,

Türkiye'de ve Dünyada Yaşanan Ekonomik Bunalım (The Current Economic Crisis in Turkey and the World) (Ankara: Yurt Yayınları) pp. 165–87.

Erdost, C., (ed.) (1982) *IMF İstikrar Politikaları ve Türkiye* (IMF Stabilization Policies and Turkey (Ankara: Savaş Yayınları).

Hobart, Lord V. H. and E. M. Foster (1862) 'Report on the Financial Condition of Turkey', Great Britain: *Parliamentary Papers*, Vol. 64, No. 2972.

Issawi, C., (ed.) (1966) *The Economic History of the Middle East, 1800–1914* (Chicago: The University of Chicago Press).

Kıray, E. (1987) 'Foreign Debt and Structural Change in the "Sick Man of Europe": The Ottoman Empire, 1850–1875', PhD dissertation, Massachusetts Institute of Technology.

Kopits, G. (1987) 'Structural Reform, Stabilization, and Growth in Turkey', International Monetary Fund Occasional Paper 52 (Washington DC: IMF).

Krueger, A. (1974) *Foreign Trade Regimes and Economic Development: Turkey* (New York: Colombia University Press).

Okyar, O. (1983) 'Turkey and the IMF: A Review of Relations, 1972–1982', in J. Williamson, (ed.) *IMF Conditionality* (Cambridge, Mass.: Massachusetts Institute of Technology Press) pp. 533–62.

Pamuk, Ş. (1984) *Osmanlı Ekonomisi ve Dünya Kapitalizmi, 1820–1913* (The Ottoman Economy and World Capitalism, 1820–1913) (Ankara: Yurt Yayınevi).

Schick, I. C. and E. A. Tonak (1987) 'The International Dimension: Trade, Aid, and Debt', in I. C. Shick and E. A. Tonak, (eds.), *Turkey in Transition: New Perspectives* (New York: Oxford University Press) pp. 333–63.

Taylor, L. (1983) *Structuralist Macroeconomics* (New York: Basic Books).

Tekeli İ., *et al.* (1984) *Türkiye'de ve Dünyada Yaşanan Ekonomik Bunalım* (The Current Economic Crisis in Turkey and the World) (Ankara: Yurt Yayınevi).

TÜSİAD (1987) *Dış Borçlar: Tahmin ve Analiz* (Foreign Debt: Estimation and Analysis) (Istanbul: Turkish Industrialists' and Businessmen's Association).

World Bank (1988) *World Development Report, 1988* (New York: Oxford University Press).

12 The Turkish Experience: Summary and Comparative Notes

Lance Taylor

I will try here to draw a few lessons from the preceding papers about the stabilization and adjustment process in Turkey, and add some comparisons with other countries. The goal is to point out potential political and economic problems for the foreseeable future, which may not stretch very far.

Let me begin with a sketch of what has happened since 1980, as I see it. On the whole, Turkish policy has been partly, but *only* partly, orthodox in its design and implementation. It is clear that Turkish policy-makers have been on a long leash from the IMF and World Bank, far longer than people in other countries enjoying the ministrations of these Bretton Woods institutions. There are fairly non-standard elements in Turkish policy as it has evolved, despite the fact that the country received massive capital inflows orchestrated by the Fund and Bank. I do not think that there is any question that the flows were tied to policies sanctioned from Washington; the money would not have arrived otherwise. The point is that conditionality was loose in Turkey as compared to other places that one can think of.

Relative to GDP, in the early 1980s Turkey got at least as much external support as other countries the Bretton Woods agencies label as showcases: Ghana a couple of years after Turkey, Tanzania now, and India in the 1970s (although the Indians did everything in macro policy 'right' in official eyes, but did not get much benefit out of it). The economy got ample capital inflow initially, but subsequently the new money dried up. Now, debt is mounting and there is increasing recourse to short-term, high-cost finance, borrowing from Mastercard and Visa so to speak. The politics of how this debt relationship will evolve is terribly important. Commercial bank capital is not going to flow to Turkey unless there is a signal from Bretton Woods. The Fund and Bank in turn will favor or disfavor Turkey in light of the political situation, since the US State and Treasury Departments ultimately call the shots. This is a key question that one has to look at in the future.

The main orthodox aspect of Turkish policy — and there are obvious parallels to places like Chile and Sri Lanka which also acted in collaboration with the Fund — was a massive effort to reduce domestic absorption, essentially by imposing some degree of austerity and pursuing policies such as incomplete wage indexation to inflation and cutting support prices for peasant farm products that led to regressive income redistribution. Both moves, I am sure, were premeditated. They had several effects, but one was opening a vent for manufactured exports by reducing the level of domestic demand.

Now, in fact, the exports did respond, for reasons complementary to the cut in local consumption. There was steady devaluation, and there was a whole collection of non-liberal interventions to push up foreign sales, for example the subsidies amounting to 25–30 per cent of export value and bilateral trade deals. There was the Iran-Iraq war next door, and a bit earlier the high oil prices after 1979. There was a fortunate conjuncture of external demand increases to go hand-in-hand with demand cuts at home, *and* it is essential to recognize that if Turkey had not gone through its previous phase of import-substituting industrialization, then the capacity to export would simply not exist. The ISI model was surely coming to an end by the mid-1970s, and while it was in force it had been roundly criticized for all its distortions and such nonsense, but the key point is that it put an industrial base in place. It is vital to recognize that. The export miracle would never have happened without the preceding 20 years of ISI.

The bulk of new exports, as I understand it, were medium quality manufactures and items like steel and cement going to the Middle East. But more recently most of the growth has taken the form of increased sales to Europe, and that creates another set of problems. There is a question about what share of Europe-bound exports is made up of low-wage products, things made in sweatshops, so to say. How far the country wants to go in the direction of specializing in sweatshop manufacturing has to be determined. Such operations do not build much capacity for the future and are often at risk of removal at the whim of transnational corporations.

An even more important query is how rapidly export momentum can be built up. Will there be enough investment in new plant so that there can be steady productivity increases which will allow wages to rise? Long-lived export-led growth as in South Korea rests upon exports feeding into new investment and Kaldor/Verdoorn style productivity increases and then more exports. This sort of process has not started in Turkey so far. If it does not, the export boom will ultimately peter out. One might add that indiscriminate trade liberalization will not help exports either, despite frequent Bretton Woods advice to the contrary. The current team has had enough sense not to emulate the disastrous liberalization experiments in South America's Southern Cone, and you have to give them credit for that.

Another intriguing feature of the Turkish experience is how the economy got over the financial boom and crash of the early 1980s. Such outbursts occur frequently when there is regressive income distribution and slack domestic demand. Both these factors set up potential excess saving in the system. There is a lot of money in the hands of rentiers without a productive investment outlet; the funds flow naturally toward capital flight and fun and games with speculative assets, in the Turkish case manipulated by the brokers. Elsewhere during the early 1980s, there were conglomerate groups borrowing from their own banks to bid up their own share prices in Chile, or people floating post-dated checks to buy offshore dummy corporations or real estate in Kuwait. But the speculative fever was basically the same, leading to a boom and inevitable crash. After the crash, there has to be an expensive bailout of the financial system (especially the bigger actors, who can not be allowed to fail). This certainly occurred in the Turkish case, and it may be that productive enterprise balance sheets have not yet completely recovered. In contrast to the Southern Cone, another interesting aspect is that there was not much capital flight.

Speculation in financial assets is more likely when real investment is low, that is, an important outlet for loanable funds is lacking. Although capital formation has increased a bit since 1980, it is not on a rapid growth path. Why not? High interest rates certainly have contributed to the investment crawl, but there is perhaps a more fundamental issue which I do not think any of the chapters brings up. I suspect that the fall in absorption and the export boom are a 180-degree reversal from the traditional stimuli to investment in Turkey. In the good old days of ISI, private investment probably responded mostly to public sector capital formation (in a crowding-in process which many people are talking about now and which has pretty good econometric support) as well as domestic consumer demand according to an accelerator. Both these motors were taken away for most of the past decade, so it is not surprising that private capital formation has been flat.

Why has the export growth not led to extra investment demand? Probably a fairly lengthy learning process is holding capital formation back. As Charles Kindleberger has observed, people making financial and investment decisions tend to scan familiar horizons, and if events in those directions do not look promising they may opt for speculation of just sitting on their funds. Sooner or later, of course, they may turn their heads toward new vistas, say toward opportunities in the export sector. But if exports now stagnate because they are pushing against capacity limits — which seems to be the case — then an export-led investment push may never occur because investors have not learned to be stimulated by export growth. One way or another, the Turkish state is going to have to make heads turn, perhaps by pursuing export investment on its own accord. But here other difficulties arise.

One apparent problem with an aggressive public investment strategy is that the government itself is consuming large quantities of loanable funds since it has been borrowing less from the central bank and more from the private sector. Now it may be that this change is just an apparition, since there seems to be an ongoing structural inflation (I will have more to say on that later on). What happens when prices grow steadily for a while is that money itself begins to bear interest, effectively protecting its real value from inflation. But then base money in turn has to be indexed, and in Latin American cases the corresponding interest payments on this component of the government debt nowadays amount to several per cent of GDP. Such explicit monetary indexation is not happening in Turkey, but something very similar is. The state is bypassing the banking system and borrowing directly from rentiers, with the inflation forcing it to pay high nominal interest rates. The big interest component in government spending does not look very different from similar outlays in Mexico, Agentina, and Brazil. The interest payments are all transfers to rentiers to offset the effects of inflation on the real worth of the government's liabilities that they hold.

The key question is whether such interest transfers have real effects, since if they don't, the government may be pursuing restrictive fiscal policy (and in particular not undertaking enough public investment) even though the nominal public sector borrowing requirement is huge. After all, rational rentiers should save the inflationary component of the interest they receive, or else they will just be running their own real wealth down. If their nominal saving offsets the government's nominal dissaving, the whole thing is a wash and no demand injection results from government interest. None of the chapters here attempted to make an inflation-corrected estimate of the fiscal deficit. Somebody probably should do that, since if the Fund returns in force the PSBR is going to be a major bone of contention. And even if the Fund does not arrrive, the state may have to nerve itself to keep exports growing through investment despite the big nominal PSBR. One has to learn to live with inflation, if it shows no inclination to go away.

Even without the inflationary component, interest rates still look high. Why should they be so steep? I suspect the causes involve the rapid real depreciation, exchange liberalization, and the fact that the government has to get its hands on foreign exchange to meet payments on the external debt. This last obligation means that a double transfer problem appears. The first transfer is the traditional need to generate forex through trade to meet external obligations. The second transfer is necessary because the private sector earns the DM or dollars while the public sector owes the debt — the government has to get its hands on the corresponding resources.

Exchange liberalization and depreciation make the second transfer costly by putting a floor under the real interest rate structure. Basically, liberalization permits enough arbitrage to force domestic interest rates to be close to external rates plus the rate of depreciation plus a premium. Hence, to borrow money from the exporters who earn it, the state has to pay high real rates which are its own policy creation. An open capital market plus steady devaluation makes the Finance Minister's job very hard, without much chance of getting easier. Once the capital market is opened — once financial investors' heads turn in that direction — it can be terribly difficult to shut it down. This is an aspect of liberalization the government surely has cause to regret.

Now we see a vicious circle beginning to close. Exports may stagnate because of lack of investment, which the state may have to undertake to crowd private animal spirits into action. But the state faces large nominal interest obligations which make its own accounts look bad. Part of the big PSBR may not have real effects since it just reflects inflation, but real interest rates are also high. Major causes are surely accelerated exchange depreciation coupled with external capital market liberalization, but the depreciation is now part of the export sector's world view. Unless export entrepreneurs also undertake capital formation, Turkey may not grow out of its present situation.

At least one heartening aspect is that there has not yet been enough local stagnation to provoke capital flight. Here, a crucial issue centers around the mentality of the Turkish bourgeoisie. Some examples may illustrate what I have in mind. Brazil has never relaxed capital controls and does not have much capital flight. One important factor behind this success is that Sao Paulo industrialists — the dominant wealth-holder class — are basically interested in industry in Sao Paulo. They do not now scan financial horizons in London or New York in part because they never have. This attitude contrasts sharply with the views of the upper bourgeoisie elsewhere in Latin America whose lifestyle is strongly centered around the United States. They send their kids to Ivy League schools, keep a big house in Miami, and at an appropriate age fly to Houston to get a triple bypass. All this requires a big stack of onshore American assets.

I do not know how rich Turks measure up on this scale. The Prime Minister's exhortations to industrialists to sell their villas and put the proceeds into their firms are fascinating. Would they rather sell their villas (to whom? other industrialists?) than their flats in Geneva? Do they have flats in Geneva to sell? Or have they not become as worldly as the Latins, preferring to hold their assets at home? These social considerations will play a strong role in determining whether the country will be subject to capital flight. If the financial system is indeed fragile — if a few corporate balance sheets are subject to collapse — adverse capital movements could become an acute policy pain.

Let me return for a moment to inflation. There are numerous parallels between Turkish and Latin American economic thought, and for this reason I found it surprising that there was no analysis in the papers of structural inflation processes. None looked at inflation from the side of costs, asking how it might be nourished by various forms of indexation propagating price increases arising from class conflict throughout the system. It seems clear that if one were to decompose the present Turkish inflation in this fashion, a major finding would be that exchange depreciation and public enterprise price increases are putting a lot of upward pressure on the overall price index. Cost push from expensive working capital finance tied to high interest rates could be another positive item, while negative contributions would come from incomplete wage indexation and possibly falling real agricultural prices.

Having a baseline decomposition like this would be a beginning toward looking forward. Suppose that there is liberalization (perhaps de-repression is a better word) of the wage-setting process. Nominal wages might begin to rise at a faster pace, closer to 100 per cent of recent inflation. At the same time, if exporters finally feel that the real exchange rate has depreciated enough, the nominal rate might stop increasing at more than 100 per cent of inflation. What would be the implications for costs, given that public enterprise prices will probably continue to be fully indexed as well? The outcome with full indexation of most cost compo-nents is that inflation would become highly inertial, and unresponsive to reductions in money supply growth or other moves toward austerity. If inflation becomes a political issue, it may be very difficult to make it go away.

Finally, there is the question of trade liberalization. Turkey has done what most countries do when the Bretton Woods agencies insist on liberalization. It has followed what you could call a Duke of York strategy, after the good old chap in the nursery rhyme who had 10 000 men, and marched them up the hill and marched them down again. The country liberalized, and then deliberalized again through the creation of the 'funds' — not the most rational way to retain a controlled trade regime.

What this episode illustrates, I think, is that there are strong pressures in any semi-industrialized economy for trade controls. They are essential to the import substitution process, and then of course there are positive feedbacks from the import substituters to the trade regime. This is not a situation an economy breaks out of until it is essentially fully competitive on world terms, which Turkey is not. This lack of industrial maturity also raises problems for integration with the EEC, if that ever takes place. There are political reasons to suspect that Turkey will not get into the Common Market, and its economic position makes the probability of entering even less.

Just to summarize, there seem to be many problems on the horizon: the absence of truly export-led growth based upon new investments in export capacity and rapid productivity gains, the high interest rates and financial fragility, the double transfer problem, increasingly inertial inflation, and the smoldering possibility of massive capital flight. The current policy management has had a good run, but may be forced increasingly toward austerity and extreme liberalization as these problems mount. And of course, austerity and liberalization will not make the sorts of difficulties that Turkey faces go away. The challenge for Turkish economists, and indeed for economists all around the Third World, is to come up with new ideas to attack problems that the old remedies cannot touch.

Index

adjustment: conflicts in adjustment policy, 53–5; and fiscal policy in the 1980s, 39–42; impact on domestic credits, 48–50; and the public sector, 43–7

Akyüz, Yılmaz, 98–131, 192, 259

Anand, Ritu, 87, 94, 157–82, 261, 262

Arıcanlı Tosun, 1–7, 230–53

Atiyas, Izak, 132–56

austerity: impact on Turkish labor migration, 234; measures and economic aid, 244–6; and the Social Democrats, 237–8

balance of payments: crises and exogenously imposed stabilization measures, 254–7, 266; and foreign debt, 31–2; and trade in the 1980s, 28–31

banks, commercial banks: and interlocking ownership, 114; response to the 1982 financial crash, 99–100; foreign, 102. *See also* Central Bank

Banker, Kastelli, 136

Baysan, Tercan, 9–36, 246, 247, 259

Blitzer, Charles, 9–36, 246, 247, 259

bonds, 106–9; corporate, 99; government, 102, 192; private, 102, 106–8. *See also* borrowing

Boratav, Korkut, 199–229, 246, 260, 264

borrowing, 235, 248, 271–2; domestic, 57, 184; foreign, 37, 41, 171–9

capital formation, 88, 120, 163, 177, 271. *See also* investment

capital inflows, 4, 5, 25, 230, 260–2, 266, 269. *See also* borrowing

capital markets, 102, 244, 273; Capital Markets Board (CMB), 102, 108, 115, 119

Celâsun, Merih, 37–59, 84, 85, 186, 188, 235, 245

Central Bank, 14, 38, 41, 43, 48–9, 55–6, 99–103, 110, 120–1, 133, 137

CGE models, 89

Chibber, Ajay, 4, 87, 94, 157–82, 261, 262

comparative advantage, 10, 263–5

consumption, 118, 122, 125, 168, 264; private, 161–3, 169; public (also government), 43, 47, 58, 160, 165–6, 169, 180

Conway, Patrick, 78–97

creditworthiness, 1, 4, 41, 61, 171–80, 186–8

crowding-out, 32, 167

current account, 166, 177–9, 183; deficit, 24–5, 166, 168, 172–3, 177–9; surplus, 25, 157, 160, 232

Cyprus, 239–42, 244–6

debt, 6, 151, 171–2, 256, 265–6; crisis, 1, 5–7, 39–40, 184, 230, 241; external, 4–6, 11, 24–5, 37, 55–6, 110, 171–6, 185–90, 257; internal, 5, 56, 109–10, 127, 173–4, 179, 194; short-term, 119, 186–8, 241, 261; debt-to-assets ratio, 133, 150–1; debt-equity ratio, 118–19; debt-to-exports ratio, 25, 171–2, 186; debt-to-GDP ratio, 186; debt-to-GNP ratio, 25; debt-to-output ratio, 157, 164, 171–9, 186, 189; debt-resource ratio, 4, 172; debt-service ratio, 25, 186; debt-servicing, 37–8, 56–7, 183–8, 261. *See also* borrowing

deficit: budget, *see* fiscal deficit

deficit: fiscal, *see* fiscal deficit

deposits, 4, 25, 55, 102, 120, 132–44, 191–4, 259; foreign exchange, 3, 103, 192–4, 221–2; time, 3, 106, 110–13, 123, 162, 191–4, 221–2

devaluation, 11–12, 24, 31, 39–40, 90–3, 110, 147, 191, 254, 257, 259, 270

direct foreign investment (DFI), 60, 64–5, 71, 82–6, 257–60, 266

Dresdner accounts, 25

EEC, 62, 65–72, 230–5, 239; exports